4/3/13
$90.95

STRATEGIC PARTNERS

Advance Praise for *Strategic Partners*

"Jeanne L. Wilson skillfully traces the evolution of Russian-Chinese relations from the hostility of the late Soviet period to the 'strategic partnership' of the late 1990s. She persuasively argues that Russian policy toward China, from the Gorbachev reforms through the Yeltsin years and into the Putin era, has been remarkably constant. For Wilson, Russia's economic and military decline, its demography and geographic constraints, explain Russian foreign policy far better than political structure or personalities. America's global dominance after the Cold War has pushed Moscow and Beijing toward an alignment of mutual interest, promoting multilateralism in opposition to Washington's hegemony. Wilson devotes considerable attention to Russian and Chinese reactions to the 9/11 attacks, their perspectives on the war on terrorism, and the promise of energy cooperation. *Strategic Partners* is quality scholarship—succinct, thoroughly researched, and readable. It is a valuable contribution to our understanding of Russian-Chinese relations."

—Charles E. Ziegler, *University of Louisville*

"Wilson's book on Russia and China can serve as a model for any analyst who seeks to explore a complex bilateral relationship. Richly layered in its exploration of political, economic, and military dimensions, deeply insightful into the cultural and historical perspectives of both actors, and fully in command of all of the relevant source material, Wilson's analysis will become an essential foundation for any further research on this important, but often puzzling, relationship."

—Robert H. Donaldson, *University of Tulsa*

STRATEGIC PARTNERS

RUSSIAN-CHINESE RELATIONS IN THE POST-SOVIET ERA

JEANNE L. WILSON

M.E.Sharpe
Armonk, New York
London, England

Library of Congress Cataloging-in-Publication Data

Wilson, Jeanne Lorraine, 1948–
  Strategic partners : Russian-Chinese relations in the post-Soviet era
/ by Jeanne L. Wilson
    p. cm.
  Includes bibliographical references and index.
  ISBN 0-7656-0939-8 (alk. paper)
  1. Russia (Federation)—Foreign relations—China. 2. China—Foreign relations—Russia
(Federation) I. Title: Russian-Chinese relations in the post-Soviet era. II. Title.
DK68.7.C5 W55 2004
327.47051′09′049—dc22

                                                        2003025163

Printed in the United States of America

The paper used in this publication meets the minimum requirements of the
American National Standard for Information Sciences—
Permanence of Paper for Printed Library Materials,
ANSI Z39.48-1984.

BM (c)   10   9   8   7   6   5   4   3   2   1

To Bernard S. Morris,
mentor and dear friend

Contents

List of Tables and Maps

Tables

Maps

List of Acronyms

ABM	Anti-Ballistic Missile Treaty
APEC	Asian Pacific Economic Cooperation
ARF	ASEAN Regional Reform
ASEAN	Association of South East Asian Nations
AWACS	Airborne Warning and Control Systems
CAST	Center for the Analysis of Strategies and Technologies (Russia)
CCP	Chinese Communist Party
CNPC	China National Petroleum Corporation
CPSU	Communist Party of the Soviet Union
DPRK	Democratic People's Republic of Korea (North Korea)
FRY	Federal Republic of Yugoslavia
G-8	Group of Eight
GATT	General Agreement on Tariffs and Trade
GDP	Gross domestic product
GNI	Gross National Income
IAEA	International Atomic Energy Agency
IISS	International Institute of Strategic Studies
KAPO	Kazan Aviation Production Association
KMT	Kuomintang
MAC	Military Affairs Commission (China)
MFER	Ministry of Foreign Economic Relations (Russia)
MOFTEC	Chinese Ministry of Foreign Trade and Economic Cooperation
NATO	North Atlantic Treaty Organization

NMD	National missile defense
NNPT	Nuclear Non-Proliferation Treaty
PfP	Partnership for Peace
PRC	People's Republic of China
ROC	Republic of China
ROK	Republic of Korea (South Korea)
SCO	Shanghai Cooperation Organization
SIPRI	Stockholm International Peace Research Institute
THAAD	Theater High-Altitude Air Defense
TMD	Theater missile defense systems
TRADP	Tumen River Area Development Program
WTO	World Trade Organization

Acknowledgments

In the course of writing this book, I have benefited from the assistance and support of many people. First I would like to thank those individuals in Moscow—in research institutes and in the Russian government—who met with me to discuss issues of the Russian-Chinese relationship. I appreciate their willingness to give so generously of their time and expertise, which greatly enhanced my understanding of the topic. Closer to home, I would like to thank the Davis Center for Russian and Eurasian Studies at Harvard University. The Davis Center has been a constant source of intellectual stimulation and fellowship, and access to the Harvard University libraries an invaluable aid in my research. In addition, I want to thank Robert Donaldson for his meticulous and constructive reading of this manuscript. His criticisms were very useful to me in making the final revisions. I am quite certain that he will not agree with all of my conclusions, but I hope that he will feel that his comments contributed positively to the final product.

The mechanics of writing this book have been greatly eased by Patricia Kolb and Amy Albert at M.E. Sharpe. I want to thank Pat for her counsel on matters of presentation—based on a deep reservoir of accumulated wisdom—and Amy for her willingness to respond quickly to my numerous editorial queries. I also want to thank and credit the Geography Department of Brigham Young University, Provo, Utah, for the use of its maps of Russia and Central Asia; the International Boundaries Research Unit of the University of Durham, Durham, Scotland, for granting copyright permission to use its map of disputed islands in the Khabarovsk region; and the Russian Far East Advisory Group, LLC, Seattle, Washington, for granting copyright permission to use its map of the administrative regions of the Russian Far East.

The presence and encouragement of my family and friends have also been instrumental in the realization of this project. Linda Cook and David Powell have been good friends as well as colleagues, which has been a beneficial synthesis. My husband, Allan Shwedel, has helped me with a number of technical computer issues, including the preparation of the maps and the tables. More important, however, has been his encouragement and his sustaining personal support, demonstrated by an unwavering faith in my abilities. I cannot thank him enough. I also want to thank my daughter Anna for her presence, and her patience and tolerance, especially during the final stages of this project. Most of all, I would like to thank Bernard S. Morris. It is difficult, in fact impossible, to come up with a fitting tribute to Bernie. His guidance and friendship have enriched my life immeasurably. His academic career has been a testimonial to the importance of ideas and a critical understanding of the social and political order. As a person, he has taught me a great deal about how to live and to enjoy life. This book is dedicated to him.

STRATEGIC PARTNERS

1

Introduction

With the collapse of the Soviet Union, the leadership of the emergent Russian Federation set out on a deliberate task of reconstruction, seeking to forge a new identity in both the domestic and foreign policy spheres. This endeavor was reminiscent of efforts by the Soviet regime itself three-quarters of a century earlier and was similarly doomed to partial defeat, suggesting the existence of certain immutable constraints encountered by any Russian government, irrespective of its ideological and political orientation. The Yeltsin leadership, anxious to demonstrate its membership in the Western cohort of nations, sought to downscale its interactions with those states—a greatly reduced number in any case—that continued to uphold Marxist-Leninist precepts and communist party leadership. Thus, at the onset of the Russian Federation, the Russian foreign policy orientation toward the People's Republic of China (PRC) was marked by suspicion and an often not-well-concealed hostility. It did not appear to be an auspicious beginning for the bilateral relationship between the two states.

Throughout the 1990s, the ties between Russia and China intensified. The Yeltsin leadership carried on the Gorbachev legacy in a number of areas. The Russian-Chinese border was demarcated according to the terms of the 1991 border agreement. Talks on the demilitarization of the border continued, leading to agreements in 1996 and 1997 on increased transparency and reduction of military strength in the border regions. In July 2001, Chinese president Jiang Zemin arrived in Moscow to sign the Russian-Chinese Treaty of Good-Neighborly Friendship and Cooperation. In the span of less than a decade, Russia and China had forged a "strategic partnership," with the two sides resolving that their friendship "would pass down for all generations."

Russia and China found a common cause in the establishment of the Shanghai Cooperation Organization (SCO), an outgrowth of these negotiations. The Yeltsin presidency also elected to continue discussions initiated in the late Soviet period on the sale of weaponry, which resulted in the large-scale transfer of arms and their related technologies to China in the 1990s and early 2000s. As Russia's initial expectation for acceptance by the West as a full and equal partner was dashed, Russia and China found themselves increasingly united by a largely convergent view of issues in the international realm.

In 1992, few observers anticipated the emergence of close ties between Russia and China in the 1990s. Yet its very development testified to the existence of explanatory factors, more evident in retrospect than at the time. The evolution of Russian-Chinese foreign policy relations in their first decade (specifically from January 1992 to mid-2003) is the subject of this investigation. The primary focus is on Russia and Russian foreign policy behavior, but some attention is directed to China and Chinese foreign policy behavior as a matter of necessity. It is not possible to analyze the dynamic of Russian interactions with China without considering the interactive effect of China itself on the bilateral relationship. In format, this book is a case study that examines the basic issues and events that shaped Russia's behavior with China. In so doing, I address two interrelated questions: (1) what was the process by which Russia and China established their relationship? and (2) why was Russia motivated to develop cordial ties with China? The first question frames the subsequent chapters. The second question provides a subtext for the investigation in its assessment of factors that were determinant in structuring the evolution of relations. This analysis considers Russia's motivation in its foreign policy behavior with China as threefold: bilateral, regional, and international issues have all contributed to its development. It is not possible to gauge precisely the relative importance of each factor as an input, for they have also shifted over time. However, if the modes of interaction are considered as a concentric circle, then bilateral considerations constitute the core of the relationship, reflecting the contiguous geographic location of Russia and China. In this sense, geography exercises a decisive impact on the Russian-Chinese relationship.

In the 1990s, the Yeltsin administration considered its foreign policy with the United States as a primary concern, a preoccupation that was largely shared by analysts of Russian foreign policy behavior. In comparison, less attention was given to Russia's relationship with China. By the late 1990s and early 2000s, Western scholars had published several books (as well as a number of articles) that focused in whole or in part on Russia's relationship with China in the post-Soviet era.[1] Yet overall, Russia's interactions with China remained a relatively unemphasized aspect of Russian foreign policy behavior in the post-Soviet era. This disregard has been unfortunate, for both practical and theoretical reasons. Russia's relationship with China is of enormous importance to Russian security interests. Moreover, propositions set forth about Russian foreign policy behavior during its first decade were largely constructed with reference to Russia's relationship with the United States and Europe. Whether these propositions were generalizable remained largely unexamined. This study thus seeks to analyze the extent to which Russia's interactions with China conformed to or deviated from other documented patterns of Russian foreign policy behavior, an endeavor that also mandates an identification of forces impelling the Russian-Chinese relationship.

Russian-Chinese Relations: A Russian Foreign Policy Success Story

In the 1990s, the Russian Federation met with a series of disappointments, as hopes for a rapid economic and political transition from socialism proved unfounded. In the domestic sphere, the value of the gross domestic product fell precipitously, accompanied by a corresponding decline in living standards for the majority of the Russian population. Russian foreign policy objectives were also often unrealized. The expectation that Russia would join the Western alliance as a cordial and full-fledged partner was not fulfilled, and its relationship with the states of the former Soviet Union was fraught with tensions. Debate will long continue on the Yeltsin presidency and its place in a historical accounting. In fact, anyone assuming the position of Russian president in 1992 would have been faced with a series of virtually insurmountable obstacles. Nonetheless, the Boris Yeltsin who mounted a tank in August 1991 in courageous defiance of the plotters of the coup attempt against Mikhail Gorbachev was more attractive than the seriously ill and often inebriated figure who served as the first president of the Russian Federation. It is easy to caricaturize the Russian political scene in the 1990s, but it is also the case that a caricaturist would be hard pressed to exaggerate certain grim realities of the Russian situation. The Russian Federation faced an environment of severe economic constraints, which sharply limited its range of options, but the Russian leadership in the Yeltsin era was loath to abandon the pretense that Russia was still a global power. In addition, the Yeltsin administration failed to institute a defined process of foreign policy decision making. These resultant deficiencies have been well chronicled: they included an absence of institutionalized structures for the formation and implementation of foreign policy, a constant turnover of administrative personnel, and the presence of ongoing power struggles within the Yeltsin leadership.[2] These problems were compounded, moreover, by the erratic behavior of Yeltsin himself.[3]

Russian interactions with China in the 1990s and early 2000s were subject to the same set of strains and constraints that beset the general course of Russian foreign policy. Russia's economic circumstances impeded the development of economic linkages between the two states, which remained largely stagnant in the 1990s. In addition, Russian-Chinese relations were affected by specific tensions that were a consequence of geographic proximity. Russian residents of the Russian Far East and Transbaikal area, accustomed to an autarchic existence, feared the opening of the Russian-Chinese border. Protests escalated concerning the transfer of territory to China following the 1991 border agreement and the emergent migration of Chinese across the border, a process that had been effectively proscribed since the Stalin era. However, despite these obstacles, the Russian Federation established a cordial foreign policy relationship with China, distinguished by a continual upgrading of its format. The two states established a "constructive partnership" in September 1994 and a "strategic partnership" in April 1996, moving on to formalize their relationship through the Friendship Treaty in July 2001. Some commentators would likely question the wisdom of Russia's foreign policy interactions with China, noting that Russian arms sales to China posed a potential security risk to Russia in the future.[4] Others have downplayed the significance of the relationship, pointing to the superficial nature of relations between the two states, which barely disguised the inherited legacy of mistrust.[5] There is no doubt that Russia and China lacked an underlying foundation of shared norms and values. The warming of ties between the two states was based not on trust but on convergent assessments of their mutual interests. Nonetheless, in comparison to Russia's foreign policy performance in a number of other venues, Russia proved proficient in developing ties with China. While Russia experienced frustration and setbacks in its interactions with NATO member states and was unable to resolve its long-standing issues with Japan, the Russian-Chinese relationship improved. In this regard, the Russian-Chinese relationship must be considered, at least in a relative context, as a Russian foreign policy success story, arguably Russia's most substantive foreign policy success story in its first decade. This situation, moreover, raises the obvious question as to why and how Russia attained a success with China that it did not achieve with other states. What circumstances facilitated the development of the relationship?

The Decisive Role of the Ministry of Foreign Affairs

In the Soviet era, a well-developed infrastructure existed for the formation of foreign policy under the centralized direction of the Central Committee of the Communist Party. During Yeltsin's tenure in office, despite repeated efforts, no comparable set of institutional mechanisms was constructed to fill this void. The Russian constitution delegated primary authority for the setting of a foreign policy agenda to the president, whose task was to be assisted by a series of structures including the Security Council, the Presidential

Council, the Ministry of Foreign Affairs, legislative committees dealing with international affairs, and foreign policy specialists located in both government and private (or quasi-private) institutes. In fact, even during the increasingly rare periods when Yeltsin was relatively healthy, he displayed little interest in devoting the time and effort necessary to create an effectively coordinated foreign policy apparatus. Although the establishment of the Security Council in 1992 was greeted with apprehension and viewed as an ominous replacement for the Politburo, such fears proved unfounded. The Security Council in practice turned out to be ineffective and largely powerless, meeting only infrequently and largely devoting its attention to issues of internal security rather than foreign relations. In practice, in the absence of a viable alternative, the day-to-day responsibility for the coordination and implementation of foreign policy devolved to the Ministry of Foreign Affairs.[6] The Ministry of Foreign Affairs clearly played a central role in the orchestration of Russian foreign policy toward China. Although Boris Yeltsin apparently made key decisions regarding the overall policy line to be adopted, specific issues of Russian-Chinese relations did not garner much individual attention from the president. Yeltsin's appointees to positions in the executive branch also tended to be uninterested in Russia's relationship with China, instead focusing their attentions on the United States or the near abroad as a foreign policy priority.[7] Lacking clear-cut directives from Yeltsin or his presidential staff, the Ministry of Foreign Affairs by default became active in the de facto formulation as well as the implementation of Russian foreign policy toward China.

The Ministry of Foreign Affairs lost a number of dedicated, knowledgeable specialists on China in the purge of the ministry that accompanied the Yeltsin transition to power and was further impeded by problems of low morale and high turnover among its staff. Nonetheless, the ministry retained in the China area a number of competent and experienced staff members from the Soviet era. Primary among them was Igor Rogachev, who served as a vice premier under Gorbachev, and was the Russian ambassador to China from 1992 onward. Similarly, Genrikh Kireev, formerly the chief of the Directorate of Socialist Asian Countries of the USSR Foreign Ministry and the initial head of the Sino-Soviet talks on border troop reductions, continued to act in that capacity in the Russian Foreign Ministry. Kireev headed the Russian delegation in negotiations during the 1990s on both boundary demarcation and border troop reductions.[8] During the first decade of the Russian Federation, the First Asian Department of the Russian Foreign Ministry (encompassing the states of China, North Korea, South Korea, and Mongolia) was also headed by career diplomats with extensive experience in Asia dating back to the Soviet era.

To a greater extent than was often acknowledged, the Ministry of Foreign Affairs conducted foreign policy toward China building upon the foundation provided by the Gorbachev administration. The ability of the staff of the ministry to carry out traditional tasks of diplomacy gave evidence of inherited reserves of professionalism and expertise that transcended the often chaotic conditions of the decade. At the same time, the organizational structure of the Foreign Ministry made it ill suited for the substantive task of coordinating Russian foreign policy, as it lacked mechanisms to ensure compliance with government policy or to punish deviant actions. The Foreign Ministry was also not well equipped to perform tasks—well beyond its traditional range of operations—associated with the transition to a market economy and the development of economic linkages with China.[9] But the Foreign Ministry deserved more credit than it generally received for its almost singular ability to provide a semblance of order to Russian foreign policy toward China in the initial years of the Russian Federation.

Elite Perceptions of the Russian-Chinese Relationship

As previously noted, in the 1990s, the question of how to define the Russian relationship with the United States was a subject of intense interest on the Russian political scene. Although the Yeltsin administration eventually moved away from its overtly pro-Western foreign policy orientation, interactions with the United States nonetheless remained the primary preoccupation of the foreign policy establishment. This situation stood in marked contrast with the Russian-Chinese bilateral relationship. To a considerable extent, moreover, discussions on Russian-Chinese relations were conducted within a geostrategic framework that revived the concept of the strategic triangle, focusing on interactions between Russia, China, and the United States. In effect, the United States was still the main referent. A parallel displacement existed on the domestic scene. The leftist politicians who extolled the virtues of the Chinese economy in fact displayed little knowledge of its operation. For example, Arkadii Vol'skii, president of the Union of Industrialists and Entrepreneurs, advocated the Chinese economic model, but his promotion of China emphasized its features—such as state industries—that were slated for radical restructuring, if not outright elimination, by the Chinese government under the leadership of Premier Zhu Rongji. Vol'skii's ultimate interest was not China but the defense of the state sector of Russian industry.

Regarding the attitudes of Russian elite toward China, two points are of particular importance. First, there was a nearly consensual agreement across the political spectrum at the national level that Russia needed to maintain an amicable relationship with China. In the words of the Russian academic

Evgenii Bazhanov, Russia's policy toward China was "probably the only issue on which there is a consensus within the turbulence of Russian society."[10] At the same time, however, many Russian politicians lacked an interest in China, or for that matter, in the nuances of the Russian-Chinese relationship, which tended to be a topic of investigation for Russian academic specialists.[11] Various politicians did criticize Chinese actions, typically regarding allegations that China was deliberately moving migrants into Russia in an effort to regain lost territories. State Duma committee investigations, however, ended up substantially endorsing the government policy.[12] Liberal Democratic Party of Russia leader Vladimir Zhirinovskii's efforts in the Duma to pass a law on establishing diplomatic relations with Taiwan received little support and went down to defeat.[13] Compared with the impassioned debate that developed over the Russian relationship with the United States, Russia's relationship with China was virtually a nonissue, receiving limited attention. The Russian relationship with China was not a topic of sustained inquiry in either the 1996 or the 2000 presidential elections. The only Russian candidate to offer some semblance of an alternative platform on Russian-Chinese relations was Zhirinovskii, and his credibility on this matter was compromised by widely disparate statements.[14] The lack of dissension—and the seeming disinterest—meant that the Russian government's foreign policy behavior toward China was not subjected to intense scrutiny.

China: A Willing Partner

The ability of Russia to establish friendly ties with China was obviously dependent on Chinese acquiescence to this arrangement. China, moreover, often acted as the initiator of linkages with Russia, functioning more as the pursuer than the pursued in the development of the Russian-Chinese strategic partnership. Despite the antipathy that it initially felt for the Yeltsin regime, the Chinese leadership, apparently acting on the direct orders of paramount leader Deng Xiaoping, perceived that it had nothing to gain—and much to lose—from a policy of outright condemnation.[15] Rather, Chinese interests dictated a policy of accommodation with the Russian Federation.

With the onset of the Chinese economic reforms in 1978, Chinese foreign policy had been subordinated to an overwhelming domestic imperative directed toward the transformation of China into a modernized advanced industrial state. The collapse of the Soviet Union was apparently also a factor motivating Deng in his decision to relaunch China's economic reforms, on hold since the Tiananmen events of June 1989. Deng's celebrated inspection tour of South China in the winter of 1992 was a clear challenge to party conservatives who opposed the continuation of the reforms, seeing them as harbingers of "bourgeois liberalization," "spiritual pollution," and the eventual demise of the Chinese Communist Party. Deng's victory over his opponents reestablished economic growth as a top priority on China's domestic agenda with consequent implications for foreign policy pursuits.

The legacy of Deng Xiaoping, his crowning achievement before he died, was symbolized by his 1992 southern tour, which set China irrevocably upon the path of economic reform and made integration into the world capitalist economy China's foremost national goal. The identification of economic growth as the preeminent Chinese priority dictated the adoption of a foreign policy strategy that placed a premium on stability, both domestically and externally. China's interest in seeking good relations with Russia was an effort to ensure a stable environment with a very large contiguous neighbor. In his July 2001 speech at Moscow University, Jiang Zemin noted:

> Our objective is by the middle of this century, we will basically achieve modernization, build a prosperous, strong, democratic, civilized, and socialist modern country, and realize the great rejuvenation of the Chinese nation. To fulfill this grand objective, China needs a long-term peaceful and stable regional and international environment.[16]

While the original impetus for the establishment of harmonious ties with Russia was the maintenance of a secure environment, it subsequently became evident to the Chinese leadership that there were additional benefits to be gained from the relationship. Russian collaboration was necessary in China's parallel quest to maintain stability in Central Asia and also served a geostrategic function in China's ongoing efforts to offset the hegemonic position of the United States. China, moreover, benefited considerably from Russian arms sales, which enabled it to circumvent the arms embargo imposed by the Western states in the aftermath of Tiananmen. Russia proved willing to sell some of its most sophisticated weaponry, which notably enhanced the military capabilities of the Chinese air force and navy.

The strengthening of Russian-Chinese ties was also facilitated by China's willingness to treat Russia as an equal in a mutually beneficial partnership. This was precisely the sort of relationship that Russian elites had—incorrectly and unrealistically—envisioned with the United States in the post–Cold War era. Despite their constant reiteration of "equality and mutual benefit"—one of the Five Principles of Peaceful Coexistence—as a cardinal precept of Chinese foreign policy, the Chinese leaders more typically displayed a thoroughly Confucian appreciation of hierarchy and status gradations. It would seem, moreover, that the Soviet Union's unwillingness to accord China equal treatment was a key factor in the Sino-Soviet split (see Chapter 2). Nonetheless, the Chinese were highly solicitous of Russia in the 1990s, displaying a tolerance that indicated a confidence as to their superior position in the relationship. Chinese leaders politely chose to ignore the diplomatic blunders of the struggling Russian government. In the late 1990s, as Boris Yeltsin's health deteriorated, summit meetings between Russia and China were routinely canceled and rescheduled. Jiang Zemin's 1998 meeting with Boris Yeltsin brought diplomatic protocol—important to the Chinese—to a new low: the thirty-minute session between the two presidents took place in Yeltsin's hospital room. Chinese foreign minister Qian Qichen apparently reacted with equanimity in March 1997 when he was left waiting at the airport for twenty minutes for his hosts to come pick him up.[17] In contrast, when U.S. vice president Al Gore was late to a meeting with Chinese premier Li Peng, Li walked out of the room, leaving Gore in a position of having to apologize.[18] The Chinese forbore behavior on the part of the Russians that they would not have accepted by the United States. As Dmitri Trenin has noted, "Chinese leaders have behaved themselves nearly impeccably with regard to Russia. China is one of the few countries that spare Russia's injured vanity."[19]

Russian Motivations for a "Strategic Relationship" with China

The Russian motivation to establish a peaceful relationship with China was more inchoate and less consciously or eloquently articulated than the Chinese rationale for the bilateral relationship. But, as in the Chinese case, it was similarly rooted in domestic conditions that reflected the convergence of geography and economics. Simply stated, the Russian leadership (like the Chinese leadership) soon came to perceive that the establishment of a cordial bilateral relationship was a matter of national interest. The militarization of the border at the height of the Sino-Soviet conflict had been immensely costly to the Soviet Union. In the 1990s, the Russian state, saddled with a crumbling military in disarray, could not afford a hostile relationship with China. Russia was no longer a superpower—whether it was even a global power was a matter of debate. And except for its possession of nuclear weapons, Russia was weaker than China on virtually all traditional indicators of national power capabilities. In this sense, Russia's foreign policy strategy toward China was dictated by its domestic economic circumstances. Prudence—or rationality—mandated the cultivation of a friendly relationship with the increasingly powerful state on its border. Both the Yeltsin and the Putin administrations indicated—although Putin was more steadfast in this regard than Yeltsin—that excessively harsh criticism of China (of the type that would elicit formal complaints by the Chinese Ministry of Foreign Affairs) would not be tolerated.

The bilateral aspect of Russian-Chinese relations has often been overshadowed by geostrategic assessments. But bilateral issues constituted the core element of the relationship. It is difficult, for example, to underestimate the importance to Russia of the 1991 border agreement and the 1996 and 1997 agreements on the reduction of military strength in the border regions. It is notable, moreover, that the July 2001 Friendship Treaty, unlike its predecessor, explicitly referred to the geographic position of Russia and China in its title: the Treaty of Good-Neighborly Friendship and Cooperation between the People's Republic of China and the Russian Federation.[20] While Russian arms sales to China—another aspect of the bilateral relationship—served to link the states together and provided fiscal benefits to some enterprises in the military-industrial complex, it was not the driving force of the relationship.[21] Russia, even absent of selling arms to China, had a strong incentive to develop relations with its neighbor.

At the regional level, Russia and China have shared an interest in the maintenance of stability in Central Asia, resulting in the establishment of the Shanghai Cooperation Organization (SCO). The SCO's establishment, however, has been more important to China than to Russia, which has had other avenues through which to exercise influence in the region. The Yeltsin administration more or less left the organizational details of setting up the SCO to the Chinese. But Vladimir Putin indicated an active intent for Russia to take a more assertive role in the structure, acting as a co-equal with China. The original orientation of the organization was to preserve security and combat terrorist activity at the regional level. However, the entrance of the United States into Central Asia in the aftermath of the terrorist attacks on the United States on September 11, 2001, injected a new geostrategic element into Russian and Chinese calculations, leading them to look upon the SCO as a means of counteracting an increased U.S. presence in the region. Elsewhere in Asia, Russia and China have had fewer overlapping interests. Russia persistently but unsuccessfully tried to gain Chinese support for Russian participation in negotiations on the status of the Korean peninsula in the 1990s. However, Putin's efforts to renew ties with North Korea led to increased Russian influence in the region in the early 2000s, creating an atmosphere more conducive to Russian-Chinese joint collaboration. Neither Russia or China, moreover, welcomed a nuclear North Korea or, as the United States sometimes appeared to desire, the collapse of the North Korean regime.

Russia, like China, considered that their strategic partnership could serve as a means of promoting an international vision of a multipolar world order. The joint communiqué issued at the end of Boris Yeltsin and Jiang Zemin's first meeting in 1992 noted their conviction (or possibly their hope) that the world was heading toward multipolarity. By the late 1990s, Russian and Chinese efforts to check U.S. foreign policy behavior had intensified, manifested in their joint opposition to the U.S.-led NATO intervention in Kosovo and U.S. plans to develop missile defense systems. Many analysts, including Russian and Chinese commentators, interpreted the strengthening of ties between Russia and China in the 1990s as a marriage of convenience rooted in geostrategic calculations.[22] In fact, the international dimension of the Russian-Chinese relationship was highly instrumental, envisioned as a means of counteracting the hegemonic power of the United States, which both states viewed as their foremost foreign policy priority. There is no doubt that efforts to check U.S. predominance played a role in the strengthening of ties between Russia and China. However, this analysis argues that the Russian-Chinese relationship cannot be considered simply in its international dimension, which is not in itself sufficient to account for the development of Russian-Chinese ties in the 1990s and early 2000s. The restrained approach to international issues in the July 2001 Friendship Treaty—the term "multipolar" is not mentioned—suggested, for example, that realpolitik considerations were not foremost in its implementation.

Organization of the Book

This book chronicles the development of Russian-Chinese relations from the establishment of the Russian Federation in January 1992 through mid-2003, or in shorthand form, approximately its first decade. With the exception of Chapter 2 (a historical and chronological overview) and Chapter 8 (the conclusion), each chapter deals with a specific aspect of Russian-Chinese relations. These include border and regional relations (Chapter 3), economic linkages (Chapter 4), military-technical ties (Chapter 5), the China factor in the Russian Far East and Transbaikal regions (Chapter 6), and interactions in the international realm (Chapter 7). Each chapter is written to stand on its own as an inquiry into a distinct aspect of the Russian-Chinese relationship. At the same time, the topics are evidently interrelated. The demarcation of the Russian-Chinese border, for example, is presented as a bilateral concern for the Russian-Chinese governments in Chapter 3 and as a regional issue with reference to the attitudes and behavior of politicians in the Russian Far East and Transbaikal area in Chapter 6.

The effort to deal with political events in the post-Soviet era can be akin to chasing a moving target. This is accompanied by the fear—by no means unrealistic—that one's analysis will be rendered almost instantaneously obsolescent, outpaced by the sweeping forces of history. Most issues of relevance to the Russian-Chinese relationship, however, are not highly susceptible to rapid fluctuations in policy, but rather have reflected incremental changes accruing over time. The major exception is the international dimension of the Russian-Chinese relationship, which is subject to external—

often unpredictable—systemic influences. The focus of this inquiry is on explanation, not on prediction of the future, which appears well beyond the capabilities of social science inquiry. Nonetheless, it is to be hoped that this analysis contributes to the understanding of the Russian Federation's inter-actions with China in its initial decade.

Russian language materials are transliterated in this book according to the Library of Congress system. Some variant spellings, however, appear with respect to well-known figures and place names (e.g., Boris Yeltsin, Tumen River). Citations from translation services (such as World News Connection) also retain the original translation. The *pinyin* romanization system is used for most Chinese names, places, and references. Certain prominent excep-tions, however, apply, notably in the discussion in Chapter 2 of the pre-1949 era. In this case, I follow the more familiar usage (e.g., Chiang Kai-shek, Kuomintang) rather than the *pinyin* equivalents. I also retain the original romanization in citations that appear in translation, typically from the Hong Kong press (e.g., *Ta Kung Pao*, *Pai Hsing*, etc.).

2

Russian-Chinese Relations
A Chronological Overview

Historical Antecedents

The first sustained contact between the Russian and the Chinese empires took place in the seventeenth century as Russian explorers, on a colonizing mission, made their way across Siberia toward the Pacific coast. The Treaty of Nerchinsk, signed between Russia and China in 1689, was the first treaty China concluded with a European state. It checked Russian territorial ambitions and designated the Amur region as within the Chinese domain, while granting Russia provisions to conduct trade. However, China was not able to maintain its ascendant position in Russian-Chinese interactions. This situation was less a reflection of Russian prowess than the declining fortunes of the Qing dynasty, under assault from within by domestic insurgencies and from without by a host of European states seeking to encroach on Chinese sovereignty. Following upon the extraterritorial concessions wrested from China by Britain and France in the mid-nineteenth century, Russia procured some 665,000 square miles of land, extending Russian territory in northwestern Xinjiang and in the region of the Amur and Ussuri rivers in northern Manchuria to the Pacific Ocean, through the Treaty of Aigun in 1858, the Treaty of Peking in 1860, and the Treaty of Tarbagatai in 1864. Subsequent Russian efforts to enlarge its territorial domain at Chinese expense were less satisfactory. China managed both to dislodge Russian forces from the Ili Valley in the Xinjiang region and to quell a regional Muslim revolt, incorporating the area as a province in 1884. The Treaty of St. Petersburg in 1881 largely negated Russian territorial concessions won at the Treaty of Livadia in 1878. The Russian foray into big power politics in Manchuria from 1896 to 1905 ended in disaster. Russia managed to secure two railways—a 900–mile stretch cutting through Manchuria connecting Chita to Vladivostok, and a 700–mile track in South Manchuria—and the lease of two ports, Lu-shun

(Port Arthur) and Ta-lien (Dairen) on the Liaotung peninsula from the Chinese. But Russia underestimated the political strength of Japan and ignored Japanese demands that the two delineate spheres of influence in the region. Russia's defeat in the Russian-Japanese war of 1905 was costly to Russia, leading to the destabilization of the tsarist government and the transfer of Manchuria, save some restricted railway operations, to Japan, as well as the surrender of the southern half of Sakhalin island.[1]

Geography exerted a strong impact on Russian-Chinese contacts in a manner that distinguished the pattern of Russian interactions with China from that of the other European powers. Whereas the other Europeans arrived by sea, the Russians approached China by land. To a certain extent, the Chinese leadership tended to treat the Russians as a variant of the northern barbarians who had appeared on China's doorstep for centuries. The trading privileges extended to the first Russian envoys, for example, were more extensive than those allotted to the Europeans sequestered in the coastal regions. In addition, both Russia and China were involved in complex and sometimes overlapping efforts to extend their frontiers in Central Asia. For China in particular, this meant granting Russia occasional concessions in its quest to subdue various tribal groups. In addition, the Qing government's efforts to isolate China from outside contacts rebounded in the long term to Russia's advantage.[2] As a foreign Manchu dynasty, the Qing leadership faced a certain crisis of legitimacy from the onset. Its decision to prohibit Han Chinese migration beyond the Great Wall into the frontier regions of the empire, including Inner Mongolia and the three northernmost provinces of Manchuria—Liaoning, Jilin, and Heilongjiang—contributed to the dynasty's eventual inability to retain control of sparsely populated lands. These geographical and demographic factors, not readily susceptible to political or socioeconomic intervention, have continued to play an important role in structuring interactions between the two states.

The Bolshevik Revolution and Its Aftermath: Soviet Policy Toward China

The Bolshevik revolution had momentous consequences for China as well as for Russia. Shortly after the establishment of the Comintern, its agents arrived in China orchestrating the founding of the Chinese Communist Party (CCP) in Shanghai in July 1921. Under Comintern tutelage, CCP members were educated in the basics of Marxism-Leninism, and the party was organized according to precepts of democratic centralism. Comintern efforts to dictate CCP policy, including the unsuccessful formation in the 1920s of a United Front with its chief rival the Kuomintang (KMT) (also the object of

Comintern attentions), were eventually superseded by the ascendance of Mao Zedong to the party leadership. Under Mao's direction, the party adopted a rural strategy based on peasant support and the development of a military structure oriented toward waging guerilla warfare.[3] The extent to which CCP policy was formulated in Moscow has been a topic of considerable debate in Western scholarship. Although the CCP evolved into a largely autonomous actor through the embrace of a distinctly unorthodox—at least according to tenets of Marxism-Leninism—set of doctrinal precepts, it also nonetheless appears to have remained deferential to outright commands emanating from the Soviet Union. For example, Mao Zedong was reluctant to form a Second United Front with the KMT, a position outlined in 1935 at the Seventh (and final) Comintern Congress. But eventually, amid factional feuding (and maneuvers on the part of Moscow), the CCP fell into line.[4]

As elsewhere, Soviet interactions with China were famously dualist. Coterminous with its contacts with the CCP, the Soviet Union maintained a formal diplomatic relationship in the 1930s and 1940s with the KMT (Nationalist) leadership, which had emerged after 1928 as the internationally recognized government of China. In August 1937 (one day prior to the formal initiation of the second CCP-KMT United Front), the Soviet Union signed a nonaggression pact with the KMT regime, specifying neutrality in the event of an attack on one of the parties by a third power, in addition to providing monetary, technical, and advisory assistance in its war against Japan. In September 1945, the Soviet Union signed a thirty-year Treaty of Friendship and Alliance with the KMT government—formally the Republic of China (ROC). In addition to a Soviet promise to withdraw its troops from Manchuria, the two states pledged "to work together in close and friendly cooperation" and "to act according to principles of mutual respect . . . and noninterference in the internal affairs of both contracting parties."[5] This did not preclude the Soviet Union, however, from resurrecting tsarist-era claims on China. Agreements concluded at the Yalta conference had provided for the Soviet Union to share port facilities with China at Dairen, for joint Chinese-Soviet ownership of the Manchurian railway, and for a Soviet naval base at Port Arthur.

Soviet interactions with China in the Stalinist era, whether with the CCP or the KMT, were invariably conducted in the context of an overall assessment of Soviet national interests. This involved an intricate calculation of the international environment and distribution of forces, with a focus on Japan in the 1930s and the United States in the aftermath of World War II. Beginning in 1946, the Soviet Union provided invaluable aid to the CCP through its transfer of military equipment in Manchuria, which vastly strengthened the CCP's position in the ensuing civil war between the CCP and the KMT.

But Stalin was possibly not convinced of the inevitability of the CCP's final victory or completely sanguine about the prospect. As a number of analysts have noted, Stalin—ever the consummate realist—had reasons to prefer dealing with the KMT leader Chiang Kai-shek rather than Mao Zedong and to seek a disunited or divided China that would be vulnerable to Soviet territorial demands and unlikely to pose a challenge to its northern neighbor.[6]

The Soviet Union and China as Communist Party States: Alliance and Split

Whatever the latent tensions between the CCP and its Soviet patron, Mao Zedong announced in June 1949 the intention of the CCP, upon coming to power, to "lean to one side" and follow the Soviet path.[7] The Chinese Communists proclaimed the necessity of "learning from the Soviet Union," explicitly identifying the Soviet state, in traditional Confucian terms, as the "big brother" in a hierarchically defined relationship. The Treaty of Friendship, Alliance, and Mutual Assistance Between the USSR and the People's Republic of China, signed in February 1950, committed the two states to mutual assistance against aggression by Japan (or any other state in league with Japan). The Soviet Union promised to transfer the Manchurian railway to China by 1952, agreed to Chinese administration of Dairen, and noted the eventual removal of Soviet troops from Port Arthur. The treaty also provided for Soviet credits of 300 million dollars to China with the Soviet Union providing support in the establishment of an industrial base in China modeled along Soviet lines.[8] During the 1950s, thousands of Soviet technicians complete with blueprints arrived in China to aid in the construction of a select 156 enterprises meant to serve as the foundation of China's industrialization effort.

Chinese deference to the Soviet Union, however, did not last long. By the mid-1950s, cracks were beginning to appear in the edifice of a relationship heralded as an eternal friendship. The events of the Sino-Soviet split have been well chronicled.[9] Nikita Khrushchev's speech criticizing Stalin at the Twentieth Party Congress of the Communist Party of the Soviet Union (CPSU), the Chinese movement away from the Soviet model and its embrace of communes (alluded to as representing "sprouts of Communism"), the USSR's renunciation of its agreement to provide nuclear technology to China (fostered by a perception that Mao Zedong showed no respect for the destructive capabilities of nuclear weapons), and Chinese criticism of Khrushchev for his overly slavish obeisance to the West all contributed to the worsening of the relationship. In 1960, the dispute between China and the Soviet Union became public as the Chinese published a 15,000-word article entitled "Long Live Leninism" (purportedly written by Mao himself) in the party theoretical journal *Hongqi* (Red Flag). Ostensibly written in honor of Lenin's ninetieth birthday, the article was a critique of the sins of the Khrushchev leadership. A few days later, the Soviet reply appeared in *Pravda*, the newspaper of the CPSU, sparking off an escalating ideological battle between the two states which was waged in part through the media. In retaliation, the Soviet Union also withdrew its technical experts from China, further exacerbating the Chinese economic crisis that had developed following the collapse of the Great Leap Forward.

As the quarrel between China and the Soviet Union intensified, China began to raise complaints regarding the Sino-Soviet boundary, claiming that the territories acquired by Russia during the Qing dynasty unfairly allocated Chinese land to the Soviet Union.[10] Both states began a massive deployment of troops along the border, accompanied by ensuing border skirmishes. In March 1969, large-scale fighting between Chinese and Soviet troops occurred in the area of Damanskii island (Zhenbao to the Chinese) in the Ussuri River. By some accounts, the Soviet Union seriously contemplated launching a nuclear strike against China as a preventive strategy.[11] The deterioration of Sino-Soviet relations to an all-time low prompted China to reassess its global strategy and its position of virtual isolation, leading the China leadership to initiate overtures to the United States. The fruits of this endeavor were manifest in Richard Nixon's historic visit to China in February 1972. According to Li Zhisui, Mao's longtime personal physician, Mao considered that the mutual interest drawing China and the United States together was the threat of the "polar bear" to the north.[12]

The Normalization of Relations

Movement toward the normalization of relations between the Soviet Union and China was a protracted process.[13] Progress was hindered by crises of leadership succession in both states—for China in the 1970s and for the Soviet Union in the 1980s—as well as the intrusion of international factors. By the mid-1970s, both Mao Zedong and longtime Premier Zhou Enlai were virtually incapacitated; their deaths in 1976 sparked a struggle for power in China that was resolved with Deng Xiaoping's (unofficial) assumption of leadership in July 1977. Although the Soviet Union and China agreed in 1979 to discuss issues in their relationship, the talks, initiated in September 1979, were soon suspended by the Chinese after the Soviet Union invaded Afghanistan in December of that year. A few hopeful signs emerged in the early 1980s. In 1980, the Chinese leadership renounced—no doubt because of its own economic reforms—its former characterization of the Soviet Union as a "revisionist" state. On the Soviet side, General Secretary Leonid Brezhnev made a speech in Tashkent, Uzbekistan, in April 1982 calling for Sino-Soviet cooperation. Negotiations between the Soviet Union and China resumed in late 1982, but made little progress. Huang Hua, the Chinese foreign minister, presented his Soviet counterpart Andrei Gromyko with a list of the "three obstacles" (later to evolve into the "three demands") to the normalization of relations while visiting Moscow to attend Brezhnev's funeral in November 1983: these involved the buildup of Soviet troops along the Sino-Soviet border, the Soviet presence in Afghanistan, and Vietnamese troops in Cambodia.

Although the development of bilateral linkages between the Soviet Union and China intensified in the mid-1980s—First Vice Premier Ivan Arkipov's December 1984 trip to China marked the highest ranking visit of a Soviet leader in fifteen years; the final reconciliation of relations was not achieved until the ascension of Mikhail Gorbachev to the Soviet leadership. Improving ties with China (as well as with the United States) was a notable goal of the Gorbachev foreign policy strategy. To these ends, Gorbachev's July 1986 speech in Vladivostok went a significant distance in addressing issues raised by China as a prerequisite to normalization. Gorbachev announced that the Soviet Union would begin withdrawing regiments from Afghanistan, that some troops might be removed from Mongolia, and that the Soviets were prepared to discuss the reduction of force levels along the Sino-Soviet border.[14] Subsequent negotiations between the Soviet Union and China concentrated on the major remaining stumbling block between them—the withdrawal of Vietnamese troops from Cambodia. The announcement by the Vietnamese government in April 1989—surely not a purely independent decision—that it would remove its troops from Cambodia by September 1989 set the stage for Mikhail Gorbachev's May 1989 visit to Beijing.[15]

The circumstances of Gorbachev's trip to Beijing in May 1989 were, to say the least, awkward. Gorbachev arrived to a Beijing in tumult, gripped by the Tiananmen crisis. The presence of demonstrators on Tiananmen Square necessitated that Gorbachev and his entourage enter the Great Hall of the People for state meetings via a side door rather than the main entrance. Gorbachev's meeting with General Secretary Zhao Ziyang (under attack by conservatives for his overly liberal policies) was particularly inauspicious. It turned out to be Zhao's last high-profile public appearance before being purged, while his comments to Gorbachev that Deng Xiaoping was the paramount leader of China earned him criticism for revealing a "state secret" to a foreigner. The validity of Zhao's remark was duly confirmed by the Chinese leadership's dating—seemingly without irony—the normalization of Sino-Soviet relations to the meeting between Deng and Gorbachev.[16] Following the summit, the two states issued a joint communiqué summarizing their relationship. The Soviet Union and China noted that the normalization of relations was not directed against any third countries, pledged to refrain from force or the threat of force in their interactions, agreed to reduce armed forces in the border regions, and to intensify work on the deliberation of the border.[17]

The long-term dispute—at times threatening to erupt into violent conflict—between the world's two largest communist party states refuted both Marxist-Leninist precepts of socialist solidarity and Cold War preconceptions of a monolithic communist movement. A number of explanations have been advanced as to the underlying causes of the Sino-Soviet conflict, most of which are plausible and no doubt contributed to the intensification of antagonisms between the two states to a greater or lesser degree.[18] Xenophobia and ignorance existed on both sides. The Chinese resented tsarist occupation of disputed territories and Stalin's treatment of the CCP in the pre-1949 era. Khrushchev and Mao came to detest each other, although the demise of Khrushchev brought no immediate improvement to relations between the two countries. China's claims to have staked out an alternative path to socialism eventually merged into an effort to assert leadership over the international communist movement, causing great offense on the Soviet side. Despite the massive onslaught of polemics and counterpolemics launched in the course of the dispute, the Chinese leadership, assessing the situation in retrospect, did not identify ideology as a predominant factor. According to Deng Xiaoping, "the Soviet Union put China in a wrong position." This sentiment was echoed in the 1990s by Li Fenglin, the outspoken former Chinese ambassador to Russia, who noted that "the substance of the issue is that the Soviet Union did not treat China on an equal footing."[19]

The Interval Between Regimes: June 1989–December 1991

For both states, the significance of the Sino-Soviet reconciliation was immediately overshadowed by a series of domestic and international events. Subsequently, the Gorbachev regime was too besieged by internal conditions at home—seen in economic collapse, the rise of Boris Yeltsin in Russia, the emergence of separatist movements in other republics—and the collapse of communist party states in Eastern Europe to devote much attention to orchestrating foreign policy toward China. For its part, the Chinese leadership, still struggling to reassert political authority in the wake of events at Tiananmen, also found itself confronted with the specter of the collapse of communism in Eastern Europe and the steady erosion of communist party control in the Soviet Union. Such events inevitably cast a pall on the task of institutionalizing a normalized Sino-Soviet relationship, especially on the part of the Chinese.

In a first test of the parameters of a normalized relationship, the Soviet leadership responded to the Tiananmen events with tact and discretion. The Congress of People's Deputies released a statement that noted that the events in China were an internal affair, and that "any attempts at pressure from outsiders would be inappropriate."[20] Gorbachev indicated his "regret" over the situation in China but maintained a distinctly low-key response.[21] This tempered reaction, however, was not sufficient to allay Chinese apprehensions. Initially, the CCP tended to blame Gorbachev personally for the troubles in the socialist bloc.[22] In July 1989, China's leaders were reported to have decided to censor publications dealing with Mikhail Gorbachev as politically too explosive.[23] By December 1989, China's leaders identified Gorbachev as responsible for "the disappearance of socialism" in Eastern Europe.[24] After the decision made by the CPSU to abandon its monopoly of power in February 1990, Jiang Zemin, the successor to Zhao Ziyang as CCP general secretary, called Gorbachev a "traitor to communism."[25]

In spite of the vindictiveness heaped upon the CPSU and Mikhail Gorbachev in particular, the Chinese leadership elected to keep its criticisms internal, while simultaneously asserting its commitment to noninterference in other countries' affairs. In the bilateral sphere, Sino-Soviet relations expanded and intensified in the wake of Gorbachev's visit. The pace of negotiations on the delineation of the border increased, while talks on reducing troop strengths along the border were initiated in November 1989. Military linkages between the two states resumed after a thirty-year hiatus, with China beginning discussions over the purchase of military hardware, specifically Su-27 fighter aircraft. Party-to-party exchanges were reinstated and formal state visits by government leaders began to take place on a routine basis. Premier Li Peng's visit to the Soviet Union in April 1990 marked the highest-level exchange in Sino-Soviet relations since Gorbachev's trip to Beijing almost a year earlier.

The continued unraveling of CPSU control, marked by the exodus of reformers—including Boris Yeltsin—from the party at the Twenty-eighth CPSU Congress in June 1990 further unnerved the Chinese leadership. Nonetheless, plans to go public with a mass criticism campaign of the Soviet Union in early 1991 were halted as China's leadership reassessed its options. On the one hand, the easy victory obtained by the U.S.-led coalition in the Gulf War demonstrated the ascendancy of the United States as the predominant global actor, leading China to pursue closer ties with the Soviet Union as a means of counterbalancing U.S. global influence. On the other hand, Chinese leaders concluded that they had little choice but to support Gorbachev in the increasingly fractionalized struggle for power in the Soviet Union. Chinese investigations had concluded that their first choice, the conservative

Igor Ligachev, lacked any foundation of support, leaving Gorbachev, for all his faults, still far preferable to his main challenger, Boris Yeltsin.[26] This decision was further reinforced by Gorbachev's own move toward the conservatives in the CPSU in the fall of 1990.

Thus, Jiang Zemin's trip to Moscow in May 1991 took place in a relatively cordial atmosphere. The joint communiqué released by the two states at the conclusion of Jiang's visit noted their "identical views on socialism" and reaffirmed their commitment to the development of "relations of friendliness, good-neighborliness, mutual benefit and cooperation."[27] A *People's Daily* editorial following the visit lauded the trip as "completely successful" and a "new milestone in Sino-Soviet Good-Neighborly and Friendly Relations."[28] Chinese equanimity, however, was destined to be short-lived. Following the abortive coup attempt by Communist hardliners in August 1991, Gorbachev lost his precarious hold on power, eclipsed by Boris Yeltsin as the president of the Russian republic. Although Chinese leaders no doubt had hoped for the success of the coup instigators, it does not appear—despite widespread assertions to the contrary—that the CCP was involved in efforts to overthrow the Gorbachev leadership.[29] Formally, the Chinese response to events in Moscow stressed that changes in the Soviet Union were "its own internal affair."[30] Following the failure of the coup, Foreign Minister Qian Qichen noted, in virtually identical language, that "the internal affairs of the Soviet Union should be handled by the Soviet people themselves."[31]

By the end of the year, the Soviet Union lay in tatters, to be replaced by the Russian Federation and the other newly independent states that emerged from the former Soviet republics. The collapse of the Soviet Union was an incalculable loss to China's shaken leadership. Whatever the level of discord between the two states, the Soviet Union had nonetheless stood as a symbol, by virtue of its existence as the first socialist state, of legitimacy and affirmation for China's adherence to Marxist-Leninist precepts. By late 1991, however, after two years of viewing the inexorable demise of the socialist bloc, China's leaders determined that they could not afford themselves the luxury of polemics and recriminations. The Chinese survival strategy consisted of bolstering its domestic position through a multipronged (and somewhat contradictory) policy of combating "peaceful evolution" and maintaining political stability, while simultaneously pursuing economic reform and opening up to the West in the economic realm. Although the Chinese leadership had initially identified external factors, in particular the pernicious influence of the United States, as a motive force in the Tiananmen events, it later came to endorse the position (most notably articulated by Deng Xiaoping) that the main threat to the Chinese regime did not come from abroad but was a reflection of China's internal challenges.[32] Correspondingly, the Chinese foreign policy strategy was oriented toward the preservation of conditions necessary for political stability and economic modernization. As an internal document circulated in the wake of the failure of the August 1991 coup attempt noted: "Even if Yeltsin is a reactionary, we can internally curse him and pray for his downfall, but we still have to maintain normal state-to-state relations with him and have to endeavor to maintain good-neighborly ties with the Soviet Union. This is for the sake of our country's peace, stability, and social development."[33]

Russian-Chinese Relations: Initial Contacts

The onset of Russian-Chinese diplomatic contacts, while adhering to the niceties of diplomatic protocol, was marked by an undercurrent of hostility and suspicion on both sides. Despite its disapproval of Yeltsin and his fledgling government, the Chinese leadership opted for pragmatism. China recognized the government of the Russian Federation (along with the eleven other members of the Commonwealth of Independent States [CIS]) on December 27, 1991.[34] Russia and China agreed to their willingness to fulfill obligations previously concluded between the Soviet Union and China, including the terms of communiqués signed with the Gorbachev leadership in 1989 and 1991. The Russian leaders, for their part, took fewer pains to hide their distaste for China. Boris Yeltsin initially showed little inclination to be accommodating to a Chinese leadership that had previously snubbed him. Not only had Jiang Zemin declined Yeltsin's request to meet with him during his May 1991 trip to Moscow, but the Chinese had compounded the insult a month later. After Yeltsin's victory in the Russian presidential election, the Chinese leadership invited Ivan Polozkov, the head of the Russian Communist Party and a Yeltsin rival, to China where he was received by Jiang Zemin. In any event, despite the entreaties of his diplomatic corps, Boris Yeltsin adamantly refused to accord the newly appointed Chinese ambassador to Russia the courtesy of a separate meeting to present credentials.[35] Andrei Kozyrev, the new foreign minister, was oriented toward an overtly pro-Western, and specifically pro-American, foreign policy path for Russia. Whereas Soviet foreign policy in the Gorbachev era had been essentially evenhanded in its simultaneous pursuit of normalized Sino-Soviet ties and the improvement of relations with the West, Russian foreign policy at the beginning of the Yeltsin era, while acknowledging the maintenance of diplomatic links with China as a practical necessity, nonetheless envisioned a significant downgrading of the relationship. The new order was tangibly in evidence at the reconstituted Foreign Ministry, symbolized by the exodus of members of the First Department of the Asia-Pacific Region from their offices in the Foreign Ministry headquarters on Smolenskaia Square to considerably less dignified quarters above a food shop across the street.

Nonetheless, the Russian leadership soon came to take increased notice of China. Boris Yeltsin and Chinese premier Li Peng met briefly at the United Nations in New York in January 1992, agreeing that Russia and China should strengthen relations and contacts in the future. The institutional structures and policy venues inherited from the Soviet era were reconfigured and reconstituted without major substantive alteration. In February 1992, Chief of Staff of the Joint Armed Forces of the CIS Viktor Samsonov became the first high-ranking Russian official to visit Beijing. Samsonov's itinerary included both the status of negotiations on the reduction of armed forces in the border areas and forms of military-technical cooperation, with Samsonov confirming the Russian commitment to providing China with previously contracted armaments, including the delivery of twenty-four Su-27 fighter jets. In March 1992 both Minister of Foreign Economic Relations Petr Aven and Foreign Affairs Minister Kozyrev visited Beijing. Aven concluded a five-year intergovernmental trade and economic agreement, followed in August by the convocation of the Russian-Chinese Intergovernmental Commission for Trade, Economic, Scientific and Technical Cooperation, a successor to the Soviet-Chinese commission. Although Kozyrev took the opportunity to castigate the Chinese for their human rights record, he also laid the groundwork for Yeltsin to undertake a formal trip to Beijing. Border negotiations regarding the status of the former Sino-Soviet boundary along its western flanks and the reduction of troop strengths resumed in the fall of 1992, including the incorporation of Kazakhstan, Kyrgyzstan, and eventually Tajikistan as sovereign states in the process.

Russian-Chinese relations suffered a setback in September 1992, the consequence of a temporary Taiwanese diplomatic coup that highlighted the lack of coordination in Russian governmental structures. Unbeknownst to the Russian Foreign Ministry, Oleg Lobov, a longtime member of Yeltsin's inner circle, had signed an agreement with Taiwanese vice foreign minister Chang Hsiao-yen to exchange representative offices to handle bilateral affairs. This action by the freelancing Lobov provoked a sharp protest from the Chinese government. Kozyrev was compelled to pay a courtesy call on the Chinese ambassador to reassure him that Russia had no intention of establishing formal links with Taiwan. Kozyrev's actions were reaffirmed by a decree issued by Boris Yeltsin on September 15, 1992, clarifying that Russia, in recognition of the one-China principle, would not enter into official interstate relations with Taiwan and would only engage in interactions with Taiwan at the nongovernmental level.[36]

Boris Yeltsin's trip to Beijing in December 1992 was a seminal event in setting the course of subsequent Russian-Chinese interactions. The president's behavior was vintage Yeltsin, virtually a paragon of unprofessional and indiscrete conduct, initiating a pattern that was to become all too familiar to his Chinese hosts in the coming years. In press conferences, Yeltsin disclosed that he had previously considered China as a country "very much in one mold, under the Party's heel," that he had not believed "that the prosperity level was improving in real terms," and that the eighty-eight-year-old paramount leader Deng Xiaoping "was not in good health."[37] Subsequently, Yeltsin cut short his visit by a day, canceling a planned trip to the Special Economic Zone of Shenzhen in Guangdong province in order to return to Moscow and deal with an internecine political struggle taking place within his cabinet. Nonetheless, the Chinese leadership reacted with tact and forbearance, and both states described Yeltsin's visit as a diplomatic success that signified the development of a new stage in Russian-Chinese relations. A package of twenty-four documents was signed outlining a diverse array of cooperative activities. Many of these agreements—especially those in the economic sphere—were destined to remain unrealized or to move forward with excruciating slowness, but several were of substantive importance. These included a memorandum on mutual reduction of armed forces and strengthening of trust in the military sphere in the border areas; a memorandum of military and technical cooperation, which, according to Yeltsin, was urged upon him by an insistent Li Peng; and a joint declaration laying out the basis for mutual relations between the two states.[38] According to the declaration, Russia and China were "friendly states" that would not allow differences in social systems or ideology to obstruct the normal development of state-to-state relations. In keeping with the intent of Yeltsin's decree of September 15, the declaration also included a clause that affirmed Russia would not establish "governmental relations and ties with Taiwan," dictating that the PRC existed as the sole legitimate government representing the Chinese state.[39]

Upgrading the Relationship: 1993–1996

Russian-Chinese relations were subordinated to Russian domestic concerns during 1993, as Boris Yeltsin was increasingly preoccupied by a power struggle with members of the Russian legislative branch over control of the government. Military contacts, however, continued to expand. In July 1993, Liu Huaqing, the vice chair of the Chinese Military Affairs Commission, arrived in Russia, followed by the November 1993 visit to Beijing of Russian minister of defense Pavel Grachev. Both trips focused on Chinese arms purchases and the transfer of military technologies. Grachev's visit culminated in the signing of a five-year agreement on forms of military-technical cooperation between the two states. While Russia expressed "deep regret" over China's decision in the fall to resume underground nuclear testing, this sentiment did not extend to the level of formal protest. For its part, despite covert sympathy for the anti-Yeltsin forces, China adhered to a strict formal neutrality in its reaction to the political events of the fall of 1993, marked by efforts of the Russian Duma to impeach Yeltsin and an attempted parliamentary insurrection. Displaying a distinct respect for the survival skills of Boris Yeltsin, the Chinese leadership reiterated its commitment to noninterference in the domestic affairs of another sovereign state, while expressing hopes for the return of stability on the Russian domestic scene. The wisdom of this strategy was confirmed in December 1993 as Boris Yeltsin triumphed over his opponents with the passage of a constitutional referendum providing for a strong Russian president.

In contrast, 1994 was a year of intensive diplomatic activity between the two states. In a New Year's letter to Jiang Zemin, Boris Yeltsin proposed that Russian-Chinese relations be upgraded to the status of a "constructive partnership," a theme elaborated upon by Foreign Minister Kozyrev during a January 1994 visit to Beijing. According to Kozyrev, the concept included the strengthening of mutual trust, cooperation in the United Nations Security Council, and an increase in trade and economic cooperation, especially between the border areas. Prime Minister Viktor Chernomyrdin took up the topic of trade and border relations during his May 1994 visit to Beijing. While the results of his trip were not particularly substantive (a package of microlevel agreements was signed primarily addressing issues of trade cooperation in the border regions), Chernomyrdin was personally assessed by the Chinese to be a more sympathetic figure, and more in tune with Chinese sensibilities, than Yegor Gaidar, his predecessor.

In September 1994, Jiang Zemin arrived in Moscow to participate in the second Russian-Chinese summit meeting. Jiang and Yeltsin signed several documents, including a declaration specifying that the two states would not target their strategic nuclear weapons against each other and an agreement (negotiated without controversy) outlining the fifty-five-kilometer western section of their border. The key result of the summit, however, was a joint statement that formally elaborated Russian-Chinese relations as a "constructive partnership." The statement specified four areas of focus for the development of Russian-Chinese relations: political, economic, military, and international. Relations between the two states were said to be "based on the principle of nonalignment and not directed against any third country." In the international realm, the world was described as moving toward multipolarity, with Russia and China motivated by a joint desire to "permit no expansionism and oppose hegemony, power politics, and the establishment of antagonistic, political, military, and economic blocs."[40] The statement represented a major shift in the bilateral relationship from its inauspicious beginnings, which was essentially reflective of shifting perceptions on the part of the Russian leadership. By 1994, the pro-Western orientation of the early days of the Russian Federation had lost a great deal of its allure, and the Russian leadership was far less concerned to stress ideological differences separating the two states. In particular, Russian elites discovered a correspondence of interests with their Chinese counterparts in their appraisals of the international system. The "constructive partnership" was a Russian initiative, but it tapped into consensual Chinese assessments. As Chinese Foreign Minister Qian Qichen noted in a trip to Moscow to prepare for the summit: "the views of Moscow and Beijing 'either coincide or are similar' on many important international problems."[41]

By the mid-1990s, Russian-Chinese relations were increasingly affected by the physical reality of their 4,250–kilometer border. While the 1991 border agreement had been negotiated by a Soviet leadership without domestic input, the more pluralistic and markedly weaker Russian state was not able to prohibit domestic criticism of the border agreement and the subsequent demarcation of the border. Regional leaders in the Russian Far East in particular launched protests against the agreement, which was seen as an abdication of Russian territory. The protests were partly a means of attracting the attention of a distant center that had largely cut off the subsidies that had kept the region afloat in the Soviet period. The Chinese took a negative view of such activities, with the Chinese Ministry of Foreign Affairs lodging a number of protests over the efforts of Russian politicians to amend the border agreement. The task of defending the agreement fell largely to the Russian Ministry of Foreign Affairs, with Kozyrev dispatched to reassure the Chinese that Russia had no intention of renouncing it.

In the Soviet period, the heavily militarized border had acted to separate the two states, placing artificial constraints on cross-border interactions. But the resolution of the border conflict meant a sizable increase in the movement of goods and people across the border. By the mid-1990s, the Russian press was filled with reports—most of them vast exaggerations—detailing Chinese illegal immigration into Russia, especially the Russian Far East. The topic was deemed critical enough to be placed on the agenda for discussion during Jiang Zemin's 1994 visit to Russia, with Jiang denying the existence of any sort of formal Chinese plan to colonize the area.[42] Efforts to constrict the movement of Chinese into Russia were a motivating factor in the Russian revision of visa regulations in January 1994. As a consequence, the number of Chinese entering Russia dropped substantially, but so did Russian-Chinese trade. Trade figures for 1994 (see Table 4.1, page

62) plunged precipitously, decreasing about one-third compared to 1993, a source of concern for both states. Li Peng's June 1995 visit to Russia focused on trade issues, although without any dramatic results. In fact, the most promising venue for trade was implicitly recognized to be in the military-technical sphere. Liu Huaqing's visit to Moscow in December 1995 attained a notable success for the Chinese, as the Russian side, after years of negotiation, agreed to sell China the license to produce Su-27 fighter aircraft, in addition to the purchase of twenty-four Su-27 planes.

Despite the emergence of tensions on border issues and the seemingly intractable weakness of economic interactions between the two states, Russia and China began taking steps in the mid-1990s to intensify their relationship. Strategic calculations played an undeniable role in this development. In the summer of 1995, China initiated a series of missile "exercises" off the coast of Taiwan, an action that was repeated during Taiwanese president Lee Teng-hui's reelection campaign in March 1996. These movements were apparently meant to deter Lee from pursuing a diplomatic strategy seeking greater international recognition of Taiwan, as well as to intimidate Taiwanese voters in Taiwan's first democratic presidential election, therefore ensuring the victory of a more compliant candidate. The campaign was a massive miscalculation as the Taiwanese electorate rallied around Lee who easily won. China's actions also aroused intense international alarm, especially on the part of the United States. For its part, Russia in 1995 felt increasingly threatened by the plans, now well under way, to expand the North American Treaty Organization (NATO), a move viewed in Russian political circles, even by the most liberal advocates, as a means of subordinating Russia to the United States and its European allies. Thus, both Russia and China came to share a worldview that identified the United States as a hegemon seeking global domination. The initiation of Russian military operations in Chechnya in December 1994 further served to cement the Russian-Chinese relationship, as Russia found increased meaning in China's longtime insistence on the principle of noninterference in internal affairs and the primacy of state sovereignty. Chechnya also served to put an end to Russia's tendency to moralize to the Chinese about human rights abuses. The two states agreed to an arrangement, codified in subsequent joint statements, in which neither would criticize the internal domestic policies of the other: China would support Russian policy in Chechnya in return for Russian support of China's right to sovereignty over Taiwan and Tibet.[43]

A third Russian-Chinese summit meeting, scheduled to be held in November 1995 in Beijing, was ultimately postponed due to the recurrent health problems of Boris Yeltsin.[44] Yeltsin's eventual trip to China in April 1996 resulted in two significant accomplishments. Meeting in Beijing, Yeltsin and

Jiang signed a joint communiqué updating the 1992 and 1994 renditions that announced Russia and China's commitment to developing a "strategic partnership of equality, mutual confidence and mutual coordination toward the twenty-first century." The statement elaborated upon geopolitical concepts laid out in the 1994 statement, stressing the development of the trend "toward a multipolar world," and maintaining that "the desire for peace, stability, cooperation, and development has constituted the mainstream of the present international life."[45] At a second regional summit in Shanghai, Yeltsin and Jiang, along with the leaders of Kazakhstan, Kyrgyzstan, and Tajikistan signed the Agreement on Strengthening Mutual Military Confidence in the Border Regions, which provided for levels of transparency in military operations along the former Sino-Soviet border.

Developing the Strategic Partnership

Unofficially, Russian-Chinese relations were also affected by the January 1996 replacement of Andrei Kozyrev with Evgenii Primakov as the foreign minister of the Russian Federation. Primakov's appointment did not alter the actual content of Russian-Chinese bilateral relations, but it did have a notable impact on the tenor of relations. The same qualities in Primakov that aroused suspicion and distrust in the West were welcomed by China's leaders, who looked upon Primakov's career in the Soviet and Russian intelligence services as proof of his competence and expertise. In the Chinese view, Primakov was a consummate professional. Officially, both Russia and China acknowledged that their commitment to a strategic partnership necessitated more attention to the development of institutionalized procedures. During Li Peng's December 1996 visit to Moscow, the two states unveiled their plans to convene regularized meetings. These included yearly summit meetings at the presidential level, biannual meetings between the prime minister of Russia and the premier of China, and regular exchanges between the foreign ministers. A series of subcommittees were established to promote the growth of economic interactions. Simultaneously, the two states announced their intent to raise the total level of bilateral trade to 20 billion dollars by the year 2000. The military-technical relationship also continued to expand. At a December 1996 meeting of the Bilateral Commission on Military-Technical Cooperation, the two sides hammered out specifications of the Su-27 licensing agreement, agreed to the sale of two Sovremennyi class destroyers to China, discussed the potential sale to China of Su-30MKK fighter jets, and signed a Memorandum of Military-Technical Cooperation updating the provisions of the 1993 agreement.

During 1997, bilateral contacts increased, with two presidential summits and a host of lower-level interactions. In April 1997, Jiang Zemin arrived in Moscow on a state visit, which included the signing of a follow-up agreement by the members of the "Shanghai Five" (China, Russia, Kyrgyzstan, Kazakhstan, and Tajikistan) on the Mutual Reduction of Military Strength in Border Regions. The agreement provided for the large-scale reduction of troop and equipment levels along the former Sino-Soviet border. While the ceilings imposed reflected levels greater than those any side was inclined (or able) to support, the agreement represented another important milestone, indicating the official demise of border issues as a flash point of conflict in the region. In addition, Jiang held a series of meetings with Russian officials, including a hasty meeting with an apparently ailing Boris Yeltsin, who returned to Moscow from his vacation spot in the Crimea for the occasion. Yeltsin and Jiang signed yet another joint declaration, which in its outline of mutual views on the international situation included an implicit reference to NATO expansion. The document pointedly noted that "both sides express concern over the attempt at enlarging and strengthening military blocs, because such a tendency may pose a threat to the security of certain countries and aggravate regional and global tension."[46]

These precepts were reaffirmed during Boris Yeltsin's reciprocal visit to China in November 1997. The most important result of Yeltsin's visit—although mainly as a symbolic gesture—was the announcement of the official completion of the demarcation of the eastern section of the Russian-Chinese border. In fact, this announcement was premature: the actual work of border demarcation continued on the Russian side until early 1999, but reflected pressures on the Chinese side to prod a lagging Russia into acquiescence with the framework of the original 1991 border agreement. In addition, the joint statement signed by Yeltsin and Jiang included plans to resurrect a Sino-Russian Committee for Friendship, Peace, and Development; agreements on guiding principles of joint economic use of certain islands and surrounding waters on border rivers; measures for joint economic cooperation between Chinese and Russian regions; and a memorandum on preparing a feasibility study for the construction of a gas pipeline from East Siberia to China. The Russian-Chinese economic relationship received a major boost in December 1997 when, after years of discussion, the two states finalized the plans for Russia to construct a nuclear power plant in Lianyungang in Jiangsu province.

By the late 1990s, high-level contacts between Russian and Chinese officials had become largely routinized although somewhat hobbled by the exigencies of Russian domestic politics. The collapse of the ruble in August 1998 impeded the already difficult task of establishing economic links and also contributed to a high rate of turnover among personnel in government positions. From March 1998 to August 1999, Russia had four prime ministers, with Evgenii Primakov earning the distinction of the longest duration in office, at a brief seven months. Presidential contacts were complicated by the chronic health problems of Boris Yeltsin. Jiang Zemin's trip to Moscow in November 1998 took place under circumscribed conditions. The planned unofficial summit—the so-called "no-neckties" approach favored by Yeltsin— was even more casual than originally envisioned: the half-hour meeting between the two presidents took place in Yeltsin's hospital room. Yeltsin's return visit to Beijing in December 1999, moreover, was undertaken immediately after his release from the hospital. Despite his evident ill health, Yeltsin nonetheless managed to meet twice with Jiang Zemin and to sign a series of documents, including a joint statement on the international situation, a protocol specifying the results of the demarcation of both the eastern and western sections of the border, and an agreement detailing specific islands and adjacent water areas scheduled for joint economic use.

Russian-Chinese Relations and the Yeltsin Legacy

By the end of the Yeltsin era, certain basic parameters of the Russian-Chinese relationship had been, or were in the process of becoming, institutionalized. First, the border issue, so contentious during the Soviet era, had largely been resolved. The protocols signed at the December 1999 presidential summit on border demarcation brought another level of closure to the border dispute. Military troop strengths along the border were no longer a political concern (see Chapter 3). Regional elites in the Russian Far East had largely ceased their protests over the 1991 border agreement, although Chinese immigration into Russia continued to be a source of tension in the Russian-Chinese relationship (see Chapter 6). Second, negotiations over border issues had led to the unanticipated establishment—largely spearheaded by China—of an incipient multinational organization in Central Asia. Emerging from the 1996 and 1997 military troop reduction agreements, the five signatories, the Shanghai Five, continued to meet on a yearly basis, in 1998 at Almaty and in 1999 at Bishkek, to discuss issues of common interest, which included ethnic disputes, religious extremism, and terrorism.

Third, during the Yeltsin presidency, the military-technical relationship continued to expand, involving the increasing transfer of Russia's technological expertise to its Chinese clients. By the late 1990s, the Chinese market was critical to the continued existence of a number of Russian armaments producers. The Russian effort to preserve a 70-to-30 ratio of arms deliveries to technology transfer was ultimately unsuccessful. The issue figured prominently on the agenda at a series of meetings in 1998: these included July

1998 talks between the Russian prime minister and the Chinese premier, a July 1998 consultation meeting of the Russian and Chinese general staffs, and a follow-up visit to Beijing in October 1998 by Defense Minister Igor Sergeyev. During Sergeyev's visit, Russia and China agreed that Russia would provide China with technological assistance in the manufacture of high-technology weaponry. With the trip of Vice Prime Minister Ilya Klebanov to Beijing in August 1999 to attend a session of the Russian-Chinese Commission for Economic Cooperation, the two states agreed to intensify their coordination of joint projects in the military realm. Faced with insistent Chinese pressures and extremely limited prospects for domestic procurement orders—a situation exacerbated by the 1998 economic crisis—Russian leaders capitulated to Chinese demands to transfer increasingly sophisticated technological information and armaments.

Fourth, the Russian-Chinese economic relationship (other than in the military-technical realm) remained highly resistant to efforts at its development, plagued by seemingly insurmountable difficulties. Total trade turnover between the two states in 1998 was actually less than in 1992 (see Table 4.1, page 62). Chinese and Russian leaders had no choice but to abandon their often proclaimed goal of raising total trade turnover to 20 billion dollars by the year 2000. Russian hopes were bitterly thwarted in August 1997 when Russian firms lost out to the Western competition in their quest to provide generators and turbines for China's Three Gorges hydroelectric dam project. In fact, Russia's ability to penetrate Chinese markets was limited. Russia's overwhelming economic difficulties, as well as its incomplete transformation to the market, served to impede the development of trade and economic interactions with China. By the late 1990s, Russia and China were expanding their collaborative activities in aerospace (a sector closely related to the military-technical realm, with the actual content of collaborative agreements a highly guarded secret). The nuclear reactor project in Jiangsu province represented Russia's largest economic undertaking in China. Throughout the 1990s, Russia and China discussed a variety of potential projects in the energy sphere, which for the most part remained unrealized. Neither the Yeltsin presidency nor the Russian energy sector was inclined to focus its attention on prospects of energy collaboration with China. By the late 1990s, however, Chinese leaders, strongly cognizant of Chinese energy shortages, began to look more closely at Russia as a possible source of oil and gas. In February 1999, the two states signed an agreement for a feasibility study to consider the construction of a gas pipeline and agreed to begin negotiations regarding the construction of an oil pipeline from Siberian regions to Northern China.

Finally, Yeltsin's tenure in office was distinguished by the increasing convergence of Russian and Chinese interests in the international realm. The strategic partnership was envisioned as a means to check and counterbalance the hegemonic aspirations of the United States. In December 1998, Prime Minister Primakov, while on a state visit to India, created a furor when he proposed the creation of a "strategic triangle" made up of Russia, China, and India. Primakov apparently had in mind that the three states could act as a stabilizing influence in South Asia and a means of deterring actions such as the then ongoing U.S. (and British) military operations against Iraq, an action taken independently of United Nations (and Security Council) authorization. Primakov's proposal was predictably rebuffed by the leaderships of both India and China, unlikely partners given their longtime competitive and hostile relationship. Nonetheless, Russian and Chinese leaders concurred in their perspective on Iraq and their joint opposition to the continuation of economic sanctions, as well as the propensity of the United States to take independent action without appropriate consultation within the forum of the United Nations.

Increasingly, however, two international issues emerged at the forefront of Russian-Chinese concerns: (1) U.S. proposals to employ missile defense systems, both in Asia and on the U.S. mainland; and (2) the political crisis in Kosovo, resulting in NATO intervention in the spring of 1999 (see Chapter 7). The joint statement signed by Boris Yeltsin and Jiang Zemin at their 1998 summit meeting made explicit reference to the 1972 Anti-Ballistic Missile (ABM) Treaty, stressing the "exceptional importance of preserving and strengthening the Treaty on the Limitation of Anti-Ballistic Missile Systems, which was, and remains, one of the cornerstones in maintaining strategic stability throughout the world."[47] This sentiment was reaffirmed in a communiqué on the ABM Treaty signed by both vice foreign ministers in April 1999, which provided for regular consultations between the two states on the matter, and in the joint statement signed by Yeltsin and Jiang at their 1999 meeting. Moreover, both Russia and China viewed the deepening political crisis in Kosovo as an internal concern of the Yugoslav state, jointly opposing the eventual decision of NATO to make use of military force as ill advised and an inappropriate usurpation of the designated role of the Security Council of the United Nations. Russia originally displayed a greater interest in the conflict than China on both cultural and strategic grounds, but the NATO bombing of the Chinese embassy in Belgrade on May 7, 1999, galvanized Chinese sentiment. In its aftermath, the two states presented a united front in their denunciation of NATO military operations in Kosovo, deploring the circumvention of the United Nations, and the employment of "humanitarian intervention" as a means of exercising power politics.[48]

Déjà Vu?—The Russian-Chinese Treaty of Good-Neighborly Friendship and Cooperation

Boris Yeltsin's resignation from the Russian presidency in late December 1999 and his replacement by Vladimir Putin had no substantive impact on the Russian-Chinese relationship. Putin took up the position of acting president with the pledge that he would continue Yeltsin's foreign policy legacy, and Russian relations with China reflected the maintenance and intensification of trends set during the Yeltsin era. Putin proved to be a peripatetic leader; in his first year in office, he managed to meet with President Jiang Zemin on four different occasions. Putin, moreover, was both healthier and better organized than his predecessor, and Russian-Chinese relations came to benefit from the more systematic orientation of his government. After years of stagnation, Russian-Chinese economic ties in 2000 experienced modest growth. Russian-Chinese total trade turnover reached 8 billion dollars in 2000, its highest recorded level since the onset of the Russian Federation (see Table 4.1, page 62). Consultations on joint cooperative projects in energy intensified: During Putin's July 2001 trip to Beijing, the two states signed documents providing for a feasibility study for the construction of a 1,700–kilometer oil pipeline as well as granting the Russian gas monopoly Gazprom permission to participate in a tender for construction of a gas pipeline within China. Military-technical relations also continued to develop. In the year 2000, China was Russia's largest arms customer, the recipient of an estimated 70 percent of external arms deliveries.[49]

The Putin presidency at its onset maintained the strategic dynamics of the Russian-Chinese relationship constructed under Yeltsin. As previously, consultations between the two states devoted considerable attention to the international situation. Vladimir Putin's trip to Beijing in July 2000 resulted in the promulgation of two documents dealing with international concerns—a Joint Statement by the PRC President and the Russian Federation President on the Anti-Missile Issue and the Beijing Declaration of the People's Republic of China and the Russian Federation. The joint statement on anti-missile issues reiterated Russian and Chinese opposition to U.S. plans to construct a form of national missile defense or to deploy a regional anti-missile defense system in the Asia Pacific region. The most notable aspect of the Beijing Declaration was a clause stating the intention of the two states to begin preparations for a Sino-Russian Treaty of Good-Neighborly Friendship and Cooperation.

Subsequent bilateral consultations between representatives within the Russian and Chinese foreign ministries focused on drafting a treaty; by April 2001, a protocol on a draft treaty was signed by the Russian and Chinese foreign ministers. The completed document was signed between Presidents

Putin and Jiang in Moscow during Jiang's visit in July 2001. The treaty, officially the Treaty of Good-Neighborly Friendship and Cooperation between the People's Republic of China and the Russian Federation, was a twenty-five-article document that outlined the basic premises of the Russian-Chinese relationship for a twenty-year period (see Appendix). The two states pledged themselves to the continued development of a "strategic cooperative partnership," renounced the use or threat of force in their mutual relations, and reaffirmed the principles of national sovereignty and territorial integrity in their mutual relations. Article 5 explicitly referred to Russian support of China on the Taiwan issue, specifying Russia's adherence to the one-China policy and its opposition to Taiwanese independence. The two states declared that there were no territorial demands between them, while announcing that they would continue to hold negotiations to resolve questions of border demarcation in those areas set aside in the 1991 border agreement.[50] While the treaty did not bind the two states together in a formal alliance, it did impose certain conditions on their interactions with third parties. Article 8 specified that "neither party will participate in any alliance or bloc which damages the sovereignty, security, and territorial integrity of the other party," or to allow a third party—either a country or an organization or group—to use its territory to such ends. Article 9 provided for immediate mutual consultations in the event of a threat of aggression endangering the security interests of either state. Within the international realm, the treaty further reaffirmed the Russian and Chinese commitment to upholding the global strategic balance and maintenance of security, to promoting the process of nuclear disarmament, and to strengthening the role of the United Nations in the maintenance of peace and development.

The Russian-Chinese Treaty of Good-Neighborly Friendship and Cooperation inevitably recalled the Sino-Soviet Treaty of Friendship, Alliance and Mutual Assistance of 1950, but in fact the scope of the 2001 document was considerably more restricted than its ill-fated predecessor. Whereas the 1950 treaty provided for joint military action against aggression, the 2001 treaty noted the need for immediate mutual consultations in case of a threat to the security of either state. The vocabulary employed in the 2001 treaty to describe the international situation was restrained and seemingly deliberately nonprovocative. Certain code words, common to Russian-Chinese discourse by the late 1990s were notably absent: these included *multipolarity*, *hegemony*, and *power politics*. Nonetheless, the treaty represented a deviation from standard practice for both states.

The Chinese, following the deterioration of the Sino-Soviet relationship, had opted for nonalignment as a foreign policy strategy. While the Soviet Union promulgated treaties with a number of client states—especially in the

Brezhnev era—Russian foreign policy in the Yeltsin era was much more circumscribed. During the 1990s, Russia signed friendship treaties with a number of CIS States, but adopted a more restrained approach elsewhere. Russia concluded a vague treaty with North Korea in February 2000 while Putin was still acting president, and a brief cooperation treaty with Iran in March 2001.[51] In many respects, the Russian-Chinese Friendship Treaty was an unexpected development, all the more so because the concept originated on the Chinese side with Jiang Zemin suggesting the treaty to Vladimir Putin.[52]

For both states, a combination of international and bilateral factors played a role in their decision to promulgate the Friendship Treaty. On the one hand, geostrategic considerations were apparently of importance to both sides. The Chinese reportedly contacted Prime Minister Evgenii Primakov about a treaty shortly after the NATO bombing of their embassy in Belgrade.[53] Both Russia and China strongly maintained that the treaty was in no way directed against a third country. Nonetheless, the two states seemed to view their "strategic partnership," now upgraded to treaty status, as a means of exerting leverage on the international situation, and more specifically of constraining the activities of the United States. However, the bilateral dimensions of the treaty were also extremely important. In an interview with *Rossiiskaia Gazeta*, Jiang Zemin indicated that China viewed the treaty as a means to establish a solid legal basis to China's partnership with Russia.[54] Speaking at Moscow State University during his July 2001 trip to Russia, Jiang noted China's overriding national objective as the development of a modernized and prosperous state, a goal requiring a "long term peaceful and stable international environment." As Jiang pointedly noted with reference to the Russian-Chinese relationship: "Promises must be kept and action must be resolute. And the same also holds true for contacts between states."[55] For China, the treaty served as a means of codifying the positive gains achieved during the Yeltsin era and ensuring the commitment of subsequent leaderships to the maintenance of that legacy. The Chinese leadership's emphasis on modernization as an overarching regime goal necessitated the pursuit of cordial relations with Russia. On its part, the Putin administration also determined that Russian interests were served through the Friendship Treaty. By most conventional measures, Russia was weaker than China. Russia, no less than China, required peaceful relations with contiguous states to pursue national reconstruction. Article 6, which noted the essential resolution of the border issues, was important to both states in stating the inviolability of the border. The Chinese provided Russia with the reassurance that they had no interest in staking out claims on lost territories or in colonizing the area through direct or indirect means. In turn, the Russian government indicated that it would not tolerate efforts by regional elites to alter the 1991 border agreement.

"Brothers Forever"?: Testing the Relationship, 2001 to mid-2003

The geostrategic component of Russian-Chinese relations was tested by the terrorist attacks on the United States of September 11, 2001. Both Russia and China responded by hastening to improve their relationship with the United States, asserting their support for the anti-terrorist coalition. Nonetheless, the configuration of strategic interactions between the three states was altered as Russia moved closer to the United States than did China (see Chapter 7). Compared to Russia, which signed on as an active participant in the U.S.-led incursions into Afghanistan, China remained more wary, suspicious that the United States would seek to extend its global role under the guise of fighting terrorism. In the aftermath of the attacks, Russia and China toned down their criticisms of the United States (either implicit or explicit) while struggling to come up with a coordinated foreign policy platform suitable to newly constrained parameters.

However, both Russia and China reacted coolly to President George Bush's designation in January 2002 of Iraq, Iran, and North Korea as an "axis of evil." Russia emerged as a more assertive player as well as a more vocal critic of the United States in the flurry of diplomatic activity that accompanied the U.S.-led attack on Iraq in March 2003. Aligning with France and Germany within the Security Council of the United Nations, Russia announced its intention to veto a U.S.-sponsored resolution that would authorize the use of force against Iraq. Simultaneously, Russia and China stepped up their coordinated response to international issues: the foreign ministers of Russia and China released joint press communiqués on Iraq and North Korea during their February 2003 meeting. For Russia and China, the U.S. unwillingness to compromise on the Iraqi issue underscored the enduring relevance of fundamental precepts of their worldview. The Russian-Chinese joint declaration of May 2003 was forthright in its condemnation of "unilateralism and power politics," while maintaining the commitment of the two states to the construction of a multipolar world.[56]

The May 2003 joint communiqué indicated the continued importance of the United States as the referent for Russian-Chinese international strategy. Beyond the international sphere, Russian-Chinese bilateral interactions by mid-2003 displayed a certain degree (by no means complete, especially in the economic realm) of institutionalization, which suggested the commitment of both sides, if not to undying friendship, at least to the development and maintenance of their relationship. Quietly, the two states pledged to increase the pace of negotiations over the status of the three contested islands left out of the 1991 border agreement. In the early 2000s, China continued to purchase some of the most technologically sophisticated aviation and naval weaponry in the Russian arsenal. In 2002, this included two Sovremennyi destroyers, eight Kilo-class submarines, ten Su-27 fighter jets, and between 38 and 40 Su-30MKK fighter jets.[57] Putin's foreign policy orientation toward China did not deviate from the basic parameters laid down in the Yeltsin era (although his movement toward the West did introduce complications into the international component of the relationship). But by 2002, it was apparent that Putin's greater attention to administrative and personnel issues had positive consequences for Russian interactions with China. In contrast to Boris Yeltsin, whose managerial style bordered on the chaotic, the methodical Putin directed greater efforts to establishing structures of Russian-Chinese coordination, especially in the economic realm. In particular, Putin directed attention to the prospects for energy collaboration with the PRC.

During the 1990s, the Russian Federation faced a series of seemingly overwhelming challenges, many the legacy of the Soviet collapse. In contrast, China enjoyed unparalleled economic growth and political stability. Although Jiang Zemin assumed the position of general secretary of the CCP under highly inauspicious circumstances in the aftermath of the Tiananmen events, he proved to be proficient at the position, serving as CCP leader from 1989 until his formal retirement at the Sixteenth Party Congress in November 2002. By late 2002, however, China was facing its own set of economic and political issues, collectively not as daunting as those encountered by Russia, but sufficient to create a sense of uncertainty. Jiang Zemin's retention of the chairmanship of the Military Affairs Commission at the party congress indicated his intention to remain—in the style of his own predecessor Deng Xiaoping—the de facto leader of China. Nonetheless, the National Party Congress, followed in March 2003 by the National People's Congress, the governmental counterpart, instituted a sweeping transition of the political leadership, signaling a generational shift of power. This emergent leadership—the "fourth generation"—differed from the previous generation in its lack of familiarity with Russia. Jiang Zemin had studied in the Soviet Union in the 1950s and spoke Russian fluently. His successor Hu Jintao built his political career in the remote Chinese hinterlands (including a four-year tenure as the Communist Party leader in Tibet), making his first trip to Russia only in October 2001.

Conclusions

The onset of interactions between Russia and China took place at a relatively late date in the historical evolution of the two states and was strongly influenced by the expansionary movement of both states on their frontiers.

Despite sharing a border stretching thousands of kilometers, Russia and China developed separately, with little interaction between cultures. The lack of cultural linkages, however, was partially offset in the twentieth century by the shared political legacy of Marxism-Leninism. The CCP was a rare example of a successful Communist Party movement that attained power in a nationalist struggle. Its subsequent association with the Soviet Union— exemplified in the 1950 Friendship Treaty—was voluntary. At the same time, the nationalist character of the CCP was also an essential factor in the subsequent unraveling of the alliance, as China proved unwilling to be appropriately deferential to Soviet authority. The common political heritage of the two states was not sufficient to keep their alliance afloat and is destined to continue to erode over time. The generation of Chinese leaders who were trained in the Soviet Union was coming to a close. Nonetheless, the commitment of the Chinese leadership to the maintenance of strong ties with Russia was illustrated by Hu Jintao's announcement that his first formal presidential visit would be to Moscow.

The experience of Russian-Chinese relations during their first decade indicated the influence of a series of convergent factors that impelled them toward closer relations. In the 1990s, geopolitical considerations served to bring Russia and China closer together although Russian claims to great power status rested more on its past than its present capabilities. Geography, moreover, placed certain immutable conditions on interactions between the two states. For both Russia and China, the task of economic construction (or possibly reconstruction in the Russian case) demanded the cultivation of harmonious ties with a large contiguous neighbor. The two states were similarly motivated to cooperate on regional issues with regard to the maintenance of political stability and the deterrence of the religious extremism and terrorist activities in Central Asia. These factors appeared to transcend, at least for the present, the absence of cultural ties and the historical legacy of discord between the two states, as both Russia and China realized that cordial relations were in their national interest.

3

Russia and China as Neighbors

Border Issues and Regional Relations in Asia

Geography was a determinate factor—although acting in conjunction with other variables—in shaping the historical pattern of interactions between Russia and China. More often than not, however, issues surrounding their common border divided rather than united the two states. In the 1990s, Russian-Chinese relations with respect to border issues were largely congenial on the national level, although Russian elites in the border regions continued to voice discontent. Interactions on border questions reflected the institutional heritage of agreements concluded in the waning days of the Soviet Union. The demise of the Soviet Union, moreover, not only significantly reduced the length of the Sino-Soviet border, but also gave rise to the emergence of a number of new states, contiguous or near-contiguous neighbors to both Russia and China (see Map 3.1). Forging a relationship with these states was a preoccupation of both Russia and China in a bilateral and multilateral context. To a considerable degree, Russia and China shared complementary interests in Central Asia, notably in the preservation of regional stability, which led them to coordinate their efforts to promote the development of the Shanghai Cooperation Organization (SCO). Elsewhere in Asia, however, Russian and Chinese interests were considerably less convergent, with the two states largely pursuing their own independent foreign policy goals in regional bilateral or multilateral relationships.

Putting the Border Conflict to Rest

Despite the passions aroused over border boundaries, the actual historical claims to territory advanced by both Russia and China are rather hazy. As

42

Map 3.1   **Russian-Chinese Border**

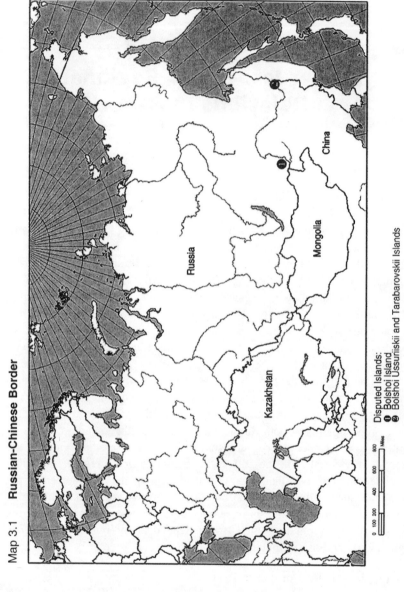

Source: Brigham Young University, Geography Department, 2002.

noted in Chapter 2, historically, the border regions lay beyond the traditional boundaries of either state. The 1689 Treaty of Nerchinsk between Russia and China vaguely distinguished the area of the Amur basin, between the Amur and Ussuri rivers, within the Chinese domain. Russia, however, was successful in obtaining some 665,000 square miles of territory from China in the Treaty of Aigun in 1858, the Treaty of Peking in 1860, and the Treaty of Tarbagatai in 1864.[1] The boundary itself was never demarcated. While the Soviet regime gave some acknowledgment to Chinese jurisdictional claims in the 1920s that sought to locate the border along the midpoint of rivers, Stalin preemptively brought an end to these efforts in 1930 by unilaterally setting the Sino-Soviet boundary along the right side of riverbanks. This move also meant that the islands within the rivers (and all river navigation) came under Soviet control.

During the era of Sino-Soviet enmity, the dispute over the 7,100-kilometer border came to symbolize in many aspects the conflict between the two states. As the quarrel intensified, the Chinese came to press their claim—by no means distinctive to the Sino-Soviet relationship but a staple of Maoist era interactions with neighboring states—that the boundary between China and the Soviet Union was inequitable, imposed upon a weak and defenseless Qing dynasty by a rapacious European power. A rapid militarization of the border ensued as each side sent troops to protect its turf, turning the border region into a heavily fortified armed camp. Relations between the Soviet Union and China reached their nadir in March 1969 when a clash between Soviet and Chinese border troops over a disputed island (Damanskii to the Soviets, Zhenbao to the Chinese) in the Ussuri River led to a number of deaths. In the aftermath of this incident, both sides agreed to a reconvocation of stalled border talks. Progress in resolving the conflict was insignificant; nonetheless, fifteen rounds of negotiations were held between 1969 and 1978, until they were broken off by the Chinese after the Soviet Union signed a Treaty of Friendship and Cooperation with Vietnam in 1978. The Soviet side put out a few tentative feelers during the later years of the Brezhnev leadership. Measurable progress was not attained, however, until Mikhail Gorbachev became general secretary of the Communist Party of the Soviet Union in March 1985. In July 1986, Gorbachev gave a speech in Vladivostok that signaled a newfound Soviet flexibility on border issues, noting Soviet willingness to discuss the reduction of force levels along the Sino-Soviet border and to acquiesce to Chinese demands that the border line in disputed river areas be set along the main navigation channels.

Gorbachev's speech provided the impetus for the resumption of border negotiations in February 1987 and the initiation of talks on reducing Soviet and Chinese border defense troops in November 1989. After their resumption in February 1987, border negotiations between the two states were held at the vice foreign minister level under the joint chairmanship of Qian Qichen (later Tian Jengpei) and Igor Rogachev. By October 1988, agreement had been reached as to the alignment of most of the eastern boundary and preparations were made to shift attention to the western part of the border. By April 1991, an agreement on the eastern section of the Sino-Soviet border had been concluded, which was subsequently signed by the foreign ministers of the two states in May 1991, and by Jiang Zemin and Mikhail Gorbachev during Jiang's June 1991 visit to Moscow.[2] Since approximately 3,550 kilometers of the border were along rivers, a key aspect of the agreement was the determination—in conformance with international law—to set the boundary along the middle line of the main fairway of navigable rivers or along the middle of the river or its main channel in the case of non-navigable rivers. The status of three islands, however, was left unresolved subject to future negotiations: Bolshoi Ussuriiskii and Tarabarovskii islands in the region of Khabarovsk in the Amur River, and Bolshoi island in the upper reaches of the Argun River in Chita oblast.[3]

In accordance with the terms agreed to upon the establishment of diplomatic relations between China and the Russian Federation, the Yeltsin government accepted the validity of the 1991 border agreement, which was subsequently ratified by the Russian Supreme Soviet on February 13, 1992, by a vote of 174 to 2, with 24 abstentions.[4]

Following the collapse of the Soviet Union, border negotiations on the western section of the former Soviet border were reconstituted to allow for the incorporation of Kazakhstan, Kyrgyzstan, and eventually Tajikistan as newly sovereign states into the process. In fact, the Russian segment of the western border is only fifty-five kilometers long. Border talks between the five states began in the fall of 1992, and by June 1994 an agreement between Russia and China on the western section of the Russian-Chinese border had been drafted. This was signed by Boris Yeltsin and Jiang Zemin during the second Russian-Chinese summit in Moscow in 1994, and ratified by the Russian Duma and the Chinese National People's Congress without controversy.

The 1991 border agreement laid out the terms for setting the boundary in the abstract, delegating the task of surveying and demarcating the border to a joint demarcation commission. Since most of the 4,250-kilometer Russian-Chinese border is along rivers, much of the work of the Boundary Demarcation Commission was occupied with the highly technical process of determining the course of river flows as a means of dividing jurisdiction and deciding which islands would remain Russian and which would be allocated to China. The 600-plus kilometers of the boundary line on land, most of it within Primorskii krai, also involved technical surveys to locate the position of the watershed line in conformance with agreements dating from the 1860s. According to the 1991 border agreement, the demarcation of the border was to have been completed by 1997. Both economic and political factors slowed the progress of border demarcation on the Russian side: Russian vessels were chronically short on fuel while regional authorities protested the reversion of territory to China (see Chapter 6). The document signed during Boris Yeltsin's trip to Beijing in November 1997 marking the completion of the demarcation of the border was more symbolic than substantive, an effort to conform to predetermined deadlines. In fact, border demarcation work continued for another seventeen months. The Boundary Demarcation Commission announced the completion of the demarcation of the western segment of the Russian-Chinese border in September 1998 and the completion of the demarcation of the eastern section of the border in April 1999. According to Genrikh Kireev, chairman of the Russian side of the commission, the commission had erected more than 2,084 border signs and markers and identified 2,444 islands, of which 1,281 were to be allocated to China, leaving 1,163 to remain under Russian sovereignty.[5] In Primorskii krai, the adjustment of the border meant the return of approximately 1,500 hectares of land to China although China agreed to let Russia retain some 140 (of approximately 300) hectares of land in the Khasan region, the site of graves of Soviet soldiers who died fighting the Japanese in 1938.[6] During Boris Yeltsin's December 1999 trip to China, the Russian and Chinese foreign ministers signed two protocols that for the first time set (except for the three contested islands) the exact specifications of the Russian-Chinese frontier.[7]

A notable aspect of Russian-Chinese border negotiations was the effort to establish arrangements for the joint economic use of border islands. For the most part, the islands within the border rivers are uninhabited and of no economic or political significance. In some instances, however, where the islands are adjacent to settled regions, the Russian local residents made use of them for hunting, fishing, grazing of livestock, and, notably, in the case of the disputed islands near Khabarovsk, the building of dachas. In these situations, Russian inhabitants of the border regions were understandably reluctant to surrender their access to these territories. The attempt to establish some framework for shared activity on disputed territory built upon proposals that were set out in the Gorbachev era, but it also owed much to regional initiatives, especially by the authorities within Chita oblast. When it became evident that Menkesili island, which covers an area of 175 square kilometers in the Argun River, was to be transferred to China, local residents, who used the island for foraging, fishing, and as a hayfield, protested vehemently. By 1995, however, the local authorities were successful in working out an arrangement with the Chinese for joint economic use of the island, which also served as a precedent for further negotiations at the national level.[8] Beginning in November 1996, the Russian and Chinese foreign ministries commenced discussion on this issue, announcing in March 1997 that they had reached agreement on a draft proposal. This agreement, formally entitled Guidelines for Joint Economic Use of Individual Islands and the Water Areas Adjacent to Them on Border Rivers, was signed during Boris Yeltsin's November 1997 visit to China. By April 1999, the Russian-Chinese intergovernmental commission had agreed upon ten islands scheduled for joint economic development, and in December 1999 the Russian and Chinese foreign ministers signed a five-year Agreement on Joint Economic Uses of Individual Islands and Border River Water Areas Adjacent to Them during Yeltsin's trip to Beijing. According to the document, Russia was to set aside an island in the Amur while China specified several islands in the Menkesili island group in the Argun, as well as an island in the Amur for joint economic use. Joint economic activity was to be restricted to the local population, with considerable administrative authority divested in the regional authorities.

The joint communiqué signed between Jiang Zemin and Vladimir Putin during their July 2000 summit specifically referred to the border situation, noting that the agreement on joint economic use of border islands and adjacent waterways was "without precedent" and that the two states would continue negotiations to resolve contested border sections.[9] Consultations on the disputed border islands were held in Beijing in March 2001. The 2001 Friendship Treaty adopted an extremely positive attitude toward the border issue, affirming in Article 6 that there were "no territorial demands" dividing Russia and China and that the two states were "resolved to actively work to turn the building of their border into a border of everlasting peace and friendship for all generations." A further clause, however, allowed that the two parties would "continue to hold negotiations to resolve questions of border demarcation." The accompanying joint statement further pledged that the pace of negotiations to resolve the border issue would be intensified. Subsequent statements by Russian officials indicated that negotiations over the islands were drawing to a close. Speaking to the Russian State Council in January 2003, President Putin predicted that the border questions with China would be resolved: "I expect the foreign ministries of the two countries to make the necessary decisions, but this will require, of course, certain compromises. However, there is every reason to presume that the problem will shortly be settled for once and for all."[10] The May 2003 joint communiqué signed by Putin and newly designated Chinese president Hu Jintao noted that the two states would resolve the border issue "as soon as possible."[11]

During the 1990s, regional leaders in the Russian Far East, especially in Khabarovsk and Primorskii krais, were vocal in their protests of the 1991 border agreement and the subsequent demarcation of the border, gaining considerable verbal support for their cause among various elites at the federal level. In Khabarovsk krai, the struggle continued into the 2000s, led by the Governor Viktor Ishaev, who pledged never to oversee the transfer of Bolshoi Ussuriiskii and Tarabarovskii islands to the Chinese.

Nonetheless, the clamor over border protests tended to obscure the very significant achievements of the 1991 border agreement and the subsequent demarcation of the boundary regions. Except for a miniscule area, the border dispute has been laid to rest. Similarly, the ability of Russia and China to initiate procedures for joint economic activity on island territories has been a relatively unemphasized and underappreciated element of the evolving Russian-Chinese relationship. Considerably more attention was directed to the flamboyant protests of the border demarcation in Khabarovsk and Primorskii krais than to the more conciliatory efforts of the Chita authorities to retain use—if not formal sovereignty—of island lands and their surrounding waters.[12] The success of Russia and China in largely resolving their entrenched territorial dispute invites comparison to the Kurile island conflict between Russia and Japan, but the situation is not wholly analogous. The Russian proposals for solving the Kurile island dispute typically offered the Japanese the prospect of joint economic activity on the islands with the retention of Russian sovereignty over them.[13] In contrast, the proposals for joint economic activity between Russia and China reflected a situation in which China assumed formal sovereignty but acquiesced to a continued Russian presence on certain islands. Since the Chinese were historically excluded from the islands, the concept of joint economic activity was something of a euphemism.

In fact, Russia's negotiating position with China over the disputed islands was not favorable. By the standards of international law, the disputed islands should be yielded to China. Russia's economic decline, moreover, has further reduced its stature at the bargaining table. Geostrategic considerations have contributed to Russia's unwillingness to surrender the disputed territories. Bolshoi island is near the juncture of Russia, China, and Mongolia, as well as serving as a site for the water supply to Krasnokamensk, the second largest city in Chita oblast. Bolshoi Ussuriiskii and Tarabarovskii islands are directly adjacent to Khabarovsk, the largest city in the Russian Far East and the capital of Khabarovsk krai.[14] In the 1990s, Russian-Chinese negotiating behavior on border issues was marked less by compromise than by Chinese willingness to grant Russia territorial concessions (as in the Khasan district) and to allow Russian citizens to retain economic use of islands legally transferred to China. This offers a potential formula for the eventual resolution of the island dispute, which has been steadfastly rejected by regional leaders in Khabarovsk. Nonetheless, Putin's reference to the need to compromise in his January 2003 statement implied that Russia would be compelled to transfer sovereignty over at least part of this territory to China.

Border Troop Reductions

As with the interrelated issue of border demarcation, Gorbachev's 1986 Vladivostok speech provided the impetus for the initiation of negotiations between the Soviets and the Chinese aimed at reducing troop strengths along the heavily fortified Sino-Soviet border. By the early 1980s, the Soviets were stationing forty-five divisions, comprising about 400,000 men, along the border, about one-quarter of their total forces. Chinese troop levels, although qualitatively inferior and dispersed over a wider geographical area, were even higher. The Chinese, moreover, had made it clear that the reduction of the Soviet military presence along the border was one of the prerequisites for the normalization of relations. Hence, Gorbachev's statement in Vladivostok that the Soviet Union would be willing to discuss the reduction of force levels along the Sino-Soviet border, as well as his announcement that the Soviet Union was considering withdrawing a large part of its troops from Mongolia, were taken as positive signals by the Chinese. Gorbachev's subsequent moves toward Soviet military retrenchment, driven by economic as well as political interests, were similarly welcomed. In December 1988, the Soviet leadership reported that the Soviet Union would be reducing Soviet military forces by 500,000 men (40 percent directed at divisions east of the Ural mountains) and that the Soviet Union and China had agreed to begin talks on border troop reductions.

The first talks on reducing Soviet and Chinese border defense troops took place in November 1989, followed by the announcement that the Soviet Union would begin withdrawing troops from Mongolia. In April 1990, during Premier Li Peng's visit to Moscow, the Soviet and Chinese foreign ministers signed an agreement on Guiding Principles for Reciprocal Armed Forces Cuts and Confidence Building in the Military Sphere in the Soviet-Chinese Border Area that pledged to reduce the number of armed forces along the Sino-Soviet border to "the lowest possible level" and to transfer remaining forces into purely defensive units. By December 1991, on the eve of the Soviet collapse, Chinese and Soviet negotiators had further refined the scope of discussion, with each side presenting their drafts of a general agreement.

As with the corollary boundary negotiations, the talks between China and the Soviet Union on military troop reductions along the border were reconstituted following the collapse of the Soviet Union to include Kazakhstan,

Kyrgyzstan, and Tajikistan, along with Russia, as the four representatives of the delegation from the Commonwealth of Independent States (CIS). The basic resolution of the boundary issue, accompanied by an overall warming of relations, removed the fundamental rationale for the presence of heavily armed troops along the border. Russian negotiators, moreover, were strongly motivated by economic considerations. In a 1992 interview, Russian ambassador to China Igor Rogachev noted that the Soviet Union had spent no less than 60 billion rubles on strengthening its border with China in the 1960s and 1970s.[15] The Russian military, beset by financial woes and subject to large reductions of troops and armaments spending, could no longer afford to preserve the military force levels of the Soviet era.[16]

A major concern, first for the Soviets and later for the Russians, in negotiations with China was how to define the size of the border region. Because of the proximity of the Trans-Siberian railway, the Soviet Union stationed its troops closer to the Sino-Soviet border than did China. Russia thus initially sought to define the border region as a 25-kilometer zone, while China pressed for a wider area with a depth of approximately 300 kilometers. The border region was defined as a 100-kilometer zone on each side of the CIS-Chinese border at the eighth round of talks held in November 1992. Subsequent negotiations, nonetheless, bogged down over the specifics regarding armaments and troop configurations within the border regions, essentially an issue for the Russians rather than the Chinese. The Chinese military in fact did not maintain any sizable contingent of forces or equipment within the 100-kilometer zone, selecting rather to maintain troops in rear areas. By April 1996, however, significant progress had been made, enabling the leaders of China, Russia, Kyrgyzstan, Kazakhstan, and Tajikistan to convene in Shanghai to sign the Agreement on Strengthening Mutual Military Confidence in the Border Regions, which sought to provide a level of transparency in military operations along the border. A year later, in April 1997, the same leaders gathered in Moscow, signing a follow-up Agreement on the Mutual Reduction of Military Strength in Border Regions.

Included in the military force reduction agreement (which extends through 2020) was a pledge to refrain from the threat of force or use of force in the border regions and the imposition of troop and equipment ceilings for land forces, frontline aviation, and air defense forces in the 100-kilometer zone on each side of the border. Russia agreed to a maximum number of 119,400 troops on its eastern border with China.[17] The greater relevance of the agreement lay in its symbolic importance, signaling a commitment to the maintenance of peace, security, and stability in a formerly highly conflicted region. The agreement permitted force and equipment ceilings that neither side was likely to maintain.[18] On the Russian side, military troop reductions on the order of 15 percent in the Transbaikal and Far East military regions had already been scheduled before the signing of the agreement.[19] Russian minister of defense Igor Sergéyev further noted during his October 1998 trip to Beijing that Russia was in the process of disbanding or reducing in size about 300 formations and military units stationed in areas along the Russian-Chinese border.

In reality, economic constraints compelled the drastic reduction of Russian troop strengths along the Russian-Chinese border. Even maintaining basic facilities and operations was a challenge: many border posts were deserted, and power cuts—due to nonpayment of energy bills—resulted in the periodic deactivation of the alarm system along segments of the Russian-Chinese border. In December 2001, Lieutenant-General Alexander Shramchenko, commander of the Russian Radio-Technical Troops, disclosed that the Russian military had lost its ability to control air space from the Ural mountains to the Kurile islands.[20] In the Russian Far East, the number of servicemen was reduced to one-sixth of previous numbers with a commensurate decrease in officers.[21] In the late 1990s, no Russian division in the region had more than half its authorized number of officers or servicemen. As Felix Chang noted, "the Russian military in the Far East has become a shadow of its former self."[22] Russian forward deployment of troops became a logistical impossibility, a circumstance that no doubt made it easier for China to proceed with its own plans to reduce military troop strengths. At the same time that Sergeyev visited Beijing in 1998, President Jiang Zemin announced that China would be reducing the size of its army by 500,000 men.[23] Thus, by the late 1990s, the military component of Russian-Chinese border relations had diminished markedly, almost to the point of insignificance.

From "The Shanghai Five" to the Shanghai Cooperation Organization

The emergence of a regional multilateral organization in Central Asia (see Map 3.2) was an unanticipated outcome of the 1996 and 1997 agreements on military troops in the border areas. Since 1996, the leaders of the five states that signed the border agreements—originally christened the "Shanghai Five"—have met on a yearly basis, redefining their mission with an expanded agenda that has moved away from traditional indicators of military prowess to embrace a broad-based conception of regional security. Beginning in 1998, the four CIS states began to participate in meetings as separate entities, rather than as a joint delegation that was effectively under Russian leadership. At the July 2000 meeting Uzbekistan took part for the first time as an observer, formally joining at its June 2001 session, which resulted in the inauguration

Map 3.2 **Central Asia**

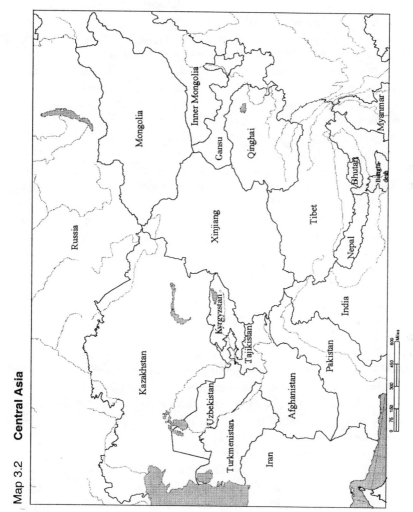

Source: Brigham Young University, Geography Department, 2002.

of the institution as the SCO.[24] A number of other states in the region—India and Pakistan in particular—also expressed interest in joining the organization.

The terms of the 1996 and 1997 border agreements provided for yearly meetings of the heads of state and defense ministers, as well as the establishment of a joint supervisory group to verify that agreements were implemented. By July 2000, the "Shanghai Five" had agreed to broaden the scope of their interaction. The joint statement signed by the heads of state at their July 2000 meeting in Dushanbe set out the task of establishing institutional structures, with the development of multilateral links in a number of spheres, including the economy and trade, culture, environmental protection, law enforcement, and diplomacy. The Dushanbe Statement planned for the appointment by each state of a special envoy to the group, regular meetings of foreign ministers and prime ministers of the member states, the establishment of a coordinating council, the adoption of a constitution, and the development of cooperative arrangements to coordinate law enforcement activities, including the establishment of a regional anti-terrorist agency in Bishkek.[25] By the early 2000s, the association had held meetings between representatives of a number of governmental ministries of the participating states; these included convocations of ministers of trade, culture, the interior, and border guard chiefs. At its June 2002 meeting, SCO member states approved a constitutional charter laying out the legal basis for the organization, with the permanent secretariat to be located in Beijing.[26] Further institutional details regarding the operation of the SCO were confirmed by the heads of the member states at its May 2003 meeting. These included approval of a financial charter specifying budgetary arrangements, regulations on the various operative councils (heads of state, government, foreign ministers, etc.), and the establishment of the SCO Secretariat in Beijing and the Regional Anti-Terrorist Structure in Bishkek. In addition, Zhang Deguang (as of May 2003 the Chinese ambassador to Russia) was appointed the first secretary general of the SCO. According to the declaration, the permanent bodies of the SCO were to begin functional operations by January 1, 2004.

Well before the events of September 11, 2001, the member states of the SCO had identified Islamic extremism and the Taliban regime in Afghanistan as major threats in the region. The joint statements released at the conclusion of both the 1998 meeting in Almaty and the 1999 meeting in Bishkek identified ethnic disputes, religious extremism, international terrorism, cross-national crimes, weapons smuggling, drug trafficking, and illegal immigration as common areas of concern. At their July 2000 meeting, the participants agreed to an initiative proposed by Kyrgyzstan to set up an anti-terrorist center in Bishkek. As the Dushanbe Statement noted, "all sides are deeply concerned over the continued military and political confrontations in Afghanistan and hold that these have constituted a serious threat to regional and international security."[27] The Shanghai Convention on Rebuffing Terrorism, Separatism, and Extremism was enacted by the heads of the SCO in June 2001, followed up by the Agreement of the Member States of the Shanghai Cooperation Organization on a Regional Mechanism for Countering Terrorism in June 2002.[28] These agreements served as the framework for the erection of the SCO regional anti-terrorist center in Bishkek. Although the focus of the SCO had expanded in the early 2000s to include a range of economic and environmental issues, regional security nonetheless remained a priority for the organization. As Article 1 of the charter noted: "The fundamental goals and tasks of the SCO include . . . the development of multi-profiled cooperation with the goal of supporting and strengthening peace, security and stability in the region" as well as "joint action again terrorism, separatism, and extremism in all of its manifestations."[29] One planned measure announced in May 2003 by SCO defense ministers regarded plans to conduct two joint anti-terrorist exercises in the fall of 2003 in Kazakhstan and China.

The endurance and subsequent evolution of the Shanghai Five since 1997 largely reflected the interests of China in creating a regional structure to foster security and stability in the Central Asian region.[30] While Russia had recourse to the CIS as a means of maintaining a foothold in Central Asia, China sought to promote the SCO in order to develop linkages in the area. Russian foreign policy in the late 1990s, under the increasingly enfeebled direction of Boris Yeltsin, simply did not pay much attention to the SCO. At the 1998 meeting, Russia was the only state not represented by its president, leaving Foreign Minister Evgenii Primakov to serve in Yeltsin's place. A shaky Yeltsin did eventually materialize (in the midst of considerable speculation as to his presence) for the 1999 meeting in Bishkek, but he was clearly upstaged by the energetic activities of Chinese president Jiang Zemin, who used the occasion to deliver a speech outlining his four-point proposal for the development of the organization. Russia similarly was the last state to appoint a special envoy to the organization in February 2000, a decision made not by Yeltsin but by Acting President Vladimir Putin. China has taken the initiative in hosting a number of SCO meetings: for example, the first meetings of culture and trade ministers, and an unscheduled meeting of foreign ministers, took place in Beijing. The placement of the SCO Secretariat in Beijing and the selection of a Chinese national to serve as the first secretary general similarly testified to the interests of China in the development of the organization. China's actions, moreover, were facilitated by its affluence, at least relative to the other SCO members. In his speech to the SCO in May 2003, President Hu Jintao announced that China would make office space for the SCO Secretariat available free.

With the ascendance of Putin to the Russian presidency, Russian-Chinese interactions on the SCO become considerably less asymmetric. In contrast to Yeltsin, Putin displayed a greater interest in the SCO and recognition of its potential utility. The July 2001 Friendship Treaty reflected the commitment of China and Russia to the SCO as a means to maintain political stability. Article 14 noted that the two states should "promote stability with their peripheral regions, establish an atmosphere of mutual understanding, trust, and cooperation, and spur efforts to establish a mechanism for multilateral cooperation suited to the actual security and cooperation issues in these regions." Russia hosted the SCO meetings of heads of state in both 2002 and 2003, and Russia and China agreed to bear the largest share of the economic burden in financing the operation.[31] Russia and China, for example, were reported to have each pledged to provide about twenty-five percent of the financing for the regional anti-terrorist center in Bishkek.[32]

China's original desire to promote the SCO appears to have been largely driven by a fear of the perils of ethnic separatism and the threat it posed to continued Chinese hegemony over politically restive Muslim—primarily Uighur—ethnic groups in Xinjiang province. But China has also been committed to the development of economic development in the region, not only because of its potential benefits to China, but also because it has been viewed as a stabilizing factor that serves to mitigate ethnic unrest. As noted by Chinese academic Pan Guang: "Cooperation in security must have an economic basis. If Central Asian countries can greatly improve their economies, the room of maneuver for terrorists will surely be greatly reduced."[33] Although Russia faced no comparable challenge along its borders with SCO member states, it nonetheless shared Chinese concerns regarding ethnically based separatist movements—Chechnya being an obvious example—and Islamic fundamentalism. Both Russia and China considered the maintenance of stability a key goal for the Central Asia region. The convergence of Russian and Chinese interests, moreover, was further reinforced by the movement of U.S. troops into the region in the aftermath of the September 2001 terrorist attacks on the United States. Three of the SCO member states—Kyrgyzstan, Uzbekistan, Tajikistan—became basing areas for the U.S. assault on Afghanistan. With the sudden appearance of the United States on the scene, Central Asia was transformed almost overnight from a peripheral backwater to the near epicenter of U.S. efforts to dislodge al-Qaeda and its Taliban patrons from Afghanistan (see Chapter 7). Despite its active (and prescient) anti-terrorist stance, the SCO did not emerge as a visible player on the international scene in the aftermath of September 11, 2001. The SCO's still-embryonic status—as of September 2001 it had yet to set forth a constitutional charter or establish an anti-terrorist center—inhibited the ability of the organization to assume a prominent role in response to the terrorist attacks. But the presence of the United States in the region also undercut cohesion within the organization and reduced the influence of Russia and China as some Central Asian states came to view the United States as a potentially more attractive protector.[34] In particular, Uzbekistan appeared to distance itself from the SCO. The Uzbek government failed to send a representative to SCO meetings of border guard chiefs, emergency situation ministers, and defense ministers held in April and May of 2002, although Uzbek president Islam Karimov did attend the June 2002 meeting of heads of state. Uzbekistan, however, also declined to take part in the joint anti-terrorist operations scheduled for the fall of 2003.

Russian and Chinese support of the international war against terrorism made outright opposition to the U.S. presence in Central Asia politically awkward. But it also increased the motivation of the two states, both wary of the long-term consequences of an extended U.S. role in the region, to seek to develop the SCO as a counterweight to expanding U.S. influence. The power disparity between the members of the SCO ensures that Russia and China, at least for the present, have a disproportionate voice in orchestrating its activities, although the Uzbek example indicated that they could not be certain of automatic compliance. Prior to attending the May 2003 SCO meeting, Uzbek president Islam Karimov warned against the possible emergence of "internal blocs" within the SCO.[35] However, the declaration signed by the heads of state at their May 2003 meeting appeared to reflect Russian and Chinese sensibilities in its lengthy critique of the international situation.

Beyond the SCO: Russian-Chinese Interactions in the Asian Pacific Region

While Russia and China pursued a coordinated foreign policy strategy in the development of the SCO in Central Asia, the two states had notably fewer overlapping interests elsewhere in Asia. By virtue of geography, Russia was an Asian state, but its historical development oriented it predominantly toward the West. A number of factors—historical, political, and economic—served more to separate Russian and Chinese foreign policy interests in the region than to unite them. While both states had a problematic relationship with Japan, their specific grievances were sufficiently disparate that they found little common ground for a joint foreign policy approach.[36] On the contrary, Japan's status as the third major power in the region injected a certain competitive dynamic into interactions between the three states. The concept of the strategic triangle played itself out at the regional level insofar as each actor feared the possibility that improved relations between the other two could rebound to its disadvantage. In the early 2000s, this scenario was evident in Japanese and Chinese competition, accentuated by the U.S. invasion of Iraq in March 2003, to emerge as the destination point for Russian energy resources (see Chapter 4).

An equally complex set of circumstances prevailed on the Korean issue. In the 1990s, Russia persistently (and unsuccessfully) sought to participate in multilateral negotiations over Korea, first in 1994 when allegations surfaced that North Korea was developing a nuclear weapons capability and second in the late 1990s during the Four Party Peace Talks conducted between China, the United States, and North and South Korea. Although Russian-Chinese communiqués noted their shared commitment to the maintenance of peace and stability on the Korean peninsula, China in fact politely but consistently rebuffed Russian efforts to gain a seat at the bargaining table. In the early 2000s, however, the Chinese motivation to formulate a joint foreign policy strategy with Russia increased, a consequence of two interrelated factors. First, Russia's relationship with the Democratic Republic of North Korea improved with the ascent of Vladimir Putin to the Russian presidency, resulting in a presumably enhanced Russian influence over its furtive neighbor. Second, both Russia and China reacted negatively to U.S. president George W. Bush's depiction of North Korea as a member of the "axis of evil" in January 2001, viewing it as an unnecessary provocation (see Chapter 7).

During the 1990s, both Russia and China sought to escape the isolationist orientation of their socialist past through participation in Asian regional multilateral structures. China became a member of the Asian Pacific Economic Cooperation (APEC) forum in 1991, Russia in 1998. China supported Russia's membership in APEC, and the two states have stressed, as in their December 2002 joint declaration, their intent to "conduct regular consultations and coordinate their views and positions in connection with APEC affairs."[37] In fact, the vastly divergent economic circumstances of Russia and China meant that the two states lacked common interests regarding participation in the organization. In 2000, China's GDP (assessed at 991 billion dollars) ranked third among APEC members, behind that of the United States and Japan. Russia's GDP, however (estimated at 185 billion dollars), placed it in the vicinity of Indonesia (141 billion dollars) and Thailand (122 billion dollars), well behind such APEC members as Mexico (484 billion dollars) and South Korea (407 billion dollars). Russia's relative impoverishment was further highlighted by the disparities in per capita income: Thailand's GDP per capita (1,954 dollars) exceeded that of Russia (1,729 dollars).[38] China was a major player in APEC circles, while Russia had far less influence. Relative to the other APEC members, Russia was something of an anomaly with its historical legacy of state socialism, its still incomplete status as a market economy, and its decaying manufacturing sector rooted in heavy in-dustry.[39] Whereas a number of APEC states—including China—pursued trade strategies based on the export of manufactured goods, Russia's export earn-ings were predominantly derived from the sale of raw materials, specifically energy resources (see Table 4.2, page 63).

In addition to APEC, Russia and China attended meetings of the Associa-tion of Southeast Asian Nations (ASEAN) in the 1990s. Both states partici-pated in their first meeting of ASEAN in 1991 and were accepted as full dialogue partners in 1996.[40] The two states also took part in the ASEAN Regional Forum (ARF), dealing with issues of security in the Asian Pacific region. China's linkages with ASEAN were more extensive than Russia's. As a major economic actor in Asia, second only to Japan, China had more interactions with ASEAN on economic issues. Moreover, in June 2003, China became the first state outside of Southeast Asia to join ASEAN's Treaty of Amity and Cooperation. But Russia and China shared overlapping and largely convergent interests with respect to security questions with the ARF. In their joint communiqués issued in the early 2000s, the two states indicated their intention for jointly coordinated activity with the ARF.[41] The sorts of mea-sures promoted by the ARF were in fact evocative of socialist diplomacy familiar to both states. China and Russia were enthusiastic in their endorse-ment of principles of good neighborliness, embodied in the concept of the Declaration of the Zone of Peace, Freedom and Neutrality, and the Southeast Asia Nuclear Weapons–Free Zone. Moreover, efforts of the ARF to promote confidence-building measures and a level of transparency were similar to arrangements developed by the SCO. In June 2003, moreover, Russian for-eign minister Igor Ivanov suggested that ASEAN and the SCO institute di-rect contacts in a joint struggle against terrorism.[42]

Conclusion

In less than ten years, Russia and China succeeded in fundamentally resolv-ing the border dispute that had obstructed Sino-Soviet relations for decades. The relative ease with which this issue was put to rest raises some obvious questions about whether it was more a symptom than an underlying cause of the conflict in the first place. But the ability of the two states to come to an amicable settlement in the midst of the transformation from Soviet to Rus-sian authority was a notable achievement. Russia made use of the inherited Soviet institutional apparatus in negotiating a settlement with China. The Yeltsin leadership finished what the Gorbachev regime had initiated without any apparent deviations in policy. The border demarcation completed by the Russian government during the 1990s was a specification of the 1991 border agreement. The 1996 and 1997 agreements regarding border troops and the reduction of military strength along the border similarly followed a trajectory that had been initially set forth in draft form in the Gorbachev era. Although the Ministry of Foreign Affairs was subjected to a large-scale turnover —more accurately, purging—of Soviet staff with the onset of the Russian Federation, key individuals retained their positions with respect to the negotiation of border issues with China. Specifically, Genrikh Kireev, formerly the chief of the Directorate of Socialist Asian Countries of the USSR Foreign Ministry and the initial head of the Sino-Soviet talks on border troop reductions, continued to serve in that capacity in the Russian Foreign Ministry, heading the Russian delegation in negotiations on both boundary demarcation and border troop reductions.

The Yeltsin leadership's decision to adhere to the path previously outlined under Gorbachev was not preordained. The Russian government could have made different choices, with far less positive outcomes for Russia. The acquiescence of the Yeltsin leadership to decisions mediated by its Soviet predecessor indicated a pragmatic acknowledgment of the concrete realities facing Russia, as well as a willingness to abide by international norms and procedures. The Russian-Chinese border was demarcated according to standard precepts of international law regarding the determination of boundaries. The reduction of force levels along the border was motivated by more than a newfound Russian commitment to peaceful coexistence: it was also spurred on by sheer economic necessity.

At present, however, the border issues that confront Russia and China are qualitatively different from those that framed the Sino-Soviet dispute. The Soviet institutional legacy served Russia and China well in negotiating an end to the border dispute with China, but it is of little use as a guide to the future. The collapse of the Soviet Union has given rise to the emergence of a new series of issues (some actually recycled from the tsarist past) relevant to border relations between Russia and China. Even during the decade of Sino-Soviet friendship in the 1950s, movement across the border was tightly controlled. The Soviet institutional heritage has left Russia ill prepared for developing border relations with China characteristic of a market economy. Russian resistance to increasing economic integration with China, moreover, has been accentuated by a not entirely unreasonable fear of large-scale Chinese immigration into the Russian Far East (see Chapter 6).

It is notable, moreover, that the border issue as a post-Soviet phenomenon appears significantly different to China than to Russia. China must now coordinate border relations with four states where previously there was one monolithic entity. The transparency of the Russian-Chinese border has contributed to the emergence of such issues as illegal immigration, crime, smuggling, and drug trafficking as factors affecting Russian-Chinese bilateral relations. However, issues of ethnic separatism and religious extremism, which loom large in China's relations with neighboring states in Central Asia, are not a significant component of Russian-Chinese border relations. The 2001 Friendship Treaty alludes to the separatist issue in Article 8 which notes that neither side will permit "the establishment on its territory of an organization or group which harms the sovereignty, security and territorial integrity of the other party, and will prohibit such activities." The statement is similar in wording to those China has concluded with the states of Central Asia as a means of preventing Xinjiang-based insurrectionist movements—notably Uighur groups promoting an independent East Turkestan—from establishing operating bases across the border. However, Russian-Chinese relations are largely absent of the tensions arising from the existence of separatist groups pursuing an irredentist agenda across state boundaries: unlike Kazakhstan and Krygyzstan, Russia lacks an established Uighur population.[43]

Both internal and external factors encourage Russia and China to map out a coordinated foreign policy approach in Central Asia. The two states have a strong interest in both the domestic and foreign policy orientation of states in the region. On the one hand, Russia and China seek to prevent what the Chinese call the "three evil forces"—terrorism, separatism, and extremism—from making inroads in Central Asia.[44] Simultaneously, the prospect of the United States establishing a permanent U.S. presence in the area is a worrying prospect for the two states. The SCO serves as a mechanism for Russia and China to exert influence over the Central Asian region through setting the SCO agenda and channeling the issues of discourse, thereby encouraging the smaller member states to adhere to the program. As the heir to the Soviet Union, Russia has other avenues available for pressuring Central Asian regimes, a factor that partially explains Boris Yeltsin's initial relative disinterest in the organization. For China, however, the SCO is its main entry point into the affairs of Central Asia. Russian influence in the region has been greatly diminished with the collapse of the Soviet Union, but it is still substantial. In this context, China needs Russia and Russian support in its quest to develop the SCO as a regional security organization.

During the Soviet era, the Soviet Union was an international superpower exercising a decisive role on Asian affairs, but it was not an Asian regional power. Interactions in Asia were played out in the tradition of great power politics. With the demise of the Soviet Union, Russia has struggled to define its role in the Asian Pacific region. For all the discussion in Russian domestic circles of Russia as an Eurasian power, Russia does not have much of a consciousness of itself as an Asian state, nor did it delineate a specifically Asian foreign policy strategy in the first decade of the Russian Federation.

Russia's interest in participating in negotiations on the Korean peninsula is largely (although not entirely) a function of its desire to retain the status of a great power.

Russia's economic weakness reduces its influence in Asia, as well as the extent of convergence of Russia and Chinese foreign policy interests in the Asian Pacific region as a whole. Despite its greatly diminished stature, Russia remains a significant actor in the European regional context. Russia, however, lacks the ability to play a comparable role in Asia. In contrast to Russia, China suffers from no crisis in its identification as an Asian state and is positioned as a major, arguably the preeminent, actor in the Asian regional context. The disparities in influence between the two states—as well as the Chinese disinclination to adhere to a foreign policy that is not rooted in self-interest—indicates that a coordinated foreign policy approach between the two states is likely to focus predominantly on Central Asia in the near future.

Yet ultimately geography is a form of destiny that exerts a determinant influence on Russian-Chinese relations. The 2001 Friendship Treaty explicitly acknowledged the importance of the border issue for both Russia and China. Article 6, which noted the essential resolution of the border conflict, provided a degree of security for both states in ruling out efforts in the future for redistribution of the border. At present, the foreign policy orientation of both Russia and China argues for the maintenance of cordial relations. Russia cannot afford to antagonize its increasingly powerful neighbor to the south. At the same time, the Chinese leadership has seen the maintenance of stable relations with Russia as a necessary condition for the all-consuming domestic task of economic development. The physical reality of the 4,250-kilometer border demands that each state regard its relationship with the other as a critical component of its overall foreign policy strategy.

4

The Weakest Link

Economic Relations
Between Russia and China

Throughout the 1990s, Russian-Chinese relations steadily developed in a number of venues. Political relations became closer, culminating in a "strategic partnership" in 1996; the border was demarcated and demilitarized; and the two states collaborated in the establishment of a regional multilateral structure in Central Asia, later to evolve into the Shanghai Cooperation Organization. In comparison, Russian-Chinese economic linkages remained largely stagnant. The value of total Chinese-Russian trade in 1999 (5.620 billion dollars) was less than in 1992 (5.862 billion dollars), the first year of the Russian Federation. By the late 1990s, Russian and Chinese officials admitted that the goal, set in 1996, of bilateral trade figures reaching 20 billion dollars by the year 2000 was unattainable. In the early 2000s, however, Russian-Chinese trade values had increased significantly, reaching 10.671 billion dollars in 2001 and 11.927 dollars in 2002 (see Table 4.1).

The difficulties encountered by Russia and China in forging an economic relationship were largely attributable to the weakness of the Russian economy. On January 1, 1992, the Russian Federation marked its establishment with the initiation of a bold series of neoliberal economic reforms aimed at transforming Russia into a full-fledged participant in the global capitalist economy. The reformers' expectations for a rapid transition to capitalism—something like the First Five-Year Plan in reverse—turned out to be rooted in an overly optimistic set of assumptions that seriously underestimated the constraints involved in moving toward a market economy. During the 1990s, the Russian gross domestic product (GDP) declined precipitously, perhaps by as much as 50 percent.[1] The Russian economy was especially hard hit in 1998 by the reverberations of the Asian financial crisis. Falling oil prices led to the collapse of the ruble, debt default by the government, and sharply negative

Table 4.1

Chinese-Russian Trade, 1992–2002 (in US$ billions)

Year	Export	Import	Total
1992	2.336	3.526	5.862
1993	2.691	4.988	7.679
1994	1.581	3.495	5.076
1995	1.665	3.798	5.463
1996	1.693	5.153	6.846
1997	2.032	4.086	6.118
1998	1.839	3.641	5.480
1999	1.497	4.222	5.720
2000	2.233	5.769	8.002
2001	2.711	7.959	10.671
2002	3.521	8.406	11.927

Source: Zhongguo duiwai jingji maoyi nianjian 1996/97, 1997, 1997/98, 2000, 2002 (Almanac of China's foreign economic relations and trade). (Beijing: China Foreign Trade Publishers, 1998, 1999, 2001, 2003): 538, 465, 394, 495, 340.

growth.[2] The Russian economy began a partial rebound in 1999 with GDP estimated to grow at 5.4 percent in 1999, 9.6 percent in 2000, and 5.0 percent in 2001.[3]

Nonetheless, by the early 2000s Russia could not claim the status of a major economic player in the international arena. Its GDP in 2001 was estimated at 310 billion dollars, less than that of Mexico (617.8 billion dollars) or the Netherlands (380.1 billion dollars). According to World Bank classifications, Russia was considered a lower middle income economy with a 2001 gross national income (GNI) per capita of 1,750 dollars.[4] Income inequality, moreover, had been exacerbated by the transition to the market. According to an estimate made in 2000 by Sergei Karaganov, chairman of the Russian Council for Foreign and Defense Policy, about half of the Russian population lived on less than a dollar a day, placing the citizens of Russia among the one billion poorest inhabitants on earth.[5]

Moreover, as Table 4.2 illustrates, the commodity composition of Russian trade fit that of a Third World state detailed in the dependency literature, with Russia acting as an importer of finished goods and an exporter of raw materials. In 2002, fuel and energy products constituted 56.4 percent of Russian exports with states outside of the Commonwealth of Independent States (CIS), while machinery and equipment made up the single largest category— 38.7 percent—of imports.[6]

Russia's economic situation starkly contrasted with that of China, which experienced one of the world's highest sustained rates of growth over the last two decades. In many years, Chinese economic growth attained double-digit

Table 4.2

**Commodity Composition of Russian Exports and Imports with States
Outside of the CIS, 2002** (as a percentage)

Product	Percent	
	Exports	Imports
Fuel/energy products	56.4	<1.0
Metal/metal products	14.7	4.9
Machinery, equipment, and transport	7.9	38.7
Products of chemical processing	6.4	17.8
Precious stones and metals	5.2	<1.0
Forestry, pulp, and paper products	4.8	4.3
Other goods	2.2	5.3
Foodstuffs, agricultural products	1.8	23.9
Textiles, textile products, and shoes	<1.0	4.4

Source: Tamozhennaia statistika vneshnei torgovli Rossiiskoi Federatsii, 2002 (Foreign trade customs statistics of the Russian Federation, 2002) (Moscow: Customs Committee of the Russian Federation, 2003) pp. iii–iv.

figures, resulting in a GDP in 2002 that was quadruple that of the late 1970s.[7] China's GDP in 2002, estimated at 1.2 trillion dollars, was about four times larger than that of Russia, while its per capita GNI, estimated at 890 dollars, placed it, along with Russia, in the ranks of a lower middle income economy.[8] The Chinese trade profile, however, differed substantially from that of Russia. Like many of its East Asian neighbors, China pursued a strategy of export-oriented growth, initially concentrating upon the export of labor-intensive goods in which it possessed a comparative advantage.

In the process, China evolved into one of the world's premier trading nations, with a total trade volume in 2002 of 581.4 billion dollars, a figure that was over three and a half times greater than the volume of Russian trade, reported at 165.3 billion dollars.[9] Table 4.3 indicates the commodity composition of Chinese imports and exports in 2001. Unlike Russia, major exports of China were concentrated in the manufacturing sphere. Textile goods and related products (handbags, shoes, etc.) made up 26.5 percent of exports, machinery and mechanical appliances (including television sets and electronics) constituted 31.9 percent of exports, and forms of miscellaneous manufacturing (including furniture and toys) were another 6.9 percent of exports, to comprise over 65 percent of China's total exports. As in Russia, however, China's largest category of imports lay in the realm of machinery and mechanical devices, consisting of 39.6 percent of total imports.

Compared with Russia, as well as most of its Asian neighbors, China managed to weather the Asian financial crisis relatively unscathed, even reporting a 7.8 percent GDP growth rate for 1998.[10] Nonetheless, by the late 1990s,

Table 4.3

Commodity Composition of Chinese Exports and Imports, 2001
(as a percentage)

| | Percent | |
Product	Exports	Imports
Foodstuffs, agricultural products	5.8	4.0
Products of chemical industry	7.9	14.9
Textiles, textile products, shoes, leather	26.5	8.9
Forestry, pulp, and paper products	1.8	4.2
Glass, ceramics, etc.	1.6	<1.0
Precious stones and metals	<1.0	<1.0
Base metals	6.0	9.0
Machinery and mechanical devices	31.9	39.6
Transport	1.8	4.1
Optical and precision goods	3.4	4.4
Mineral	3.7	9.2
Misc. manufactured (including toys)	6.9	<1.0
Miscellaneous	<1.0	<1.0

Source: Extrapolated from *China Customs Statistics Yearbook, 2001* (Beijing: Customs General Administration of the People's Republic of China, 2002): 64–68.

China was experiencing a multitude of serious economic problems, including bankrupt state-owned enterprises, an underdeveloped banking industry, the collapse of thousands of town and village enterprises (previously the most dynamic realm of the economy), and the existence of serious sectoral problems in agricultural. China's entrance into the World Trade Organization (WTO) in December 2001 exacerbated the situation, but the Chinese leadership considered that membership in the WTO, while a risky venture, was essential to the final transformation of the Chinese economy to market mechanisms.[11] Numerous analysts have doubted the veracity of Chinese economic statistics, considering Chinese projections of the GDP growth rate to be inflated. Nonetheless, the Chinese economy in the early 2000s continued to grow, even after factoring in downward adjustments. Official Chinese statistics set GDP growth at 7.3 percent in 2001, while the CIA considered the growth in GDP more likely to be around 5 percent.[12]

Russian-Chinese Trade Structure

As previously noted, Table 4.1 indicates that bilateral trade turnover between China and Russia remained at low levels throughout the 1990s, but began an upward trajectory in the early 2000s. In the year 2000, Russian trade with China comprised just 2.2 percent of Russia's total trade turnover. However, by 2002, this percentage had increased to about 6 percent, a notable rise, with China emerging as Russia's fourth largest trading partner, after the United States, Germany, and Italy.[13] In contrast, Chinese trade with Russia in 2002 was only 1.9 percent of its total trade turnover. Russia ranked eighth on the list of China's trading partners, but the value of Chinese-Russian trade (11.927 billion dollars), was dwarfed by Chinese trade with Japan (101.905 billion dollars) and the United States (97.181 billion dollars), its two largest trading partners.[14]

Nonetheless, Russian-Chinese trade volume was higher than recorded in official statistics, especially Russian trade statistics, which underestimated the substantial trade in commodities carried across the border through informal channels. These included the shuttle and border trade, forms of barter exchange, and smuggling and illegal unregistered activities. Throughout the 1990s, Russia invariably experienced a balance of trade surplus with China, although not to the extent indicated in the official statistics, which did not take into sufficient account informal economic transactions. By some estimates, including a 1997 assessment by the Russian Ministry of Trade, the Russian trade imbalance with China virtually disappeared when the shuttle trade was included. The ministry estimated Russian exports at 4.93 billion dollars and imports at 4.55 billion dollars, with the shuttle trade accounting for 3.36 billion dollars in the calculation of exports.[15] Official Russian statistics underestimated the volume of Chinese exports to Russia and simultaneously underreported the extent of Russian exports to China. Significant quantities of unrecorded goods flowed to China from the Russian Far East. These included raw materials (such as timber) and seafood products.[16] Other aspects of the Russian-Chinese economic relationship were cloaked in secrecy (or at least semi-secrecy), deliberately unrecorded in official trade statistics. In 2001, Chinese customs statistics indicated that China imported almost 1.5 billion dollars of aircraft, spacecraft, and related parts from Russia, which constituted China's largest commodity purchase for the year. Russian statistics, however, omitted this category, resulting in a substantial undervaluation of Russian exports to China.[17] Neither Russia nor China, moreover, officially record the value of Russian arms sales to China or other forms of military-technical cooperation in their official statistics. By the late 1990s, Russian arms and technology transfers to China were estimated to be in the vicinity of one billion dollars a year (see Chapter 5).[18]

Table 4.4 provides the commodity composition of Chinese exports and imports to Russia in 2001 in percentages calculated according to the value of trade. Russia's largest export share in 2001 was comprised of transport equipment (23.4 percent). As previously noted, China purchased almost 1.5 billion dollars worth of aircraft and spacecraft from China, with another 360,000 dollars allocated to transport vessels. This was followed by base metals (20.8 percent), predominantly comprised of iron and steel; products of the chemical

Table 4.4

Commodity Composition of Chinese Exports and Imports to Russia, 2001
(as a percentage)

	Percent	
Product	Exports	Imports
Foodstuffs, agricultural products	9.1	6.9
Products of chemical industry	5.1	16.3
Textiles, textile products, shoes, leather	64.8	<1.0
Forestry, pulp, and paper products	<1.0	15.0
Glass, ceramics, etc.	1.0	<1.0
Precious stones and metals	<1.0	<1.0
Base metals	1.8	20.8
Machinery and mechanical devices	9.3	4.9
Transport	<1.0	23.4
Optical and precision goods	<1.0	<1.0
Mineral products	2.5	10.8
Misc. manufactured (including toys)	3.5	<1.0
Miscellaneous	<1.0	<1.0

Source: Extrapolated from *China Customs Statistics Yearbook, 2001* (Beijing: Customs General Administration of the People's Republic of China, 2002): 130–31.

industry (16.3 percent), including chemical fertilizers; forestry, pulp, and paper products (15.0 percent); and mineral products (10.8 percent). Mineral product exports—mostly fuel oil—to China were low relative to their preeminent position in Russia's global export mix but represented a significant rise since the late 1990s. In 1998, the value of Russian mineral product exports to China was only 115,539 dollars, compared to 860,483 dollars for 2001.[19] These figures indicated China's increasing demand for energy imports, as well as China's interest in targeting Russia as a major source of energy supplies. By the late 1990s, moreover, Russia had attained a certain success, not readily achieved in other venues, providing machinery and equipment to China, largely due to cooperative agreements with the nuclear, aviation, and aerospace industries. Certain distinctive characteristics of the Chinese economy—residual traces of the Soviet legacy, Chinese aspirations to develop its space program, and so forth—made it possible for Russia to penetrate the Chinese market, with the delivery of goods making use of Russia's most advanced technology. In general, however, the commodity composition of Russian exports to China conformed to Russia's global profile as a supplier of raw materials, metals, and semi-processed goods. These constituted almost 63 percent of Russian exports to China in 2001.

As Table 4.4 indicates, China exported mainly consumer items to Russia: almost 65 percent of Chinese exports in 2001 consisted of textiles, textile products, leather goods, and shoes. China, of course, was internationally recognized as a leading exporter of textiles and related products. However, as Table 4.3 notes, textiles and related products comprised only 26.5 percent of China's total exports in the year 2001. China's largest export category in 2001, constituting 31.9 percent of all exports, was machinery and mechanical devices (including electronic goods, televisions, etc.). Chinese exports of these items to Russia, comprising 9.3 percent of exports, were disproportionately lower than its overall share in the Chinese export mix. Chinese exports to Russia thus tended to concentrate in its lower-technology sectors, absent the range of products that flowed to higher-income economies such as the United States and Japan. Moreover, although it is not evident from the data, a disproportionate percentage of Chinese consumer good and foodstuff exports had a destination point in the Russian Far East (see Chapter 6).

Bilateral Initiatives Regarding Trade

As with other aspects of Russian-Chinese relations, initial efforts to develop economic links rested on the institutional remains of the bilateral arrangements developed by the Gorbachev leadership in the 1980s. The various trade commissions that had been established underwent a name change, and bilateral agreements under consideration largely remained on the table. Shortly after the establishment of the Russian Federation, Petr Aven, the minister of Foreign Economic Relations, concluded a five-year intergovernmental trade and economic agreement during his March 1992 visit to China.[20] The first session of the Russian-Chinese Intergovernmental Commission for Trade, Economic, Scientific and Technical Cooperation—the successor to the Soviet-Chinese Commission—was held in August 1992. A number of documents relevant to trade were among the twenty-four intergovernmental agreements signed during Boris Yeltsin's December 1992 trip to China: these included agreements on scientific and technical cooperation, an agreement on cooperation in space exploration, an agreement on cooperation in building nuclear power stations in China, and a contract for delivery from Russia of equipment for the Shantou thermal power station in China. Subsequently, however, Russian-Chinese institutional initiatives stalled, yet another casualty of the dislocation of the Russian government. After its inaugural session in August 1992, the subsequent meeting of the Russian-Chinese Intergovernmental Commission for Trade, Economic, Scientific and Technical Cooperation was postponed four times, at Russian request, not meeting until May 1994. Most of the economic projects formalized during Yeltsin's 1992 visit remained unfulfilled. The Ministry of Foreign Economic Relations, formally in charge of orchestrating the bilateral relationship on the Russian side, received little guidance from the Yeltsin leadership and was institutionally inclined to follow, insofar as possible, the method of operation inherited from its Soviet predecessor.

During Premier Li Peng's December 1996 visit to Moscow, the two states announced their decision to raise economic interactions to a higher official level, which would involve regular (at least once a year) consultations between the heads of government.[21] Simultaneously, a Russian-Chinese Committee, operating at the vice prime minister level, was constituted to prepare for these talks, including three standing subcommittees specifically focusing on developing forms of cooperation in the areas of (1) trade, science and technology; (2) energy; and (3) transportation. With considerable fanfare, Premier Li Peng and his Russian counterpart Prime Minister Viktor Chernomyrdin declared their intention to raise the total level of bilateral trade to 20 billion dollars annually by the year 2000. The decision to elevate economic discourse to the prime ministerial level seems to have been motivated in part by the desire to place Russian-Chinese relations on the same plane as those between Russia and the United States. The Chernomyrdin–Li Commission was envisioned to parallel its Russian-U.S. counterpart, the Chernomyrdin–Gore Commission.[22] But this was also seen as a way to stimulate bilateral ties through focusing more attention on the relationship. In reality, these hopes were misplaced. It took Boris Yeltsin four months to appoint a chair for the Russian side of the Commission to Prepare Regular Meetings of the Russian and Chinese Prime Ministers. The high levels of turnover within the Russian leadership—five prime ministers occupied the position between 1998 and 1999—further impeded its work. The standing committees were similarly inert, lacking an institutionalized existence and hastily mobilized for bilateral meetings.

By the time Premier Zhu Rongji met with Prime Minister Evgenii Primakov in February 1999, the goal of raising trade to 20 billion dollars annually by the year 2000 had been abandoned. Both sides acknowledged that the major impediment to its realization lay with the chronic difficulties of the Russian economy. They differed, however, in their prescription for how best to increase trade. China's leaders advocated greater efforts to promote local and private forms of bilateral cooperation through the establishment of joint ventures and special economic zones within the border areas. Russian officials, meanwhile, remained loyal to the promotion of large-scale government-initiated bilateral projects in the areas of energy (including nuclear power), space, machine building, and civil aviation.

The arrival of Vladimir Putin on the Russian political scene, first as prime minister and then as president, was accompanied by a notable shift in the tenor of Russian-Chinese economic relations. Putin's first several years in office coincided with the improvement of Russia's domestic economy, making it difficult to specify cause and effect. However, Putin's administration was more attentive to the establishment of bilateral mechanisms with China and their subsequent institutional development.

Compared to the structures established during the 1990s, which were often recycled from the Soviet era (e.g., the Sino-Russian Friendship, Peace, and Development Committee), these organizations were more oriented toward dealing with the challenges of the market economy. Previously existent subcommittees—such as the initially dormant energy subcommission—sprang to life and began to meet on a yearly basis as originally planned. Additional subcommittees were established dealing with banking, aerospace, and communications and information technology. Working groups were set up to deal with specific economic issues, including groups to resolve contentious trading issues, to establish standards for quality control in the border trade, and to deal with joint civil aviation projects. Russian and Chinese joint communiqués issued at meetings of the presidents and the prime ministers stressed the necessity to establish trading practices in such areas as banking, investment, insurance, loan guarantees, and legal operations "compatible with international standards."[23]

Putin showed more interest in economics than Yeltsin and exhibited a greater understanding that Russia's economic rejuvenation was dependent on Russia's thoroughgoing integration into global—that is to say capitalist—economic practice. Nonetheless, the Putin administration remained wedded to the establishment of large-scale high-technology collaborative projects as a major means to increase trade ties between Russia and China. As the 2002 joint communiqué between the heads of government noted, "work should be done to lay a foundation for long-term stability of trade cooperation by increasing the share of high-technology, mechanical-electrical and other high value added products so as to improve the product mix and develop economic ties of advanced forms."[24] Simultaneously, however, the Putin leadership was more attuned to collaborative projects in the energy sector than the Yeltsin administration. In March 2000, Acting President Putin identified the construction of an oil pipeline with China as a top priority for the Russian energy sphere. Nonetheless, the Putin presidency indicated its intention of remaining in control of the evolution of future collaborative projects with China, rather than relying on the whims of the marketplace. In August 2002, Russian prime minister Mikhail Kasyanov stated during a visit to China that he and his Chinese counterpart, Premier Zhu Rongji, had agreed to take the largest joint projects planned between Russia and China—including in the oil and gas sector—under their personal control.[25]

Impediments to the Development of Economic Ties

A host of reasons can be adduced to explain the low level of economic trans-actions between the Russian Federation and China in its first decade. Most of these were not distinctive to China, but similarly served to constrain Russia's economic interactions with other states. Many reflected the linger-ing impact of the Soviet legacy and the incomplete status of Russia's eco-nomic transformation. Although China had traveled further down the capitalist road than Russia, its economic transformation was nonetheless also a work in progress. Certain economic problems were common to both states, which acted—sometimes in negative bilateral synergy—to impede the development of bilateral economic links.

The Economic Legacy of the Sino-Soviet Split

The Sino-Soviet split has mostly been interpreted in terms of its political implications but it also had a dramatic impact on Sino-Soviet economic trans-actions, which declined precipitously because of the dispute. Table 4.5 indi-cates the value of trade between the Soviet Union and China between 1950 and 1990, which more or less parallels the state of their relationship.

Bilateral ties developed markedly during the early years of the People's Republic of China (PRC), with the Soviet Union providing China with mate-rials for plant construction and technological expertise during China's First Five-Year Plan. Economic interactions, however, declined sharply after the Sino-Soviet split in the early 1960s. Total trade turnover in 1970 had fallen to about 3 percent of the 1960 level. Trading links revived in the 1980s with the improvement of political relations. Border trade between the Soviet Union and China resumed in 1983. The visit to Beijing of Soviet vice premier Ivan Arkhipov in December 1984 resulted in several trade related initiatives: a Sino-Soviet Agreement on Economic and Technical Cooperation, a Sino-Soviet Agreement on Scientific and Technical Cooperation, and an Agree-ment on the Establishment of a Sino-Soviet Commission on Economic, Trade, and Scientific and Technical Cooperation. In 1985, China and the Soviet Union signed an agreement on trade arrangements for 1986–90 that speci-fied the building of seven new industrial enterprises and the renovation of seventeen other enterprises with Soviet participation. According to the data presented in Table 4.5, the value of Soviet trade with China in 1990 was almost ten times higher than in 1980.[26]

Despite the advances in bilateral trade relations during the Gorbachev era, the net effect of the Sino-Soviet dispute, which turned the border region into a kind of impenetrable fortress, was to preclude the possibility of normal

Table 4.5

Soviet Trade to China, 1950–1990: Selected Years (in millions of rubles)

Year	Total	Exports	Imports
1950	518.9	394.4	169.5
1960	1,498.7	735.4	763.3
1970	41.9	22.4	19.5
1975	200.9	93.1	107.8
1980	316.6	169.6	147.6
1985	1,604.9	778.8	826.1
1990	3,038.0	1,378.0	1,660.0

Sources: Vneshniaia torgovlia SSSR 1922–1981 (Foreign trade of the USSR, 1992–1981) (Moscow: Ministry of Foreign Trade, 1982): 16–17; *Vneshniaia torgovlia CCCP v 1985* (Foreign trade of the USSR in 1985) (Moscow: Ministry of Foreign Trade, 1986): 11; *Narodnoe khoziaistvo SSSR v 1990 g* (Economy of the USSR in 1990) (Moscow: State Statistical Committee of the USSR, 1991): 658.

commercial transactions for decades. Consequently, the infrastructure necessary to transport goods across the border was wholly inadequate to meet demand. In the early 1990s, only two railway crossings existed (at Zaibaikalsk-Manzhouli and Grodekovo-Suifenhe) along the Russian-Chinese border, leading to daily pileups of thousands of freight cars standing idle on the Russian side of the tracks.[27] In a 1994 interview, Minister of Foreign Economic Relations Oleg Davydov noted that 25–30 percent of all signed contracts between Russian and Chinese participants went unfulfilled because of transportation problems.[28] Telecommunication facilities were also rudimentary. Until 1993, only two telephone channels connected China and Russia, with all telephone calls routed between Moscow and Beijing.

Some progress was made in alleviating transportation bottlenecks, as China and Russia worked to open up new border crossings, increase air and shipping links, build bridges, lay rail track, and develop communication facilities. In January 1997, a 970-kilometer fiber optical cable (constructed with equipment from the German telecommunications firm Siemens) became operational connecting Harbin in Heilongjiang province to Khabarovsk in the Russian Far East. In 1998, a new fourteen-lane motor vehicle crossing point opened between Zabaikalsk and Manchuria, which became the site of up to 60 percent of all cargo passing from Russia to China. Rail traffic also began passing through the Russian-Chinese border crossing connecting Kamyshovaia in Primorskii krai to Hunchun in Jilin province. The lack of infrastructure, however, remained a serious impediment to the development of trade relations. The rail link at Kamyshovaia-Hunchun was only twenty-two kilometers long with the proposal to extend it to link Hunchun to the Russian border city of Makhalino still in the planning stages. The inability of the Russian oil company Yukos to fulfill its contract shipping oil to China compelled then Prime Minister Vladimir Putin to sign an ordinance in September 1999 instructing relevant ministries and the State Customs Committee to coordinate their actions to ensure that the oil reached China. A Russian-Chinese agreement formalized in 1995 to build a bridge and highway connecting Blagoveschensk in Amur oblast to Heihe in Heilongjiang province remained stalled for years, a fatality of regional fears of increased Chinese immigration into the area. Highways connecting the Russian Far East to other parts of Russia were virtually nonexistent, and transportation tariffs on the Trans-Siberian Railroad tripled in the 1990s. The costs of moving goods from the Russian Far East to western Russia on average exceeded their value, which had a predictably dampening effect on the transfer of Chinese products to the European areas of Russia.[29]

Money and Banking

The heritage of the Communist past also continued to exert a strong influence on Russian-Chinese trade in the sphere of financial transactions. As was commonplace throughout the socialist world, Soviet-Chinese trade transactions were pre-monetary, in the sense that they rested on barter. Trade between the Soviet Union and China consisted largely of a protocol trade consisting of bilateral contracts concluded between governmental structures. In the 1990s, the Russian government did not succeed in setting Russian financial transactions on a monetary basis, with the exchange of money as payment for goods and services. Barter remained commonplace for both domestic and foreign interactions. According to a 1997 report, Russia's largest companies conducted 73 percent of their business in barter and other nonmonetary means.[30] The Russian government, moreover, was not able to implement a systemic banking reform.

Despite the notable achievements of the Chinese economic reform movement, its economy in the 1990s still displayed considerable divergence from market indicators in the financial sphere. Chinese efforts at banking reform were in an initial phase of implementation. Banks operated under the direction of administrative authorities, were unresponsive to market stimuli, and often performed as conduits for the dispersal of funds to keep bankrupt state-owned enterprises afloat. The entrance of China into the WTO in December 2001, however, posed a distinct challenge to China's unreformed fiscal system, as it meant the entrance of foreign banks into the Chinese domestic market and the acceleration of the movement to full convertibility of the Chinese monetary unit, the renminbi.

   With the collapse of the Soviet Union, bilateral trade between Russia and China rapidly decentralized into several formats. The protocol trade characteristic of the Soviet era declined sharply. At the same time, individual enterprises, granted permission to forge direct linkages, began entering into trading relationships. A substantial "shuttle trade" developed, comprised of individual traders plying their wares, and the border trade rapidly increased. Initially, Russian-Chinese trade was predominantly conducted according to barter, continuing the practice of the Soviet era. As of 1995, Russian-Chinese trade transactions were to have been conducted in hard currency. However, the absence of an institutionalized banking reform, the nonconvertibility of the renminbi, the volatility of the ruble, and the lack of regularized settlement agreements between banks of the two states all served to restrict the use of cash transactions as well as to impede the overall growth of trade volume. Statistics on the extent of the barter trade are fragmentary and of questionable reliability, but it seems apparent that the use of barter between Russia and China to settle trade transactions was extensive in the first decade of Russian-Chinese relations. According to Chinese sources, barter trade constituted over 60 percent of Chinese-Russian trade volume in 1992, but by 1998 had fallen to approximately 20 percent of total trade volume.[31]

   Moreover, a range of Russian-Chinese trade interactions was conducted by means of barter. In the border trade, barter was commonplace, although Hu Chusheng, director of the European Department of the Ministry of Foreign Trade and Economic Cooperation (MOFTEC), claimed in July 1998 that cash payments made up half of the total border trade volume between China and Russia.[32] Much of the illegal trade across the Russian-Chinese border was conducted in barter, with Russian enterprises exchanging raw materials for Chinese consumer goods. The head of the Federal Security Service in Primorskii krai complained in 1998, for example, that the actual volume of timber felled in the krai in 1998 was several times larger than that indicated by official records, with much of it surreptitiously smuggled into China.[33] Barter continued to play a key role in Russian-Chinese bilateral protocol trade. The 1999 intergovernmental agreement on trade and economic cooperation between Russia and China provided that Russia would deliver equipment, materials, and services to China to the sum of 115.2 million Swiss francs (9.2 million dollars), with the share of China's payment made in Chinese goods amounting to 90.2 million Swiss francs, or 78 percent of the total.[34] In the initial years, Russian-Chinese arms deals were routinely made involving barter (see Chapter 5). Russia, moreover, was not able to abandon barter even in transactions involving its most technologically advanced civilian industries. Russia was eventually successful in edging out the Western competition to secure a contract to construct two pressurized water reactors for the Tianwan Nuclear Power Plant. But its ability to do so was evidently linked to its willingness to accept bartered goods—reportedly at the level of several hundred million renminbi a year—as payment from China.[35]

The collapse of the ruble in August 1998 was a setback to efforts to put bilateral trade interactions between Russia and China on a monetary basis. A number of Russian banks involved in business with China went bankrupt, withdrawing from the Chinese market after the August financial crisis. Chinese distrust of Russian banks, which had defaulted on a number of bilateral contracts, allegedly led to a secret ban prohibiting the Bank of China from establishing further ties with them.[36] Traders on both sides of the border, moreover, found barter preferable to the risks involved in holding on to the unstable ruble. In the early 2000s, however, Russia and China renewed their efforts to institute credit arrangements in their trade. The two states agreed to set up a subcommittee dealing with banking cooperation during Vice Prime Minister Ilya Klebanov's visit to Beijing in March 2000. By July 2001, twenty-three Russian banks had established correspondent accounts with banks in China, while fourteen Chinese banks had established correspondent accounts with banks in Russia.[37] During Prime Minister Mikhail Kasyanov's visit to China in August 2002, Russia and China signed a series of interbanking cooperation agreements. This included an accord dealing with interbank settlements in the border region between the Amur region of Russia and Heilongjiang province in China allowing Russian and Chinese businesses the opportunity of the direct conversion of the ruble and the renminbi.

Old Thinking: The Marxist-Leninist Inheritance

The economic reform program adopted at the onset of the Russian Federation was the handiwork of a small number of reformers, led by Egor Gaidar, the first prime minister of the Russian Federation. A select group of elites constructed a reform program absent of input from other sectors of Russian society, including other members of the political establishment.[38] It is doubtful that Boris Yeltsin, not known for his grasp of economics, had a detailed understanding of the reforms. It is equally dubious that the majority of the Russian population would have endorsed the economic reform package if their opinions been solicited in a democratic manner through a vote or a referendum. The top-down nature of the Russian economic reforms, enacted by the president without advance preparation, meant that the majority of officials involved in making Russian-Chinese economic policy possessed little knowledge and less enthusiasm for a transformation of foreign trade operations to correspond with capitalist practice. In particular, the Ministry of Foreign Economic Relations in its earliest years served as a bastion of conservative thinking.

Just as Russian politicians (as well as the Russian citizenry) clung to the image of Russia as a political superpower at the onset of the Russian Federation, so too were they reluctant to abandon their perception of Russia as an advanced industrial economy. Russian officials, including Yeltsin himself, tended to adhere to the psychologically comforting but inaccurate view, rooted in the 1950s, of Russia as the technologically superior economy ready to come to the aid of a weak and backward China.[39] In this scenario, Russian-Chinese trade relations involved the Russian supply of high-technology products and services to China in exchange for Chinese consumer goods. Russian officials, in discussions with their Chinese counterparts, steadfastly sought to establish cooperative economic arrangements based on large-scale bilateral government-supervised contracts in a manner distinctly reminiscent of the protocol trade of the Soviet Union. In this respect, the prospect of concluding agreements in the energy sphere evoked a certain ambivalence on the Russian side. On the one hand, Russian elites were reluctant to see Russia's role in the global marketplace reduced to that of a lowly raw materials exporter. On the other hand, the scope and structure of such projects appealed to Russian sensibilities insofar as they necessitated a large-scale commitment of resources and a high degree of government involvement, reminiscent of socialist-style planning.

In addition, Russian economic interactions with China in its first decade indicated a decided unease, if not outright hostility, toward the unfettered operation of market forces, that reflected the persistence of attitudes retained from the Soviet era. Many Russians, including high-ranking members of the Russian leadership, viewed the extensive shuttle trade and small-scale commodity border transactions characteristic of the Russian-Chinese trade relationship as an embarrassment. Capitalism at a later stage of its evolutionary development—such as the United States, Japan, and Western Europe— appeared more palatable than the format of Russian-Chinese trade interactions, which was widely viewed as anarchic, uncivilized, and reflective of the worst aspects of petty bourgeois commodity exchange. The shuttle traders were subjected to a barrage of criticisms from both Russian officials and the Russian media, who often depicted them as criminal elements and parasites who profited from selling inferior goods to hapless and destitute Russian citizens.[40] In a speech in Shanghai in August 2002, for example, Prime Minister Mikhail Kasyanov launched an attack on the shuttle trade, criticizing the quality of goods brought in by the shuttle traders and calling on Chinese businesses to improve the quality of items brought onto the Russian market.[41] Over the years, a variety of governmental decrees were enacted that sought with some success, through the constriction of visas and the imposition of heavy import duties, to reduce the scope of the operation of the shuttles. Russian policymakers, especially within the Russian Far East, were also often resistant to initiatives to establish bilateral small and medium-sized cooperative ventures with China, displaying a distinct lack of enthusiasm for the development of Special Economic Zones in the border regions.

The Russians' hostility toward small-scale commercial ventures and the perception that such transactions were unseemly for a former superpower exasperated their Chinese counterparts. Economic negotiations between the two states were infused with a considerable irony in that the Chinese side, ostensibly still socialist, was an unapologetic defender of market norms and values. Over time, the Chinese leadership became outspoken in its support of the shuttle trade and other forms of small-scale commercial activity that were often the object of derision in Russia. In the Chinese view, the shuttle traders were engaged in a wholly legitimate activity that contributed to the development of market relations. During his tenure as Chinese ambassador to Russia, Li Fenglin made it a point to uphold the shuttle traders, a position that Chinese premier Zhu Rongji reiterated. During his February 1999 trip to Moscow, for example, Zhu praised the shuttle traders as making an important contribution to the development of Russian-Chinese trade links in a speech to Russian business leaders.

Moreover, the Chinese leadership's dedication to capitalist precepts meant that it assessed potential economic transactions with Russia according to market criteria. The unwillingness of the Chinese to grant Russia a special status in its bid for contracts with Chinese firms caused consternation, as well as a sense of disappointment, among Russian leaders, who originally hoped—and apparently believed—that the parameters of the strategic partnership extended to the economic realm. The Chinese were well aware of the perils of doing business with Russia. The short history of Russian-Chinese economic relations was replete with examples of unfulfilled agreements; even projects that were eventually initiated often inched along with a glacial slowness. The Russians, for example, continued work throughout the 1990s on the modernization of two thermal power stations—the Suizhong and the Yimen—that were a component of an agreement signed between China and the Soviet Union in 1985. Chinese vendors were concerned about problems regarding quality, cost overruns, and the ability to meet deadlines in their contemplation of economic contracts with Russian enterprises. Consequently, in civilian markets that were exempt from the constraints imposed by the arms embargo, Russia faced difficult, and in some cases seemingly insurmountable, competition from Western firms. During the 1990s, the Russians invested considerable effort in attempting to convince the Chinese to agree to a joint venture agreement to coproduce civilian aircraft. The Chinese ambassador to Russia, Li Fenglin, expressed Chinese reservations about the project when he undiplomatically noted: "The Russians want to sell us civilian airliners like the Ilyushin-96 and the Tupolev-204. But even Aeroflot doesn't want them, so there must be something wrong."[42] Russia suffered its biggest disappointment, however, in August 1997 when its bid to provide generators and turbines for China's massive Three Gorges hydroelectric dam project was rejected. Russian participation in the construction of the dam had been a regular topic of discussion in bilateral meetings between the two states in the mid-1990s, and many Russians assumed that Russia would be awarded a contract, especially after the 1996 upgrading of their bilateral relationship to a strategic partnership. Russian lobbying for the Russian consortium included two letters sent by Prime Minister Viktor Chernomyrdin to Chinese premier Li Peng.[43] China, however, selected Western European firms over the Russian bid, reportedly because it was concerned over Russia's ability to supply equipment and meet project deadlines, and because Russian cost projections were too high to be competitive. The Chinese subordination of politics to economics came as a shock to a Russian leadership that bore the ideological heritage of a system in which profit was largely a meaningless category in the courting of friendship. But the subsequent lesson was not lost on Russian officials: there were no free lunches in doing business with China.

By the late 1990s, moreover, there was some evidence that Russians—both the leadership and ordinary citizens—were scaling down their expectations as to Russia's political and economic status in the international realm. Initial hopes for a rapid and virtually painless transition to capitalism had not been fulfilled. But the transition itself had brought about a greater exposure to the external world, apparently leading Russians to a more accurate assessment of Russia's relative global economic capabilities. In a 1998 survey, a greater percentage of Russian citizens considered Russia to be an underdeveloped country than China: Whereas 52.3 percent of those polled considered Russia to be an underdeveloped country, only 33.5 percent ranked China as underdeveloped. Correspondingly, 36.1 percent ranked Russia as at an average level of development, compared to 49.9 percent for China.[44] Thus, by the end of the 1990s, Russian attitudes regarding China's economic status seemed to have undergone a substantial transformation, with Russians less inclined to view China as the "little brother" in a hierarchically structured relationship.

Russian-Chinese Economic Collaboration: Selling Russian Technology

During its first decade, Russian exports to China were oriented toward the supply of raw materials and semi-finished products. The commodity composition of exports varied on a yearly basis, but such items as fertilizer, base metals (specifically steel), and forestry products typically constituted a high percentage of overall exports. Textiles, clothing, shoes, and leather products remained the predominant export items for China to Russia. Russian consumers either could not afford to purchase China's more technologically sophisticated goods—such as televisions, electronics, and video equipment—or preferred to buy alternative brands manufactured in other countries. The Russian leadership's interest in promoting high-technology exports to China was not simply an indication of a lingering ideological proclivity for large-scale, capital-intensive projects. In Russia's ailing economic climate, there was little domestic demand for technologically advanced products; the penetration of foreign markets was seen as necessary for survival. By the early 2000s, joint communiqués released by Russia and China spoke increasingly of their intent to increase forms of economic collaboration, including the establishment of joint ventures involving technology transfer, but these plans remained for the most part vaguely articulated and undefined. Russian chances of entering the domestic Chinese market were greater than in many other locations due to the shared structural heritage of the two economies, but the areas of Russian industry that had some claim to comparative advantage were limited. China selected in a number of instances, for example, to hire Western firms to carry out the renovation of industrial plants originally built according to Soviet specifications in the 1950s. Apart from arms sales and military-technical cooperation, Russia was able to attract Chinese interest in three technologically advanced venues in the first decade of the Russian Federation: the nuclear industry, aerospace, and in the early 2000s, civil aviation.

Russian Initiatives with China in the Nuclear Sector

Russian initiatives with China in the nuclear sector were based upon negotiations begun by the Gorbachev leadership. The Soviet Union and China signed an agreement on cooperation in building a nuclear power station in China in 1985, and a further memorandum on the topic in 1990. Subsequently, Russia and China signed two agreements relating to nuclear cooperation during Boris Yeltsin's December 1992 trip to Beijing, specifying the Russian construction of a nuclear power plant and a gas centrifuge uranium enrichment plant in China. In 1996, the two states signed an intergovernmental agreement on the peaceful uses of atomic energy. The Russian-Chinese Commission on Cooperation in the Nuclear Energy Field was created in 1996 when the two states decided to upgrade their economic interactions, and it proceeded—unlike some of the other commissions—to hold meetings on a yearly basis.

By the early 2000s, Russia and China had established a number of projects involving nuclear cooperation. Russia completed the first stage of a gas centrifuge uranium enrichment plant in Shanxi province in 1996. Russian experts from the Kurchatov Institute in Moscow participated in installing a Tokamak-7 fusion research reactor at an institute in Hefei province. Russia and China collaborated on the construction of China's first experimental fast neutron reactor in Guizhou province, with Russia scheduled to deliver enriched nuclear fuel. Russia also lobbied China assiduously to participate in joint venture undertakings involving nuclear waste processing and to sign on as a customer for nuclear waste shipments to Russia.[45]

However, Russia's biggest breakthrough came in December 1997, when China and Russia finalized the plans—after a decade of negotiation—to construct a nuclear power plant in Jiangsu province, with Russia contracted to provide two pressurized water reactors for the site.[46] The Tianwan project, estimated to involve a capital outlay of about 2.5 billion dollars, represented the largest joint venture undertaking between the two states.[47] Russia's involvement in the project was reported to be providing work for 700 Russian factories and job opportunities for 220,000 workers over a three-year term.[48] The project was not only Russia's largest economic undertaking with China, but also its largest international nuclear venture. In the early 2000s, Russia was working on several other international projects, including the completion of a nuclear power station at Bushehr in Iran, the construction of two blocks of the Kudankulam nuclear power plant in India, and the modernization of a nuclear power plant in Bulgaria. In addition, Russia hoped to expand its contract to allow for the construction of additional reactors (six reactors were scheduled to be built) at the Jiangsu site. However, Russian officials were well aware that its initial performance there presented a vital test case for Russia that would determine not only the future development of Russian-Chinese nuclear initiatives but also the ability of the Russian nuclear industry to perform as an international player. As Vice Minister of Nuclear Energy Yevgeny Reshetnikov noted at the 1999 ceremony launching construction: "Pushing our technologies to China, we win a foothold not only on that market but also on markets of nearby Asian countries."[49]

Bilateral Initiatives in Aerospace

Details regarding the specific content of Russian-Chinese aerospace collaboration, as well as the extent of financial reimbursement provided to Russia by China for its services, have been cloaked in secrecy.[50] Nonetheless, Russian aid to China in the area of aerospace technology in the 1990s was extensive and apparently served as a decisive factor in China's ability in November 1999 to launch an unmanned space capsule. Although China presented its

Shenzhou space capsule as "completely indigenous," Western analysts noted that it appeared to be a slightly abridged version of the Soviet Soyuz model.[51] As with nuclear initiatives, Russian-Chinese discussions regarding cooperative ventures in aerospace date to the Gorbachev era. During Boris Yeltsin's December 1992 visit to China, the two states signed an intergovernmental agreement on space, which was updated by a 1994 protocol. Following Yeltsin's 1996 visit to Beijing, Russia and China reportedly signed a secret accord on space cooperation that intensified Russian assistance to the Chinese space program.[52] Russia began training two Chinese cosmonauts at the Yuri Gagarin Cosmonaut Training Center outside Moscow in 1996 and provided considerable assistance in China's quest to launch a manned space flight. In the late 1990s, Yuri Koptev, director general of the Russian Aerospace Agency, was a regular participant in Russian delegations visiting China.[53] In October 1999 Koptev acknowledged that Russia and China were in the process of discussing a series of proposals involving space cooperation.

During Vice Prime Minister Ilya Klebanov's March 2000 visit to Beijing, Russia and China agreed to set up a subcommission on aerospace cooperation, as well as signing a protocol that included an elaboration of bilateral space initiatives. Items on the agenda for Russian-Chinese space cooperation included joint programs in navigation, manned space missions, space communications, and space research. The Russians attempted to convince China to join in a bilateral partnership making use of their Glonass space satellite system.[54] The Chinese, for their part, floated a number of prospects involving joint cooperation in space flight, including possible collaborative use of the Mir space station.[55] In July 2001, the two states signed a five-year space cooperation agreement, which included joint endeavors in the areas of research, the construction of space complexes, and instruments.[56] Hu Jintao's visit to the Khrunichev Space Research and Production Center during his May 2003 trip to Russia underscored the importance of forms of aerospace cooperation between the two states.

Nonetheless, Russian-Chinese interactions in the aerospace sector were impeded by the widely disparate motivations of the partners. In the 1990s, the Russian aerospace program, once the pride of the Soviet Union, was sorely strapped for funding and in dire need of externally generated income. Russia participated in space cooperation programs with the United States and other European states, but these tended not to be revenue-generating ventures. Russia thus turned to commercial activities, attempting to form joint ventures with Western firms to tap into the commercial market. Russian aerospace also moved into hitherto unexplored realms of space advertising and space tourism. The Pizza Hut logo appeared on the side of a Proton launch rocket, and the Russian Aerospace Agency began offering visits—for a price—to the International Space Station.[57] In contrast to these activities, aerospace collaboration with China appeared almost dignified, but it still was an action primarily born out of financial desperation. For the Chinese leadership, however, development of its space program, and the launching of manned space missions in particular, was a national mission. In 1992, President Jiang Zemin formally announced the goal of placing a human in space, which was presented as a matter of national prestige, as well as impending evidence of great power status.[58] China established collaborative arrangements in space technology with the United States and European states, but considered the Russian relationship more promising, partly because Chinese technological conditions more closely approximated those of Russia, but mostly because Russia was prepared to provide more technological assistance.

Despite the veneer of outward cordiality, the Russian-Chinese relationship in aerospace cooperation was marked by notable tensions lurking beneath the surface. These were more manifest than in the military-technical sphere, which was impelled by a similar dynamic, seemingly due to the strong nationalistic sentiments harbored by both sides. The Chinese quest to place a human in place was not justified on grounds of national security but was essentially a demonstration of national prowess. China's attainment of this goal diluted the significance of the Soviet achievement, in addition to serving as a reminder of lost glory. Efforts undertaken in the early 2000s to develop a joint space program foundered due to China's interest in establishing its own independent system.[59] The two states, moreover, disagreed over the topic of costs and reimbursement, with the Russian side arguing that the Chinese were not willing to pay adequately for their services. In March 2000, Russian vice prime minister Klebanov, speaking of difficulties in negotiations noted: "The problem is in the prices. The Chinese think the prices that we offer are too high even though they are formidably lower than world prices." Klebanov added that while the two sides had agreed to thirty-six projects, only eleven had resulted in contracts.[60]

Civil Aviation

In the early 2000s, after years of negotiation, Russia made some progress in convincing the Chinese to commit themselves to joint projects in civil aviation. In September 2001, the Chinese agreed to purchase five Tupelov Tu-204–120C cargo planes with the option to buy an additional ten planes at a later date. The deal was estimated at 500 million dollars (including, however, the potential purchase of ten more planes).[61] Chinese willingness to

sign on to the deal was enhanced by the presence of international participants. The Egyptian firm Sirocco held the exclusive rights to market the Tu-
204–120s abroad, which were to be fitted with Rolls Royce engines and
Honeywell avionics. Sirocco also promised product support for the planes
(long a problem area for Russian exports), including a warehouse for spare
parts, and a pilot training center. Spurred by the success of Tupelov, the Kazan
Aviation Production Association (KAPO) initiated efforts to interest the Chinese in their mid-range Tu-214 aircraft. The major—in fact possibly the only—
advantage of Russian airline manufacturers was price. The Tu-214 was offered
to the Chinese for 30 million dollars a plane, less than half the cost of the
equivalent Boeing and Airbus aircraft.[62] Although the prospects of selling
planes on the Russian domestic market had improved in the early 2000s,
with Russian domestic airlines looking to replace their aging Soviet-era capital
stock, aircraft manufacturers nonetheless concluded that their survival also
dictated selling products abroad, with China viewed as an attractive market.
In April 2002, moreover, China and Russia announced the conclusion of a
deal jointly to develop a new generation of civilian aircraft. The decision to
launch joint production was codified in the August 2002 joint communiqué
between Russian prime minister Kasyanov and Chinese premier Zhu Rongji,
which called for the two states to start work on compiling Cooperation Guidelines for the Manufacture, Production and Provision of Promising Aviation
Technologies.[63]

In November 2002, a newly established bilateral commission for cooperation in civilian aircraft met, with the Kamov corporation, which manufactured helicopters, coming to an agreement with the Haifei aircraft firm in
Harbin to begin studies of potential joint projects. Working groups were set
up to assess the project in early 2003.

Prospects for the Future: Collaboration in the Energy Sector

While Russia had some success in its first decade concluding contracts with
China drawn from its high-technology sector, it seems unlikely that Russia
will come to occupy more than certain specialized niches on the highly competitive Chinese domestic market. In the long term, the most promising av-
enue for the development of bilateral economic links between Russia and
China lies, rather, in the realm of energy transfers. Both states have been
motivated to increase their economic interactions in the energy sphere. As of
1993, China became a net importer of oil, and China's energy demands as a
whole were estimated to grow at an annual rate of about 4.5 percent through
2010.[64] China's dependence on energy exports, moreover, was increasing. In
1999, China imported over 40 million tons of oil, a record figure that was

surpassed in 2000 when China imported over 70 million tons of oil, or about 20 percent of total consumption.[65] In the late 1990s, Chinese relied on coal to supply approximately 75 percent of its energy needs. While Chinese supplies of coal were adequate to meet demand, the adverse ecological consequences of the large-scale use of coal were also a consideration in China's search for alternative energy resources. Confronted with disappointing results in domestic explorations in the area of oil and gas, the Chinese government embraced an assertive strategy of seeking out foreign markets, with Russia and Central Asia identified as prime targets. The March 2003 U.S.-led attack on Iraq, moreover, further solidified China's commitment to searching for alternative energy supplies beyond the Middle East.

Despite the ambivalence that many Russians felt about Russia serving as a raw materials provider in the international marketplace, Russian leaders across the political spectrum generally endorsed the prospect of developing bilateral and multilateral projects involving energy. As Table 4.2 (page 63) indicates, energy resources were vital to Russia's domestic economy, with their export comprising 56.4 percent of Russia's total exports in 2002. In 2000, Vice Prime Minister Viktor Khristenko noted that monies derived from energy provided about 30 percent of the revenues of the state budget and about 45 percent of Russia's total hard currency revenues.[66] In this context, bilateral collaboration in energy with China not only held out the potential for sizable revenues on the Russian side but also addressed the issue of the paucity of economic linkages in the Russian-Chinese relationship.

Small-scale Russian-Chinese energy initiatives regarding oil and gas were initiated in the Gorbachev era.[67] In 1987, the Sino-Soviet Commission on Economic, Trade, Scientific and Technical Cooperation agreed to establish a permanent working group on cooperation in energy, foreshadowing later discussions under Yeltsin. In the 1990s, Russia and China concluded a number of bilateral agreements in energy cooperation, but these were accompanied by simultaneous multilateral initiatives seeking to involve other Asian states, notably Japan and South Korea, in energy exploration. Beginning in the mid-1990s, energy assumed an increased importance in bilateral discussions between Russian and Chinese leaders.[68] In April 1996, Russia and China signed an intergovernmental agreement on cooperation in energy. The establishment of the Bilateral Commission on Cooperation in the Energy Sphere followed in December 1996. During Prime Minister Chernomyrdin's June 1997 trip to Beijing, Russia and China signed an agreement for gas exploration in the Kovytkinskoe gas field in Irkutsk and the construction of a pipeline to China. Subsequently, however, the two states failed to make significant progress on the development of energy initiatives. The Bilateral Energy Commission, for example, did not hold its first meeting until January 1999.

The Yelstin administration was adrift and the oligarchs who headed the newly privatized energy companies were not particularly interested in developing large-scale infrastructure projects in Asia, as long as there were easier ways to make money elsewhere.[69] The Russian gas industry, which remained a state-dominated monopoly as Gazprom, oriented its efforts toward the sale of gas to Europe. The newly emergent oil barons who headed Russia's major oil firms were more interested in quick profits than reinvesting their capital in the extensive infrastructure necessary to develop an energy relationship with China.

Beginning in 1999, however, bilateral energy consultations received a new stimulus due to a series of interrelated economic and political factors: these included China's growing reliance on energy imports, lowered input costs for Russian energy producers with the devaluation of the ruble, and a dramatic rise in world energy prices. As Vice Prime Minister Yuri Maslyukov noted in his position as chair of the Russian side of the Russian-Chinese Commission to Prepare Regular Meetings Between the Prime Ministers in February 1999: "Cooperation in oil and gas is issue number one."[70] Vladimir Putin's assumption of the Russian presidency in January 2000 also meant a reorientation of governmental priorities. Putin set out to reassert state control over the energy sphere, putting his own appointees into positions of authority and pushing energy companies toward expansion into the Asian market.[71] In July 2001, Russia and China agreed on basic principles for carrying out a feasibility study for the construction of an oil pipeline from Angarsk in Irkutsk oblast to Daqing in northeastern China. Subsequently, the rhetoric of Russian-Chinese joint communiqués was ratcheted up a notch with respect to energy cooperation signaling a new degree of importance to the endeavor: The 2002 joint communiqué noted the "great importance of bilateral energy cooperation," while the 2003 joint communiqué pointed out that "cooperation in the energy field is of tremendous significance to the two countries."[72]

Despite the notable escalation in rhetoric, the fact remained that Russian-Chinese negotiations on energy cooperation had not achieved a great deal over the course of a decade. The potential benefits of energy collaboration for both states were matched by an imposing set of obstacles. Transporting oil and gas to China necessitated the construction of pipelines, which raised questions of cost and financing. The Byzantine nature of business interactions within the Russian energy sector and the absence of legal guarantees made investing in the Russian energy sphere a risky business, as Western oil corporations had discovered to their detriment. The technical problems alone encountered in Russia's energy industries were legion: these included out-of-date equipment, mismanagement and corruption, inadequate capital, and a fundamental lack of infrastructure.[73] More than 60 percent of equipment in oil extraction and more than 80 percent of equipment in oil processing were estimated in 2000 to be obsolescent.[74] In 2002, Mikhail Khodorkovsky, president of Yukos oil, stated that the average cost of production in the Russian oil industry was nine to eleven dollars a barrel; this compared with fifty cents to three dollars a barrel in other major oil-producing states.[75] The Chinese leadership was well aware of these problems, which made them wary of committing investment funds in the face of considerable uncertainty.

Electrical Power

At the onset of the Russian Federation, Russia and China discussed a collaborative arrangement in which Russia would supply electricity to China. Russia's industrial decline in the 1990s led to a sharp decrease in electricity consumption and excess production, while China faced electricity shortages. A working group to discuss electrical energy exports was set up in 1997, with attention to the construction of a power transmission line to bring electricity from the Irkutsk region of Siberia to northern China. Subsequently, however, the two states were not able to make much headway on the project. In the Chinese view, Russian prices were too high to warrant investment. In April 1999, a Russian delegation headed by Anatolii Chubais, acting in his capacity as chairman of the board of the Unified Energy System of Russia, arrived in China to hold electricity talks with China's State Energy Corporation. Two protocols were signed at the session. One reiterated that work would continue on the Irkutsk project, while the other set forth a considerably more modest plan in which Russia would export electricity from the border regions of Amur, Chita, Irkutsk, Khabarovsk, and Primorskii to northern China.

Like other cooperative efforts in the energy sector, various projects to export Russian electricity to China were deterred by the lack of financial resources. Regional leaders in Irkutsk were anxious to see the power transmission line put into operation, but this was also dependent on the completion of two unfinished hydroelectric sites at Bureyskaia and Bogunchanskaia in Irkutsk. The Ministry of Fuel and Energy was an advocate of increasing electricity supplies to China and President Yeltsin discussed the project during his December 1999 visit to Mongolia, securing agreement to the construction of a power transmission lines through Mongolia en route to China.[76] However, Unified Energy Systems, under the leadership of Chubais, turned away from the Chinese market, focusing its attention on Japan and the potential construction of a hydroelectric power plant on Sakhalin island. The Chinese, for their part, also lost interest in Russian electricity, deterred both by a concern over costs and a reduced demand for imports due to the expansion of their own hydroelectric capacity.

Bilateral Initiatives in Gas

The initial focus of Russian-Chinese energy discussions in the 1990s was on the Russian supply of natural gas to China and the construction of a gas pipeline. Russia and China signed an agreement for gas exploration in the Kovytkinskoe gas field in Irkutsk and the construction of a pipeline to China in June 1997.[77] Although the actual route of the pipeline was undefined, discussions had focused on a 4,500-kilometer pipeline transporting natural gas from Kovytkinskoe through Mongolia to Rizhao in Shandong province in China. During the February 1999 meeting of the Bilateral Energy Subcommission, Russia and China signed an agreement, building upon previous accords, specifying a feasibility study regarding the project, including the possible future extension of the pipeline to Korea and Japan. The feasibility study agreement was signed by Russia-Petroleum—in which the Russian oil giant Sidanko held a majority stake—and the China National Petroleum Corporation (CNPC). The Republic of Korea agreed to join Russia and China in supporting feasibility studies on the project in October 1999, with a feasibility study agreement signed between the three states in November 2000.

Subsequently, however, enthusiasm for the project waned. In addition to the magnitude of the projected costs of the pipeline, a major impediment was the lack of a domestic infrastructure within China to transport and use natural gas. Geography also had a constraining influence. China's most prosperous regions, with the greatest energy demands, were located in the coastal areas of southern China. In 2002, China concluded an agreement to buy 11 to 13 billion dollars' worth of liquefied natural gas from Australia over twenty-five years for Guangdong province and made arrangement in talks with Indonesia for the purchase of similarly large quantities of liquefied natural gas from Indonesia for Fujian province. On the Russian side, Russia-Petroleum had begun arguing for a pipeline route that ended at the port of Nakhodka in Primorskii krai.[78] Nonetheless, Russia and China insisted on their continued interest in the pipeline. Representatives from China, Russia, and the Republic of Korea continued to work on the feasibility study, discussing issues of resources, the pipeline route, time and volume of delivery, and gas prices.

With the Kovytkinskoe gas project more or less stalled, the major bilateral gas initiative between Russia and China involved the participation of Gazprom, the Russian gas monopoly, in the construction of a 4,100-kilometer gas pipeline from the Tarim gas fields in Xinjiang province to Shanghai. Under arrangements worked out in 2001–02, Gazprom (along with its junior partner, the Russian pipeline construction company Stroitransgaz) was awarded a 15 percent share in the project as part of an international and domestic consortium that included Shell, Exxon-Mobil, and PetroChina.[79]

Gazprom was not new to the Chinese gas market; in 1997 it had signed a bilateral cooperation agreement with CNPC, but its selection nonetheless came as a surprise to many observers.[80] A number of analysts questioned the economic feasibility of the pipeline, with estimates of its cost ranging up to 20 billion dollars. This also raised the issue as to the ability of heavily indebted Gazprom to finance its share of the endeavor.[81] Nonetheless, the Russian government strongly supported Gazprom's participation in the pipeline, based in part on the hopes that it might be extended in the future to include Russian gas deposits in western Siberia. However, Gazprom was an outspoken advocate of a rival pipeline to China stretching from the Urengoy deposits in the Tomsk region of Siberia across Altai territory through Xinjiang province to Shanghai.

By the early 2000s, Russia had proposed a variety of initiatives to China involving collaborative efforts in gas fields in Siberia and the Russian Far East. These included the development of gas fields in Yakutia, with the construction of a gas pipeline stretching to China; various proposals to construct gas pipelines to connect China to the Sakhalin gas and oil fields; and the shipment of liquefied natural gas from Sakhalin to China.[82] A plethora of schemes was suggested by competing energy firms, with alternative destinations. As part of a recentralizing move, Putin began to promote Gazprom as the dominant gas producer and exporter in dealing with China.[83] In July 2002, the government went further and instructed Gazprom and the Energy Ministry to develop a program for gas exports to China and other Asian Pacific states, calling upon them to prepare a plan to provide a coherent and unified strategy for the extraction and transport of gas.[84] While the short-term chances of Russian-Chinese collaboration in gas exploitation were not particularly promising, the stark realities of resource allocation indicated brighter prospects for the future. China had very limited domestic gas reserves but a seemingly insatiable growing demand for more environmentally friendly energy resources, factors that compelled it toward the establishment of partnerships with Russia, the world's largest depository of natural gas.

Bilateral Initiatives in Oil

In the late 1990s, Russian-Chinese energy discussions had shifted their predominant emphasis to various initiatives involving the delivery of oil from Russia to China. Bilateral cooperation in oil offered several short-term advantages over gas. In comparison to natural gas, crude oil and its derivatives were relatively portable. Smaller quantities of oil could be transported to China by rail without the construction of pipelines or large-scale processing facilities. As previously noted, China was largely lacking in a domestic infrastructure to support the supply of natural gas. The estimated costs for the construction of oil pipelines were less than those projected for gas. By the late 1990s, moreover, China had encountered unanticipated difficulties penetrating the energy market in the newly independent states of the CIS, which increased its motivation to conclude deals with Russia. A 1997 agreement signed between CNPC and Kazakhstan to construct an oil pipeline between western Kazakhstan and China became mired in difficulties and was subjected to numerous delays. In addition, CNPC became embroiled in a bitter labor dispute in a case involving the dismissal of workers at a Kazakh energy company in which it held a majority of the shares.[85]

Forms of cooperation in oil exploration between the Soviet Union and China had been initiated in the mid-1980s during the Gorbachev leadership but remained on a small scale. In the 1990s, Chinese companies signed agreements to participate in oil exploration in several different sites in Siberia. In bilateral forums related to energy cooperation, Russian officials began to raise the prospect of constructing pipelines to facilitate the export of oil to China. During Premier Zhu Rongji's February 1999 trip to Moscow, Russia and China concluded an agreement specifying that the Russian oil company Yukos and CNPC would begin negotiations on terms for the delivery of Russian oil to China, with the possibility of constructing a pipeline from oil fields in Angarsk in East Siberia to China. Under the terms of the agreement, Yukos was scheduled to deliver one million tons of oil a year to China.[86] Transportation difficulties impeded the shipment of oil to China, but Yukos was able to increase its oil deliveries from 430,000 tons in 2000 to 1.4 million tons in 2001.[87] Despite challenges raised by other oil companies, Yukos managed to remain the dominant participant in negotiations between Russia and China over the pipeline project. In July 2001, an agreement on basic principles for carrying out a feasibility study was signed between Yukos, the Russian state pipeline monopoly Transneft, and CNPC. The pipeline was proposed to run 2,400 kilometers from Angarsk in Irkutsk oblast to Daqing in northeastern China, eventually providing 30 million tons of oil a year to China at an estimated cost of 2.5 billion dollars. The project drew closer to reality in May 2003 when Yukos and CNPC signed a general agreement on the long-term supply of oil from Russia to China through the construction of a pipeline. In a separate agreement, Yukos committed to providing China with 6 million tons of oil by rail over a three-year period.

As with the gas sector, Russian-Chinese negotiations on oil included a number of alternative projects in addition to the pipeline proposal. The Chinese government actively encouraged Chinese oil companies to pursue an aggressive policy of overseas oil exploitation, making investments in geographically diverse locales. To these ends, Chinese oil firms initiated discussions with a variety of Russian oil companies regarding oil explorations in

Irkutsk, Sakha, Tomsk, Yakutia, and Primorskii krai.[88] The high degree of competition in the Russian oil industry, however, meant that not all Russian oil firms supported the construction of a pipeline to China. An alternative preference, advocated by Yukos competitor Rosneft and by the Russian pipeline monopoly Transneft, was for the construction of a pipeline that would be laid from Angarsk to the Pacific port of Nakhodka, targeting the Japanese and more broadly the Asian Pacific market. The project was given an additional stimulus in January 2003 with the visit to Russia of Japanese prime minister Junichiro Koizumi, who offered to provide 5 billion dollars in investments for a pipeline ending in Nakhodka, which would reduce Japanese dependence on Middle Eastern oil.[89] In March 2003, the Russian Energy Ministry, in a Solomon-like decision, recommended that the Japanese and Chinese proposals be combined into a single project, with a spur off the Nakhodka route heading to China.

Russian-Chinese Economic Relations:
The International Context

Forswearing the socialist model of economic performance, both Russia and China aspired to participate in the structures of the global market economy. China, however, considerably outdistanced Russia in its efforts to realize this quest. While Russian-Chinese economic interactions in the 1990s still relied heavily on barter and the small-scale commodity transactions of the shuttle trade, China's economic relationship with its major trading partners indicated the increasing importance of market precepts and Chinese compliance with international norms and standards. In the 1990s, China's Ministry of Foreign Trade and Economic Cooperation (MOFTEC) steadily gained influence as economic issues became an increasingly important component of China's overall foreign policy. MOFTEC, however, had little to do with Russia focusing its attentions on the United States and Europe, as well as the global financial institutions.[90]

In the early 1980s, the Soviet Union applied for observer status in the General Agreement on Tariffs and Trade (GATT), the precursor to the World Trade Organization (WTO), an endeavor that was rejected. In 1992, the emergent Russian Federation applied for membership in GATT, with a working group on accession formed in 1993. China, meanwhile, had filed an application for membership in GATT in 1986, initiating an arduous process of accession negotiations that culminated in its membership in the WTO in December 2001. China's entrance into the WTO had momentous significance for its economic relationship with the United States and other developed market economies. As a condition of accession, China was required to open up its domestic markets to foreign investment in a number of areas, including telecommunications, banking, and service industries. It also required compliance with WTO tariff-rate quotas in agriculture, allowing for increased imports of agricultural products onto the Chinese domestic market.[91] Chinese membership in the WTO was of lesser import for China's economic interactions with Russia. In comparison with other members of the Group of Eight, Russia had a limited presence on the Chinese domestic market. However, market liberalization of the Chinese economy meant that Russian firms seeking to develop collaborative manufacturing projects in China—such as a joint venture to produce Ural trucks—would face increasingly intense competition from Western corporations. The terms of Chinese accession to the WTO, moreover, required the elimination of some preferential tax policies in Chinese border areas, with consequent negative implications for Russian-Chinese border trade.[92]

In a gesture of friendship and solidarity befitting "strategic partners," China went on record as supporting Russia's entrance into the WTO "as early as possible."[93] However, joint communiqués between the two states did not mention the WTO as a topic of mutual consultation until 2002. In April 2002, Vice Prime Minister Viktor Khristenko announced that Russia and China had agreed to begin negotiations on the terms surrounding Russia's accession to the WTO. The first round of talks was held in June 2002. In the initial negotiations, China pressed Russia for the reduction of customs tariffs, the opening up of domestic markets, and an increase in economic and trade transparency. In particular, China wanted to secure Russian compliance to the movement of Chinese labor onto the Russian domestic market, an especially sensitive issue on the Russian side.[94] The Russian government considered bilateral negotiations with China to be a crucial element of the Russian accession process. In a June 2003 interview, Russian Economic Development and Trade Minister German Gref stated that talks with the United States, the European Union, and China were the most important aspects of the negotiating process for Russia's entry into the WTO.[95]

Conclusion

Russian-Chinese economic interactions in their first decade constituted the weakest link in their bilateral relationship. Russia's ongoing economic travails imposed a fundamental constraint on trade between the two states, which was further impeded by the structural and ideological legacy of the Soviet era. Whereas geostrategic concerns had an impact on Russian-Chinese interactions in the political sphere, domestic circumstances were predominant in structuring the policy agendas of Russian and Chinese leaders in their struggle to develop bilateral economic relations. Russia promoted the export of the products and expertise of its high-technology sectors to China largely as a means of preserving industries, formerly the pride of the Soviet Union, that were on the verge of collapse. In marked contrast, China was interested in the development of small- and medium-scale economic ventures between the two states, the establishment of special economic zones in the border areas, and the expansion of linkages with the Russian Far East and Siberian regions. Such proposals were born out of Chinese experience, reflecting the institutional format of the Chinese economic reforms. But they met with resistance on the Russian side. The widespread interest in the Chinese economic model, prevalent during the Gorbachev era, was markedly attenuated with the birth of the Russian Federation.[96] Russia's first prime minister, Egor Gaidar, was perhaps the most dismissive of the relevance of the Chinese economic reforms for Russia, but his general view was shared by a wide spectrum of Russian political elites.[97] The Chinese model, despite its evident achievements, exposed in stark outline the painful process of primitive capitalist accumulation, a condition that Russians believed—possibly mistakenly—was behind them in the evolutionary scheme of historical development.[98]

Moreover, the expansion of economic linkages with China was often viewed with suspicion and outright hostility, with China viewed as a threat to Russia's economic independence. Such views were not entirely unfounded. By the early 2000s, China had emerged as an economic colossus with a GDP that greatly surpassed that of the Russian Federation. The indications were, moreover, that the economic differential between the two states would expand in the future. The Russian propensity, reinforced by decades of Soviet autarchy, was to consider economic transactions as a zero-sum affair in which one actor's gain meant another's loss. Such calculations, however, were contrary to basic precepts of capitalist economics rooted in the concept of comparative advantage. Russia's application to join the WTO indicates—especially if Russia is accepted as a market economy—the necessity of compliance with neoliberal trade practices, including the lowering of tariffs and the opening up of the economy to foreign investment. This does not mean the invasion of Russia by Chinese entrepreneurs, who will be guided in their investment choices by sober assessments of potential risk and profits. But it does connote the increasing opening up of the Russian market—especially in the border areas—to Chinese trade and the expansion of economic linkages.

Despite the tensions and multiple difficulties, Russia was able to achieve certain successes in its economic relationship with China during its first decade. During the 1990s, formal economic interactions between the two states were based on institutional arrangements initiated in the Gorbachev era. Russia managed to penetrate the Chinese domestic market in several high-technology sectors, exporting equipment and the professional expertise of its labor force. Russian-Chinese collaboration in aerospace appeared to bring disproportionate rewards to China relative to Russia, but bilateral agreements in the nuclear and civil aviation spheres conformed more closely to the often-touted precepts of equality and mutual benefit. Under the Putin administration, Russia and China inaugurated greater efforts to develop economic interactions based on market, rather than administratively ordered, precepts. The growth in the value of Russian-Chinese trade in the early 2000s was indicated by China's emergence as one of Russia's major trading partners. Taking into account the extent of trade unrecorded in official Russian trade statistics, Russian-Chinese trade in 2002 exceeded that of Russia with Italy and possibly surpassed Russian trade with Germany, formally Russia's second largest trading partner.[99]

By the early 2000s, the most prospective venue for Russian-Chinese economic interactions, which also offered the fastest means of increasing the value of trade turnover, lay in the area of energy transfers. The two states intensified their discussions regarding joint forms of energy exploitation, specifically focusing on the construction of an oil pipeline stretching from Irkutsk in Siberia to northern China. Russia's dependence on energy resources—which intensified in the early 2000s—posed a number of risks to the Russian economy, but simultaneously appeared indispensable as a means of growth, capital, and government revenues. The U.S.-led incursion into Iraq in March 2003 provided additional confirmation to an uneasy Chinese leadership of the perils of overreliance on the Middle East as a major source of energy imports. The national interests of both states pointed toward collaboration in energy exploitation, although it appeared that China would be compelled to compete with a newly assertive Japanese government that had reached similar conclusions about the need to diversify its energy supplies. Oil and gas pipelines linking the Siberian regions to China would contribute substantially to the growth of bilateral trade between Russia and China, although it would also exacerbate the existing trade imbalance and reinforce trade patterns in which Russia served primarily as a supplier of raw materials and semi-finished goods to China. The pipelines, moreover, would presumably be constructed making use of Chinese labor. This development could increase already present tensions and heighten fears in Russia about the threat posed by an influx of Chinese across the border. But the construction of oil and gas pipelines would also increase the level of economic ties between Russia and China, with consequent spillover effects in both the political and economic realms. The commitment to construct pipelines would join the two states in a web of economic interdependence from which neither could easily extricate itself. This development would also presumably simultaneously serve as a powerful incentive for both states to maintain harmonious and amicable relations.[100]

5

Russian-Chinese Military and Military-Technical Relations

Since the establishment of the Russian Federation, the Russian and Chinese military establishments have steadily expanded and deepened their contacts. The format of these contacts, however, has been fundamentally impelled by a starkly commercial imperative. What the Russians and Chinese preferred to label as military-technical cooperation in essence referred, less euphemistically, to the Russian sale of weaponry and its related technologies to China. Russia in the post-Soviet era witnessed the symbiotic—if sometimes reluctant—interaction of a series of domestic actors united in a common goal of selling Russian armament systems to foreign purchasers. This included, as a matter of necessity, the Ministry of Defense. The business of the transfer of armaments and their related technologies constituted an integral aspect, in fact *the* integral aspect, of Russian transactions with China in the military sphere. It has been difficult to distinguish bilateral interactions that might be said to fall within the realm of conventional military activities from those connected with the business of selling arms, so thoroughly have the two been interpenetrated.

The Initial Development of Military-Technical Links

Interactions between Soviet and Chinese defense structures were virtually nonexistent during the decades of the Sino-Soviet conflict, only resuming in the latter period of the Gorbachev era. After the official renewal of military ties in 1989, an entourage headed by Song Wenzhong, director of the Foreign Affairs Bureau of the Chinese Ministry of Defense, arrived in Moscow in April 1990, marking the first visit of a Chinese military delegation in thirty years. In June 1990, Liu Huaqing, the first vice chairman of the Chinese Military Affairs Commission (MAC), headed another Chinese military delegation to Moscow.[1] Liu and his delegation were intent to discuss terms for the purchase of Soviet military equipment, in particular, the procurement of twenty-four Su-27 fighter jets. In May 1991, Dmitri Yazov became the first Soviet minister of defense to pay an official visit to China as the head of a military delegation. Yazov's delegation continued discussion over the Chinese purchase of Su-27s as well as other Soviet military hardware. This task was continued with the August 1991 arrival in Moscow of Chi Haotian, chief of general staff of the People's Liberation Army (PLA).[2]

By the waning days of the Soviet Union, military delegations representing both states were trekking back and forth across the border on a regular basis. The focus of their energies, however, was not on the reestablishment of the sort of military contacts characteristic of the Soviet Union in its heyday, but on the negotiation of arms sales and technology transfers. Thus, the absence of military ties during the three decades of the Sino-Soviet conflict meant that the institutional legacy of the Soviet experience was very limited in the military sphere. Those linkages that did exist were established after the normalization of Russian-Chinese relations in 1989 and were largely directed toward the sale of armaments and weapons technologies. In marked contrast to bilateral interactions in other sectors, Russian-Chinese military relations did not undergo any notable downgrading of emphasis in the initial period following the Soviet collapse. At the same time that Foreign Minister Andrei Kozyrev was seeking to distance Russia from China, the members of the Russian military were making plans to confirm Russia's commitment to the fulfillment of military-technical agreements negotiated by the Gorbachev leadership.

Colonel General Viktor Samsonov, chief of staff of the Joint Armed Forces of the Commonwealth of Independent States (CIS), selected China as the destination for his first international visit, arriving in February 1992 shortly after the founding of the Russian Federation. One of Samsonov's goals was to discuss the status of negotiations on the reduction of armed forces in the border regions, a matter of evident interest for both China and the newly emergent CIS states along the former Sino-Soviet border. But bilateral discussions also dealt with forms of military-technical cooperation, with Samsonov confirming the Russian decision to provide China with previously contracted armaments, specifically the delivery to China of twenty-six Su-27 fighter jets.[3] For its part, the Chinese leadership was anxious to step up negotiations on arms and technology sales with Russia, which were seen, according to an internal report issued by the MAC in May 1992, as a means of breaking the arms embargo imposed by the Western states after the Tiananmen events of June 1989.[4] In November 1992, the State Council of the People's Republic of China (PRC) approved the purchase of 1.2 billion dollars' worth of Russian military equipment.[5]

The issue of Russian-Chinese military relations appeared on the agenda during Boris Yeltsin's December 1992 visit to Beijing. The two states signed a memorandum on principles of military-technical cooperation that reportedly dealt with the continued delivery to China of spare parts for armaments formerly supplied by the Soviet Union, as well as reaffirming the Russian commitment to provide China with Su-27 fighter jets and S-300 air defense systems.[6] While in Beijing, Yeltsin also disclosed—no doubt to the consternation of those who had labored to keep such figures secret—that Russian arms supplies to China had totaled 1.8 billion dollars for the 1992 calendar year.[7] Talks in November 1992 had focused on the Russian transfer of certain military technologies to China as a means of repaying one-half of a one billion dollar loan provided by China to the Soviet Union in the Gorbachev era.[8] During 1992, moreover, Russia and China reached a series of agreements regarding training programs providing for the dispatch of Russian military instructors and technicians to China as well as the admittance of Chinese military personnel to Russian military institutes.

Thus, from the very onset of the Russian Federation, military contacts between Russia and China centered upon arms and technology transfers as a primary preoccupation. Interactions between military personnel of the two states began to assume certain distinctive characteristics: Chinese military delegations visiting Russia often appeared to be on a large-scale shopping expedition, so assiduously did they incorporate on-site visits into their itineraries, checking out military hardware for potential purchase (preferably at bargain basement prices). In 1993, a notable increase in bilateral contacts between the Russian and Chinese navies—especially the April visit to Russia of Vice Admiral Zhang Lianzhong, the commander of the Chinese navy—signaled Beijing's interest in purchasing naval armaments. In July 1993, a Chinese military delegation led by Liu Huaqing arrived in Russia with the primary, if unannounced, purpose of procuring advanced weaponry. The Chinese were especially interested in Kilo-class submarines, S-300 missile systems, and the purchase of another consignment of Su-27 jet fighters.[9] The following November, during Minister of Defense Pavel Grachev's visit to Beijing, the Russian and Chinese Ministries of Defense signed a five-year agreement on forms of military cooperation. The details of the most significant segment of the agreement, the Sino-Russian Agreement on Military-Technical Cooperation, remained a closely guarded secret but evidently laid out a series of armament sales from Russia to China, as well as forms of technology transfer and arrangements for the technical training of Chinese personnel. One key topic of the negotiations was reported to be China's possible acquisition of a licensing agreement to produce the Su-27 fighter aircraft.[10] Subsequently, Russia was also reported to have sent to China a list of forty-four advanced weapons systems for possible purchase, which included Su-27, Su-30, and MiG-31 fighter jets and air defense systems.[11]

By the mid-1990s, Chinese weapons purchases from Russia included orders for four Kilo-class submarines and a variety of missiles including those of the S-300, Sa-15, and Tor-M1 series. Bilateral negotiations, however, encountered their greatest obstacle on the question of technology transfer. The Chinese were strongly interested in acquiring licensing rights for their own domestic production, especially with respect to the Su-27 fighter jet, a scenario that was obviously less appealing to Russia than direct weaponry sales. China, however, attained a breakthrough on this issue in December 1995 with the visit of Liu Huaqing to Russia. Liu's agenda included a series of meetings with high-ranking personnel connected with the military-industrial complex and with members of the government, resulting in an intergovernmental agreement on cooperation in defense technology. Both states sought to maintain an aura of secrecy on the subject of their negotiations. Liu's trip was portrayed as a "good will" visit focused upon cooperation in defense conversion. The content of the cooperation agreement was not disclosed. In February 1996, however, Colonel Petr Deinekin, commander-in-chief of the Russian air force revealed—against Chinese wishes—that Russia had sold China the license for Su-27 production. Subsequent details indicated that the agreement involved the Chinese purchase of forty-eight Su-27 fighter planes (including the twenty-six already contracted) from Russia.[12] China was authorized to produce 200 Su-27s in China in a fifteen-year time period without the right of exportation to third countries. Russia would import a production line and the aircraft would be furnished with Russian engines and avionics. Chief contractors were the Sukhoi Design Bureau and the Sukhoi aviation plant located at Komsomolsk-na-Amur in Khabarovsk krai. Reports of the price paid by China for the license varied markedly, ranging from over 1 billion to 2.5 billion dollars.[13]

Expanded Linkages: Toward the Increased Transfer of Technology

In December 1996, Russian and Chinese representatives met in Beijing at a session of the Bilateral Commission on Economic Cooperation. The technical specifications of the Su-27 licensing agreement, the sale of two Sovremennyi-class destroyers to China, the modernization of armaments and navigation systems on Chinese naval ships, and the potential sale to China of Su-30MKK fighter jets (an updated variation of the Su-27 series specifically developed for the Chinese market) were among the items of negotiation. In addition, representatives of the two states signed a Memorandum of Military-Technical Cooperation revising the provisions of the 1993 agreement. Several weeks later, during Premier Li Peng's visit to Moscow, these two arrangements were reiterated in a confidential military and technical cooperation agreement.

By the mid-1990s, the Chinese were pushing Russia toward expanding the range of technology transfers as a component of their military-technical interactions. This development was a logical outcome of the Su-27 licensing agreement. Once this symbol of national pride, representing the highest technological achievements of Soviet military prowess, became reduced to the status of a commodity on the marketplace, the barriers to similar transactions were correspondingly diminished. Still, the Russians sought to hold the line on escalating Chinese demands, seeking to preserve a 70 to 30 ratio of arms deliveries to technology transfers. The January 1998 visit of Defense Council Secretary Andrei Kokoshin to China was partly in response to these issues, as Kokoshin pressed China to buy more Russian arms.[14] By Kokoshin's account, his talks had included a "frank and serious discussion of the problems of military cooperation."[15] Issues of military-technical cooperation were also contemplated at the meeting of the Russian and Chinese prime ministers and at consultation talks between the Russian and Chinese general staffs, both of which took place in July 1998. Speaking after the consultations, Colonel-General Valeriy Manilov, the head of the Russian delegation, stated that the two sides would work to develop joint research and weaponry projects, as well as to increase the number of Chinese military personnel trained in Russia.[16]

Manilov's comments implied a Russian concession to Chinese demands, but the specifics of technological transfer continued to be a dividing point in Russian and Chinese negotiations. Russian Minister of Defense Igor Sergeyev acknowledged the existence of "problems" connected with military-technical cooperation during his October 1998 trip to Beijing, adding that a group of experts had been instructed to spend a "sleepless night" in order to resolve the issue.[17] Ultimately Russia, beset by increasingly severe economic problems with the August 1998 collapse of the ruble, yielded to China, jettisoning the 70 to 30 ratio. During Sergeyev's visit, the two states agreed that Russia would provide China with the technological assistance it needed to initiate domestic manufacture of high-technology weapons. The agreement reportedly provided for the expansion of a list of Russian licenses to be transferred to China for the production of a series of armaments, as well as an increase in the training of Chinese military personnel—in both Russia and China—in the operation of these systems.[18] Other notable outcomes of the meeting included the conclusion of a preliminary agreement about deliveries of Su-30MKK fighters to China and the acceleration of cooperation on nuclear and diesel-electric submarines. As the academician Georgy Arbatov noted, "We have made it much easier for them because of the absolute failure of our economic reform. . . . For us the weakest point is the state of our economy."[19]

The reception accorded to MAC First Vice Chairman Zhang Wannian during his June 1999 trip to Russia starkly highlighted the reliance (if not outright dependence) of segments of the Russian military-industrial complex on bilateral links forged with China. Zhang engaged in talks with his Russian hosts about future armaments purchases—estimated in the range of 5 to 6 billion dollars over a six-year period—as well as the prospects for establishing joint programs of basic research in the applied sciences to further the development of defense technologies.[20] The two states also signed an agreement on cooperation in military education and training, providing for training Chinese servicemen in Russian military institutes within the Ministry of Defense. On his return to China, Zhang made several stopovers that highlighted some of the potentials for military-technical interaction. Zhang attended a demonstration of the Topol M-1 missile in Novosibirsk, viewed production facilities at the Sukhoi aircraft plant in Komsomolsk-na-Amur, and made an excursion in Vladivostok to a missile destroyer stationed with the Russian Pacific Fleet where he extolled the myriad possibilities for bilateral cooperation. Issues of joint cooperation in the defense realm were also reiterated with the August 1999 visit of Vice Prime Minister Ilya Klebanov to Beijing to attend a session of the Russian-Chinese Commission for Economic Cooperation. Military-technical ties quite obviously dominated the agenda of the meeting: Zhang Wannian served as the chairperson on the Chinese side. The session, described by Zhu Rongji as "very successful" and by Klebanov as "the most effective meeting" of the commission, formalized the Russian sale of 38 to 40 Su-30MKK fighter jets to China worth a total of about 2 billion dollars.[21] After the session, an effusive Klebanov characterized the Russian-Chinese relationship as that of "brothers forever" in the area of military-technical cooperation, noting that "there will be many joint projects in science and technology."[22] Shortly thereafter, in December 1999, China also purchased twenty-eight Su-27UBK combat trainers to instruct Chinese pilots in the operation of fighter planes of the Su-27 and Su-30 series.

Military-Technical Cooperation in the Putin Era

Military-technical cooperation between Russia and China in the first years of the Putin presidency was characterized by the continuation and deepening of trends laid down in the Yeltsin era. During Chinese minister of defense Chi Haotian's January 2000 visit to Russia, the Ministries of Defense of the two states signed a Memorandum of Mutual Understanding on Further Strengthening Cooperation in the Military Field. A large delegation of representatives from Russian military-industrial structures accompanied Putin on his first presidential trip to China in July 2000. Despite earlier reports that the July 2001 Friendship Treaty would call for increased cooperation in the military-technical realm, a direct statement to this effect was not included in the completed document. Article 7 only noted that military and military-technical cooperation between the two states was not aimed at a third country, while Article 15 listed military technology as an area of joint cooperation. Nonetheless, in 2001–02, Chinese arms purchases from Russia accelerated. In 2001, the two states signed a contract for the Chinese purchase of thirty-eight Su-27MKK fighter jets and four S-300PMU-4 long-range anti-aircraft missile systems.[23] In addition, a contract was prepared but not signed for the Chinese purchase of four A-50E early warning aircraft, which the Russians promoted to the Chinese after Israel canceled its agreement to provide China with four phantom airborne warning and control systems (AWACS) aircraft in July 2000.[24] China continued its buying spree in 2002, signing contracts to purchase eight additional Kilo-class (Project 636) submarines and two 956EM destroyers.[25] This was followed in January 2003 by a contract in which China purchased an additional twenty-four Su-30MK2 fighter jets equipped with Kh-31A anti-warship missiles for the Chinese navy.[26]

Motive Factors of Military-Technical Cooperation: The Politics of Economics

The factors that shaped the evolution of Russian-Chinese military linkages in the 1990s were not complex for either state, although, as with other aspects of the Russian-Chinese economic relationship, they were impelled by different motives. Geopolitical calculations rooted in balance-of-power alliances were not a major consideration—occasionally obfuscating rhetoric to the contrary—in the expansion of military linkages between the two states. Since 1975, when Chinese Premier Zhou Enlai unveiled the Four Modernizations, the modernization of the Chinese military has been advanced as an essential goal of the Chinese state. The specific circumstances of the Gulf War in 1991, waged as a high-technology battle that culminated in a swift Allied victory, provided an abrupt shock to the Chinese military, exposing the backwardness of the PLA and leading to a revision of doctrine and training. The Chinese defense doctrine of the 1990s was rooted in the conviction that any future military engagement would take place as a "limited war under high-technology conditions." Liu Huaqing, the longtime first vice chairman of the MAC (and a close associate of Deng Xiaoping) was a strong and powerful proponent of military modernization who viewed arms and technology purchases from Russia as an important means to this end. An admiral in the Chinese navy, Liu was especially committed to the development of a blue-water navy, seeking to expand China's naval range in the Asian arena beyond a coastal capacity.[27]

Nonetheless, the post-Mao leadership's rejection of the Maoist model of military operations was not accompanied by a corresponding abandonment of the Maoist precept of self-reliance. As previously noted, China sought to make use of the most advanced technology that Russia had to offer in order to establish its own domestic armament production. This reliance on Russian technological prowess was largely dictated by the Western arms embargo imposed on China after Tiananmen, but it also had certain advantages: Russian arms and Russian technology were relatively inexpensive, and they did not pose major problems of adaptation to Chinese operational systems, which were largely replicated on the Soviet model. Thus, Russia served as the major source of arms and forms of military technology available to China.

As Table 5.1 illustrates, Russia was the largest supplier of arms to China during the 1990s and the early 2000s. According to assessments made by the Stockholm International Peace Research Institute (SIPRI), Russia on average provided 91 percent of the arms imported to China between 1993 and 2002. In the early 2000s, the percentage was even higher, with Russia the source of 94–97 percent of arms delivered to China between 2000 and 2002. In the absence of the lifting of the Western arms embargo, the Chinese reliance on Russia as its major external source of armaments does not appear likely to abate.

In contrast to China, the Russian motivation to pursue bilateral military-technical linkages was devoid of any underlying strategic goal save the most fundamental impulse toward self-preservation. In the words of Pavel Felgenhauer, Russia's preeminent military analyst, on the sale of Russian arms and their related technologies to China: "First of all, it's money. Second of all, it's money, and third of all, also money."[28] While arms deliveries declined in the 1990s by over 90 percent compared to the Soviet era, they continued to be an important export and source of foreign exchange earnings for the Russian Federation in its first decade.

Table 5.2 provides data on the estimated value of Russian arms and technology exports from 1994 to 2002.[29] Russia managed to retain a hold on the world armaments market, increasing the value of its arms deliveries from a low of 1.72 billion dollars in 1994 to 4.80 billion dollars in 2002. In the early 2000s, a number of arms analysts considered Russia to have emerged as the second largest exporter of armaments, behind the United States.[30] Although Russian customs statistics did not report arms exports, it was nonetheless

Table 5.1

Arms Transfers to China, 1993–2002, by Major State Suppliers (in US$ millions and as a percentage)

	1993	1994	1995	1996	1997	1998	1999	2000	2001	2002	Total
Russia	772	79	376	945	430	111	1,334	1,642	2,948	2,185	10,822
	91%	55%	90%	89%	80%	49%	89%	94%	97%	95%	91%
Ukraine	55	22	—	73	73	73	73	78	73	113	633
	6%	15%	0%	7%	14%	32%	5%	4%	2%	5%	5%
Israel	18	18	18	18	18	18	18	18	18	—	162
	2%	13%	4%	2%	3%	8%	1%	1%	1%	—	1%
France	5	19	14	21	15	7	18	7	7	9	122
	1%	13%	3%	2%	3%	3%	1%	<1%	<1%	<1%	1%
Italy	—	5	11	5	3	—	11	—	3	—	38
	—	3%	3%	0%	0%	—	1%	—	<1%	—	0%
U.S.	1	—	—	—	—	—	31	—	—	—	32
	<1%	—	—	—	—	—	2%	—	—	—	2%
U.K.	—	—	—	—	—	16	10	—	—	—	26
	—	—	—	—	—	7%	1%	—	—	—	<1%
Total	851	143	419	1,062	539	225	1,495	1,745	3,049	2,307	11,835

Source: SIPRI (Stockholm International Peace Research Institute) arms transfers database at http://projects.sipri.se/armstradeTrnd_Ind_CHI_TAI=impts_93–02.pdf.

Note: Figures are trend indicator values expressed in US$ millions at constant (1990) prices. SIPRI values indicate the volume of arms transfers, not the actual financial values of such transfers. Percentages extrapolated.

Table 5.2

Russian Arms Deliveries, 1994–2002 (in US$ billions)

Year	US$ billions
1994	1.72
1995	3.05
1996	3.52
1997	2.60
1998	2.60
1999	3.34
2000	3.68
2001	3.71
2002	4.80

Source: Figures for 1994–2001 from Ruslan Pukhov, Konstantin Makienko, and Maxim Pyadushkin, "Preliminary Estimates of Russia's Arms Exports in 2002," *Eksport Vooruzheniy* (January–February 2003): 2; 2002 figures from Konstantin Makienko, "CAST Comments," 9 June 2003 at http:www.cast.ru.

evident that Russian arms transfers occupied an important niche in Russia's export earnings.[31] Russian weaponry ranked among the most technologically advanced products that Russia had to offer, occupying a place on a very short list of manufactured items potentially competitive within the global marketplace. In February 2000, for example, Foreign Trade Minister Mikhail Fradkov acknowledged that arms and other military hardware accounted for 40 percent of all exports by the engineering sector of the economy in 1999.[32]

With the collapse of the Soviet Union, Russia lost a number of client states that had been large-scale recipients of Soviet weaponry. Table 5.3 notes the value of Russian arms transfer deliveries to major customers from 1987 to 1999. Certain states such as Afghanistan, Syria, and Iraq essentially disappeared as a market for Russian armaments, while arms shipments to Vietnam and Angola were sharply curtailed both in terms of volume and percentage share. In contrast, whereas China received less than 1 percent of Soviet arms exports in 1987–91, it emerged in the mid-1990s as the source of almost one-quarter of all Russian arms deliveries. The Chinese share of Russian arms deliveries, moreover, increased substantially in the early 2000s. According to data compiled by SIPRI, Russia arms transfers to China in 1997–2001 constituted 37 percent of the value of its total deliveries, followed by India with 22 percent.[33] In the early 2000s, these trends were accentuated by China's emergence as a purchaser of large volumes of high-technology weaponry, specifically Su-27 and Su-30 fighter jets, with their accompanying operational systems, and naval equipment, including destroyers and submarines. In the year 2000, it was estimated that 70 percent of Russian arms exports were transferred to China, with another 20 percent

Table 5.3

Value of Russian (Soviet) Arms Transfer Deliveries to Selected Major Customers: Cumulative Years 1987–1999
(in US$ millions and percentage shares)

	1987–91	%	1991–93	%	1993–95	%	1995–97	%	1997–99	%
Total	84,350	100	11,555	100	7,925	100	9,225	100	7,950	100
China	550	<1.0	1,700	15.0	1,200	15.0	2,200	24.0	1,300	16.0
India	10,200	12	1,100	9.5	675	8.5	700	7.5	1,300	16.0
Kuwait	240	<1.0	—	—	240	3.0	775	8.0	—	—
Malaysia	—	—	—	—	550	7.0	550	6.0	—	—
Iran	2,100	2.0	2,300	20.0	1,000	13.0	480	5.0	675	8.0
Vietnam	5,900	7.0	220	2.0	290	4.0	320	3.0	290	4.0
Afghanistan	13,200	16.0	1,900	16.0	—	—	—	—	—	—
Iraq	7,400	9.0	—	—	—	—	—	—	—	—
Angola	4,100	5.0	50	<1.0	525	7.0	160	1.0	280	4.0
Poland	2,400	3.0	—	—	—	—	—	—	—	—
Syria	5,500	6.5	950	8.0	120	1.5	—	—	260	3.0

Source: World Military Expenditures and Arms Transfers, 1991–92, 1993–1994, 1996 (Washington, DC: U.S. Arms Control and Disarmament Agency, 1993, 1995, 1997): 131–43, 128–32, 151–54. Data for 1995–97 from the Web site maintained by the U.S. Department of State at http://www.state.gov/www/global/arms/bureau_ac/wmeant98/table3.pdf. Data for 1997–99 from *World Military Expenditures and Arms Transfers, 1999–2000* (Washington, DC: U.S. Department of State, Bureau of Verification and Compliance, 2001): 155–59. Percentages extrapolated.

destined for India.[34] Although the Chinese share in Russian arms deliveries declined in 2001–02, China still remained Russia's largest arms customer. In 2002, aircraft manufacturers were estimated to account for between half and three-quarters of all Russian arms exports, with their deliveries comprising up to three-quarters of Russian export revenues.[35] In January 2003, for example, Rosoboronexport general director Andrei Belyaninov announced that the arms agency had received a record 4.3 billion dollars from arms exports in 2002, indicating that "most of this came from aircraft contracts—mainly for Sukhoi fighter jets."[36]

By the late 1990s, moreover, the Chinese market was more advantageous to Russia than a number of other venues. Sizable Russian shipments of armaments in the 1990s—notably to Finland, Hungary, South Korea, and Slovakia—did not generate revenue for Russia but were employed as a means of paying off debt.[37] Initially, a number of Russian-Chinese arms deals made use of barter as a major component of exchange, provoking considerable chagrin, if not outright despair, among Russian observers who were compelled to watch their sophisticated weaponry being exchanged for low-quality consumer items and foodstuffs from China. For example, 75 percent of the first contracts to provide Su-27 fighter jets and Kilo-class submarines was paid in barter.[38] Bartered commodities included 24,000 tons of canned meat delivered to the Sukhoi aircraft plant in Komsomolsk-na-Amur and plastic lighters sent to the Admiralteiskie Wharf shipyards in St. Petersburg producing Kilo-class submarines.[39] The Russian ability to place transactions with China on a strictly monetary basis, however, improved markedly with time. By the late 1990s, virtually all of the Russian arms arrangements with China that involved the transfer of advanced technology were negotiated in hard currency payments. During his February 2001 visit to China, MAC's first Vice Chairman Zhang Wannian held talks with Prime Minister Kasyanov about issues relating to Chinese payments for Russian equipment and technology. In August 2002, Kasyanov announced that China would transfer payments in hard currency in matters of military-technical cooperation, implying that the era of barter had come to an end.

Staying Alive: Arms Transfers and the Military-Industrial Complex

With the former Soviet military-industrial complex in grave financial straits, arms sales abroad became a key means for a segment of Russia's defense industry to remain operational in the post-Soviet era. The enormous declines in arms procurement orders from the Russian Ministry of Defense in 1992 made export sales a necessity for the military-industrial complex. Between

1992 and 1999, defense enterprises produced 2 ships for domestic procurement and 11 for export sales, 31 tanks for domestic use and 433 for export, and 7 aircraft for the domestic sector and 278 for export.[40] By the early 2000s, budgetary allocations for domestic defense purchases had increased, but 80 percent of the financing of the military-industrial complex still came from export earnings.[41] The difficulties of economic reform in Russia, accompanied by the prevalence of barter, nonpayments, and the maintenance of Soviet-style accounting procedures, made hard currency income derived from arms sales vital to the continued operation of a number of defense enterprises and design bureaus.[42] A 1996 report estimated that military-technical cooperation with foreign countries provided work for over 400,000 employees of defense enterprises, while up to two-thirds of the working assets of enterprises of the military-industrial complex were produced by arms exports.[43]

The dependence of Russian defense enterprises on export earnings meant that China (along with India) was the main source of financial support for some of Russia's largest arms producers. As Russian Defense Minister Sergei Ivanov candidly stated in November 2002: "Russia's defense industry complex can be preserved only by supplying military equipment and arms to China."[44] This reliance gave rise to certain understandable but dysfunctional behaviors on the part of defense enterprises, born out of financial desperation. Lacking a domestic market for their output, defense enterprises often appeared willing to sell virtually anything to anyone. In the early years of the Russian Federation, moreover, export controls over the sale of weaponry and related technologies were in a state of disarray, making it a relatively simple matter to sell advanced weaponry, licensing technology, and classified information to foreign customers independently of formal government approval. By the mid-1990s, allegations had surfaced, for example, that the Sukhoi Aviation Complex had sold the production license to China to manufacture Su-27 fighter jets without official authorization, that the Chinese obtained classified information on Kilo-class submarines, and that personnel in the Russian Ministry of Defense sold upper-stage nuclear powered rocket engines to China bypassing formal channels, an action that was in violation of the Missile Technology Control Regime.[45] In fact, enterprises had good reason to deal directly with foreign clients independently of official channels because it provided a means of ensuring that revenues paid for their products actually ended up in their own accounts. The state arms export agency, Rosvooruzheniye, was notorious for its corruption.[46] By some accounts, at least 40 percent of the revenue from contracts with China did not reach the specific manufacturers.[47]

Perhaps no other Russian defense industry exemplified the complexities of a reliance on the export market as much as the aviation sector manufacturing Sukhoi fighter jets. By Russian standards, the ability of Sukhoi producers to sell their planes abroad in the 1990s was a rare post-Soviet success story. But it was a relative success story that illustrated the limitations of dependence on a foreign patron. In 2003, Sukhoi production operations included AHC Sukhoi, comprised of the Sukhoi Design Bureau and two production facilities in Novosibirsk and Komsomolsk-na-Amur, and NPK Irkut, located in Irkutsk. NPK Irkut was AHC Sukhoi's main competitor (although AHC Sukhoi held a 14.7 percent share of its operations), breaking away from its parent corporation in the early 2000s. In its quest to reinvent itself as a Western-style corporation, NPK Irkut became the first Russian defense enterprise to have its books audited (by PricewaterhouseCoopers) to international standards, raising cash through corporate bonds. In 2002, AHC Sukhoi was Russia's top defense company with revenues of 1.04 billion dollars, while NPK Irkut ranked in the number two position with revenues of 562 million dollars.[48]

Most of China's orders for fighter jets were filled at the Komsomolsk plant, while the Irkutsk facility was oriented toward the construction of the Su-30MKI fighter jets destined for India. However, the Su-27UBK trainers (six in 1992, six in 1995, and twenty-eight in 1999) purchased by China were manufactured at Irkutsk. As Yuri Baturin, the secretary of the Defense Council, noted in January 1997, the Sukhoi plant at Komsomolsk-na-Amur would not have survived without orders from China.[49] In addition, foreign revenues, which reportedly accounted for 70 percent of the Sukhoi Design Bureau's income, served as the main source of capital to pursue critically necessary product development. In a May 1996 interview, Vladimir Konokhov, the chief designer of the Su-37 fighter aircraft, the upgrade to the Su-27 series, noted that its development as a prototype had been financed through the sale of Su-27 fighter jets to China and Vietnam, and the sale of the Su-27 production license to China.[50] The Sukhoi plant in Irkutsk also received funding from the Indian government to develop a more advanced variant of the Su-27 series, the Su-30MKI, tailored especially to Indian specifications.

The orientation of both AHC Sukhoi and NPK Irkut toward the export market as their main source of revenues was successful, at least in the short run. In 1998 AHC Sukhoi announced net profits of 22.4 million rubles, compared with 213 million rubles in 1999 and 445 million rubles in 2000.[51] At the end of 2001, Mikhail Pogosyan, the head of the Sukhoi Design Bureau, stated that the company had achieved its best year since the collapse of the Soviet Union, with financial revenues on a par with those of Soviet times. However, while AHC Sukhoi was rated Russia's top defense company for export earnings in 2002, these earnings indicated a decrease by about one-third compared with 2001, a consequence of fewer aircraft deliveries to China.[52] Although the sale of Su-30MK2 naval fighters to China in January 2003 ensured production for the mid-years of the decade at the Komsomolsk-na-Amur plant, Sukhoi faced the problem in the longer term of market saturation. There was a limit to how many aircraft fighters China or India could purchase, a dilemma compounded by the sale of licensing technology to both states. Beside the sale of the license to China to manufacture Su-27 aircraft, Russia sold a license to India to produce 140 Su-MKI fighter jets and was involved in negotiations with China over the transfer of a license to produce fighter jets of the Su-30MKK series.

In addition, the Sukhoi producers faced the urgent problem (one encountered by enterprises throughout the Russian defense sector) of product obsolescence. Sukhoi was involved in a race against time to update its weaponry in order to remain competitive on the international market. The Su-27 and its assorted modifications were designed in the 1970s and coming to the end of their product life. On their own, the aircraft manufacturers did not possess the resources to finance this project, and were trying to interest both China and India in investing in some sort of collaborative venture for research and development. NPK Irkut, considered Russia's most promising company in terms of securing international partnerships, signed on with the HAL Corporation, an Indian firm, to study the prospects of developing and producing a tactical transport aircraft for military use. AHC Sukhoi managed to win a 1.5–billion-dollar government tender providing government support for a fifth-generation aircraft, now renamed the Su-47. This endeavor, however, necessitated cooperation with rival aircraft firms MiG and the Yakovlev Design Bureau, with analysts expressing doubts about the overall feasibility of the project.[53] Besides its battles with external competitors, AHC Sukhoi was beset with internal conflicts that cast serious doubt on the ability of the firm to pursue product development. In July 2002, for example, the Komsomolsk-na-Amur production plant sued the Sukhoi Design Bureau, complaining that the bureau was diverting revenues earned from the sale of fighter aircraft to China to subsidize the project to develop a fifth-generation fighter aircraft.

Russian Military Interactions with China: Domestic Circumstances

The dire conditions of the Russian military-industrial complex in the 1990s meant that arms and technology exports to China were a matter of economic survival for a number of defense firms. In addition to the Sukhoi enterprises, arms sales to China were critical for such arms producers as the Severnaia

Wharf (destroyers) and Admiralteiskie Wharf (submarines) shipbuilding firms, as well as a number of firms supplying radars and missile systems. Unsurprisingly, defense producers were fervent advocates of arms sales to China.[54] But defense lobbyists did not seem to have to work too hard to promote their cause. Personnel throughout the Russian governmental apparatus embraced the policy. In January 1992, immediately after the establishment of the Russian Federation, Boris Yeltsin began urging arms producers to seek out foreign customers, noting that "the weapons trade is essential for us to obtain the foreign currency which we urgently need and to keep the defense industry afloat."[55] After coming to office, Vladimir Putin moved to restructure the arms export hierarchy and broaden the scope of Russian military assistance in an effort to increase Russian arms and technology sales abroad. In interviews with officials from the Russian government and defense industries in 1999, Kevin O'Prey reported that virtually all respondents strongly defended arms sales to China as being of critical importance to Russian enterprises and design establishments as a means of procuring revenue.[56]

During the 1990s, the Yeltsin government failed to establish clear lines of authority between a myriad of domestic actors involved in military-technical cooperation with China. In the first years of the Russian Federation, the Ministry of Defense acted as the central body conducting negotiations with the Chinese on arms sales and technology transfers. The 1993 Russian-Chinese Agreement on Military and Technological Cooperation was signed between the Russian and Chinese Ministries of Defense. By the mid-1990s, authority over military-technical cooperation had shifted to the civilian sector of the government, under the direction of a vice minister in charge of defense affairs within the prime minister's cabinet. In contrast to the 1993 agreement, Vice Minister Aleksei Bolshakov signed the 1996 Memorandum on Military-Technical Cooperation on the Russian side. In January 1998, President Yeltsin sent a delegation led by Andrei Kokoshin, the Defense Council secretary, to China to negotiate over arms purchases, further blurring the institutional lines of command. In 1999, however, the Russian and Chinese ministers of defense signed an updated Russian-Chinese Memorandum on Military-Technical Cooperation. In contrast, the Putin administration set out to centralize controls over arms exports, granting an increased role to the Ministry of Defense. In November 2000, Putin reorganized arms export institutions, merging them through the creation of Rosoboronexport, which was placed under the supervision of the Ministry of Defense. In June 2002, Minister of Defense Sergei Ivanov replaced Vice Minister Ilya Klebanov as the chairman of the Russian side of the Russian-Chinese Military-Technical Cooperation Commission.

As a practical matter, the Russian military had information regarding the operation and functioning of weapons systems that made it an essential participant in arms sales. The various edicts, statutes, and decrees issued by the Yeltsin leadership on military-technical cooperation in the 1990s acknowledged the role of the Ministry of Defense in the process of preparing proposals, demonstrating weaponry, training foreign military personnel in the operation of Russian weaponry, and rendering technical assistance in the adaptation of weapons systems.[57] Moreover, when the business at hand involved arms and technology transfers, the Chinese government relied exclusively on military personnel. Although the Chinese military did not generally intrude into issues of foreign policy (with the notable exception of Taiwan), it did possess considerable autonomy to make its own decisions with minimal interference on arms and technology purchases. In the 1990s, the MAC set up an office in the Chinese embassy in Moscow to deal with the acquisition of arms and technologies from Russia.[58] Under these circumstances, interactions between the Russian and Chinese militaries became inextricably interconnected with arms sales and technology transfers.

During the Soviet era, the military had prided itself on its professionalism, an orientation it was hard pressed to maintain in the post-Soviet era. The Yeltsin government was not interested in preserving the military as a Soviet-style institution, an action that would have been impossible in any case given the state of the Russian economy. It was dubious that Russian military personnel, inheritors of a proud Soviet tradition, embraced the role of salesmen hawking their wares on the international market. But grim economic circumstances and near budgetary famine made it difficult for the Russian military not to adopt this new position. The military-technical relationship with China provided the Ministry of Defense with much needed revenues derived from the training of Chinese military personnel both in Russia and in China, commissions on orders placed on the export of arms, and the sale of used weaponry.[59] Moreover, the Ministry of Defense had a vital interest in the ability of defense enterprises to invest arms sales revenues in the development of new weapons systems. The authority to supervise arms exports granted by the Putin administration in November 2000 was warmly received by the Ministry of Defense insofar as it provided the ministry with increased input into the development of specified weapons systems for eventual deployment by Russian military forces.[60] The Ministry of Defense also pushed the government to divert monies used from arms exports to equip the Russian military. As Minister of Defense Sergei Ivanov noted in December 2001: "I believe—and many people support me on this issue—that our [arms] exporters should forward some small part of their incomes to equipping our army with modern weapons. Otherwise, it is an ironic situation: we sell up-to-date weapons abroad, while the Russian army does not have anything from this."[61]

From a geostrategic perspective, the Russian transfer of weapons and technology to China was not a wholly rational behavior, as it exposed Russia to the possibility of future retaliation from its erstwhile partner.[62] In fact, members of the Russian military, especially within the echelons of the top leadership, voiced concerns as to the potential risks involved with the sale of advanced weapons technologies to China.[63]

Russian Minister of Defense Igor Rodionov voiced an apprehension reportedly shared by others within the Russian military leadership when he referred to China as a potential military threat to Russia in December 1996. Rodionov, however, did not single out China; his remarks identified NATO as well as a number of bordering states as sources of military danger. In general, however, Russian military experts tended to downplay China as a significant military threat to Russia, at least for the time being. The prevalent reasoning was that China's technological capabilities still lagged considerably behind those of Russia and that China's geostrategic orientation was not directed toward Russia but toward the projection of its military capabilities in the Taiwan straits and the South China Sea. At various times, moreover, the Ministry of Defense blocked Chinese access to technology incorporating Russia's most up-to-date weapon systems.[64] This included prohibiting the sale of most high-technology land systems in the name of national security.[65] Russia was also more willing to sell its most highly advanced weapons models to India than to China. The technology embodied in the Su-30MKI—Russia's most advanced fighter jet—was more advanced, for example, than the Su-30MKK.[66] In any event, other concerns loomed as more pressing than the long-term threat posed by China to Russia's beleaguered military establishment. The potential dangers of the transfer of arms and technology to China were superseded by short-term imperatives.

Beyond the Arms Trade: Bilateral Military Interactions

Relations between the Russian and Chinese militaries in the post-Soviet era were driven by the sale of armaments and related technologies. Military relations—as opposed to military-technical relations—were subordinated to this exigency. Nonetheless, in the 1990s Russia and China established a series of military interactions of a more conventional variety. At the highest level, the defense ministers of the two states met on a regularly scheduled basis, although their discussions also included military-technical relations as a major theme. Military exchanges and goodwill visits emphasized the development of military ties as a means to strengthening relations between the Russian and Chinese militaries. These exchanges, however, often were not completely disassociated from commercial impulses. The development of exchanges between the Russian and the Chinese navies, for example, coincided with China's growing interest in purchasing naval armaments.

In the early years of the Russian Federation, Russia and China concluded two intergovernmental agreements of military and political significance. In July 1994, the Russian and Chinese defense ministers signed an agreement on the prevention of dangerous military activity that sought to identify and avoid the potential for inadvertent accidents and conflicts in the border regions. In September 1994, the Russian and Chinese presidents signed a joint communiqué in which the two states pledged not to target each other with their strategic nuclear missiles, nor to be the first to use nuclear weapons against the other. Both of these agreements paralleled analogous agreements that Russia had concluded with other states.[67] In addition, Russia and China signed two multinational agreements of military significance: the 1996 Agreement on Strengthening Mutual Military Confidence in the Border Regions and the 1997 Agreement on the Mutual Reduction of Military Strength in Border Regions (see Chapter 3). These documents mandated the yearly meeting of defense ministers, an arrangement that was subsequently incorporated into the Shanghai Cooperation Organization.

Beginning in the early 1990s, Russia and China resurrected the practice of military exchange visits. In August 1993, a group of ships of the Russian Pacific Fleet paid a visit to the Chinese port of Qingdao, the first such visit in thirty years. Subsequently, Chinese naval ships visited Vladivostok and a convoy of Pacific Fleet destroyers docked at Shanghai in October 1999 to take part in joint naval exercises with China as part of the celebration of the fiftieth anniversary of the PRC. In 1996, Russian and Chinese air force commanders agreed to step up exchanges and cooperation, while the Russian and Chinese navies signed a cooperation protocol in 1999. However, cooperation between the naval forces of the two states included sending Russian instructors to China to train Chinese military personnel in the operation of Sovremennyi destroyers bought by China. Various arrangements were established for military exchanges—including border guards—between commanders of the Siberian and Russian Far East military districts and their Chinese counterparts.

Russian and Chinese military interactions at the national level also included discussions of regional and international issues, following an agenda laid out in presidential summit meetings. During his tenure as minister of defense, Pavel Grachev persistently tried to interest Chinese defense officials in his vision of a joint security system in the Asian Pacific region without any success. In 1997, the general staffs of the PLA and the Russian army established consultations on strategic and security issues. These discussions included aspects of military-technical relations, but they also dealt with regional and international issues, as well the consolidation of confidence-building measures between the two states and the status of Russian military reform. Discussions between the Russian and Chinese defense ministers invariably included international and regional issues. In the late 1990s and early 2000s, these included the Kosovo situation, missile defense, the 1972 Anti-Ballistic Missile Treaty, and—even before September 11, 2001—terrorism at the regional level.

In the summer of 2002, reports of planned joint maneuvers between Russia and China received considerable publicity, fueled by speculation that they involved the large-scale organization of land, sea, and air forces directed against the United States. In fact, the reality appears to have been considerably less sensational. Russia and China were involved in joint radio training of the personnel of radio stations in the border regions between Siberia and Inner Mongolia, reported to be a yearly event connected with their 1994 agreement on the prevention of dangerous military activities.[68] Russian-Chinese military interactions did not focus extensively on strategic-political issues, nor were they distinguished for a high degree of institutionalization in the development of military exchange programs. The latter was presumably partly a reflection of the impoverished circumstances of the Russian military, which lacked the funds to pay for goodwill visits and military exchanges.

Conclusion

Some analysts have interpreted the expansion of military-technical relations between Russia and China as an indication of an outright military alliance.[69] In fact, formal military contacts between the two states absent a financial impetus were limited and often superficial. According to Dmitri Trenin: "Bilateral military contacts [between Russia and China] are probably less profound than those between the Chinese and U.S. militaries."[70] The legacy of the Sino-Soviet dispute—which terminated contacts between the Soviet and Chinese militaries for decades—left Russia and China without an institutionalized heritage to draw upon in the construction of formal military linkages. Rather, the limited contacts that were initiated in the waning days of the Soviet Union were oriented toward the sale of Su-27 fighter aircraft, setting the framework for the arms and technology transfers undertaken by the Yeltsin leadership. Moreover, the salience of traditional military issues as a component of border relations diminished significantly in the 1990s, superseded by a broader conception of security concerns that included ethnic separatism, religious fundamentalism, and terrorism.

The burgeoning growth of Russian arms and technology sales to China in the 1990s was undoubtedly a factor in the increasingly friendly ties between the two states. Arms and technology transfers served immediate Russian economic and political interests. For both the Yeltsin and the Putin administrations, arms sales served as a means to avoid painful and politically costly reforms of the defense sector entailing the closure of numerous enterprises. Although Putin attempted to assert control over the arms industry—an essential measure if the government was to attain much needed revenues lost to corruption—his actions did not indicate an abandonment of the fundamental policy of promoting arms exports.[71] Nonetheless, the Russian-Chinese military-technical relationship differed from most forms of economic interaction between the two states insofar as it did little to foster economic linkages, but rather contributed to China's eventual ability to attain self-sufficiency in arms production. The increasing dependence of Chinese weapons systems on Russian prototypes helped to ensure Russia's presence on the Chinese arms market as a supplier of spare parts and component equipment. Russian-Chinese cooperation in arms production held the promise of an increased economic interdependence between the two states. But this prospect was far from assured. Despite bilateral discussions between the two states on joint co-production, the Putin administration lacked an overall policy for promoting collaborative projects, leaving Russian enterprises on their own in finding foreign partners.[72] Ultimately, moreover, China aimed for self-reliance and the acquisition of the technological prowess to build its own high-technology weapon systems.

The Russian contribution to Chinese military modernization obviously had strategic implications not only for Russia, but the Asian Pacific region and, in a broader sense, the entire international system. Russian weapons transfers to China altered power balances in the region, with potentially destabilizing implications. The pattern of Chinese arms purchases from Russia implied China's clear intent to acquire the military capability in order to exert significant diplomatic and political pressure on Taiwan, as well as to enhance its dominance in Southeast Asia through the development of a blue-water navy.[73] The increase in Chinese military prowess presented a potential threat to Russian security interests, especially in the vulnerable Russian Far East (see Chapter 6). Nonetheless, even a militarily weakened Russia continued to possess overwhelming superiority relative to China in the nuclear realm, a situation that presumably acted to deter potential aggressive action. Whatever the unsettling long-term implications, the Russian leadership perceived that its immediate interests were served by the development of a military-technological relationship with China.

6

The China Factor in the Border Regions

The Russian Far East and Transbaikal Area

Not only do Russia and China share a 4,250-kilometer border, but for the 7.2 million citizens of the Russian Far East, Beijing is a closer geographical destination than Moscow. Among the ten administrative regions in the Russian Far East, four—Primorskii krai, Khabarovsk krai, Amur oblast, and the Jewish autonomous oblast (Birobidzhan)—border directly onto China (see Map 6.1). In addition, Chita oblast, one of six administrative territories in the East Siberian Administrative Region, and a small segment of Altai krai in the West Siberian Administrative Region share a border with China.[1] During most of the Soviet period, and particularly during the decades when the Sino-Soviet conflict reached its apex, linkages between the two states were tightly constrained as Russians lived in an artificially constructed world of geographical isolation from the rest of Asia. In the autarchic days of the Soviet Union, moreover, the Russian Far East was heavily subsidized at great expense to the center. In the 1990s, much of the Russian Far East was brought to the point of economic collapse, with a sharp decrease in industrial production and living standards. In fact, Primorskii krai achieved the dubious distinction of experiencing the most significant economic decline in all of Russia.[2] At present, moreover, given the cessation of subsidies and the vast distances from European Russia, residents of the region are confronted, to an even greater extent than elsewhere in Russia, with the prospect of globalization, in the form of increased economic integration with the Asian Pacific region, and the development in particular of cross-border linkages with China. Such a transition necessitates sweeping changes in the traditional economic, social, and cultural orientation of the region, and has evoked considerable fears of being overwhelmed by China, either in a relationship of economic dependency or, more literally, by waves of immigrants.

Map 6.1 **The Russian Far East: Administrative Regions**

Source: Copyright Russian Far East Advisory Group, LLC. Seattle, WA. Reprinted with permission.

In the aftermath of the collapse of the Soviet Union, neither the Russian state, regional elites, nor residents of the border areas were prepared to deal with a multitude of issues that arose regarding regional relations with China. To compound these problems, Russian regional leaders, operating in an environment of lax federal control, often contested nationally formulated policies regarding China, on occasion pursuing their own deviant course of action. In the Russian Far East, however, Russian-Chinese relations emerged as a tactical issue that leaders sought to use in their ongoing struggles with the center. It was not always clear to what extent the objections posed by regional authorities to Russian foreign policy toward China reflected a principled opposition or were simply attempts to increase political leverage, or more modestly, attract the notice of a largely inattentive center. Nonetheless, since the establishment of the Russian Federation, three interrelated topics of Russian-Chinese relations have been especially salient for the Russian Far East and Transbaikal area: (1) border demarcation; (2) migration; and (3) economic and trade relations in the border regions. Through their treatment of these issues, regional leaders have been able to exert some influence on the shaping of Russian policy toward China with respect to its formulation as well as its implementation.[3]

Border Demarcation

As previously discussed in Chapter 3, the Soviet Union owned all river islands and controlled all river traffic along the Sino-Soviet border prior to the adoption of the 1991 border agreement. According to the terms of the agreement and the subsequent demarcation of the border, 1,281 islands were allocated to China, leaving 1,163 under Russian control. In correspondence with international law, the border was reset along the main navigation channel of rivers, with Chinese vessels accorded navigational rights along the waterways. In addition, Russia also turned land over to China in Primorskii krai. This shift in the longtime status quo indicated a sizable alteration of the balance of power—or more precisely, the imbalance of power—in the border areas to the disadvantage of Russia. It was difficult, in particular, for regional residents within the border areas to come to terms with this evident diminishment of Russian sovereignty. The 1991 border agreement was widely viewed as an unfair and inequitable concession concluded by a distant government insensitive to local interests. This perception was reinforced by the secrecy surrounding the border negotiations. The specific points of the 1991 agreement were not provided to the public beforehand, thus creating consternation and anger, especially in the Russian Far East and Transbaikal areas, when the population realized that Russian territory would be handed over to China.[4] Although the 1991 border agreement was ratified by the Russian Supreme Soviet in February 1992 by a vote of 174 to 2, with 24 abstentions, the ensuing demarcation of the border proved to be more complicated than originally envisioned. Regional leaders were quick to jump on the populist bandwagon, using the border demarcation as a means of rallying support against federal authorities. Regional authorities mobilized to protest the border agreement in four regions in particular: the Jewish autonomous oblast, Chita oblast, Primorskii krai, and Khabarovsk krai.

Regional politicians in the Jewish autonomous oblast reacted adversely to the announcement that five islands in the Amur River used by local residents were to be ceded to China. In response, Nikolai Volkov, the oblast governor, signed a resolution recommending that village administrators create voluntary militias and Amur Cossack troops be deployed to defend the border region. Subsequently, the oblast Duma sent a proposal to the Russian government and the Federation Council demanding a halt to demarcation in the area of the Amur islands, calling for a regional referendum on the question. The representatives continued to raise objections even after Yeltsin signed the Russian-Chinese border demarcation agreement in November 1997. Initially, a similar situation prevailed in Chita oblast when it was learned that Menkeseli island in the Argun River was to be given over to China. Villagers had made use of the island (actually a sandbar) for agricultural purposes. But this situation was resolved when local activists themselves put forward a suggestion for a compromise solution in which they would retain the right to use the island but formal ownership would reside with China.[5] This arrangement was formalized during Yeltsin's November 1997 trip to China, where Menkeseli was included, along with other adjacent islands, among the areas that were earmarked for joint economic activity (see Chapter 3).

During much of the 1990s, however, the most vocal criticisms of the 1991 border agreement were raised in Primorskii krai under the leadership of the governor, Evgenii Nazdratenko. In Primorskii krai, the territorial dispute involved the transfer of approximately 1,600 hectares of land to China: 410 hectares in Khankaiskii raion, 960 hectares in Ussuriiskii raion, and, most controversially, 328 hectares in Khasan raion along the Tumen River. Opponents of the land transfer marshaled a litany of objections. The Chinese were alleged to be irresponsible environmentalists who would wreck havoc on the delicate ecological balance of the region. Patriotic nationalists protested that the land to be transferred in the Khasan region contained the hallowed graves of Soviet soldiers who died fighting the Japanese in 1938. The most prevalent objection, however, was that the transfer of land in the Khasan region would allow China access to the Sea of Japan, thus enabling it to build a port in direct competition with Primorkskii's ports in Vladivostok and Nadhodka. In the words of Valeriy Rozov, an aide to Nazdratenko and the former chairman of the Russian-Chinese Border Demarcation Commission for the krai:

> With the loss of this land, Russia will lose its strategic positions in the Far East. It will be losing not only, and not so much, Primorskii krai as our entire state. . . . The Chinese side intends to invest twenty-five billion dollars in these territories over the next few years. And this would have the most negative impact on Primorksii krai.[6]

Nazdratenko orchestrated an elaborate campaign against the 1991 border agreement, a struggle that was interconnected with his political battles with the Yeltsin government which was seeking his removal from office. In 1994, Nazdratenko promised to resign if even a span of Russian land was given over to China. Under his direction, the work of border demarcation in the krai was obstructed for several years and the Ussuri Cossacks were mobilized to picket disputed sections of the border. In April 1996, Nazdratenko was successful in providing a maximum level of embarrassment to the Yeltsin administration, strategically timed to coincide with Yeltsin's upcoming visit to Beijing. First, Valeriy Rozov, the head of the Russian-Chinese Border Demarcation Commission for the krai, resigned from his position, announcing that the transfer of land was injurious to the national interest of Russia.[7] A few days later, Nazdratenko made an unauthorized announcement that Yeltsin had called for a moratorium on the demarcation of the border.[8] The latter provoked a sharp response by Vice Foreign Minister Aleksandr Panov, who harshly criticized the governor, accusing him of seeking to undermine Russian-Chinese relations.[9] Naztradenko himself was an awkward member of Yeltsin's delegation to China who reaffirmed upon his return that he had upheld his views in front of the president, the Russian Foreign Ministry, and his Chinese hosts.[10] In January 1997, Yeltsin ordered (without any notable short-run success) Nazdratenko to restrict his comments on China to those in conformance with the position of the Russian Foreign Ministry. Subsequently, however, Yeltsin and Nazdratenko patched up their political differences—Yelstin even rewarded Nazdratenko with an order for "service to the Fatherland" during a March 1999 visit to Moscow—and Nazdratenko sharply curtailed his objections to the 1991 border agreement. By the late 1990s, dissension over the transfer of land in Primorski krai had largely receded as an issue.[11]

The regional leadership in Khabarovsk krai was also outspoken in its opposition to the realignment of the border (see Map 6.2). Both the governor, Viktor Ishaev, and the krai Duma expressed an unremitting hostility to any prospect that Bolshoi Ussuriiskii and Tarabarovskii islands, located near Khabarovsk—two of the three islands excluded from the 1991 border agreement—be given over to China. Nor were the authorities in the krai willing to accept the right of the Chinese to navigate along the Amur River. In September 1993, Ishaev sent a letter to Prime Minister Chernomyrdin demanding that the agreement be rescinded, claiming that Chinese fishermen were routinely violating fishing regulations. Subsequently, in May 1994, Khabarovsk officials unilaterally issued a decree requiring that Chinese vessels seeking to navigate along the Amur River inform a Russian border official about their plans one day in advance, with nighttime sailing prohibited. Boris

Map 6.2 **Disputed Islands in Khabarovsk Region**

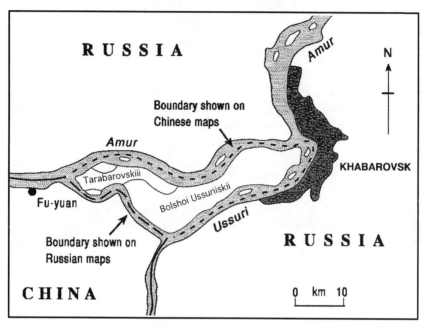

Source: *Boundary and Security Bulletin* 5(3), 1997. Reprinted with permission of the International Boundaries Unit, University of Durham.

Yeltsin's tacit acquiescence to this measure was signaled by his authorization in February 1995 to provide for an Amur border flotilla as part of the Russian border troops.[12] Krai Duma hearings in December 1998 continued to press the issue, claiming that Chinese vessels were impeding the navigation of Russian vessels in the Amur. A related concern of the Khabarovsk authorities was the status of the Kazak'evichev channel, along which the border was drawn, in the southern arm of the Amur River near the city of Khabarovsk. Over time the channel had become steadily shallower and was in danger of disappearing completely, a situation that would indicate the shifting of the border to the northern arm of the Amur and the transfer of the two disputed islands to China. China rejected Russian suggestions for a joint project to deepen the channel. In fact, residents of Khabarovsk, including Ishaev, charged that the Chinese were deliberately and surreptitiously working to fill in the channel to ensure the redrawing of the border to their further advantage.[13]

By the early 2000s, with the demarcation of the border completed and regional complaints more or less abated, the status of Bolshoi Ussuriiskii and Tarabarovskii islands in Khabarovsk was the major border issue that remained unresolved between Russia and China. Khabarovsk authorities were unyielding on the question, insisting that the sovereignty of the islands remain with Russia. Ishaev steadfastly rejected any joint economic activity on the islands, engaging in a series of seemingly deliberately provocative statements and actions. Local leaders built an Orthodox church on Bolshoi Ussuriiskii island, in addition to claiming that archeological research had uncovered artifacts proving its indisputable native Russian origins. Plans were made to step up the economic development of the island and to build a pontoon bridge linking the island to the mainland, thus preventing Chinese travel along the waterway.

Russian and Chinese Reactions to Regional Dissent

Regional politicians who objected to the 1991 border agreement enjoyed some success in publicizing their dissatisfaction and garnering support at the federal level, especially among members of the government opposition. National politicians with presidential aspirations, such as Vladimir Zhirinovskii and General Aleksandr Lebed, identified themselves as opponents of the surrender of territory to China. Both the Russian Duma and the Federation Council conducted hearings on the demarcation of the border in the Russian Far East. In general, the Federation Council, reflecting its regional orientation, was more sympathetic to complaints of Far Eastern officials. In December 1996, for example, Federation Council Vice Chairman Vasilii Likhachev stated that the border agreement inflicted "damage on Russia's geostrategic interests."[14] The Foreign Relations Committee of the Duma, under the chairmanship of Vladimir Lukin upheld the validity of the 1991 border agreement, but Duma Chairman Gennadii Seleznev assured the Khabarovsk authorities during a June 1998 visit that Russia would not hand over the disputed islands to China.

Under the Yeltsin government, the thankless task of defending the border agreement largely fell to the Ministry of Foreign Affairs.[15] Unlike its critics, who often seemed oblivious to Russian vulnerabilities, the Ministry of Foreign Affairs displayed a consistent recognition that any renegotiation of the 1991 border agreement might well be detrimental to Russia. The Foreign Ministry sought to justify the 1991 border agreement through recourse to international law, arguing that the document conformed to internationally recognized principles and that it was impermissible to seek changes after the agreement had been ratified.[16] The Foreign Ministry, however, was not obligated to adhere to a position of neutrality on the issue of the disputed islands that lay outside of the domain of the border agreement. Russian negotiators sought to demonstrate that the islands belonged to Russia, but left open the possibility of compromise. In July 2000, Foreign Minister Igor Ivanov visited Bolshoi Ussuriiskii island before traveling to Beijing. Konstantin Pulikovskii, Putin's presidential representative in the Far Eastern Federal District, accompanied him. Pulikovskii's comments were unequivocal: "These islands are ours."[17] Ivanov's comments, however, were more measured, indicating that his purpose was to study the situation, noting that "it is necessary to find mechanisms of solving all problems."[18]

For their part, Chinese officials adopted a relatively restrained reaction to internal dissent within Russia over the border agreement, choosing to view the behavior of Nazdratenko and other regional politicians as one more indication of the breakdown of central authority in Russia rather than as the deliberate actions of covert spokesmen for the Kremlin. China proved willing to compromise on its border with Russia, agreeing to adjust the borderline in the Khasan region so that the graves of the Soviet soldiers would remain within Russian territory. Nonetheless, the Chinese also let it be known that there were limits to their patience. The Chinese Foreign Ministry lodged protests on a number of occasions over the efforts of Russian politicians to amend the border agreement, an action that the Chinese viewed as impermissible under its terms. In 1996, the Chinese Foreign Ministry issued an ultimatum that Russia conclude its demarcation of the border by the end of 1997, a condition that was laid out in the original agreement. In August 1997, Foreign Minister Primakov acknowledged that the pace of the border demarcation was one of the key problems in Russian-Chinese relations. In fact, the Russian side was engaged in foot-dragging in its demarcation of the border, and not only because of the obstacles imposed by regional leaders. The Yeltsin leadership also sought to slow the pace of the demarcation prior to the 1996 presidential elections in a conscious effort not to provoke additional controversy that would be harmful to Yeltsin's reelection.[19] In addition, the demarcation was impeded by financial constraints. Russian vessels, for example, often lacked fuel and were consequently unable to take measurements to determine river flows. Although Yeltsin and Jiang Zemin managed to adhere to the technical requirements of the 1991 agreement by signing a document marking the completion of border demarcation during Yeltsin's 1997 trip to Beijing, the work of mapping the border and establishing boundary markers was not in fact concluded until April 1999, when the Boundary Demarcation Commission held its last meeting and announced the precise border line between the two states.

During the 1990s, the regional protests of local elites against the border demarcation served to constrain and limit the scope of negotiations for the Russian government at the center. But the Yeltsin administration was able to silence its most vociferous critic, Primorskii krai governor Nazdrentko, through a policy of cooptation. After the demarcation was completed and the final determination of the border delineated, the furor over the agreement subsided. China's willingness to permit Russians to continue small-scale farming, hunting, and fishing activities on islands and their related waterways also provided an impetus to cooperation. By the time Vladimir Putin became president, the Chinese had indicated that it was time to move toward a final resolution of the border issue. China had also exhibited its irritation with Khabarovsk authorities by lodging an official protest against the decision of the krai Duma to build a pontoon bridge. Khabarovsk governor Viktor Ishaev was a powerful regional politician but not invulnerable to federal pressures. Ishaev's commitment to Russian sovereignty as an immutable precept was also compromised by remarks that he made in May 2001 on the Kurile islands issue. According to Ishaev: "It's obvious from a historical point of view that these islands should be handed over. There is nothing we can do about it."[20] A similar assessment could be applied to Russia's island disputes with China. Chinese behavior during the demarcation of the border in the Khasan district of Primorskii krai indicated that they were agreeable to compromise, but the prospects of complete acquiescence to the Russian position seemed unlikely.

Chinese Migration to the Russian Far East

During the first decade of the Russian Federation, the illegal entry of Chinese into Russia, especially the Russian Far East, became a significant political issue with a consequent impact on Russian-Chinese relations. In particular, regional politicians in the Russian Far East—most notably in Khabarovsk and Primorskii krais—expressed alarm at the influx of Chinese into their territories. However, concern over Chinese migration was a political issue that transcended regional politics and resonated among politicians at the national level across the political spectrum, extending into the ranks of the Russian government. Russian antipathy to the entrance of Chinese into Russia was rooted in the fear that it would lead to the Sinification of the Russian Far East and the eventual loss of Russian sovereignty over the area. The demographic situation, in fact, did lend some plausibility to this scenario. The population of the Russian Far East in 2000 was 7.20 million and in decline, with 900,000 people estimated to have fled the region in the 1990s.[21] Meanwhile, Heilongjiang province alone across the Russian-Chinese border had a population of 38 million in 2000, with over 105 million people living in the three northeastern provinces of Manchuria (Heilongjiang, Jilin, and Liaoning).[22] According to a 1994 estimate made by the Russian politician Sergei Shakrai, if current economic and demographic trends continued in

Russia, the entire Russian population east of the Urals would have shrunk from 32 million to 8–10 million by the year 2010.[23]

Historically, moreover, the Chinese were a significant presence within the population of the Russian Far East. Estimates are that as many as 500,000 Chinese lived in the Russian Far East at the end of the nineteenth century, comprising approximately one-third of the population.[24] Large numbers of Chinese (and other Asians) continued to live in the region until the 1930s, when they were expelled as one facet of the Stalinist purges. Chinese (and also Koreans) again began to enter the Russian Far East in notable numbers during the Gorbachev era.[25] In 1988, visa-free border crossing was introduced along the Sino-Soviet border, leading to an influx of Chinese traders. With the breakdown of the Soviet economic system, residents of the Far East turned to China as a source of basic necessities that had previously been shipped from European Russia. The larger cities of the region, especially within Primorskii krai, began to acquire visible Chinese populations, a cause of consternation for a population that had lived in isolation for decades. In addition, the release of large numbers of prisoners from the Soviet Gulag increased the demand for Chinese (and North Korean) workers to fill their places. In 1990, about 15,000 Chinese were legally working in the Soviet Far East under cooperatively concluded labor contracts.[26]

With the dissolution of the Soviet Union, the number of Chinese entering Russia increased markedly, provoking antagonism among Far Eastern residents. Anti-Chinese sentiment was greatest in Primorskii and Khabarovsk krais, and considerably less prevalent in the Amur and the Jewish autonomous oblasts, where there were correspondingly fewer migrants. Chinese migrating to Primorskii krai tended to concentrate in urban areas and were thus more visible than in Khabarovsk, where many found employment in agriculture. In the 1990s, both Primorskii krai governor Evgenii Nazdratenko and Khabarovsk krai governor Viktor Ishaev emerged as outspoken critics of Chinese migration to the region. Like demarcation of the border, this issue produced political reverberations to the federal level, with a number of national politicians and government officials ready to jump on the anti-migration bandwagon. Structures of Russian officialdom such as the Federal Border Service, the Federal Migration Service, the Ministry of the Interior, and the procuratorial offices often exhibited an institutional hostility toward a Chinese presence in the Far East. Nationalist political movements incorporated opposition to Asian migration as a hallmark of their platforms. But the range of national politicians who denounced Chinese migration ran the political gamut, from the ultra-nationalist Vladimir Zhirinovskii to reformists such as Yabloko leader Grigory Yavlinskii. Chinese-Russian relations were also tested by the indiscreet statements of members of Yeltsin's own cabinet, such as Minister of Defense Pavel Grachev, who expressed the view in August 1995 that "Chinese citizens are peacefully conquering Russia's Far East."[27]

In fact, the extent of Chinese migration into Russia was not known with any precision. Estimates of the number of Chinese illegally living in the Russian Far East varied (in fact, wildly) and were highly speculative, not to mention often inflammatory. Typically, Russian sources in the 1990s, including those well established within reform circles, suggested a Chinese presence of well over one million persons. Thus, Boris Nemtsov estimated the Chinese population in Russia at one million, while Sergei Rogov, director of the Institute of the United States and Canada, claimed that "half a million Chinese immigrants settle every year in the largely empty Russian land between Lake Baikal in Siberia and the Pacific Ocean."[28] Perhaps the highest estimate was provided by Yabloko leader Yavlinskii, who maintained that over 5 million Chinese had illegally settled in Russia.[29]

The willingness of Russian politicians and analysts to embrace these figures was especially striking given the lack of evidence to substantiate their veracity. Few empirical studies of the scope of Chinese migration into Russia existed, but those that were conducted presented far lower estimates of the Chinese presence. Emil Pain, a presidential advisor to Boris Yeltsin, concluded in a 1997 article in *Rossiiskie Vesti* that less than 200,000 Chinese were living in the Russian Far East.[30] In the 1990s, the most comprehensive investigation of Chinese migration into Russia was undertaken by the Moscow Center of the Carnegie Foundation under the auspices of a project on migration and citizenship. In 1996–97, researchers conducted field studies in six regions of the Far East and Eastern Siberia (Khabarovsk krai, Primorskii krai, Amur oblast, Chita oblast, Irkutsk oblast, and the Buryat republic); analyzed registration data of the Federal Migration Service, the Federal Border Service, and local passport-visa services; surveyed Chinese migrants and local residents, including local experts; and observed local conditions on a first-hand basis. A further study was conducted in 1998–99 in Moscow, Khabarovsk, Vladivostok, and Ussuriisk.[31]

According to Galina Vitkovskaia, the Moscow co-director of the Migration and Citizenship project, the more realistic assessment of the Chinese presence in Russia as of 1999 was in the vicinity of several hundred thousand people.[32] The Carnegie report noted that official data often double counted the number of shuttle traders who entered and reentered Russia several times a year, and that regional data indicated that the overwhelming percentage of Chinese who entered Russia on tourist visas did not overstay their allotted time. Moreover, law enforcement agencies in border areas were rigorously active in expelling Chinese who remained illegally. In summary, large communities of Chinese in the Russian Far East, which were in any case easily detectable among the local population, simply did not exist.[33] In fact, Vitkovskaia noted that the largest Chinese population in Russia was located not in the Russian Far East, but in Moscow, where 20,000–25,000 Chinese constituted a stable community among 30,000–40,000 Chinese inhabitants of the city.[34] The Chinese population of Russia, moreover, was highly sensitive to economic indicators; migration flows decreased dramatically with the August 1998 collapse of the Russian economy.[35]

Regional Responses to Chinese Migration During the Yeltsin Administration

As increasing numbers of Chinese began to move into the Russian Far East, regional leaders were successful in pressuring the federal authorities to revise Russian visa regulations. In January 1994, the Russian government unilaterally and without prior consultation with China canceled visa-free crossing for Chinese citizens. The cost of a visa—set at $150—was meant as a further deterrent to entry. Subsequently, the Russian and Chinese governments signed a consular agreement specifying that only those on diplomatic and official passports would qualify for travel without a visa. Border controls regulating the presence of Chinese in the area were also stepped up. Over the years, the Russian Border Guards, the Interior Ministry, and the Federal Counterintelligence Service carried out a series of movements—codenamed "Operation Foreigner"—to identify and deport Chinese illegal aliens. In addition, the federal government introduced a system of quotas restricting the legal hiring of Chinese workers. In the short run, these policies achieved their immediate aim: the number of Chinese entering Russia plummeted, but such actions also contributed significantly to the downturn in bilateral trade between the two states in 1994. This created particular economic difficulties in Amur and Chita oblasts, which had become heavily dependent on imports from China. In the longer term, the new visa regime proved to be only a temporary impediment, as Chinese discovered a loophole for entrance into Russia through the visa-free exchange of tourist groups.

Russian immigration policy, which lacked a firm institutional basis to begin with, was further complicated by the decentralization of controls over the border to the regional authorities. The regional authorities ultimately decided who would receive a visa and for what length of time. Regional leaders also independently set their own quotas for the legal entry of Chinese into their localities. Primorskii krai set the most stringent conditions for Chinese hoping to do business in Russia, limiting tourist visas to a three-day period. Khabarovsk krai was considerably more lenient, allowing shuttle traders to remain for a term of one month, with possibilities for extension. A substantial illegal trade also developed in the sale of tourist visas to Chinese, whether to shuttle traders, or to those who were simply seeking transit to migrate to a third country, by all accounts a sizable number.[36] In the late 1990s, officials throughout the region began further tightening visa requirements in an effort to restrict the Chinese presence. Even areas less hostile toward Chinese workers such as the Jewish autonomous oblast reduced the number of Chinese allowed to work in the region.[37] Throughout the Russian Far East, the number of Chinese contract workers hired was typically fewer than the mandated quotas. By the late 1990s, regional officials appeared to have largely succeeded in their quest to keep out the Chinese. In 1997, Khaborovsk krai registered 2,930 foreign contract workers, 772 of whom were from China. The krai security services recorded 91 Chinese citizens in 1997 who had exceeded their legal stay. In 1998, over 10,000 Chinese tourists entered Khabarovsk, many of them in transit.[38] The statistics were similar in Primorskii krai. According to the Primorskii krai visa registration service, the percentage of visitors from China who remained illegally dropped from 34 percent in 1994 to 0.4 percent in 1998.[39] In 1998, only 39 Chinese were listed as permanent residents.[40] According to Mikhail Alexseev, the percentage of Chinese citizens in Primorskii krai between 1996 and 1998 was unlikely to have been more than 0.3 to 1.1 percent of the population.[41]

Regional officials combined their efforts to reduce the Chinese presence in their localities with inflammatory and often xenophobic anti-Chinese rhetoric disseminated in the government-controlled media. These measures appeared to intensify an already existent antagonism toward Chinese residents. Public opinion polls invariably indicated that Russians did not hold favorable attitudes toward Chinese living in the border areas. Russians complained that the consumer goods brought in by the Chinese shuttle traders were of a low quality and that Chinese were taking jobs away from Russians. While Chinese were grudgingly credited with being hard working and entrepreneurial, they were also widely viewed as dishonest and rude, with a desire to displace the Russian presence in the Far East.[42] While Khabarovsk governor Viktor Ishaev was more tolerant of Chinese business activities in Khaborovsk than his counterpart in Primorskii krai, he maintained an unflagging hostility to the notion of permanent Chinese settlement in the region. Ishaev condemned the privatization of land in the krai on the grounds that "all the land in Russia's Far East will be bought up by Chinese," and similarly emerged as a vocal foe of intermarriage—"assimilation" in his words—between Russians and Chinese, seeking to deny the Chinese spouse the right to remain on Russian soil.[43] Ishaev, moreover, was explicit in describing Chinese migration as a deliberate expansionist ploy of the Chinese government. According to Ishaev:

The peaceful capture of the Far East is under way. . . . . The main problem is that in the years of market reforms, more than 800,000 persons, which constitutes more than 10 percent of the population, have left Khabarovsk krai.[44] Their place has been taken by a mass influx of Chinese and Koreans, who take up compact residence. They are even now exerting a certain influence on the economy and policy in the region. All this is strictly planned. As we all know, China has some official program in this connection. They do not intend to fight us; they plan, availing themselves of the transparency of our borders, to come to our region and take up residence and live here. . . . The threat of the nonmilitary takeover of the Far East lands is real.[45]

Russian-Chinese Bilateral Contacts on Migration

As Chinese migration to Russia emerged as a domestic political issue in Russia, it also became a topic of bilateral discussion between the Russian and Chinese governments. As an official position, the Chinese government acknowledged and condemned the illegal migration of Chinese to Russia. Speaking at Moscow University in June 1994, Chinese foreign minister Qian Qichen noted that "the Chinese government has persistently opposed illegal immigration and will not allow any Chinese citizens to engage in affairs harming good-neighborly and friendly relations between the two countries."[46] Chinese officials subsequently reiterated these sentiments on numerous occasions. The Chinese, however, flatly disputed Russian assessments of the extent of the illegal migration of Chinese into Russia. In 1995, a Chinese estimate considered that there were 1,000–2,000 illegal Chinese residents in the Russian Far East.[47] Chinese ambassador to Moscow Li Fenglin responded to Yavlinskii's claim that 5 million Chinese were living in Russia with the retort that the problem of Chinese immigration to Russia "simply does not exist."[48] In an interview with *Nezavisimaia Gazeta* given during his February 1998 trip to Moscow, Premier Li Peng adopted a similar approach, denying that Chinese workers were settling in Russia's Far East and establishing Chinatowns there.[49] The Chinese government largely chose to ignore the inflammatory comments of some Russian politicians on Chinese migration, but the Chinese Ministry of Foreign Affairs issued a number of protests over the mistreatment of Chinese nationals in the periodic sweeps launched to deport illegal aliens.

In fact, the allegation of Russian nationalists that the Chinese leadership had an explicit plan to colonize the Russian Far East was unsubstantiated. The root cause of Chinese migration to Russia was a matter of demography, not Chinese state policy. In the first part of the decade, customs officials in Heilongjiang province, eager to stimulate trade with Russia, allowed Chinese traders to enter Russia on official passports, circumventing the need to procure a visa and thereby contributing to the influx of Chinese into Russia. These policies, however, incurred the wrath of the center, led to reprimands by the Chinese Ministry of Foreign Affairs, and were apparently a factor in the removal of the governor of the province in 1996 and the subsequent tightening of visa policy.[50] By the late 1990s, Russian and Chinese officials were working to develop institutional structures to coordinate their activities to stem the illegal flow of Chinese into Russia. Immigration issues had become a standard item on the agenda at the meetings of the Russian and Chinese prime ministers. Article 19 of the 2001 Friendship Treaty reiterated the commitment of the two states to "cooperate in cracking down on illegal immigration." In May 2003, Presidents Putin and Hu indicated their intent, formalized in their joint communiqué, to set up a working group on the problems of Sino-Russian immigration to promote joint law enforcement and regulate the entrance of Chinese into Russia.

The two states also sought to coordinate the actions of their border guard services, previously a point of considerable discord. Pavel Tarasenko, head of the Pacific Branch of the Russian Border Guard Service, acknowledged in a March 1999 interview that relations with his Chinese counterparts had improved and that the Chinese themselves had stepped up efforts to detain illegal entries on their own side of the border.[51] According to the Chinese ambassador to Russia, Wu Tao, the Chinese were also tightening their control over Chinese citizens traveling to Russia.[52] Consular talks were held on a yearly basis. A major unresolved issue for the two states, however, was the negotiation of a visa regime that would control illegal migration without simultaneously choking the development of trade relations and economic cooperative links. The Chinese were enthusiastic proponents of visa-free entry in the border areas as a means of stimulating economic growth. In contrast, a number of Russian officials sought a revision of the visa regulations to restrict further the ability of Chinese legally to enter Russia.

Immigration Issues in the 2000s: What Is to Be Done?

By the early 2000s, some Russian elites—government officials, politicians, and policy-oriented intellectuals—had begun a reassessment of immigration policy for the Russian Far East. Such a trend was visible at the national rather than the regional level, where leaders continued to exhibit hostility toward an influx of Chinese into Russia. In 2000, the Putin administration agreed to continue visa-free exemptions for tourist visits and signed an accord that standardized and (to a certain extent) liberalized the conditions for hiring Chinese workers on a contract basis. The Putin administration responded aggressively to press reports in the summer of 2002 claiming that the number of Chinese in Russia had reached 5 million people. Andrei Chernenko, the head of the Federal Migration Service, stated in June 2002 that "migration to Russia from China did not constitute a big threat," and that there had been no change in immigration levels over the past five years.[53] Defense Minister Sergei Ivanov reiterated this position noting that he saw nothing wrong with Chinese citizens coming to work in Russia under regulated conditions. In September 2002, the Foreign Ministry issued a statement criticizing domestic and foreign reports about Chinese expansion into Russia. According to the Ministry, there were no more than 150,000–200,000 Chinese living in Russia: the sensationalist reporting was "not true" and was detrimental to the development of relations with China.[54]

The Putin administration's resolutely nonalarmist attitude toward Chinese immigration was echoed by a small but growing number of policy analysts who were prepared to go even further and to assert that Russia needed to accept as necessary a sizable inflow of Asians, primarily Chinese, into the Russian Far East. Under Yeltsin the preferred solution to the demographic crisis of the Russian Far East—semi-enshrined in official policy—had been the adoption of a "Stolypin approach," along the lines of tsarist Russia, in which Russian settlers (displaced ethnic Russians from other former Soviet republics) would be brought into the region, lured by attractive financial incentives and subsidies. This view, however, was rejected by a small cadre of Western-oriented intellectuals who promoted the revisionist (and in certain Russian circles heretical) thesis that the demographic situation was so bleak, and the prospects for a Stolypin solution so unlikely, that immigration from Asia offered the only hope for economic regeneration of the region.[55] In a March 2001 interview, for example, the demographer Zhanna Zaionchkovskaia noted that Russia needed to attract more than a million immigrants a year to sustain its economy, with China the most likely source of labor power.[56] A report by the Council of Foreign and Defense Policy reiterated this perspective in a project dealing with Siberia and the Far East in the twenty-first century. According to its assessment:

> The steady and progressively intensifying combination of the aging of the population along with its exodus due to the absence of work is creating conditions under which the huge Siberian–Far Eastern expanse can be saved from depopulation only by migration from abroad, which is the only means capable to improve the age and gender structure of the population. Since such migration realistically is possible and has already begun from the states of the Asian Pacific Region (primarily China), it is necessary to consider it as socially significant and welcome from the point of view of the state.[57]

Russian assessments of the number of migrants have typically not distinguished between those legally authorized to reside in Russia and illegal aliens. According to figures released by the Federal Migration Service, 205,400 Chinese were granted permission to work in Russia between 1994 and 2001, comprising 21.2 percent of the total number of foreign workers. In the first half of 2002, 40,866 Chinese arrived in Russia to perform labor, constituting almost 18 percent of the total number of recruits, second only to Ukraine.[58] The impediments to the legal entry of migrants into Russia served to constrict their numbers. Local authorities placed tight restrictions on hiring, and arcane federal laws contributed to the difficulties faced by would-be employers. For example, it was necessary to travel to Moscow to apply for a labor import license to hire foreign workers. In addition, the maximum length of stay for an agricultural import license was three months, less than the growing season for many crops.[59] These conditions thus operated to ensure that the vast majority of Chinese migrants arriving in Russia lacked legal authorization. The Russian advocates of increased Chinese immigration to the Russian Far East and Siberian regions have been fully cognizant of the simultaneous imperative need to restructure and institutionalize Russian immigration law to ensure that Chinese who reside in Russia, whether temporarily or on a permanent basis, do so legally in conformance with prescribed procedures.

Economic and Trade Relations with China in the Border Areas

With the collapse of the Soviet Union, the Russian Far East—bereft of its traditional support system—was forced to turn to foreign trade as a matter of survival. In the early 1990s, regional trade rapidly expanded between the Russian Far East and adjoining Chinese regions, most notably with Heilongjiang province.

Table 6.1 presents the foreign trade of the Russian Far East and trade turnover with China from 1992 to 1997. These trade figures should be seen as approximations that do not reflect the considerable volume of trade conducted through informal channels not accounted for in Russian official statistics. Nonetheless, it is clear that the revision of visa regulations in 1994 had a large impact on bilateral trade. Trade with China comprised 36 percent of the total trade turnover of the Russian Far East in 1992 and 1993, but fell markedly in 1994 and 1995 to 11 percent and 8 percent of the total. Subsequently, Far Eastern trade links with China revived, only to fall again sharply with the advent of the Russian financial crisis in 1998. Total trade turnover for the Russian Far East in 1999 was estimated at 3.2 billion dollars, less than in 1993, with China the destination point of 16.7 percent of exports and the source of 13.2 percent of imports.[60]

Table 6.1

Foreign Trade of the Russian Far East/Foreign Trade of the Russian Far East with China, 1992–1997 (in US$ billions and as a percentage)

	1992	1993	1994	1995	1996	1997
Total trade	2.728	3.238	2.260	4.180	4.568	4.146
Exports	1.539	2.048	1.610	2.426	2.831	2.034
Imports	1.189	1.119	0.649	1.753	1.738	2.112
China	0.984	1.181	0.250	0.328	0.926	0.620
% Total	(36)	(36)	(11)	(08)	(20)	(15)
Exports	0.564	0.575	0.156	0.172	0.707	0.358
% Total	(37)	(28)	(10)	(07)	(25)	(18)
Imports	0.419	0.606	0.094	0.155	0.219	0.262
% Total	(35)	(54)	(15)	(09)	(13)	(12)

Source: Foreign trade figures for the Russian Far East compiled from *Regiony Rossii Tom 2, 1992–1997* (Regions of Russia: vol. 2, 1992–1997) (Moscow: Goskomstat, 1993–1998). Figures for Russian Far East trade with China for 1992–1995 are from Nadezhda Mikheeva, "Foreign Trade of the Russian Far East with the People's Republic of China: Development and Problems" at http://srch.slav.hokudai.ac.jp/sympo/Proceed97/MIKHEEVA.html. Figures for Russian Far East trade with China for 1996–97 are from Andrei Admidin and Elena Devaeva, "Economic Cooperation Between the Russian Far East and Northeast Asia," *Far Eastern Affairs*, no. 1 (1999): 34. Percentages extrapolated.

During the 1990s, Japan was the largest export market for the Russian Far East as a whole. In the early 2000s, however, China overtook Japan as the leading destination point for the exports of the region. Between 1997 and 2002, the level of trade between Japan and the Russian Far East and Transbaikal regions fell by 38 percent.[61] As Table 6.2 indicates, 45 percent of exports from the Russian Far East were delivered to China in 2001, with China also serving as the source of 18 percent of imports, comprising 40 percent of total trade turnover. In contrast, only 15 percent of the region's exports were delivered to Japan. A similar trend continued in 2002: China accounted for 34 percent of total trade turnover in the Russian Far East and Transbaikal areas, compared to 20 percent for South Korea and 17 percent for Japan.[62]

Within the Russian Far East, moreover, there was considerable variation in regional trade patterns. Geography exercised a strong influence on trade interactions, although other factors—such as the location of defense enterprises—also played a major role in structuring trade relations with China. During the 1990s, the leadership of Primorskii krai deliberately pursued a policy of reducing its dependence on China as a trading partner, a strategy made possible by its maritime position. China's share of foreign trade in Primorskii krai was 58 percent of total trade turnover in 1992, but only 24 percent of total trade turnover in 1997.[63] Primorskii krai, however, was a

Table 6.2

Trade Turnover of Russian Far East in 2001 by Country of Origin
(in US$ millions and as a percentage)

Country	Export	%	Import	%	Total	%
China	1,716.3	45	170.9	18	1,887.2	40
South Korea	643.9	17	206.5	21	850.41	18
Japan	560.4	15	186.1	19	746.5	16
Singapore	498.1	13	3.1	<1	501.2	10
USA	46.6	1	125.9	13	172.5	4
Switzerland	73.3	2	1.9	<1	75.2	1
Germany	8.9	<1	52.9	5	61.8	1
United Arab Emirates	61.4	1	0.0	0.0	61.4	1
Virgin Islands	44.3	1	0.0	0.0	44.3	1
Austria	43.2	1	0.8	<1	44.0	1
Vietnam	13.7	<1	21.1	2	34.8	1
Other	83.7	2	197.1	20	280.8	6
Total	3,793.7	100	966.3	100	4,760.1	100

Source: Compiled and extrapolated from Elena Borodina, "Russian Far East: International Trade in 2001" at www.bisnis.doc.gov/bisnis/country/020509trade_rfe.htm.

beneficiary of arms sales to China. Several plants in the krai, including the Progress plant in Arsenyev, produced electronics and anti-ship missiles for placement on the Sovremennyi destroyers purchased by the Chinese navy. In contrast to Primorskii krai, the landlocked southern border regions were heavily dependent on trade with China. In 1993, China's share in foreign trade turnover was 91.9 percent of the total in Amur oblast and 94.6 percent of the total in the Jewish autonomous oblast.[64]

In the 1990s, Khabarovsk krai, which shared a longer border with China than any other Russian region, became increasingly integrated with China in trade interactions. In 1998, 64 percent of Khabarovsk's exports were to China while China's share in the krai's total trade turnover was 59 percent.[65] While geography naturally inclined Khabarovsk krai toward economic links with China, this tendency was accentuated by the Russian-Chinese military technical relationship. In 1996, the volume of exports to China for the krai reached 500 million dollars, largely due to Chinese orders for Su-27 aircraft.[66] As of 1999, it was estimated that about 85 percent of the output of Khabarovsk krai was exported.[67] In 2001, total exports for Khabarovsk krai reached over 2 billion dollars, which constituted almost 53 percent of total exports for the Russian Far East for the year. Moreover, the leading export sector in the krai—comprising 62.4 percent of the total—was transport, machines, and equipment.[68] In effect, this indicated the shipment of Su-30MKK fighter jets from the Komsomolsk-na-Amur plant to China. The economy of the krai

Table 6.3

Heilongjiang Province Total Trade Turnover/Trade with Russia 1992–2001 (in US$ millions and as a percentage)

	1992	1993	1994	1995	1996	1997	1998	1999	2000	2001
Total Trade	2,880	3,053	3,093	3,429	3,517	3,582	3,812	2,191	2,986	3,385
Exports	1,831	1,884	1,837	2,095	1,811	2,001	2,034	950	1,451	1,612
Imports	1,049	1,169	1,255	1,334	1,706	1,583	1,778	1,241	1,535	1,772
Total Trade/Russia	1,585	1,900	1,610	1,530	1,420	1,418	1,642	916	1,372	1,799
%	55	64	52	45	40	43	43	42	46	53
Exports/Russia	839	1,066	752	852	699	718	864	231	463	780
%	46	57	41	41	39	36	42	24	32	48
Imports/Russia	745	885	858	675	720	700	777	684	908	1,019
%	71	76	68	51	42	44	68	55	59	57

Source: Heijongjiang tongji nianjian, 1994, 1996, 1997, 1998, 1999, 2000, 2001 (Heilongjiang statistical yearbook,1994, 1996, 1997, 1998, 1999, 2000, 2001) (Heilongjiang: China Statistical Bureau of Heilongjiang Province, 1995, 1997, 1998, 1999, 2000, 2001, 2002): 414–15, 380–81, 352–53, 343–44, 351–52, 331–32, 354–56.

was not only dependent on the export market but on the specific shipment of Sukhoi fighter aircraft to the Chinese military.

On the other side of the border, Heilongjiang province also underwent a substantial restructuring in its trade patterns in the 1990s as Russia emerged as a major trading partner. Heilongjiang province did not play a significant role in the overall foreign trade of China; in 2001, its total trade turnover comprised just .07 percent of the national total.[69] In 2001, however, the province accounted for 17 percent of total Chinese trade turnover and 29 percent of exports to Russia.[70] As Table 6.3 on the previous page indicates, trade with China was of critical importance to Heilongjiang: in 2001, 53 percent of its total trade was with Russia, comprising 48 percent of exports and 57 percent of imports. Despite efforts at diversification, Heilongjiang's foreign trade continued to be heavily reliant on Russia as a trade partner. Between 1992 and 2001, the Russian share in Heilongjiang's total trade turnover ranged between 42 and 64 percent.

Bilateral Initiatives to Develop Trade in the Border Regions

In the 1990s, as bilateral trade stagnated, Russian and Chinese officials pointed to regional trade between Russia and China as a bright spot in an otherwise gloomy trade picture. The initial growth in regional trade in the early 1990s was partly a consequence of short-term circumstances that could not be sustained in the face of numerous economic and structural impediments. But political factors, reflected in a disparity of outlooks between Chinese and Russian regional officials, also impeded efforts to develop economic and trade relations in the region. On the one side, Chinese leaders at both the national and the provincial level were enthusiastic adherents of regional integration. Across the border, Russian leaders at the national level acknowledged—at times with resignation—the necessity of becoming full-fledged members of the Asian Pacific region, but they could not necessarily count on their regional counterparts to share this sentiment or to work toward its realization.

In the Chinese context, Heilongjiang province was considered something of an economic backwater that lagged behind the faster growing and more developed coastal and southern regions of China. Beginning in the early 1980s, Chinese officials, both at the center and at the regional level, saw the potential of developing economic links to the north as a means of redressing regional inequities.[71] With the rise in trade between Manchuria and the Russian Far East, the Chinese intensified their efforts in the 1990s seeking to provide a system of grants and privileges to stimulate economic growth and to develop external trade links, akin to the sort of open-door strategy pursued with considerable success in other regions of China. Border trade cooperation zones, providing reduced tariff rates, were established on the Chinese side of the border in Heilongjiang in the cities of Heihe and Suifenhe. A 1996 State Council circular set forth guidelines for the growth of the border trade between China and Russia. During his July 1999 inspection tour of Heilongjiang province, Vice Premier Qian Qichen reaffirmed the importance of developing border trade and tourism with Russia.

In contrast to the Chinese situation, the Yeltsin government largely lacked a strategic plan for the development of external links to the Russian Far East. A design that existed on paper—the Special Federal Program on Integrating the Far East and the Transbaikal Area into the World Economy via Economic Cooperation with the Asian Pacific Region Countries—was essentially inoperative in practice. Meeting with governors of the border regions in July 1999, Prime Minister Sergei Stepashin acknowledged that Russia lacked the legislative base to regulate such key aspects of economic cooperation in the border areas as the creation of free economic zones, the establishment of joint ventures, the regulation of visas, and the organization of a common infrastructure. In fact, the declining authority of the federal government vis-à-vis the regions was implicit in the very convocation of the meeting, in which Stepashin sought to garner support from regional governors in advance of the upcoming parliamentary elections. Discussion at the meeting further indicated, moreover, that numerous border crossing points, most notably in Primorskii krai, had evolved into the private fiefdoms of nonstate entities that were imposing their own illegal fees for financial gain.[72]

Thus, initiatives to develop cooperative and trade links along the Russian-Chinese border largely came at the behest of the Chinese leadership. A Russian-Chinese Working Group on Inter-Regional and Cross Border Cooperation was formed in 1996 as a permanent body under the Russian-Chinese Economic and Trade Cooperation Committee. Subsequently, the Russian-Chinese Border and Local Economic and Trade Cooperation Coordination Committee was formed, holding its first meeting in January 1998 in Blagoveshchensk. Delegates to these meetings were constituted from local administrative heads from the regions along the Russian-Chinese border, representatives of relevant ministries at the national level, and representatives of business interests. The major focus of the committee was on developing and coordinating forms of border trade. Measures under discussion included increasing the number of enterprises authorized to conduct foreign-currency trade, setting up various types of free trade zones, and developing joint enterprises in forestry, wood and fish processing, and agricultural production. In November 1999, the two states signed an agreement on setting up a system to mediate problems and disputes arising in the border trade. At its third meeting, held in May 2000 in Vladivostok, the committee adopted a two-year economic cooperation program aimed at promoting Chinese investment in the Russian Far East, focusing on energy, shipbuilding, and timber. At the Vladivostok meeting, the Altai, Irkutsk, Sakhalin, and Sakha regions of the Far East and Siberia jointed the bilateral committee as members.

Interregional trade, on a somewhat broader geographical scale, was a major focus of discussion during Zhu Rongji's February 1999 trip to Moscow, where the two sides signed a Sino-Russian Local Cooperative Agreement that provided for the establishment of partnership agreements between several Russian and Chinese regions.[73] In conjunction with this arrangement, which originated at China's request, the Chinese organized two seminars, held in Beijing in January and June 1999, to examine means of developing regional cooperation. The two sides also sought to develop free trade zones along the border that would allow for the visa-free movement of Russian and Chinese citizens. In an effort to stimulate trade, Chinese authorities worked to reduce fees and tariffs, as well as to simplify visa arrangements to facilitate the entry of Russians into trading complexes on the Chinese side of the border. Arrangements were made for the visa-free entry of Russian citizens to the Inner Manchurian city of Manzhouli and to trading complexes in Heihe and Suifenhe in Heilongjiang province. Bilateral discussions also were conducted regarding the reciprocal visa-free entry of Chinese to the Zaibaikalsk trading complex in Chita oblast located on the other side of Manzhouli, to the Russian town of Pogranichnyi in Primorskii krai bordering Suifenhe, and to Blagoveshchensk in Amur oblast bordering the Chinese town of Heihe.

The July 2001 Friendship Treaty noted (in Article 16) the commitment of the two parties to "promote the development of border and local economic and trade cooperation, and create the necessary good conditions for this in line with their national laws." During the first several years of the Putin administration, discussions continued regarding visa-free crossing without any final resolution. The Russian government, however, did make some incremental changes in visa requirements that allowed Chinese to work in Russia on a contract basis for a longer period of time. Moreover, the banking cooperation agreement concluded in August 2002 provided for interbank settlements in the border region on a trial basis. The joint communiqué signed at the August 2002 meeting of the prime ministers of Russia and China also indicated their intent to intensify work on developing communication links between the two states.

Local Reactions to Prospects of Economic Integration

Bilateral efforts to stimulate economic cooperation in the border areas were hampered by the same economic constraints that impeded the overall growth of Russian-Chinese trade. These factors were accentuated, however, by regional hostility to economic integration with China. The anti-Chinese sentiment that was demonstrably in evidence in the Russian Far East was expressed in an antipathy to the development of economic cooperative links. Russian regional officials often showed little enthusiasm for the establishment of free trade zones along the Russian-Chinese border and engaged in various ploys to delay their operation. Regional leaders were also reluctant to improve transportation links, fearing that it would contribute to the influx of Chinese into the area and increase cross-border economic integration. The 1995 agreement to build a bridge connecting Heihe and Blagoveshchensk remained stalled for years, with the Russians even turning down an offer from the Chinese side to fund its entire construction.[74]

Many residents and regional leaders in the Russian Far East, seeing integration into the Asian Pacific region as inevitable, nonetheless favored the establishment of economic links with Japan or South Korea over China. In part, this reflected a disdain for the small-scale undercapitalized commercial ventures characteristic of Chinese joint ventures and entrepreneurial undertakings, as well as a pervasive preference for Japanese and South Korean consumer goods. But it was also an indication of concerns that Chinese economic penetration would facilitate Chinese immigration into the Far Eastern regions.

Regional officials in the southern border regions—specifically in Chita, Amur, and the Jewish autonomous oblasts—were generally supportive of the development of economic ties with China, which were viewed as a pragmatic necessity. These officials expressed their strong opposition to the alteration in visa requirements in 1994 that resulted in a sharp reduction in trade, and consequently revenue, with China. Regional politicians based in locations that stood to benefit from the export of raw materials and natural resources also tended to be favorable toward economic interactions with China. After domestic demand for timber collapsed, the Siberian Buryat republic responded by attempting to strengthen economic contracts with the Chinese border regions, oriented toward the export of timber. Similarly, Sakhalin authorities pressed to be included in the Russian-Chinese Border and Local Economic and Trade Cooperation Coordination Committee because of their desire to develop trade links with China. In addition to hopes of eventually selling natural gas on the Chinese market, Sakhalin officials were interested in increasing coal and marine exports to China in the short run.

The tensions between resistance against and accommodation with China as an economic partner were most sharply drawn in the Russian Far East's most populous regions, Primorskii krai and Khabarovsk krai. In Primorskii krai, Nazdratenko distinguished himself as a virulent critic of China who orchestrated policies specifically aimed to discourage economic interaction. This approach was effective: As previously noted, foreign trade turnover between the krai and China fell precipitously, and Chinese investment slowed to a trickle. In 1995, Chinese foreign investment into the krai totaled 417,000 dollars; by 1998 it had fallen to 15,000 dollars, compared with 171,090 dollars for South Korea and 126,670 for Japan, the two largest investors.[75] Upon coming to office in 1993, Nazdratenko indicated his opposition to the Tumen River Area Development Program (TRADP), a regional economic cooperation program located in the border area of Russia, North Korea, and China and sponsored by the United Nations.[76] Nazdratenko's hostility to the 1991 border agreement with its land transfers along the Tumen River to China was interconnected with his animosity to the TRADP, which he saw as providing China with the potential opportunity to build a port and gain access to the sea. In Nazdratenko's view, the development of the region would inevitably be detrimental to Primorskii krai and the ports of Vladivostok and Nakhodka. Thus, although the TRADP was endorsed by the Chinese and Russian governments—the topic was on the agenda during Boris Yeltsin's first visit to China in December 1992—Nazdratenko, along with many other residents of Primorskii krai, remained staunchly opposed to the plan.

By the late 1990s, however, Nazdratenko had significantly reduced the level of animosity in his comments on China. In part, this reflected his reconciliation with the Yeltsin government. But the regional economic environment had also altered such that Nazdratenko no longer saw China as a major threat. By the mid-1990s, the TRADP, never a particularly feasible endeavor, had mutated into a vaguely defined project, envisioned as a series of free economic zones in the greater region linked by upgraded infrastructure. Lacking funding, this endeavor was virtually moribund; nonetheless, its basic premises were far more congenial to Nazdratenko. Primorskii krai in its entirety was to be included within the loosely defined Tumen Region (which in fact extended to Mongolia in certain conceptualizations) and specific attention was directed toward the development of the Nakhodka Free Economic Zone, the improvement of ports at Zarubino and Vostochnyi, and the construction of a rail link connecting the Chinese city of Hunchun in Jilin province to the Russian city of Makhalino in Primorskii krai.

This revised format for the TRADP met with Nazdratenko's approval on several counts. Not only was the prospect of a port along the Tumen River (highly improbable in any case) abandoned, but Nazdratenko also had embraced a regional cooperation program that aimed to develop a transit link through the ports of Vladivostok and Nakhodka for the shipment of U.S. goods to areas within northern China. This plan, formally entitled the "East-West Intermodal Corridor," was developed by the U.S. West Coast Russian

Far East Ad Hoc Working Group, an outgrowth of the Gore-Chernomyrdin in Commission, to encourage trade between the United States and the Russian Far East.[77] Nazdratenko thus shifted gears and sought to interest the Chinese in the project, which was promoted as a faster, shorter, and less expensive alternative for the shipment of goods from north China as compared with Chinese ports further south. For their part, the Chinese found the proposal potentially feasible. Starting in 1998, the Chinese began to ship coal mined in Heilongjiang from Vostochnyi port in the Nakhodka Free Economic Zone to Japan and South Korea. A visiting Chinese delegation from Heilongjiang province in March 1999 indicated its interest in increasing the volume and scope of provincial exports from the port.[78] In June 1999 regional officials from Primorskii krai, Washington State, and Heilongjiang province signed a protocol to investigate the development of a transit link connecting Puget Sound ports to Harbin in Heilongjiang via Primorskii krai.[79]

With the abatement of Nazdratenko's criticisms, Chinese investment in Primorskii krai dramatically increased. In 1999, Chinese investment in Primorskii krai increased almost thirty-two-fold, from 15,000 dollars in 1998 to 476,900 dollars. China's share of total trade volume for the krai also increased from 21 percent in 1997 to 30 percent in 1999.[80] Chinese investors also began to direct their attentions to the development of Nakhodka as a special economic zone. Although the South Koreans were the primary investors, China provided the second largest allocation of investment funds for the project in 2000, totaling 474,500 dollars.[81] However, the economic and political conditions in the krai, which gained a notorious reputation under Nazdratenko's leadership as an outpost of corruption and criminality, continued to restrict the development of economic linkages with China.[82] Prospects improved in February 2000 with the resignation of Nazdratenko as governor, but deeply embedded structural problems continued to impede economic reform in the krai. Although China began to ship cargo to Japan in early 2001 through the Russian port of Pos'et in Primorskii krai, Chinese carriers refused to ship coal from Vostochnyi because of a doubling of the tariffs on transportation by rail.[83]

During the 1990s, Khabarovsk krai officials managed to maintain better ties with China than Primorskii krai, a situation that was not lost on the Chinese who opted to establish their consulate in Khabarovsk rather than Vladivostok, the largest city in the Russian Far East. Although Viktor Ishaev, the powerful governor of Khabarovsk krai, was outspoken in his opposition to Chinese immigration and the transfer of the disputed islands to China, he was also careful not to overstep certain boundaries in his interactions with the Chinese. This was also a concession to reality: it was estimated that as much as 70 percent of the local workforce was employed by the Sukhoi complex at Komsomolsk-na-Amur.[84] Over the years, Ishaev met with numerous Chinese military delegations on their prospective tours of the plant. After China and Russia concluded a deal to manufacture Su-30 fighter jets in August 1999, Ishaev told the press that the agreement would "ensure a normal workload for the factory over the next three years."[85] Ishaev also proved amenable to bilateral trade with China in the raw materials sector. The first Russian-Chinese joint venture for logging and wood processing was established in Khabarovsk krai in 1998. Khabarovsk officials also attempted to interest their counterparts in Heilongjiang in investing in a proposed pipeline to carry natural gas from Sakhalin to Khabarovsk and on to China. Ishaev apparently preferred to do business with the Chinese in the old Soviet style, on a bilateral basis, while keeping the physical presence of Chinese in the krai at a minimum. Yet the governor also displayed a pragmatism in his attitude toward economic relations with China that was based on a combination of geography and realpolitik. As he noted: "Our region is getting integrated into the Asia-Pacific, there is no alternative to that process. . . . We are not choosing our neighbors and we have to maintain friendly relations with China."[86]

Conclusion

To date, the fledgling Russian state has not been able to devise an effective and realistic policy that incorporates a concept of Russia as an integral part of the Asian Pacific region. The Russian Far East has played an important symbolic role in the Russian national consciousness, but the reality is that the sparsely populated area is distant from the center of power in Moscow in both the literal and figurative sense. In the 2000 presidential elections, none of the major candidates set foot in the area. Tensions in the Russian Far East directed against the Chinese state and the Chinese people are genuine, but also reflect the anxiety engendered by the unanticipated collapse of the Soviet regime and the consequent demands upon the population to embark upon a thoroughgoing restructuring of established patterns of daily life. The Russian transformation has imposed even greater challenges on residents of the Russian Far East than their compatriots living in European Russia, requesting them to give up their autarchic insular existence and accept—as Ishaev's comments above indicate—the inevitability of integration into the Asian Pacific region. Russians must become residents of Asia if not Asians.

In July 2000, Vladimir Putin noted the stark choice facing Russia: "If we do not make real efforts to develop the Far East in the very near future, the Russian population will mainly be speaking Japanese, Chinese and Korean in a few decades."[87] On a tour of the Russian Far East and Siberia a month later, Putin indicated that the area needed to be better integrated into the global economy. The implementation of an economic strategy for the Russian Far East was not simply an economic challenge, but a political one. During the 1990s, regional politicians gained considerable autonomy from Moscow and were resistant to efforts to relinquish their quasi-feudal powers. In February 2000, Putin installed Konstantin Pulikovskii as his presidential representative in the Far East District and also managed to oust Nazdratenko from office in Primorskii krai. Nazdratenko, however, continued to exercise influence throughout the region in his new job as head of the State Fisheries Committee.[88] Pulikovskii's initial attempts to wrest control from the regional governors were not particularly successful, nor did he indicate any particular expertise in implementing economic reform.

In the absence of fundamental economic reforms, the Russian Far East was not able to attract large-scale investment from abroad. Nonetheless, a decade after the Soviet collapse, incipient signs pointed to the opening up of the region. In the late 1990s, joint Russian-Chinese agricultural ventures emerged in the border districts. According to foreign trade statistics of Heilongjiang province, 71 percent of all cooperation projects between the border district regions in 1998 were in the area of crop husbandry.[89] In June 2002, 2,000 Chinese peasants arrived in Primorskii krai for the summer, many headed for the Ussuri district to work on privately owned farms.[90] Russian farmers, especially private farmers, began to take advantage of the superior agricultural knowledge of the Chinese, who were teaching them how to grow fruits and vegetables as well as how to raise pigs. Compared with Russians, Chinese were considered harder working, more knowledgeable, and more productive.[91] Although most Chinese laborers remained in the Russian Far East, they were also gradually disseminating westward into European Russia.[92] While climatic conditions made it doubtful that the Russian Far East would achieve self-sufficiency in agricultural production, productivity levels in the Soviet era were far below potential output yields.[93] By the early 2000s, Russian-Chinese bilateral initiatives in fruits, vegetables, and soybeans, as well as forms of animal husbandry, were beginning to supply an increasing amount of foodstuffs to the local population. As Konstantin Pulikovskii acknowledged in a 2002 interview:

> I recently visited the Jewish autonomous oblast. There Chinese people work on potato and soy fields. But where are our people, Russians? Our people drink vodka. Meanwhile, those guest workers live in huts right in the field and work from dawn to dusk, growing potatoes of excellent quality.[94]

Pulikovskii's comments indicated a central problem facing the Russian Far East and Siberian regions in the 2000s. Economic autarchy was no longer a viable option, and a Stolypin approach was not feasible. Russia's integration into the Asian Pacific region is inevitable, but its implementation cannot be disassociated from the related issue of Russian immigration policy. Anti-immigration rhetoric among politicians in the Russian Far East has often been used as a means to manipulate frustrated voters, with immigrants made scapegoats to obscure the failings of the political elites, and as a way to provoke Moscow.[95] But fears of immigration are real and concerns about its impact legitimate. At a minimum, the Russian government needs to develop a closely coordinated policy on immigration issues with China and to establish regularized procedures for its implementation. The establishment of an institutionalized immigration policy is a major challenge to a state like Russia in which adherence to legal norms has not been established. But this achievement in itself is not sufficient to guarantee success. Tsarist Russia was an empire and the Soviet Union, if not an empire, was at least a multinational state. Russia, however, has never been a nation of immigrants and lacks a historical conception of the assimilation and socialization of immigrant populations. The prevalence of ethnic conflict in the post–Cold War world provides a sobering reminder of the potential for ethnic violence in the Russian Far East in the event of a large-scale movement of Chinese into the area. As Mikhail Alexseev has noted, the local population appears to possess a low threshold for interethnic tolerance.[96] Any expansion of Chinese immigration needs to be combined with government-sponsored efforts to change Russian perceptions of Chinese as well as to instill in Chinese immigrants a knowledge of the values and norms of Russian society.

The demographic situation facing Russia is not amenable to any quick fix and will in all likelihood remain a difficult issue in Russian-Chinese bilateral relations and a constraint on the development of regional economic linkages. Russian fears of being overwhelmed by the large-scale settlement of Chinese immigrants and the subsequent transformation of the region into an economic appendage of China are not baseless, but neither is this scenario inevitable. Russians, bearing the heritage of a Soviet consciousness, have found it difficult to appreciate that the outcome of increased interactions with China cannot be reduced to a zero-sum calculation. Globalization and the development of bilateral economic linkages with China in particular pose a distinct set of challenges to the Russian Far East and Siberian regions. But in addition to the risks involved, there also exist significant benefits. The yet unanswered question is whether the Russian leadership is capable of devising a successful response.

7

Political Relations
Defining the Strategic Partnership

There can be no doubt that geopolitical calculations loomed large in the evolution of Russian-Chinese relations during their initial decade. The specific circumstances of Russia and China diverged—in short, Russia was a descendant and China an ascendant power—but both states sought to play a significant role in the international arena. With the unfolding of the post–Cold War world order, moreover, both states came to perceive the hegemonic position enjoyed by the United States as an obstacle to the realization of this goal. By the mid-1990s, the Russian-Chinese relationship, in its international dimension, was rooted in a joint effort to influence, and most often to constrain, the actions of the United States. In this respect, the concept of the strategic triangle, long a staple of Cold War interactions between the United States, the Soviet Union, and China, still proved to be of relevance, albeit in an updated format. The much vaunted "correspondence of interests" between Russia and China on the international front, in fact, indicated their mutual preoccupation, not with each other, but with the United States as a priority of foreign policy deliberations.

The international component of Russian-Chinese relations has evolved over time, the product of a diverse array of domestic and exogenous factors. Four approximate phases can be distinguished. At its outset, Russian foreign policy was determinedly pro-Western, pursuing a policy of outright rejection of its communist past. This endeavor could evoke only distaste on the part of the Chinese leadership, still reeling from the domestic impact of the Tiananmen events and the virtual collapse—China itself being the most prominent exception—of the international communist system. Under such circumstances, it was a struggle for Russia and China to identify convergent international interests. The Russian romance with the West proved to be short-lived and its attenuation served as a catalyst for the rejuvenation of the international dimension of Russian-Chinese relations. In this second phase, Russia and China edged closer in their appraisals of the nature of the international political order, a process that was formalized in their 1994 joint communiqué that defined their relationship as a "constructive partnership." The section of the joint communiqué dealing with international issues indicated the intention of the two states to intensify their cooperation, noting their mutual regard for each other as "major powers" with an important role to play in a world heading toward multipolarity.[1]

Subsequently, Russia and China moved further to develop a coordinated response to international issues. In April 1996, the two states formally upgraded their interactions to that of a "strategic partnership," a phrase that continues to serve as the theoretical underpinning of their relationship.[2] Joint communiqués issued by the two states stressed their convergent interests on a number of identified international issues, including opposition to "hegemonism," "power politics," the expansion of military blocs, and U.S. intentions to construct a missile defense system. The tenor of this analysis was temporarily curtailed by Russian and Chinese efforts to improve their relationship with the United States in the aftermath of the September 11, 2001, terrorist attacks. But the relentlessly unilateralist direction of U.S. foreign policy behavior during 2002 and the first part of 2003, culminating in the U.S.-initiated attack on Iraq, led Russia and China to resurrect key components of their geopolitical analysis, epitomized in their emphasis on multilateralism and a multipolar world order.

Phase One: Toward Reconciliation and Beyond

After years of hostile confrontation, accompanied by mutual charges of the betrayal of Marxist-Leninist ideology, the Soviet Union and China formally normalized their relations in May 1989, issuing a joint statement during Mikhail Gorbachev's visit to Beijing that detailed a number of points of convergence on international issues. The two states declared their mutual aversion to hegemony in the Asian Pacific region or elsewhere, indicated that "peace and development" were the two most important issues of the times, and called for increasing the authority of the United Nations (UN) as an international presence.[3] Subsequently, however, internal domestic crises—far more acute and in fact terminal in the Soviet case—preoccupied the leadership of both the Soviet Union and China. Although the Chinese were appalled by the steady erosion of the Communist Party of the Soviet Union, and contemplated launching a public criticism of Gorbachev as a revisionist and traitor to socialism, alterations in the international arena contributed to their decision to desist (see Chapter 2). The 1991 Gulf War demonstrated the overwhelming prowess of the United States as a military power and its unchallenged ascendance as the predominant global actor. In April 1991, Qian Qichen, the Chinese foreign minister, commented on the Soviet Union's decline, indicating that "the national strength of the Soviet Union has been weakened . . . there's only one superpower now in the world—the United States."[4] Despite their objections to the Gorbachev regime, China's leaders felt that they had little choice in the international realm but to maintain ties with the Soviet Union as a means of counterbalancing the United States. The joint communiqué released by the Soviet Union and China during Jiang Zemin's May 1991 visit stressed their congruent views in the international sphere. The two states declared their "identical views on socialism," their opposition to "hegemonism in international politics," and their advocacy of a stronger role for the UN, especially with reference to stabilizing conditions in the Middle East.[5]

The Chinese adopted a pragmatic response to the collapse of the Soviet Union, reasoning that the maintenance of normal state-to-state relations with the Russian Federation was a realistic necessity. Nonetheless, the geopolitical strategy that China had gingerly sought to pursue with Gorbachev lay in abeyance at the onset of the Russian Federation. The dominant voices in the newly positioned Russian leadership, as exemplified by Minister of Foreign Affairs Andrei Kozyrev, were eager to assert their solidarity with the West and consequent partnership with the United States. The Russian foreign policy approach was to be based on adherence to democratic values, pluralist institutions, respect for human rights, and Russia's full integration into the global capitalist economy. According to Boris Yeltsin, the aim of Russian foreign policy was to be "Russia's entry into the civilized world community."[6] The inference was clear that China was not a member of this body. For Russia's idealistic reformers, the existence of China as the world's largest remaining Marxist-Leninist state served as a painful reminder of an ideological heritage they now sought to disavow, which intensified their motivation to emphasize the distance separating the two states. In the foreign policy realm, interactions with China were acknowledged as necessary, but to be downgraded. Shortly before Kozyrev's first visit to China in March 1992, the Russian representative to the UN session of the Human Rights Commission in Geneva voted for the first time to place human rights violations in Tibet as a topic on the agenda. While in China, Kozyrev opted to highlight the differences between Russia and China on the issue of human rights, even justifying, under certain conditions, interference into the internal affairs of sovereign states, a position squarely antithetical to the Chinese point of view. As Kozyrev noted: "The creation of a civilized society in the Russian Federation is impossible without full protection of human rights. With this in view, we try to use international mechanisms and promote, to a certain extent, interference into internal affairs."[7]

The Chinese leadership, in pursuit of its own foreign policy goals, remained impassive in the face of Kozyrev's criticisms, extending an invitation to Boris Yeltsin to China on an official visit. As the year continued, Kozyrev's pro-Western "Atlanticist" foreign policy was also facing severe challenges, primarily from the loosely organized partisans of a "Eurasianist" strategy. The Eurasianists had serious reservations about wholesale Westernization, favored greater attention to the "near abroad" and states in Asia and the Middle East, and advocated an increased focus on traditional indicators of national power.[8] Even a number of Russian politicians located on the liberal end of the continuum—such as Vladimir Lukin, co-founder of the political party Yabloko and the Russian ambassador to the United States—attacked Kozyrev's foreign policy approach with its stress on Russian-U.S. partnership as an example of "romantic, infantile pro-Americanism."[9]

By the time Yeltsin arrived in Beijing in December 1992, the Russian political scene had experienced a significant transformation—including the removal of Egor Gaidar, the reformist prime minister—and this was reflected in the tone of Russian-Chinese interactions. The joint declaration signed by Boris Yeltsin and Chinese president Yang Shangkun acknowledged their variant political paths but further noted that "differences in social systems and ideologies should not impede normal development of state to state relations." In several respects, moreover, the declaration moved beyond the 1989 and 1991 joint communiqués in its description of Russian-Chinese interactions within the international system. The statement, for example, noted the "surfacing of a multipolar world" and condemned "hegemonism" and "power politics in any form." In addition, the two states pledged that each would refrain from joining "any military or political alliance against the other party or allow its territory to be used by a third country to infringe on the sovereignty and security interests of the other party."[10] Speaking to reporters after his visit, Boris Yeltsin affirmed that Russia and China shared similar or identical perspectives on a host of regional issues including the situation in Cambodia, the Korean peninsula, and Yugoslavia.[11]

This description of the international system, rooted in basic assumptions of political realism, presented a view of global politics that was fundamentally at odds with Kozyrev's Atlanticist foreign policy approach. It did conform, however, to time-honored concepts of Soviet foreign policy, which traditionally viewed international relations with reference to geostrategic criteria. Geostrategic calculations also dictated, according to rules familiar to all the principal players, that the United States was the primary unidentified referent in the clause condemning "hegemonism" and "power politics." The joint declaration was a foreign policy success for the Chinese leadership, reflecting Chinese efforts to secure support in their quest to constrain the virtually unipolar predominance of the United States in the post–Cold War era. Boris Yeltsin's willingness to sign this declaration, however, indicated a defeat for Kozyrev's foreign policy agenda, with his emphasis on liberal precepts and Russian-U.S. collaboration.

Phase Two: The Constructive Partnership

Boris Yeltsin's political travails reached an apex in 1993 as he struggled with the Russian parliament for control of the government, eventually surviving efforts at impeachment and an attempted uprising to emerge victorious after his constitutional proposal guaranteeing a strong presidency was approved in December of that year. In a New Year's letter to Jiang Zemin, a reemergent and (temporarily) revitalized Yeltsin proposed that the two states upgrade their relationship to a "constructive partnership."[12] Yeltsin's suggestion was unusual as initiatives in the Russian-Chinese relationship were more likely to originate with China than Russia. Nonetheless, the Chinese agreed to Yeltsin's proposal. During Jiang Zemin's September 1994 visit to Moscow, the two presidents signed a joint communiqué that identified their relationship as a "constructive partnership of a new type—namely, a relationship of complete equality, good-neighborliness, friendship, and mutually beneficial cooperation, established on the basis of the principles of peaceful coexistence and characterized by nonalignment and not being directed against any third country."[13] The section of the joint communiqué dealing with international issues reiterated familiar themes. Russia and China indicated their commitment to the UN; their mutual regard for each other as major powers with an important role to play in a world heading toward multipolarity; their intolerance for expansionism; and their opposition to hegemony, power politics, and the establishment of antagonistic political, military, and economic blocs.

By 1994, much of the gloss was off the U.S.-Russian relationship, leaving Russian leaders increasingly willing to revive the concept of the strategic triangle as a tool of Russian diplomacy. The expectation that Russia would make a rapid transition to the market economy turned out to be wildly optimistic, and Russian elites felt betrayed by what they perceived as parsimonious treatment by the West in rendering financial assistance. In particular, Russian fears of a Cold War–style encirclement were revived by the decision of the Clinton administration to keep the North Atlantic Treaty Organization (NATO) alive even in the face of Soviet collapse, offering former Warsaw Pact states membership in a limited military collaboration through the Partnership for Peace (PfP). Far from satisfying national aspirations, this action soon gave rise to aggressive lobbying efforts by a number of states for full NATO membership. In this context, the clause in the 1994 Russian-Chinese joint statement regarding antagonistic military blocs presumably was an implicit reference to NATO.

In contrast to Russia, China's relationship with the United States had actually experienced some improvement in 1994 as a consequence of President Clinton's May decision to abandon his commitment to link most-favored-nation status for China to "significant progress" on human rights issues. This action, although received positively, was not sufficient to alter China's conviction that the United States was seeking to set itself up as a global hegemon. China thus welcomed Russia as a valued accomplice in the struggle to thwart U.S. ambitions. Nonetheless, the mutual convergence of interests between the two states in the international sphere did not necessarily translate into collaborative efforts at the regional level. Unlike the 1989, 1991, and 1992 communiqués, the 1994 joint communiqué contained no specific reference to the Korean peninsula, despite the ongoing political crisis there involving allegations that the North Korean government was developing nuclear weapons capability. Russia's persistent efforts to play a role in resolving the crisis, specifically through its advocacy of an international conference on the issue, were politely but firmly rebuffed by China in favor of a scenario that limited participation to the People's Republic of China (PRC), the United States, Japan, the International Atomic Energy Agency (IAEA), and the governments of North and South Korea.

Phase Three: The Strategic Relationship

The constructive partnership between Russia and China was destined to be short-lived. By the time of the next summit meeting between Boris Yeltsin and Jiang Zemin in April 1996, the two states had decided to move their relationship to yet a higher level, announcing their resolve to "develop a strategic partnership of equality, mutual confidence and mutual coordination toward the twenty-first century."[14] In fact, Russian-Chinese interactions by the mid-1990s had begun to exhibit a format curiously reminiscent of the heyday of the communist era, with a vocabulary that explicitly envisioned their relationship as a sort of historical progression, moving in stages toward a higher level of evolutionary development.[15] The content of the joint statement also reflected a distinctly more Soviet-style sensibility. In addition to repeating by now standard maxims regarding "the trend toward a multipolar world" and the occurrence of "hegemonism" and "power politics," more attention was given to issues of arms control, the role of the UN, and issues of Third World development than previous statements. The pledge by the two states for the establishment of a "new international economic order" resurrected a commitment that had been included in the Sino-Soviet communiqués of 1989 and 1991 but was notably absent in later documents and evidently at odds with the neoliberal economic strategy adopted by the Russian Federation at its outset.[16]

In January 1996, Evgenii Primakov replaced Andrei Kozyrev as the Russian foreign minister. While Kozyrev had resisted efforts to conceptualize global politics according to geopolitical categories—and in particular to cast the United States as a unipolar actor—Primakov was thoroughly at home with realpolitik calculations.[17] In particular, he was, like his Chinese counterparts, a firm adherent of efforts to develop a multipolar world.[18] Primakov was also far closer to the Eurasianist than the Atlanticist position, leading him to place more emphasis on China as a foreign policy priority. The Chinese greeted Primakov's appointment with genuine enthusiasm, recognizing him as much more of a kindred spirit than his predecessor.[19] The intensification of relations between Russia and China in the international sphere reflected the convergence of their mutual interests, not the presence (or absence) of individual personalities. But it was the case that Primakov's appointment facilitated this process.

Russian and Chinese coincidence of interests on the international scene was further reaffirmed in April 1997 when the two presidents signed a Joint Declaration About a Multipolar World and the Formation of a New International Order. Unlike other communiqués released during presidential visits, this statement dealt exclusively with international issues, setting out a vision of the appropriate format of global interactions. In particular, the declaration stressed the critical role of the Security Council of the UN in maintaining peace and global security. As the document cautioned: "The global place and role of the United Nations as the most universal and authoritative organization of sovereign states cannot be supplanted by any other international organization." Subsequent statements further evoked the Security Council as the arbiter of international activity, while simultaneously emphasizing the necessity of adherence to state sovereignty, noting that "peacekeeping operations can be conducted only with permission of the UN Security Council and only with consent of the interested countries," and that sanctions imposed by the Security Council should be reduced to the minimum and lifted "in line with the implementation of UN Security Council resolutions."[20]

Nonetheless, the United States impeded Russian-Chinese hopes for the emergence of the Security Council as a mechanism for attaining multipolarity. As the sole superpower in the post–Cold War era, the United States enjoyed a capability for unilateral activity in the global arena relatively unfettered by institutional restraints. Increasingly, Russia and China found themselves united in their joint opposition to the U.S. foreign policy agenda. By the end of the 1990s, two issues, in particular, could be identified: (1) the role of

NATO as an international organization; and (2) U.S. efforts to develop missile defense systems and to modify the 1972 Anti-Ballistic Missile (ABM) Treaty. Russia and China did not share wholly convergent positions on these issues, nor were they of equal importance in calculations of their national interest. But both Russia and China came to view a coordinated foreign policy response as a means to reducing U.S. global influence.

The Role of NATO in the Post–Cold War Era

The survival of NATO after the collapse of the Soviet Union constitutes a prime example of organizational resilience and adaptation. It also attests to the commitment of the United States and its European allies to extending their reach and correspondent influence into the former Eastern bloc. NATO operations in Bosnia in the mid-1990s evoked an outpouring of pro-Serbian sentiment in Russian nationalist circles, but the Yeltsin regime, lacking any real leverage, ultimately acquiesced to the November 1995 Dayton Accords. In contrast, the issue of NATO enlargement inflamed Russian passions, meeting with opposition across virtually the entire political spectrum. The decision of the Clinton administration to intensify the pace of NATO expansion in late 1996 also aroused fears that a revitalized NATO was embarking upon an updated version of containment and encirclement of the Russian state. Despite U.S. efforts to portray NATO as a political rather than a military alliance, Eastern European elites clamoring to be included in the organization made it clear that they were largely motivated by anti-Russian impulses, seeking protection from a potentially resurgent Russia. The May 1997 Founding Act between NATO and Russia, creating a NATO–Russia Joint Council for consultation on issues of mutual concern, was more symbolic than substantive, providing Russia with little in the way of input into NATO decision making. Simultaneously, however, the act opened the door to NATO's enlargement, an event realized in March 1999 with the entrance of Poland, the Czech Republic, and Hungary into the organization.

The prospect that NATO's membership could include states contiguous to Russia, with NATO possibly even deploying nuclear weapons on the territory of new member states, predictably gave rise to statements by a host of Russian politicians that Russia would respond by seeking out its own partners, most notably China, in a military counteralliance. As Defense Minister Pavel Grachev noted in February 1996 on the topic of NATO expansion: "If they go east, we also will go east and find new allies."[21] Such comments, however, were empty threats, detached from reality. On the one hand, the Chinese leadership, as the Russian-Chinese joint communiqués regularly reiterated, was sympathetic toward Russia's plight regarding the expansion of NATO, viewing it as a continuation of Cold War containment policy. In the Chinese assessment, alterations in NATO's organizational structure did not indicate any commensurate shift in NATO goals. NATO in its new incarnation was still a vehicle for the realization of U.S. global hegemony. On the other hand, China's leaders looked upon NATO and NATO enlargement primarily as a European issue, worrisome to Russia but not a direct security concern for China nor necessitating any sort of reactive response. Addressing this issue in May 1997, Chinese foreign minister Qian Qichen noted: "There can be no talk about a union between Russia and China. . . . Our countries have gone through quarrels and unions, but neither brought any luck."[22] China was more preoccupied with U.S. foreign policy moves in the Asian Pacific region that it perceived as injurious to its national interest. Chinese leaders were alarmed by U.S. initiatives to strengthen its security alliance with Japan, which resulted in the 1996 revision of the Guidelines for U.S.-Japan Defense Cooperation and eventual Japanese acquiescence to U.S. pressures to join in funding and joint research for a theater missile defense system in the region.[23] U.S. actions regarding Taiwan, moreover, were regarded as even more troubling. In the Chinese view, a series of U.S. initiatives in the mid-1990s—such as the issuance of a Taiwan Policy Review in the fall of 1994, the granting of a visa to Taiwanese president Lee Teng-hui to deliver a speech at his alma mater Cornell University in June 1995, and the U.S. positioning of two aircraft carrier groups in the Taiwan Straits region in 1995–96 after Chinese missile tests in the area—cumulatively amounted to a substantive upgrading of the Taiwanese-U.S. relationship.[24] From the Chinese perspective, U.S. movements in the Asian Pacific region sought to circumvent and ultimately contain China, thus constituting another component (along with NATO enlargement) of Washington's overarching strategy to maintain global dominance.

Subsequently, however, the Chinese perspective on NATO and its importance to Chinese security interests began to shift due to the unfolding of events in Kosovo in 1998–99. China's formal role in the Kosovo crisis was limited to its—although by no means insignificant—position as a permanent member of the UN Security Council. In contrast to China, Russia was a visible and active player in seeking to resolve the situation. In addition to its permanent seat on the Security Council, Russia participated in consultations on Kosovo in a series of venues: as part of the six-member Contact Group established by the 1992 London Conference of the Former Yugoslavia; within the framework of the NATO–Russia Joint Council; and as the newest member of the Group of Eight (G-8). Both Russia and China interpreted events in Kosovo as validating their analysis of the international scene, laid out in previous joint communiqués. The Russian and Chinese perspective on Kosovo was by no means wholly convergent, but the two states nonetheless shared a common view on four fundamental points: (1) any settlement in Kosovo between conflicting parties needed to be based on respect for the sovereignty and territorial integrity of the Federal Republic of Yugoslavia (FRY); (2) the Security Council of the UN should serve as the primary structure for safeguarding international peace and security; (3) any resolution to the situation should be achieved by political means and not through the use of military options; and (4) the NATO air strikes on Yugoslavia were illegal under international law, constituting a military attack launched on a sovereign state undertaken without authorization of the UN Security Council.

As the Kosovo situation emerged as a key international preoccupation, Russia and China incorporated the topic as a matter of discussion in bilateral meetings at various levels, establishing consultative procedures and seeking when possible to coordinate a joint response befitting "strategic partners." Russia and China reacted negatively to the October 13, 1998, NATO decision to authorize air strikes against the FRY and criticized efforts by NATO members to present a resolution sanctioning the decision in the Security Council. Resolution 1203, adopted by the Security Council on October 24, 1998, was a watered-down version of the original draft that nonetheless brought NATO directly into the picture, providing approval for an Organization for Security and Cooperation in Europe verification mission in Kosovo and the establishment of an air verification mission for NATO over Kosovo. Both Russia and China abstained from voting for the resolution, which passed 13–0. In explaining China's abstention, Qin Huasun, the Chinese permanent representative to the UN stated that the resolution still interfered in the internal affairs of Yugoslavia.[25] This sentiment was reaffirmed in the joint communiqué signed by Presidents Yeltsin and Jiang Zemin during Jiang's trip to Russia in November 1998. According to the communiqué, "a mutually acceptable settlement in Kosovo must be based on respect for the sovereignty and territorial integrity of the Federal Republic of Yugoslavia and on observance of the UN Charter and the universally recognized principles of international law and the legitimate rights of the people of all nationalities who live in Kosovo."[26]

The failure of negotiations between the Serbs and the Kosovars, first at Rambouillet and then in Paris during February–March 1999, provided NATO with the rationale to announce the initiation of long-threatened air strikes on March 23, 1999. Both Russian and Chinese leaders issued harsh criticisms of the action. Russia halted its partnership program with NATO and suspended Moscow's implementation of the program for PfP. Prime Minister Evgenii Primakov, en route to Washington, postponed the trip after learning of NATO's impending air strikes. A flurry of consultations began between

Russia and China. President Yeltsin delivered a statement outlining the Russian position to the Chinese Foreign Ministry. Igor Rogachev, the Russian ambassador to China, described the two states as "constantly exchanging opinions on the Yugoslav crisis, sharing 'virtually identical positions' on the air strikes."[27] On March 26, Russia presented a draft resolution to the UN Security Council that condemned NATO's military action against Yugoslavia as illegal, in violation of international law, and undertaken without Security Council authorization. Predictably, the measure failed by a vote of 3–12, gathering support only from Russia, China, and Namibia. Remarks by the Russian and the Chinese ambassadors to the UN Security Council repeated their conviction that the strikes violated Yugoslav sovereignty and challenged the Security Council's authority.

The May 7, 1999, NATO bombing of the Chinese embassy in Belgrade provoked furious anger in China, further intensifying Chinese opposition to the air strikes and fueling suspicions (or hardening convictions) as to NATO's ultimate aims. Jiang Zemin condemned the event, which destroyed the Chinese embassy, killing three and injuring over twenty, as "an extremely barbarous act and a gross violation of China's sovereignty rarely seen in diplomatic history."[28] The Chinese, who had a very difficult time believing that the attack was an accident, demanded that NATO assume responsibility for its actions and that the United States issue a formal apology. For its part, Russia was quick to express its solidarity with China. Boris Yeltsin called Jiang Zemin on the presidential hotline to express his indignation at NATO actions. In a formal statement, Yeltsin described the bombing as an "act of outrage" that could not be justified, calling for an immediate cessation of the bombing.[29] Russian Foreign Minister Igor Ivanov canceled his trip to Great Britain to concentrate on the Russian response; a statement released by the Foreign Ministry stated that the bombing was of a "criminal character."[30] President Yeltsin dispatched his special envoy for the Balkans, Viktor Chernomyrdin, on an unscheduled trip to Beijing to discuss specifics of the ongoing negotiations for a Yugoslav peace settlement in light of the altered circumstances. Sergei Lavrov, the Russian permanent representative to the UN, supported Chinese demands that the bombing be taken up as a topic of discussion within the Security Council.

During his one-day Beijing visit, the seemingly peripatetic Chernomyrdin met with an array of Chinese leaders, including President Jiang Zemin, Premier Zhu Rongji, and Vice Premier (and former Foreign Minister) Qian Qichen. One of Chernomyrdin's goals was to convince the Chinese not to oppose a draft Security Council resolution on Kosovo worked out in G-8 negotiations. Although both sides took pains to identify common ground between them, China was less inclined than Russia to be conciliatory, arousing fears that China could veto the resolution. The Chinese placed two preconditions for their support of a negotiated settlement to the Kosovo crisis: (1) the end of all NATO air strikes; and (2) the preservation of the sovereignty and territorial integrity of the Yugoslav state. On June 8, the day that the resolution was submitted to the Security Council, Boris Yeltsin placed a telephone call to Jiang Zemin, lobbying him on the Kosovo issue. Resolution 1244, providing for the withdrawal of Yugoslav forces from Kosovo and the deployment of an international civilian and security presence in Kosovo, passed by a vote of 14–0, with China the lone abstention. While Yugoslavia's reluctant agreement to the resolution provided for an end to the bombing campaign, China argued that the resolution in effect stripped Yugoslavia of its sovereignty, establishing the preconditions for the eventual separation of Kosovo from the FRY.[31]

Although Russia and China shared largely similar views on the Kosovo situation, China's position as a relative outsider in negotiations enabled it to take a more ideologically determined stance on the conflict. In addition to Resolution 1244, China also abstained from two other Security Council resolutions dealing with Kosovo in 1998, which Russia supported. China abstained from Resolution 1160 adopted on March 31, 1998, imposing an arms embargo against Yugoslavia, while Russia voted for the measure as part of a compromise deal to ward off the imposition of economic sanctions by the International Contact Group on Kosovo.[32] China also abstained from Resolution 1199 adopted by the Security Council on September 23, 1998, calling for an immediate cease-fire and the beginning of a political dialogue between Yugoslav authorities and the Kosovar leadership.[33] However, China adopted a less purist approach when its own interests were directly at stake. While Evgenii Primakov canceled his trip to Washington in mid-air in March 1999 with the announcement of the NATO air strikes, Premier Zhu Rongji continued with his scheduled trip to the United States in April 1999. For the Chinese leadership, the prospects of reaching an agreement with the Clinton administration over China's entrance into the World Trade Organization (WTO) trumped opposition to NATO's ongoing bombing of Yugoslavia as a foreign policy priority.[34]

Russia's desire to be recognized as a still relevant international actor contributed to its eagerness to be included in negotiations regarding the Yugoslavia situation. As Evgenii Primakov announced in May 1998 upon arriving in London for a G-8 meeting: "Russia has been and remains a global power."[35] Russia's relative access to the Yugoslav leadership of Slobodan Milosevic made it a valuable participant to Western states, but the structure of negotiations, forced upon a recalcitrant Yugoslav government, ensured that Russia became a co-opted participant in an agenda laid out by the Western allies.

This process was accelerated after the initiation of the NATO bombings with Yeltsin's appointment of Viktor Chernomyrdin as Russia's envoy to the Balkans. Chernomyrdin, who enjoyed a cordial relationship with U.S. vice president Al Gore, tended to be seen as a favorable personage in the West, especially when compared to Primakov, who had previously played a dominant role orchestrating Russian policy toward Yugoslavia. In addition, Russia's economic dependence on the West, especially in the wake of the August 1998 financial crisis in Russia, made it vulnerable to pressures from the NATO states.

The Kosovo crisis played a decisive role in shaping Chinese perceptions of NATO and U.S. foreign policy aims. Whereas previously China had looked upon NATO as a structure with limited regional interests, after Kosovo China viewed NATO as a mechanism that the United States could employ in pursuit of its quest for global predominance. In this revised scenario, NATO and the potential for NATO intervention became a direct security concern for China. Chinese analysts notably began to expand upon this assessment well before the March 24, 1999, commencement of NATO air strikes. Writing in *People's Daily* in August 1998, staff reporter Zhang Baoxing noted: "The United States very much desires NATO's 'globalization,' and emphasizes that apart from protecting the territory of NATO member states from aggression, NATO should also undertake military actions outside its defensive area to protect the common interests of America and Europe."[36] Such a view was corroborated by U.S. secretary of state Madeleine Albright's assertion in April 1999 that in the twenty-first century NATO would undertake its mission beyond the territory of its membership, and that NATO operations in Kosovo constituted a test of that mission.[37] NATO's justification for its Yugoslav operations on humanitarian grounds also evoked alarm in China for its explicit inference that state sovereignty was not sacrosanct in the case of human rights violations. China was highly conscious of the parallels between the Yugoslav situation and ethnic conflicts within its own territory. As an article in *Ta Kung Pao* comparing the Kosovo crisis to the situation in Tibet and Xinjiang noted: "We cannot rule out the possibility that the U.S.-led NATO military bloc will act against China in one way or another, including using military means, under the pretext of safeguarding the human rights of minority ethnic groups."[38] The Chinese leadership's insistence on the paramount importance of sovereignty was also related to its sensitivities on the Taiwan issue. By the late 1990s the Democratic Progressive Party, a Taiwanese party that advocated an independent Taiwan, was gaining strength as residents of Taiwan increasingly came to identify themselves as Taiwanese rather than Chinese.[39]

NATO's opposition to carving out a peacekeeping sector for Russia in Kosovo served as a wake-up call for the Russian leadership, which had expected to be treated as an equal partner, or, failing that, at least to be rewarded for its diplomatic service in the negotiations. Russia's demand for a peace-keeping zone in Kosovo was a matter of symbolic recognition; conversely, NATO's rejection served to confirm Russia's status as a second-rate power, as well as indicating the lingering influence of Cold–War style animosities.[40] Nor could the Russian leadership, along with its Chinese counterparts, be immune to the disturbing implications of a transformed NATO, equipped to take on a militarily proactive role in the twenty-first century. NATO expansion was problematic enough for Russia, with the prospect of contiguous states included in the NATO family, but not nearly as disturbing as the potential for NATO intervention in former Soviet republics considered to be in the Russian sphere of influence or, in the worst-case scenario, in ethnic disputes in Russia itself. In the aftermath of the Kosovo operations, Azerbaijani officials called for NATO's "humanitarian intervention" in the Caucasus, the Armenian foreign minister compared the Nagorno-Karabakh Armenians to the Kosovo Albanians, and Chechens called upon NATO to rescue them from their Russian oppressors.[41]

Despite divergences in outlook, the result of NATO involvement in Kosovo was to bring China and Russia closer together. As an article in *People's Daily* noted: "Under the influence of the U.S. squeeze policy, the Sino-Russian strategic cooperation partnership is continually developing in depth and breadth, and the fields of their cooperation have expanded."[42] The Russian-Chinese joint communiqué adopted following the meeting of Boris Yeltsin and Jiang Zemin in Beijing in December 1999 provided a harsh critique of negative tendencies developing in the international sphere that evidently reflected the Kosovo events: these included "the attempt to force a unipolar world order, attempts to weaken the role of the United Nations and the Security Council, the replacing of international law with power politics or even resorting to force, and the jeopardizing of the sovereignty of independent states using the concepts of 'human rights are superior to sovereignty' and 'humanitarian intervention.'" The document further expressed serious concern over the "trend toward splitting Kosovo from the Federal Republic of Yugoslavia" and pledged to "fully respect the sovereignty and territorial integrity of Yugoslavia."[43] Compared with previous documents, the 1999 joint statement provided a bleaker appraisal of the international order that acknowledged, implicitly if not explicitly, the extent to which NATO actions in Kosovo challenged, and ultimately undercut, Russian and Chinese efforts to devise an alternative to U.S. hegemony.

U.S. Missile Defense: Toward a Coordinated Response

Despite the collapse of the Soviet Union, U.S. leaders in the 1990s sought to resurrect missile defense as a means to achieve national security. Whereas

Ronald Reagan had launched his Strategic Defense Initiative in 1983 as a means of shielding the United States from Soviet attack, the new proposals envisioned the threat to the United States and its allies as emanating from so-called "rogue" states headed by despotic leaders who viewed launching missile attacks upon the United States or its allies as a feasible strategic option. The identity of these "rogues" was a bit ambiguous, but North Korea, Iran, Iraq, and Libya were often suggested as potential instigators. North Korean missile tests, first in 1993 when North Korea launched several No Dong missiles into the Sea of Japan and subsequently in August 1998 when it launched its Taepo Dong intermediate-range ballistic missile over Japan, were taken as evidence of militarily threatening behavior justifying the erection of missile defense systems. In the 1990s, missile defense proposals focused on two formats: theater missile defense systems (TMD) designed to protect U.S. troops deployed abroad and U.S. allies; and national missile defense systems (NMD) set up to protect the U.S. land mass from attack. The Clinton administration, reflecting the chronic insecurities of President Bill Clinton on military matters and the prospects of attack from the political right, adopted a cautious and vacillating policy on missile defense issues that was neither a full embrace nor an outright rejection. On the other hand, missile defense initiatives found strong support in Congress. In March 1999, both the U.S. Senate and the House of Representatives passed measures committing the United States to field an NMD system; in July 1999 Bill Clinton signed the National Missile Defense Act of 1999, setting forth provisions for the employment of NMD, including a renegotiated ABM Treaty.

The Chinese reaction to U.S. initiatives to develop missile defense systems, in either a theater or national format, was unequivocally hostile. For most of the 1990s, however, the preponderant attention of China was directed to TMD as a response to regional threat. In the first instance, as previously noted, China strongly disapproved of U.S.-Japanese consultations on TMD, which culminated in an agreement in December 1998 to initiate a jointly funded research program. Second, China was even more fearful that Taiwan would succeed in either purchasing components of a TMD system from the United States or be covered by the umbrella of a U.S. regional shield. In the mid-1990s, Taiwan purchased Patriot Advanced Capability 2 (PAC-2) missiles from Raytheon (an upgrade to the Patriot missiles used during the Gulf War). In 1995, after the first round of the Taiwan Straits crisis with Chinese missile tests in the region, Taiwan inquired about purchasing the Theater High-Altitude Air Defense (THAAD) system being developed by the U.S. Army and subsequently raised the issue of cooperating with the United States on TMD development. In 1999, Taiwan sought to purchase from the United States four Aegis-equipped destroyers, which the

U.S. Navy had designated as the platform for the deployment of its sea-based version of TMD, and the latest upgrade of the Patriot missile, the PAC-3.[44] Despite the absence of formal diplomatic ties with the United States, the Taiwanese cause was popular in Congress. In November 1997, the U.S. House of Representatives passed the United States–Taiwan Anti-Ballistic Missile Defense Cooperation Act, which called upon the Department of Defense to investigate the prospects of establishing a TMD system in the Asian Pacific region that would be capable of protecting Taiwan from ballistic missile attacks.[45] Similarly, the Taiwan Security Enhancement Act, first proposed in the House of Representatives in 1999 and passed in a diluted version in 2000, sought to upgrade the U.S. commitment to Taiwanese military security through expanding the range of weapons purchases. In the Chinese view, the primary aim of TMD deployment in East Asia was not to guard against an attack from North Korea, as U.S. leaders posited, but to prevent the emergence of China as the dominant power in the region. U.S. initiatives to aid Taiwan or to include it in a regional TMD system were seen as obstructionist, in blatant violation of the Shanghai Communiqués of 1979 and 1982, and constituting explicit support for an independent Taiwan.

Although Chinese analysts were wholly aware of the difference between NMD and TMD systems in the 1990s, Chinese policy did not clearly distinguish between the two formats until mid-1999, a period coincident with the U.S. adoption of an official NMD policy.[46] To a certain extent, Chinese security concerns regarding U.S. deployment of TMD and NMD overlapped: both were seen as a means of maintaining U.S. hegemony in the Asian Pacific region, constraining China's role as an emergent power, and contributing to Taiwanese prospects for independence. Nonetheless, the U.S. development of NMD presented a security challenge to China that extended far beyond its role as a regional actor, raising questions as to the fundamental ability of the Chinese state to defend itself. With an estimated 20–25 Dongfang-5 intercontinental ballistic missiles capable of hitting the United States, it was wholly conceivable that an NMD system could be devised that would render China's nuclear deterrent inoperable, leaving China defenseless in the event of a first strike launched by the United States. Chinese concerns were not allayed by the tendency prevalent in U.S. media and policymaking circles to portray China as a "threat" or at least as a "strategic competitor," leading to the widespread conviction in China that the U.S. deployment of NMD was being orchestrated with the goal of subjecting China to a form of nuclear blackmail.[47]

Because of Russia's status as a still formidable nuclear power, U.S. missile defense proposals in the 1990s posed a somewhat different set of challenges to Russia than to China. As U.S. leaders acknowledged, construction of an NMD system would violate the 1972 ABM Treaty. In addition, it was not clear which aspects of TMD technology complied with the ABM Treaty. These topics, implicitly or explicitly, constituted an important component of discourse during the Clinton-Yeltsin era. In negotiations with the United States, Russia adopted the stance that the 1972 ABM Treaty constituted a "cornerstone of strategic stability." Acknowledgement of this position was included in a number of Russian-U.S. documents, including their March 1997 Joint Statement Concerning the Anti-Ballistic Missile Treaty. At the same time, the 1997 joint statement provided the option for the deployment of TMD systems by both states, setting forth the parameters for the testing of lower-velocity TMD systems. In September 1997, the United States and Russia, along with Kazakhstan, Belarus, and Ukraine, signed a joint agreement on TMD-NMD that demarcated between TMD and ABM systems with respect to higher-velocity TMD systems. The U.S.-Russian agreements on TMD demarcation indicated Russia's formal acceptance of TMD as a legitimate undertaking. Russia, in fact, was engaged in the development of its own TMD systems, based on S-300 missiles.

Rather, Russian objections to missile defense were directed at U.S. plans to deploy NMD systems. Although Russian analysts envisioned various scenarios in which Russia could be rendered vulnerable to a U.S. first strike, the fact is that NMD did not pose a significant challenge to Russia's strategic forces.[48] The United States was not technologically capable of devising an NMD system that would be able to intercept Russian warheads, which even after the cuts imposed by the START talks, numbered in the thousands. For Russia, NMD was more a political than a military threat. As Russian Defense Minister Igor Sergeyev noted: "We do not see any [real] motives for the deployment of this national ABM system other than the striving of the United States to achieve strategic domination in the world. We are deeply convinced that such a deployment would be primarily directed against Russia."[49] Thus, for Russia as for China, missile defense was viewed as a means by which the United States sought to deter potential competitors.

Although both Russia and China viewed NMD with alarm, the two states did not seek to present a joint response to the issue until late 1998, amid impending signals that the United States would soon make a formal commitment to the program. The Joint Statement on Russian-Chinese Relations on the Threshold of the Twenty-First Century signed by Boris Yeltsin and Jiang Zemin at their November 1998 summit provided the first coordinated reference to the 1972 ABM Treaty, "stressing the exceptional importance of preserving and strengthening the Treaty on the Limitation of Anti-Ballistic Missile Systems, which was, and remains, one of the cornerstones in maintaining strategic stability throughout the world."[50] In April 1999, Russia and China began consultations on issues of strategic stability at the vice foreign minister level, resulting in a joint communiqué on the ABM Treaty. The two states reaffirmed their commitment to the treaty, noting that the U.S. plan to deploy NMD violated the ABM Treaty and "will bring a series of negative consequences." They also expressed their "worries" over the "buildup and deployment of anti-missile systems in certain countries in the Asian Pacific region."[51] Nonetheless, a reluctant Russia was forced to concede to U.S. demands to begin negotiations on the modification of the ABM Treaty, an item that was placed on the agenda of strategic arms talks between the two states in August 1999. As a countermove, Russia and China took their case to the General Assembly of the United Nations in December 1999, co-sponsoring (along with Belarus) a resolution calling for the maintenance of the ABM Treaty. The Russian-Chinese joint statement issued at the conclusion of Boris Yeltsin's December 1999 visit to Beijing was explicit in its denunciation of U.S. efforts to deploy NMD, predicting widespread detrimental consequences including its "destructive impact upon strategic stability, the whole structure of key international agreements on disarmament and the nonproliferation of weapons of mass destruction and their carriers, and upon the possibility for progress in these regards." The statement also noted for the first time Russia's explicit support for Chinese opposition to Taiwan's inclusion in any TMD system deployed in the Asian Pacific region.[52]

Boris Yeltsin's unexpected resignation in December 1999 and the ascension of Vladimir Putin to the Russian presidency aroused some consternation among Chinese leaders, who were concerned as to the depth of Putin's opposition to missile defense. In June 2000, Bill Clinton and Vladimir Putin held their first summit meeting in Moscow. The resulting Joint Statement on Strategic Stability affirmed the commitment of Russia and the United States to the ABM Treaty as a "cornerstone of strategic stability" and to their ongoing efforts to "strengthen" it. From the U.S. perspective, however, strengthening the treaty was coterminous with its modification, expressed in the statement as "enhancing its viability and effectiveness." The statement also acknowledged the "dangerous and growing threat of proliferation of weapons of mass destruction and their means of delivery."[53] These obscure formulations, rendered in Aesopian language, in effect signaled Putin's willingness to contemplate amending the ABM Treaty, presumably in exchange for corresponding U.S. concessions on arms cuts in the START talks.[54] Shortly thereafter, Putin unveiled a proposal suggesting that Russia, Europe, and NATO set up a joint anti-missile defense system with the support of the United States. This effort was referred to by Putin as a "regionally based missile defense system" that would not require any changes in the ABM Treaty.[55] These comments prompted a reaction on the Chinese side. Sha Zukang, director of the Department of Arms

Control and Disarmament within the Chinese Foreign Ministry, emphasized that China opposed any revision of the ABM Treaty.[56] The Chinese Foreign Ministry reiterated this position, stating that China had taken note of reports about Putin's proposal for a joint European anti-missile defense system but "was not clear on the details."[57] In fact, China did not appear to have been informed in advance of Putin's proposal, which explicitly sanctioned the legitimacy—as well as, apparently, the necessity—of erecting TMD systems in a format that involved joint collaboration with the United States.

Chinese concerns that Russia was capitulating to the United States on missile defense were apparently mollified by Vladimir Putin's first visit to Beijing in July 2000.[58] In addition to the customary joint communiqué—the Beijing Declaration of the People's Republic of China and the Russian Federation—the two states released a Joint Statement by the PRC President and the Russian Federation President on the Anti-Ballistic Missile Issue. Russia and China reaffirmed their adherence to previous relevant documents, reiterating their commitment to the 1972 ABM Treaty as a "cornerstone of strategic stability," noting that "safeguarding and strictly observing the 'ABM Treaty' is of great importance." The two states maintained that the essence of the U.S. plan to build an NMD system was to seek "unilateral military and security advantages," noting that the "demand of a certain country to amend the 'ABM Treaty' under the pretext of a so-called missile threat does not hold water at all." The statement, while acknowledging the possibility of the deployment of TMD under the ABM Treaty, nonetheless cautioned that it "should not harm the security interests of other countries, should not lead to the establishment or strengthening of close-type military or political blocs, and should not undermine global or regional stability and security." In particular, the statement declared Russia's and China's firm opposition to "a certain country's plan to deploy in the Asia Pacific region a non-strategic missile defense system" and to the inclusion of Taiwan in any format whatsoever.[59] The statement presented a jointly constructed critique of U.S. efforts to amend the ABM Treaty and to deploy a TMD system in Asia, while challenging U.S. claims of a missile threat as a subterfuge employed in order to realize military and strategic aims. In this sense, it represented a coordinated attempt on the part of Russia and China to join forces impeding U.S. efforts to move forward with its plans for missile defense.

Upgrading the Strategic Partnership: The Sino-Russian Friendship Treaty

The Beijing Declaration signed by Jiang Zemin and Vladimir Putin during Putin's July 2000 visit contained the somewhat surprising announcement that Russia and China would begin negotiations to prepare a Sino-Russian Treaty of Good-Neighborly Friendship and Cooperation. After the failure of the Sino-Soviet treaty of 1950, the Chinese had steered clear of entangling alliances, pursuing a nonaligned foreign policy course. Likewise, Russia had not sought out treaty relationships in its initial decade.[60] The initiative for the treaty originated with China. In a subsequent interview with *Rossiiskaia Gazeta*, Jiang Zemin acknowledged that he had proposed the treaty to Putin, who had responded favorably.[61] Both states strongly maintained that the treaty was in no way directed against a third country; nonetheless, the timing of Chinese actions suggested that geostrategic calculations played a role in their decision to suggest it to the Russians. According to a March 1999 report in a Hong Kong journal with long-standing links to the Chinese political scene, U.S. proposals to form a U.S.–Japan–Taiwan TMD system were causing China to rethink its traditional policy of nonalignment, leading it to consider plans to form an alliance with Russia and also to pursue a multilateral approach with neighboring states, including members of the Commonwealth of Independent States, India, Pakistan, and Iran.[62] Moreover, the Chinese first reportedly raised the idea of the treaty with Prime Minister Evgenii Primakov—a highly respected figure among the Chinese leadership—shortly after the NATO bombing of their embassy in Belgrade.[63] Even before the NATO bombing of the Chinese embassy, the Chinese were moving to elaborate a closer relationship with Russia, a decision that was only reinforced by the events in Belgrade.

The Chinese apparently also viewed the treaty as a means to ensure that the institutional relationship forged between the two states in the Yeltsin era would continue under Putin. By the end of his term in office, Boris Yeltsin, for all of his dysfunctional attributes, was at least a familiar face. Altogether, Yeltsin and Jiang Zemin had presided over six presidential summits. Vladimir Putin was much more of an unknown quantity and did not show any particular affinity for China during his first few months in office. Although the Kremlin had originally announced that one of Putin's first trips abroad would be to China, the globe-trotting Putin did not actually visit China until July 2000.[64] Nor could some of Putin's statements regarding international issues have been wholly comforting to the Chinese. In March 2000, Putin announced that Russia would consider joining NATO if the opportunity presented itself; several months later, Putin was touting the benefits of a regionally based missile defense system to the Europeans, NATO, and the United States. Thus, for China's leaders, the treaty served as a means of reminding Russia of its commitments to China in the face of powerful pressures imposed upon it by the West.

Beginning in December 2000, diplomats from the Ministry of Foreign Affairs of the two states began working on the formulation of the treaty. A protocol of a draft was signed by the Russian and Chinese foreign ministers in April 2001, with the final document unveiled at the July 2001 presidential summit in Moscow. A carefully worded twenty-five-article document, it outlined the basic premises of Russian-Chinese relations for a twenty-year period, with reference to bilateral, regional, and international issues (see Appendix). It is insufficient to view the treaty simply in geostrategic terms as its bilateral and regional components are also very important. In fact, the treatment of international issues in the treaty was considerably more circumscribed than that provided in bilateral joint communiqués released during presidential summits, including the joint statement accompanying it. While the joint statement signed by Putin and Jiang at their 2001 summit meeting reiterated a commitment to promote a multipolar world and to uphold the 1972 ABM Treaty, neither issue received direct mention in the Friendship Treaty itself. The two states pledged themselves to the continued development of a "strategic cooperative partnership," renouncing the use or threat of force in their mutual relations and reaffirming the principles of national sovereignty and territorial integrity in their mutual relations. Article 5 of the Friendship Treaty explicitly referred to Russian support of China on the Taiwan issue, specifying Russia's adherence to the one-China policy. Article 11 upheld the adherence of the two states to international law and their mutual opposition to intervention in the internal affairs of sovereign states. Article 12 noted the commitment of the two parties to "preserve global strategic balance and security" and to "promote adherence to relevant basic agreements for ensuring the preservation of strategic security." Article 13 pledged their commitment to increase cooperation in the UN and to make efforts to "strengthen the United Nations as the highest authoritative and most universal international organization in handling international affairs" through the actions of the UN Security Council. While the Friendship Treaty did not bind the two states together in a formal military alliance, it did impose certain conditions on their interactions with third parties. Article 8 specified that "neither party will participate in any alliance or bloc which damages the sovereignty, security, and territorial integrity of the other party," or allow a third party—either a country, an organization, or a group—to use its territory to such ends. Article 9 provided for immediate mutual consultations in the event that a threat of aggression arises jeopardizing the security interests of either of the states.

A number of commentators (including many Russian and Chinese analysts) saw the treaty as an effort by Russia and China to join forces to counterbalance the predominant power of the United States.[65] For its part, the Bush administration selected to downplay, if not actually dismiss, the significance of the treaty. According to Deputy Secretary of State Richard L. Armitage, the treaty "was clearly designed to boost both of their international standing without adding much real substance."[66] On the one hand, both Russia and China sought cooperative relations with the United States, especially with respect to economic issues. On the other hand, the basis of the Russian-Chinese "identity of interests" in the international realm was rooted in a joint appraisal of the role of the United States as the predominant global actor in the post–Cold War era. By the late 1990s, it was increasingly apparent just how much power the United States had accumulated in the absence of counterweights. The Russian-Chinese effort to coordinate their foreign policy, as well as their unceasing emphasis on multipolarity, was a modest attempt to redress, in a manner predicted by balance-of-power theorists, U.S. power in the wake of the collapse of the Soviet Union. Strategic triangle politics as played out in the Cold War were a product of the past, but the Friendship Treaty provided an indication that the concept was not yet dead. At the same time, the Friendship Treaty's cautious and restrained approach to international issues, in marked contrast to the more provocative joint statements, indicated that it was being written to endure over the long run, leaving each state with considerable latitude to pursue its own vision of its national interest. As Russian vice foreign minister Aleksandr Losyukov noted: "The strategic partnership is not a civil or military union. Russia and China stick to this position and reserve the right to act freely, especially in international relations."[67]

Phase Four: Russian-Chinese Relations After September 11, 2001

Russia and China scarcely had time to begin to define the parameters of their relationship as treaty partners when the events of September 11, 2001, intervened. Whatever the long-term consequences of the terrorist attacks on the United States, international patterns of interaction were undeniably altered in the short run as states reconfigured their relationship with the United States. After the incident, the United States sought to organize a global coalition to combat terrorism, an action that received widespread international support. The enormity of the events, resulting in the deaths of several thousand American civilians, made Russian and Chinese criticism of the United States as the great hegemon appear unseemly (and possibly also inaccurate, given the spectacular success of the mission by a small group of terrorists armed with little more than a rudimentary knowledge of flying and box cutters). In addition, both Russia and China calculated that it was in their national interest to jump on the anti-terrorist bandwagon, joining forces with the United States and pledging their willingness to participate in the global war against terrorism.

In Russia, Vladimir Putin called U.S. president George Bush on September 11 to extend his sympathy to the United States. After a period of seeming indecision in which opponents of military cooperation with the United States—including Minister of Defense Sergei Ivanov—voiced their views, Putin moved decisively to aid the United State in its efforts to rout al-Qaeda, along with its patron the Taliban, from Afghanistan. Putin's offer included military intelligence, use of Russian air corridors, sanctioning of U.S. airbases in formerly Soviet Central Asia, and increased assistance to the Northern Alliance in Tajikistan. Putin's decision to position Russia squarely in the U.S. camp evoked considerable surprise. The move appears to have been taken largely at Putin's individual initiative in the face of substantial domestic opposition. U.S. behavior before September 11 had not been such as to encourage an overly positive response. U.S.-Russian relations, already strained by disagreement over the ABM Treaty and NATO, had been further exacerbated by references made by a number of members of the Bush administration to Russia as a "threat," and by the U.S. move to expel fifty Russian diplomats as spies in the spring of 2001.[68] Rather it appears that Putin assessed the events of September 11 as presenting an unparalleled (and hitherto unanticipated) opportunity to realign Russia firmly into the Western orbit. This endeavor was rooted not in a slavish desire to subordinate Russia to U.S. domination (as Russian domestic critics would have it), but in a pragmatic calculation of Russian national interest. As a number of commentators have noted, the rejuvenation of the Russian economy—which is a necessary precondition for the eventual resurgence of Russia as a global power—was dependent on Russia's integration with the West and its incorporation into the economic structures of global capitalism firmly under the control of the United States and its allies.[69] In this view, Putin was not a recast Soviet-style apparatchik mired in the ways of the KGB but a genuine Westernizer in the classic Russian tradition, a kind of contemporary reincarnation of Peter the Great.

The Chinese leadership, too, immediately acted to express its solidarity with the United States on September 11, 2001. Jiang Zemin extended his condolences to President Bush and strongly reaffirmed China's steadfast opposition to terrorism. The supportive response of the Chinese leadership was attributable to several interrelated factors. First, China, like Russia, viewed the terrorist attacks as an opportunity to mend its chronically strained relationship with the United States, which had been further exacerbated in the initial months of the Bush presidency. The hawkish members of the Bush administration were scarcely more favorably inclined toward China than Russia. Whereas Russia was a "threat," China was a potential "military" or "strategic competitor." U.S.-Chinese relations were further damaged in April 2001 by the collision of a U.S. EP-3 surveillance plane with a Chinese fighter aircraft in the South China Sea. George W. Bush's pledge that

the United States would do "whatever it took" to help Taiwan defend itself
served further to put a downward spiral on the relationship. The deterioration in U.S.-China interactions was alarming to Chinese leaders, who viewed
a cooperative relationship as a necessary condition for China's continued
economic development and full incorporation into the global marketplace.
Second, the Chinese leadership's antipathy toward terrorism was genuine;
they viewed it as a threat to political stability, economic development, and
even Chinese sovereignty. Although China had given aid to the mujahadeen
as a purely realpolitik move during the Soviet intervention in Afghanistan, it
had no sympathies for Islamic fundamentalism, for al-Qaeda, or for their
Afghan patrons the Taliban. In the Chinese view, Islamic fundamentalists
were instrumental in instigating separatist groups in Xinjiang province—
notably the Muslim Uighur—to set up an independent state of East Turkestan.
Even before September 11, the Chinese leaders had identified al-Qaeda leader
Osama bin Laden as a source of funds and training to Xinjiang ethnic sepa-
ratists.[70] Third, China's leaders were highly sensitive to their international
role as a global power and a permanent member of the UN Security Council.
China was not anxious to be placed in a position that condoned U.S. military
incursions into a sovereign state in the name of combating terrorism, but
neither was it satisfied to be left on the sidelines of a global undertaking. In
addition, concerned that the United States would employ the rhetoric of the
anti-terrorist global struggle as a cover for its own unilateral foreign policy
objectives, China sought to redirect the locus of anti-terrorist activities to the
Security Council of the UN.

The movement of Russia and China toward the United States in the immediate aftermath of September 11 undercut the geostrategic component of
their relationship that was rooted in a joint effort to constrain the United
States. This development necessitated a recrafting of the vocabulary the two
states had previously used to assess the international situation such that it did
not overly offend U.S. sensibilities. Both Russia and China muted their criticism of the United States. References to a multipolar world ceased, replaced
by earnest declarations of a common cause in the anti-terrorist coalition.
During the fall of 2001, Russia and China worked to construct an international agenda that would advance their national interests within newly circumscribed limits. The two states sought to develop a coordinated response
to terrorism. The first meeting of the Sino-Russian Working Group on Combating Terrorism was held in Beijing in November 2001. Conforming with
previous declarations, Russia and China emphasized that the Security Council of the UN should play the leading role in formulating a global anti-terrorist
policy and that any measures taken should be consonant with international
law and the UN Charter. Russian and Chinese leaders also seized upon the

opportunity to link their own domestic separatist struggles to the forces of international terrorism, identifying al-Qaeda as a source of support to insurrectionists in both Chechnya in Russia and Xinjiang province in China.

Asymmetry Within the Russian-Chinese Relationship: Putin's Turn to the West

While both Russia and China hastened to capitalize on the terrorist attacks by strengthening their ties with the United States, the dramatic transformation in Russian-U.S. relations placed strains on the Russian-Chinese relationship. The degree to which the two states improved their ties with the United States was not symmetrical. Both moved closer to the United States, but the distance covered by Russia was greater than that by China. In contrast to Russia, China remained more wary and suspicious of the United States and less willing to jettison its analysis, rooted in classic realpolitik assumptions, of U.S. foreign policy goals. Moreover, the behavior of the Bush administration in the aftermath of September 11 did little to alter long-standing Chinese convictions as to U.S. intentions to continue a unilateral approach as its mode of operation in the international arena.

Despite Russia's movement toward the United States and its valuable contributions to the struggle to oust al-Queda and the Taliban from Afghanistan, the United States did not provide any concessions to Russia in negotiations on the amendment of the ABM Treaty. George Bush argued that the terrorist attacks confirmed the need for missile defense, labeling the ABM Treaty "outmoded and useless."[71] Nor did Russia's position alter: In October 2001 Russia presented (along with China and Belarus) its annual draft resolution to the UN on the preservation of the ABM Treaty, maintaining that the "relevance of the goals it pursues has not only not diminished but on the contrary has increased in light of the current international situation."[72] The November 2001 summit meeting between Putin and Bush yielded progress on nuclear arms reduction but no agreement on the ABM Treaty. Subsequently, on December 13, 2001, George Bush announced the decision of the United States unilaterally to withdraw from the treaty.

Putin adopted an understated reply to Bush's announcement, labeling it a "mistake," but also noting that it posed no threat to Russia's security.[73] The Chinese leadership was similarly restrained in its formal response: the Foreign Ministry spokesperson, Zhang Qiyue, indicated that China had taken note of the relevant reports and expressed its concern, and was "worried about the negative impact."[74] The decision did not, as some reports speculated, create a rift between Russia and China. For both states, the broad outline of the U.S. action was wholly expected. As Chinese commentary on the event indicated, Russian options under the circumstances were limited. Li Gang, writing in *Ta Kung Pao*, noted: "In dealing with the United States, particularly in seeking to stop the United States from its pursuit of its strategic bid for 'sole superpower status' and 'absolute security,' Russia does not have a lot of cards to play; on the other hand, not only can the United States exert pressure on Russia on several issues but it can even turn off the economic lifeblood of Russia."[75] In strategic stability consultations held several days after the U.S. decision, Russia and China gave extensive attention to Bush's statement, declaring that they shared a "common understanding" of the issue.[76] During subsequent consultations, Russia and China emphasized the negative impact of the U.S. abrogation of the ABM Treaty on the international security environment. The two states determined to intensify their coordinated efforts to maintain and strengthen the entire international system of treaties on arms control and disarmament. This included the ratification of the Comprehensive Test Ban Treaty, preparations for a conference in 2005 on the Nuclear Non-Proliferation Treaty (NNPT), efforts to implement verification measures for chemical and biological weapons, and promotion of the need to prevent an arms race in space.

Russian accession to U.S. demands was also apparent at the next summit meeting between Putin and Bush, held in May 2002 in Moscow. A highlight of the meeting was the signing of a Treaty on Strategic Offensive Reductions to cut strategic nuclear weapons over a ten-year period from 5,000–6,000 warheads each to 1,700–2,200. Billed as a breakthrough in arms negotiations, the treaty in fact reflected the priorities of the U.S. agenda and was virtually devoid of specific procedures for verification. Except for the U.S. willingness in the end to label the document a treaty rather than an arms control agreement, Russia submitted to the U.S. position on all substantive areas of dispute. The treaty allowed the two sides to place some of their decommissioned warheads in storage rather than providing for their permanent destruction, thus ensuring that the proposed cuts would not necessarily be irreversible. Moreover, the Russians received no substantive reassurances that the U.S. deployment of an NMD system would not be targeted against them. The very brevity of the treaty, about three pages in length, revealed its lack of content. In effect, the treaty was a deathblow to Russia's final claim to parity with the United States on the nuclear issue, and indicated Russia's inability to maintain its strategic forces at current levels.[77]

The revised format of a Russian foreign policy strategy was also indicated in Putin's recasting of Russia's relationship with NATO. In this instance, Putin evidently decided that it was a waste of time to continue to protest NATO's eastward drift, including the incorporation of the Baltic states, and that it would be more profitable to attempt to reformulate the Russian-NATO relationship.

After months of negotiation, the two parties reached agreement in May 2002 on the formation of a new NATO–Russia Council providing an expanded role (but no veto power) for Russia as a participant in NATO activities, including issues of terrorism, nonproliferation, theater missile defense, and military cooperation.[78] Speaking in Rome in May 2002 at a press conference following the ceremony marking the formation of the new NATO–Russia Council, Vladimir Putin noted (echoing the comments of Boris Yeltsin a decade earlier) that "today, Russia is returning to the family of civilized nations."[79] This explicit (and Eurocentric) acknowledgment of Russia's movement into the Western fold inevitably raised questions as to the status of the international dimensions of the Russian-Chinese strategic partnership, rooted as it had been in the pursuit of a multipolar world and the constraint of U.S. influence. Putin maintained that Russia was pursuing a "balanced" foreign policy, but it was not clear how Russia would manage to combine the competing demands of a foreign policy approach with China rooted in multipolarity with the development of "new strategic relations" with the United States.

In fact, the Russian leadership took considerable pains to reassure its Chinese counterparts that Russia's growing rapprochement with the West presented no threat to Russian-Chinese relations and that the strategic partnership remained intact. Putin phoned Jiang Zemin on the presidential hotline to brief him on the progress of Russian negotiations with NATO; this topic, along with the outcome of the Russia–U.S. summit, was also reported to have been discussed in detail when Putin and Jiang met in June 2002 during a meeting of the Shanghai Cooperation Organization (SCO).[80] In an interview with the director of *Renmin Ribao*, Putin noted that the Friendship Treaty between Russia and China indicated that the nature of Russian-Chinese cooperation stood above the Russian-U.S. relationship in various respects.[81] This theme continued to be promoted by Putin and other Russian officials. Igor Ivanov, the foreign minister, emphasized that Russia and China actively coordinated their foreign policy, stressing that "there are no reasons" for China to worry about Russian ties with the United States.[82] Vice Foreign Minister Alexander Losyukov noted that Russia did not believe that the improvement of Russian-U.S. relations harmed its relations with China, stressing that "relations with China were and are of special importance to us."[83]

The formal Chinese response to Russia's strengthening of ties with the United States and Europe was to acclaim it as a positive development, contributing to the maintenance of global peace and stability, with a Chinese Foreign Ministry spokesperson indicating that China "was happy" over the development of Russian-U.S. relations.[84] However, Chinese press commentary was more acerbic. Russia's motivation for forging links with the West was attributed to Russia's economic weakness and consequent dependence on the West for the assistance—financial aid, investment, technological transfer, support for Russian entrance into the WTO, and so forth—necessary for Russia's economic development. At the same time, Chinese assessments also tended to highlight the tensions—latent or otherwise—inherent in Russia's relationship with the United States. Chinese accounts emphasized (accurately) that Russia had given in to virtually every U.S. demand on the Treaty on Strategic Offensive Reductions, rendering the final document "a mere scrap of paper."[85] Similarly, Chinese analyses of the NATO–Russia Council stressed that Russia did not have the right to participate in the major substantive issues of NATO discourse, viewing the Council as a means of "roping in" Russia and stifling its opposition to NATO's expansion to the east.[86]

Despite Beijing's official show of enthusiasm, indications existed that the Chinese leadership was troubled by Russia's deepening links with the West and concerned about their implications for China. The first meeting of the NATO–Russia Council adopted a document emphasizing the need to develop a TMD system for Europe using Russian S-300 missiles. In his speech at the Rome summit marking the founding of the NATO–Russia Council, President Putin spoke of the "possibility of the development of a single expanse of security—from Vancouver to Vladivostok," a sentiment likely to arouse apprehension among Chinese leaders.[87] Prior to Jiang Zemin's June 2002 trip to Moscow, he reportedly convened a meeting of the Chinese Communist Party's Leading Group on Foreign Affairs to discuss how Beijing should react to Moscow's shift in policy. In particular, Vladimir Putin appears to have been viewed as an unknown quantity: "We are not really sure what kind of a person Putin is—or how he thinks," Jiang reportedly remarked, giving instructions to China's Russian experts to come up with a fuller analysis of Putin and his political agenda.[88]

The War on Terrorism: Tensions in the Global Coalition

While the Putin administration's interactions with the United States on arms issues and NATO in the first part of 2002 highlighted disparities in outlook between Russia and China, the two states had a largely convergent perspective on the Bush administration's evolving strategy regarding the war on terrorism. In the first instance, Russian and Chinese enthusiasm to come on board as members of the global anti-terrorist struggle was tempered by traditional geopolitical concerns raised by the U.S. military presence in Central Asia. Prior to the terrorist attacks on the United States, Central Asia had been a peripheral backwater in the global scheme of things, only to be suddenly transformed into the near epicenter of U.S. military efforts to dislodge al-Qaeda and its Taliban patrons from Afghanistan. Both Russia and China acquiesced—Russia more willingly than China—to the U.S. use of military bases in Central Asia, but the long-term consequences of a greatly expanded U.S. presence in the region was worrisome to both parties. The fear was that the United States would take up permanent residence in the area, developing a sphere of influence and simultaneously encircling Russia and China. Chinese commentaries in particular expanded on this perspective, evoking the heartland thesis of Sir Halford MacKinder ("who rules the heartland commands the world island") to explain the U.S. quest to gain a foothold in Central Asia.[89] Russian and Chinese concerns were given further credence by the eagerness of many Central Asian leaders to welcome the United States into the region. After September 11, 2001, Uzbekistan, Kyrgyzstan, Tajikistan, and Kazakhstan all indicated their willingness to provide support to the U.S. cause. Only Turkmenistan remained officially neutral. In comparison to Russia, the traditional power in the area, the United States offered the prospect of material largesse. Kurmanbek Kakiyev, the prime minister of Kyrgyzstan, reportedly described the U.S. military presence as a "gold mine" with the United States paying 7,000 dollars for each takeoff or landing by a large aircraft.[90] Central Asian elites also viewed U.S. troops as providing a measure of security against domestic insurgents. This was especially salient for Uzbek President Islam Karimov, under siege by the Islamic Movement of Uzbekistan.

Russian and Chinese support of the anti-terrorism coalition made outright opposition to the U.S. military presence in Central Asia politically awkward. Military personnel were more vocal than their civilian counterparts in inquiring into the time frame for U.S. forces. Russian Minister of Defense Sergei Ivanov stated in February 2002 that the United States should leave Central Asia once the war in Afghanistan was over, while Xiong Guangkai, deputy chief of the general staff of the PLA, noted more obliquely in March 2002 that China "pays close attention to how long the troops of the military coalition will stay in that region."[91] Characteristically, Vladimir Putin himself insisted that U.S. troops posed no challenge to Russian security, a sentiment possibly born out of necessity considering that Russia lacked the ability to impose a different outcome. Nonetheless, Russia and China attempted to articulate an alternative vision to regional interactions in Central Asia that did not place the United States at center stage. First, Russia and China, stressing their "identical views" on the Afghan situation, called for military operations to be superseded as quickly as possible by a political settlement, implemented under the aegis of the UN in accordance with international law. Second, the two states tried to promote the SCO as a potential counterweight to expanding U.S. influence in the region (see Chapter 3).

In addition, both Russia and China questioned the validity of the Bush administration's plans for round two of the war on terrorism. During his January 2002 State of the Union Address, George Bush identified Iran, Iraq, and North Korea as an "axis of evil." In the U.S. view, all three states posed a threat as sponsors of terrorist activity and covert proliferators of weapons of mass destruction. The emergent Bush Doctrine indicated a commitment not only to missile defense as a shield against rogue states, but the shift to an active strategy condoning the use of a preventive first strike against harbingers of terrorism. Along with a number of other states, Russia and China questioned whether the Iraqi leadership of Saddam Hussein represented a terrorist threat, or whether the Bush administration's interest in removing him from power in Iraq was impelled by other motives, such as a desire to settle old scores left over from the 1991 Gulf War, or an interest in gaining control over Iraqi oil supplies.

Russian-Chinese Interactions on Iraq

Throughout the 1990s, Russia and China shared a largely coterminous position on Iraq. Both states opposed economic sanctions on Iraq and the use of force against Iraq, including U.S. and British bombing missions, but simultaneously urged Iraqi compliance with UN resolutions involving the presence of weapons inspectors. Just before Bush's "axis of evil" speech, Iraqi Vice Prime Minister Tariq Aziz traveled to Russia and China to discuss the easing of UN sanctions on Iraq. Neither state, however, reacted forcefully to Bush's axis of evil remarks. The Chinese Foreign Ministry spokesperson noted that "the Chinese side is not in favor of using such terms in international relations."[92] For his part, President Putin indicated that he was against drawing up "blacklists" of the so-called "axis of evil" countries and using force against them without permission from the UN Security Council.[93] Both Russia and China emphasized their standard position: conflicts should be adjudicated by diplomatic not military means within the framework of the Security Council.

By the fall of 2002, the Iraqi situation had materialized into a full-blown international crisis. On the one hand, the Bush administration, supported by Britain, was pushing the UN Security Council to endorse measures authorizing the use of force to overthrow the Iraqi regime if Saddam Hussein did not surrender weapons of mass destruction. On the other hand, the United States was simultaneously threatening to initiate an independent attack on Iraq in the event that it was unable to persuade the Security Council to support military actions. Russia and China voted in favor of Security Council Resolution 1441 in November 2002, which demanded the return of UN weapons inspectors to Iraq with the proviso that Iraq would face "serious consequences" in the event of "continued violations of its obligations."[94] The same day, however, Russia, China, and France issued a joint statement detailing their interpretation of the resolution, noting that it excluded any "automaticity" in the use of force.[95] Saddam's acquiescence to Resolution 1441 resulted in a temporary defusing of the crisis as UN weapons inspectors (expelled in 1998) resumed their activity in Iraq. Russia and China continued to promote a nonviolent response to the situation. In their December 2002 joint declaration, the two states reiterated their commitment to the UN Security Council as the appropriate venue for dealing with Iraq, maintaining that the crisis needed to be resolved according to diplomatic means on the basis of "strictly observing the UN Security Council resolutions."[96]

Nonetheless, although the Russian and Chinese view on Iraq was largely coterminous, the actions of the two states within the Security Council diverged markedly with respect to deliberations on the Iraqi issue. Whereas Russia took an activist stance, allying with France and Germany to prevent U.S. efforts to secure Security Council endorsement of a military attack on Iraq, China assumed a distinctly backseat—at times almost invisible—role, seeking refuge in silence. On the Iraqi issue, the dynamic of triangular relations between the United States, Russia, and China that had developed after September 11, 2001, was largely reversed, with China appearing more reluctant directly to confront the United States than Russia. On February 10, 2003, France, Germany, and Russia issued a joint statement calling for the UN arms inspectors to be given more time to complete their mission. The document maintained that "the use of force must be only a last resort."[97] On February 24, the United States, Britain, and Spain submitted a draft resolution to the Security Council that in effect authorized the use of military force against the Baghdad regime, prompting a countermove by France, Russia, and Germany. On March 5, the three states released another joint statement that noted they would "not allow to pass . . . a resolution that would authorize the recourse to force," adding that "Russia and France, as permanent members of the Security Council, will take all our responsibilities on this point," signaling their intention to veto the U.S.-led resolution.[98]

In this context, Russia's ties with China appear to have been an important factor in persuading China to drop its noncommittal stance and adopt a position supporting the trilateral French, German, and Russian position. On February 23, U.S. secretary of state Colin Powell arrived in Beijing to discuss the simultaneous political crises in Iraq and North Korea, hoping to secure Chinese support for the U.S. position on Iraq or at least to persuade China to abstain in a vote on the U.S.-sponsored draft resolution within the Security Council. Powell, however, left Beijing empty-handed, having failed in his efforts to convince the Chinese leadership to embrace the U.S. position.[99] Powell's visit was immediately followed by the arrival of Russian Foreign Minister Igor Ivanov in Beijing, intent on conducting his own lobbying efforts. By all accounts, Ivanov was more successful than his American counterpart. The Russian and Chinese foreign ministers released a joint press communiqué on the Iraqi situation that reiterated a familiar mantra: the "Iraqi crisis should be resolved through political and diplomatic means within the framework of the Security Council," while "war against Iraq can and should be avoided."[100] Responding to questions after the release of the March 5 joint statement by Russia, France, and Germany, Ivanov indicated that China shared the position of the three European states.[101] In a March 6 news conference, Tang Jiaxuan confirmed Ivanov's remarks. While Foreign Minister Tang Jiaxuan characterized a question as to whether China would use its veto within the Security Council as "premature," the foreign minister also noted that "China's position on the Iraq issue is the same as the one that France, Germany, and Russia stated in the joint statement they issued on 5 March. We endorse and support that statement."[102] During the first part of March, as the United States made clear its intent to bypass the UN Security Council and pursue an unilateralist approach in attacking Iraq—accompanied by an eclectic cohort of supporters—Russia and China maintained consultations on the Iraqi issue conducted under the auspices of the Russian and Chinese Foreign Ministries. As Tang Jiaxuan noted, China maintained close contacts with all leading states on the Iraq situation, but above all with Russia.[103]

Russia and China's coordinated approach on the Iraq issue, moreover, remained evident in the immediate aftermath of the March 2003 Iraq war. The May 2003 joint statement between Russia and China, signed during Hu Jintao's first presidential trip to Russia, contained a lengthy section on Iraq that reaffirmed standard maxims of international doctrine endorsed by the two states. The statement declared that the "sovereignty, political independence, and territorial integrity of Iraq should be guaranteed," with the UN as the relevant body to set upon the task of resolving the Iraqi crisis and providing for the post-war reconstruction.[104]

North Korea: A Terrorist Threat?

The U.S. identification of North Korea as another member of the terrorist axis also had worrisome implications for Russia and China. With the demise of the Soviet Union, China emerged as the single state with significant ties to the North Korean leadership, a factor that rendered it an indispensable actor in interactions involving North Korea in the 1990s. The Yeltsin government, in its eagerness to display an anti-communist pro-Western orientation, had severed its substantive links with the North Korean regime at the onset of the Russian Federation, a move it came to regret. Despite their coordinated foreign policy relationship (first as constructive and then as strategic partners), China was resistant to continuous Russian efforts to gain a foothold in international negotiations on the Korean peninsula.

In 1993–94, the North Korean regime prompted an international crisis with the announcement that it was withdrawing from the NNPT. The Chinese government opposed efforts to resolve the issue within the UN Security Council, as well as attempts to impose economic sanctions on North Korea. Beijing's opposition was instrumental in the eventual adoption of direct negotiations between the United States and the Democratic People's Republic of Korea (DPRK). The Agreed Framework, signed in October 1994, set forth a number of measures regarding U.S.-DPRK interactions. These included a pledge by the United States to arrange for the provision of two light-water reactors to North Korea, as well as compensatory alternative energy in the form of oil. In exchange, the DPRK agreed to dismantle its Soviet-style graphite-moderated reactors and to remain a party to the NNPT, permitting IAEA inspections of its nuclear reactors.[105] During the crisis, Russia sought to position itself as a key player in the region, suggesting an international conference to consider the issue, a proposal rejected by the other envisioned participants.[106] Russian officials stressed the congruence between China and Russia on the North Korean nuclear issue, the "almost identical" positions shared by the two sides.[107] In fact, China rebuffed the Russian position. While the 1992 joint declaration between Russia and China contained a lengthy reference to the situation on the Korean peninsula, the joint statement signed by the Russian and Chinese presidents during Jiang Zemin's September 1994 visit to Moscow made no mention of Korea.

Russia found itself in a somewhat analogous situation in 1997 with the onset of the Four Party Peace Talks between the DPRK, the Republic of Korea (ROK), the United States, and China. The talks were an outgrowth of a 1996 summit meeting between U.S. president Bill Clinton and ROK president Kim Young Sam aimed at bringing a peace settlement to the Korean peninsula. Russia had pressed to be included in the negotiations, or at least to be a party to supplementary discussions that would include Russia and Japan, a proposal that also met with rejection. In any event, the talks were suspended in 1999 without significant progress.

The Putin presidency, however, had more success than its predecessor in reviving ties with North Korea. In February 2000, Russia and the DPRK signed a Treaty of Friendship, Good Neighborliness and Cooperation during Foreign Minister Ivanov's trip to Pyongyang. In July 2000, Vladimir Putin became the first Russian or Soviet leader to visit North Korea. The joint declaration signed by Putin and DPRK leader Kim Jong-il spoke of the "friendly relations" between the two states, their mutual opposition to the deployment of a TMD program in Asia, and their joint desire for peace and stability in Northeast Asia. Regarding the issue of Korean unification, the document indicated its support for the North-South Joint Declaration signed between the ROK and the DPRK in June 2000, which designated the two states as independently responsible for resolving the problem of Korean reunification.[108] In August 2001, Kim Jong-il made a reciprocal trip to Moscow, the first official state visit for the elusive Korean leader.[109] The Russian–North Korean Moscow Declaration signed by Kim and Putin reaffirmed a commitment to the North-South Joint Declaration and to Korean reunification as a process free of external interference. At the same time, however, Russia also expressed its interest in taking an active role in multinational negotiations, noting that it was "ready to continue playing a constructive and responsible part in positive processes in the Korean peninsula."[110] The intensification of Russian linkages with the DPRK was further indicated by Kim Jong-il's subsequent trip to the Russian Far East in August 2002. During his Far Eastern journey, President Kim met with Putin in Vladivostok, where the two leaders held discussions on bilateral economic cooperation and the situation on the Korean peninsula.

Tensions were again heightened on the Korean peninsula in the fall of 2002 with the resurfacing of the nuclear issue, prompted by a charge (acknowledged by the DPRK) by the United States in October that the North Koreans were engaged in a covert program to produce weapons-grade enriched uranium. Subsequently, the DPRK announced its withdrawal from the NNPT, prohibiting access of IAEA inspectors to its nuclear sites. In retaliation, the Bush administration cut off supplies of fuel oil to North Korea and temporarily halted the delivery of food aid. The ensuing crisis left Russia once more seeking a substantive role in negotiations. Putin's success in strengthening ties with the Kim Jong-il regime put Russia and China on a more equitable basis, as the only two states with any substantive claim to influence in Pyongyang. Consequently, China became more solicitous of Russian input on the Korean situation, with the topic emerging as an item for joint discussion in foreign policy consultations. The joint communiqué signed by Putin and Jiang in December 2002 made the first direct mention of North Korea since the initial Russian-Chinese joint statement a decade earlier.[111] The declaration noted the importance of maintaining a nuclear-free Korean peninsula and the nonproliferation of weapons of mass destruction, but it also took a further unprecedented step in emphasizing the need for the United States and the DPRK to normalize relations.[112]

During the opening months of 2003, the situation on the Korean peninsula took a back seat to the intensifying crisis in Iraq, despite the persistent efforts of Kim Jong-il to engage the attention of the United States. In January 2003, the DPRK formally withdrew from the NNPT, a move that both Russia and China described as undesirable. Russia sent Vice Foreign Minister Alexander Losyukov as an envoy to Pyongyang in an effort to defuse the situation. Pyongyang's announcement in February 2003 that it was restarting a nuclear reactor at the Yongbyon nuclear complex with the potential to produce plutonium increased global anxiety levels. During his February 2003 trip to Beijing, U.S. secretary of state Colin Powell encouraged China to pressure North Korea not to develop its nuclear capabilities. Powell also sought Chinese support for a multilateral conference on the Korean issue and the adoption of a Security Council resolution condemning the DPRK's actions. As with the Iraqi issue, Powell did not convince the Chinese of the virtues of the U.S. position. China remained opposed both to multilateral talks and to the Security Council as a venue for discussion of the North Korean situation. In particular, China feared that a Security Council resolution imposing sanctions on the North Korean regime would result in the further collapse of the North Korean economy with adverse spillover effects for China. For its part, the Chinese leadership urged the United States to agree to bilateral direct talks with the DPRK, an action steadfastly rejected by the Bush administration. The Russian acquiescence to the Chinese position was indicated several days later during Foreign Minister Ivanov's trip to Beijing. In addition to their joint communiqué on Iraq, the Russian and Chinese foreign ministers released a joint communiqué on the situation on the Korean peninsula that indicated their mutual desire for a "peaceful and just resolution of the problem," pointedly noting that an "equal and constructive dialogue between the United States and the DPRK will be of great significance to resolving the 'DPRK's nuclear issue' and realizing the normalization of U.S.-DPRK relations."[113]

The appearance of the Korean issue as an item for bilateral political discussions between Russian and China can be attributed to two interrelated factors: (1) the newly emergent status of Russia as an actor with connections to the DPRK regime, and (2) the increasingly convergent interests of Russia and China in seeking a resolution to the crisis on the Korean peninsula. Compared to China, which provided North Korea with substantive food and energy aid, Russia's leverage in Pyongyang was limited to the political sphere. Nonetheless, by early 2003, indications existed that Putin's three meetings with Kim Jong-il had paid some dividends in opening lines of communication between Russia and the DPRK.[114] As in the Iraqi situation, Russian diplomacy was notably more proactive than China's on the Korean issue. Russia, unlike China, sent an envoy to Pyongyang in an effort to defuse the crisis. Russia, moreover, demonstrated a greater solidarity with the DPRK in abstaining in the February 2003 vote in the board of governors of the IAEA to refer the North Korean nuclear issue to the Security Council of the UN.[115] China, in contrast, indicated its opposition to the U.S. stance, but was loath to come forward with its own initiatives.[116] Nonetheless, Russia and China (as well as South Korea) shared a deep-seated concern for the maintenance of stability on the Korean peninsula, a condition that they viewed as dependent on averting the collapse of the precarious North Korean regime, not, as U.S. policy might have it, in precipitating its demise. Thus, both states were fearful of the adverse consequences of economic sanctions imposed by the UN, or even worse, the initiation of military actions by the United States against the DPRK. Russia and China indicated these convergent interests in their May 2003 joint statement. In addition to expressing their desire for a nuclear-free Korean peninsula devoid of weapons of mass destruction, the two states simultaneously indicated their commitment to "guarantee the security of the DPRK as well as create favorable conditions for its social and economic development."[117]

The Iranian Factor

Neither Russia nor China considered President Bush's designation of Iran as the third member of the axis of evil credible. Both viewed the Iranian state as a force of relative stability in the Afghan crisis, given its condemnation of the Taliban and extensive record of support for the Northern Alliance. Moreover, both states had developed significant military-technical links with Iran, leading them to discount the U.S. claim that Iran was a terrorist threat. Throughout the 1990s, Chinese military and technical assistance to Iran was a continuous irritant to U.S.-Chinese relations, with the United States applying pressure on China to sever or curtail its transfer of military technology to Iran. Despite Chinese agreement to U.S. demands on several occasions, Iran continued to be (along with Pakistan) a major recipient of Chinese military technology.[118] Military-technological interactions between Russia and Iran were even more robust and of correspondingly greater concern to the United States. In 1995, the United States and Russia concluded a secret accord under the auspices of the Gore-Chernomyrdin Commission on Trade and Economic Cooperation in which Russia agreed to cease arms sales to Iran, an arrangement that it subsequently renounced in 2000. In March 2001, Russia and Iran signed a cooperation treaty, followed by a military-technical agreement in October 2001 that provided for extensive transfers of Russian weaponry to Iran.[119] In addition, the United States repeatedly criticized Russia for its role in the construction of two nuclear reactors at a nuclear power plant in Iran at Bushehr, charging that the project could enable the Iranians to develop nuclear weapons through the potential extraction of weapons-grade plutonium and the transfer of sensitive nuclear technologies. U.S. pressure on Russia to curtail its military-technical linkages with Iran, however, was not effective. President Bush, for example, raised the issue of the Bushehr nuclear facility with President Putin at their May 2002 summit meeting, but Putin denied U.S. claims, noting that "cooperation between Russia and Iran is not of a character that would undermine the process of nonproliferation."[120]

Russia and China shared certain parallels in their foreign policy relationship with Iran: both had military-technical linkages with Iran that incurred extensive U.S. opposition, and both rejected the U.S. designation of Iran as an instigator of state-sponsored terrorism. But unlike their response to the Iraqi and Korean crises, the two states did not seek to establish a coordinated foreign policy response on Iran. Both Russia and China sought to reconcile differences with the United States separately through bilateral negotiations. Russian-Chinese joint communiqués dealing with the international situation did not single out Iran as a topic of direct consideration. President Bush's designation of Iran as a defined terrorist threat in early 2002, however, identified Iran as a focal point of U.S. foreign policy interests, with consequent geostrategic implications. The potential for the United States to turn to Iran as the next target of its war on terrorism after Iraq was hinted at in the Russian-Chinese joint statement of May 2003, which noted that "in the post-war arrangements and reconstruction process of Iraq, the legitimate rights and concerns of its neighboring countries and other concerned sides should be taken into account."[121]

Conclusion: Geopolitics in the New World Order

The political relationship between Russia and China in the first decade of the Russian Federation evolved in largely unanticipated directions, the product of the complex interaction of international and domestic factors. Few would have predicted in 1992 that Russia and China, distanced by decades of enmity and the strains imposed by the collapse of the Soviet political order, would become "strategic partners" united by a Friendship Treaty less than ten years later. The United States exerted a constant influence on the political dimensions of Russian-Chinese interactions, usually acting to drive the two states together. Despite their seemingly cataclysmic reverberations at the time, the events of September 11, 2001, appear not to have created a permanent realignment of the international political order. By mid-2002, it was evident that the concept of multipolarity had not been rendered obsolescent, at least as a goal of aspirant states if not as an empirical description of the international order. In his June 2002 interview with the *People's Daily*, Putin noted that state-to-state relations between Russia and China constituted a "tremendous contribution to the establishment of a new multipolar international order since the end of the Cold War."[122] Multipolarity remained embedded in the joint statement signed by Putin and Jiang Zemin at their December 2002 summit, with the two states maintaining that the "multipolarization and globalization of the world" was gaining momentum."[123] Thus, Russian-Chinese relations appeared to have weathered the tensions generated by Putin's foreign policy alignment toward the United States, finding some revised equilibrium, a process that was further bolstered by Russia's open break with the United States on the Iraqi situation, in which Russia proved to be considerably more confrontational with the United States than China. The Russian-Chinese joint declaration of May 2003 upheld the commitment of the two states to multipolarity, albeit in more measured and cautionary tones that implicitly acknowledged the paucity of restraints on U.S. behavior. According to the declaration, "power politics and unilateralism add a new element of instability to this already not peaceful world. . . . Multipolarization remains the principal trend, but it will be a difficult process and will require the joint efforts of the entire international community."[124]

The movement of the Putin leadership toward the United States and Europe was not in itself a new phenomenon in the Soviet or Russian foreign policy experience. Putin's desire that Russia assume its place within the ranks of European nations was reminiscent of Gorbachev's earlier efforts to return the Soviet Union to its "common European home."[125] The integration of Russia into the West had served as the fundamental precept underlying the foreign policy of the Yeltsin leadership at the onset of the Russian Federation. Underlying Putin's foreign policy approach, however, was a markedly different sensibility as to strategic options and possibilities. The Yeltsin leadership took the position that Russia was still a great power, deserving to be treated as a coequal in interactions with the United States. Putin discarded these unrealistic illusions, resigned to the fact that Russia was at best a junior partner in any joint endeavors. As Dmitri Trenin noted, speaking of the Russian-U.S. relationship, "it is important to bear in mind that the alternative to uneven partnership is not a partnership of equals, but no partnership at all."[126] The Putin strategy implicitly acknowledged subordination to the United States as a pragmatic necessity and as a prerequisite to Russia's full incorporation into the mechanisms of the global capitalist marketplace and its future economic rejuvenation. This did not imply that traditional geostrategic considerations rooted in Russia's calculation of its national interests no longer existed, superseded by a sweeping tide of globalization. But it did mean that their selective application would be rooted in a long-term appraisal of potential costs and benefits.

The tensions that erupted between the United States and its NATO allies—specifically France and Germany—over Iraq were something of a boon to Russia. Putin's bandwagoning strategy had not in fact gained Russia much in tangible benefits from the United States, and Putin's own background as a KGB operative in the German Democratic Republic probably predisposed him toward collaboration with the Europeans rather than the United States as a first choice. To Russian foreign policy analysts, well versed in the Soviet realist heritage, the rift between the United States and Europe opened up a number of strategic possibilities, not least of which was the opportunity to promote a conception of world order rooted in multipolarity. At the same time, Russian diplomacy was careful—more careful than French or Germans—not to engage in incendiary rhetoric or overtly to antagonize the United States. Igor Ivanov was a model of consummate tact, seeking to reassure the United States of Russia's commitment to dialogue and strengthened relations, while simultaneously attempting to undermine the U.S. position. The unilateralist actions of the United States, culminating in a rapid military victory over Iraqi forces, testified to the overwhelming predominance of the United States as the global hegemon. This situation, however, also reinforced the Russian and Chinese motivation to promote a multipolar world based on multilateral forms of cooperation as the antidote to U.S. supremacy.

Whereas Russia's economic weakness contributed to its political vulnerability, China's burgeoning economic growth, manifest in its increasing economic interdependence with the United States, also served as a factor limiting China's range of action. China's low profile in the Iraqi crisis partly stemmed from a reluctance to antagonize the United States, but it also reflected the sweeping leadership transition under way in the PRC. Jiang Zemin's retention of the position of chairman of the Military Affairs Commission at the Sixteenth National Party Congress in October 2002 indicated his resolve to remain a power—in fact, *the* power—behind the scenes, but China's emergent "fourth generation" leadership remained untested and seemingly adrift in the foreign policy sphere during its first few months in office.[127] The convocation of the Tenth National People's Congress in March 2003 meant the large-scale turnover of Chinese government officials, including the retirement of Qian Qichen, the former foreign minister and subsequent deputy head of the Foreign Affairs Leading Small Group in charge of the day-to-day orchestration of Chinese foreign policy. China's unusually quiescent foreign policy seemingly reflected the hesitations of a new generation of leaders who were more insular than their predecessors and largely inexperienced in dealing with issues that extended beyond China's borders.

The Jiang Zemin leadership had viewed the July 2001 Friendship Treaty as a means of providing China with some protection against potential U.S. efforts to isolate China and marginalize its status as a global presence. For Jiang and his cohorts, geopolitics was not an anachronism that had been made irrelevant by either economic factors or the impact of global terrorism. In contrast, the Chinese leaders were inclined toward the perspective that the terrorist attacks on the United States in September 2001 had presented the United States with the possibility to pursue its hegemonist ambitions under the guise of the war on terrorism, using its victimized status as a rationale to penetrate into hitherto uncharted regions. Chinese leaders further feared that aspects of U.S. foreign policy—such as its plans to deploy missile defense systems both in the Asian Pacific region and on U.S. territory, the U.S. presence in Central Asia, and the closer integration of NATO with Russia—were part of a concerted strategy to contain China. Ultimately, moreover, these core Chinese foreign policy interests transcended the generational shift in leadership. For the emergent Chinese leadership, geostrategic calculations continued to indicate the importance of close ties with Russia. Hu Jintao's selection of Russia as the site for his first trip abroad as president in May 2003 symbolized the intent of the new Chinese leadership to maintain its "strategic relationship" with the Russian Federation. In an interview with Russia media sources before his departure, Hu emphasized the importance that China placed on continued development of ties with Russia as a component of its foreign policy. According to Hu: "China believes that the trend toward a multipolar world is irreversible. China is ready to continue to intensify its relations with Russia in order to accelerate the process of formation of a multipolar world order together."[128]

8

Conclusion
The Emergent Partnership

The Russian Federation faced a seemingly unending series of challenges in its first decade. The task of transition from socialism to capitalism indicated an unanticipated historical progression that left states in uncharted territory as to guidelines for effecting economic change. The difficulties were greater for Russia than for many of the formerly socialist states of Eastern Europe due to such factors as Russia's overwhelming size, the length of Soviet rule, and the lack of historical traditions to support capitalist practice. In the foreign policy realm, Russia was compelled to adjust to the loss of superpower status. The Soviet regime had operated within the framework of a largely realist worldview. The revamped Russian leadership inherited this theoretical propensity, but was reluctant to admit that Russia's diminished power capabilities meant its decreased influence as a global actor. The Russian Federation was no longer able to maintain a global foreign policy but was forced to redirect its attention to regions in which it had a defined security interest. In this context, the Russian leadership soon came to recognize that its relationship with China, given the reality of 4,250-kilometer border, was a matter of considerable importance.

Russian-Chinese relations in the first decade of the Russian Federation were not tension free. The two states had limited success in establishing economic linkages, impeded by a series of obstacles. The situation of the Russian Far East and Transbaikal areas was a major—if largely ignored—domestic problem for the Russian leadership, which had consequent spillover effects on the Russian-Chinese relationship. Despite these problems, Russian ties with China multiplied in the 1990s, leading to the establishment of a strategic relationship and the formal conclusion of the July 1991 Friendship Treaty. Russian interactions with China were not unidimensional but multidimensional: bilateral, regional, and international issues shaped their content. The focus of this concluding chapter is to analyze Russian foreign policy toward China, reviewing the material presented in the previous chapters, in order to identify the causative factors that explain the evolution of this relationship. This investigation rejects the sort of constructivist perspective that international reality is socially constructed.[1] In my view, facts exist as empirical phenomena. But it also must be acknowledged that the means by which these facts are arranged and analyzed is invariably a subjective undertaking, susceptible to multiple interpretations. Any explanation of foreign policy behavior is invariably set in the context, whether implicit or explicit, of an underlying interpretive framework. Any given event, moreover, is susceptible to variant competing explanations.[2] The question is, which approach, in the final assessment, best explains a particular set of foreign policy events?

The Soviet Heritage

In 1992, the leadership of the Russian Federation had the ambitious goal of negating the legacy of seventy-five years of Soviet rule through the construction of a new state. This task, carried out by elites who themselves were indelibly the product of the Soviet era, proved to be impossible. Russian foreign policy toward China has reflected both directly and indirectly the formidable inheritance of the Soviet Union. This was both a benefit and a drawback, but on the whole the Soviet legacy provided an institutional framework and a set of guidelines for foreign policy decision makers to utilize in the first years of the Russian Federation. To a large extent, the Russian Federation adopted a foreign policy course toward China that followed in the footsteps of the Gorbachev leadership, making use in many instances of institutional structures left over from the former regime. In its heyday, the Soviet Union possessed an impressive, highly professionalized foreign policy apparatus that was partially preserved under the Yeltsin administration. As noted in Chapter 1, the Yeltsin administration came to rely heavily on the Ministry of Foreign Affairs to implement its foreign policy toward China through a number of retained officials. The Russian Ministry of Foreign Affairs continued the negotiations undertaken in the Gorbachev era on the reduction of military strength in the border region and oversaw the demarcation of the Russian-Chinese border specified in the 1991 border agreement.

The Yeltsin leadership also preserved the economic structures established in the Soviet period to conduct economic transactions with China. These were markedly less effective in their impact, reflecting their origins as Soviet institutions ill adapted to capitalist practice. Russian attitudes toward capitalism also often bore the imprint of the Soviet mentality, manifest in outright hostility toward capitalist endeavors, especially the shuttle trade and other small-scale business ventures brought into Russia by Chinese traders. In the defense sector, the Sino-Soviet rift immobilized military exchanges between the two states for three decades. The institutional legacy, such as it was, consisted almost solely of negotiations regarding arms sales conducted in the later days of the Gorbachev era, which were immediately assumed by the Yeltsin administration. By the mid-1990s, the intensification of links between the two states led to efforts to expand bilateral structures. Some of these—such as the Russian-Chinese Friendship, Peace, and Development Committee—appeared as a throwback to the Soviet era, indicating a distinct lack of imagination.[3] By the early 2000s, however, Russia and China were moving beyond a reliance on Soviet-style structures in their efforts to set up bilateral economic commissions—such as the subcommittee on banking—directed toward market operations.

The Soviet heritage, if advantageous in the institutional sphere, had a largely negative impact in the ideological realm in terms of shaping Russian attitudes toward China. As Alexander Lukin has noted: "Contemporary images of China in Russia have been formed on the basis of the Soviet image of this country, as well as historical and borrowed beliefs which have been reinterpreted under the influence of the dominant political culture of the Soviet period and Russia's geopolitical realities."[4] The prolonged and bitter rift with China legitimated—indeed encouraged—expressions of hostility toward China while restricting information about Chinese society and culture. The legacy of the Sino-Soviet split was especially apparent in the Russian Far East. The sealing off of the Sino-Soviet border enabled residents to live in an artificially constructed world, kept aloft by subsidies. The collapse of this—by Soviet standards—entitled existence brought forth a xenophobic reaction to prospects of integration into the Asian Pacific region.

While Russian leaders of the 1990s had little prior knowledge of China, their Chinese counterparts were considerably better informed about Russia. The Chinese leadership in the 1990s, the "third generation" in Chinese parlance, was the only generation that could lay a claim to an extensive—if rather dated—knowledge of Russia and Russian culture. Unlike many of his contemporaries, Mao Zedong was famously insular. His first trip abroad was to the Soviet Union in 1950, followed by a second visit in 1957. The more cosmopolitan Deng Xiaoping spent five years of his youth in France, visiting Moscow briefly. Jiang Zemin, however, studied in the Soviet Union in the 1950s. During his July 2001 visit to Moscow, Jiang delivered his speech to students at Moscow State University in Russian, and apparently felt a nostalgic enjoyment singing Russian songs with his hosts during his frequent state visits. In this sense, the legacy of the Sino-Soviet alliance might have been more manifest in Beijing than in Moscow.

The Domestic Context

In the Soviet period, analysts typically accepted as unquestioned that the Communist Party of the Soviet Union exercised a near monopoly of control over the processes of Soviet foreign policy decision making. The totalitarian model advanced by Carl Friedrich and Zbigniew Brzezinski in the 1950s was the dominant paradigm to explain Soviet foreign policy for several decades, enduring well into the Gorbachev era.[5] In the 1960s, Gordon Skilling made a spirited attempt to challenge the totalitarian model, arguing for a recognition of the role of interest groups as participants in decision making in Soviet society.[6] His efforts met with considerable skepticism, although assessments in the later part of the Brezhnev era were often willing to acknowledge the input of institutional interests—such as the Soviet military—in the policymaking process. In marked contrast to the Soviet period, analyses in the 1990s moved toward the opposite end of the continuum, tending to emphasize the domestic context of Russian foreign policy decision making, sometimes to the near exclusion of systemic factors.[7] The treatment of the state as a unitary actor, a bedrock assumption of the totalitarian model, was forsaken for an approach that considered Russian foreign policy as the product of domestic inputs.

Domestic Actors in the Russian-Chinese Relationship

Generally speaking, the Russian relationship with China was not an issue that attracted a great deal of attention on the Russian domestic scene. Nonetheless, it was possible to distinguish specific actors with a defined interest in Russian interactions with China. These included the military industrial complex (including the Ministry of Defense as a sometime reluctant partner), the nuclear industry, the aerospace industry, the energy industry, and elites in the border regions, most particularly in the Russian Far East. The groups in Russia with an interest in foreign policy toward China in the 1990s and early 2000s were distinguished—with one prominent exception—by their economic agenda. Elites in the border regions also had economic concerns, but ultimately sought to exercise influence over a broader array of foreign policy issues regarding Russia's relationship with China.

While there can be no doubt that these groups had an impact on Russia's relationship with China in its first decade, it is more difficult—perhaps impossible—to trace the means by which actors exercised influence, and the extent to which their input was reflected in foreign policy decision making. Western-derived models of interest articulation that assume the existence of regularized procedures and clearly formulated decision rules were quite evidently of limited utility in the Russian context. The interest group model of pluralist democracy, widely promulgated in the United States, often presented the leadership as a sort of honest broker, mediating between competing interests.[8] Russia in the 1990s was a weak state, with the federal government often lacking the capability to enact and—of equal importance—to implement policy decisions. Domestic actors—for example, enterprises within the military-industrial complex—were able at times to pursue their own independent linkages with Chinese representatives, often unbeknown to formal government authorities and in contravention of decreed policies. At the same time, the strong executive tradition in Russia was readily apparent. The authority of the legislative branch was highly circumscribed, and the president exercised a commanding role over the orchestration of the policy agenda. In the case of Russian foreign policy toward China, the interests of the defense-related industries (including the nuclear and aerospace sectors) and the executive branch tended to converge.

The institutional legacy of the Soviet era was highly visible in the defense industries, which suffered from the collapse of the Russian economy in the 1990s. The Russian military-industrial complex, the nuclear industry, and the aerospace industry sought linkages with China as a means of sustenance under grim domestic conditions. The Russian government simultaneously supported this approach. For example, as noted in Chapter 5, the Yeltsin administration endorsed a policy of promoting arms sales from its onset. In January 1992, Yeltsin began to urge arms producers to sell their weaponry abroad, noting that this was essential to keeping the arms industry alive. In certain instances, the Yeltsin administration placed restrictions on arms and technology transfers as a matter of national security or in response to external requests. Perhaps the most notable case of Russian acquiescence to foreign pressures was the secret agreement that Russia concluded with the United States in 1995, in which Russia pledged not to sell arms to Iran. In response, the Russian defense industry spent years lobbying the Kremlin to cancel the agreement.[9] In the early 1990s, the Taiwanese government put out feelers regarding the purchase of weaponry from Russia. Russian defense enterprises reportedly put considerable pressure on the Russian government to permit arms deals with Taiwan, a prospect quickly quashed by opposition from the People's Republic of China.[10]

In general, however, the Russian defense-related industries encountered a sympathetic Russian government eager to promote arms sales and technology transfers to China. The Ministry of Defense, however, had conflicting interests on the sale of weapons to China. On the one hand, members of the Russian military were concerned over the long-term implications of a policy of arms sales to a contiguous, rapidly developing neighbor. On the other hand, tangible material benefits accrued to the ministry through arms sales, which also offered the military some hope that profits from the sale of weaponry abroad could be used to equip and develop new weapons systems for Russian forces. The unease expressed by various members of the Russian military establishment over arms and technology transfers to China did not manifest itself in a principled opposition and organized lobbying against the policy. Objections to arms sales to China remained defuse. Domestic lobbying did play an important role in the Russian arms trade to China, but it was expressed in a fierce competition between enterprises over contract procurements. The process of awarding contracts to defense enterprises was highly politicized. In January 2001, for example, a political uproar ensued when the St. Petersburg shipbuilder Baltiiskii Zavod was unexpectedly awarded the tender to supply two Sovremennyi destroyers to China, rather than Severnaia Verf', which had previously delivered two Sovremennyi Project 636 destroyers to China. The Chinese Ministry of Foreign Affairs lodged a formal protest about the switch in contractors. Eventually the decision was reversed, with the entire debacle apparently contributing to the demotion of Vice Prime Minister Ilya Klebanov, who oversaw operations of military-technical cooperation with foreign states.

While the situation in the energy sector was no less politicized than in the defense industries, its circumstances differed significantly. Whereas firms in the defense sector (including the nuclear and aerospace industries) were engaged in a grim struggle for economic survival, survival in itself was not an issue for most energy firms. Rather, competition in the energy realm was driven by the prospect of large profits. Moreover, for most of the 1990s, executives within Russian energy circles did not push for energy cooperation with China, viewing it as a secondary market compared to alternative, more immediately remunerative venues. The exception was Yukos oil company, which emerged as the most dedicated adherent of a pipeline project linking East Siberian oil fields in Irkutsk to China. Vladimir Putin's efforts to develop bilateral energy cooperation with China did not appear to be a response to energy sector lobbying efforts, but rather an executive decision that the policy was in Russia's interest. Putin's challenge was to compel the powerful oil barons to get on board in supporting the policy. Despite the agreement signed between China and Russia in May 2003 to move toward the construction of a pipeline, segments of the Russian energy sector resisted the implementation of the project, preferring to build a pipeline to Nakhodka in Primorskii krai, which offered the prospect of multiple markets. The Japanese government's efforts to convince Russia to build a pipeline to supply oil to Japan further undercut support for China as a destination point for Russian oil.

Russia's relationship with China was more important to regional groups in the border regions than any other single constituency on the Russian domestic scene.[11] Russian defense enterprises were strong proponents of arms and technology transfers to China, but their product was readily adaptable to other markets if the opportunity presented itself. They had no sentimental affinities for China, and in fact would have preferred a more prestigious customer. For the defense-related industries and the energy sector, the development of bilateral links with China was motivated by potential revenues. In contrast, regional relationships with China were shaped by the immutable realities of geography. Regional elites, moreover, did not typically find a sponsor for the promotion of their interests on the China issue at the federal level: most often, the relationship between regional leaders and their federal counterparts was antagonistic.

On the one hand, regional elites did not play a large role in shaping policy directives of relevance to the Russian-Chinese relationship. The most prominent example of direct regional input into national decision making was the decision of the Yeltsin government, undertaken at the behest of the leaders in the Russian Far East, to revise visa regulations in 1994. But the issue of the influence of the regional elites on Russian-Chinese relations was more complex than indicated by a quantitative accounting of policy decrees. First, regional leaders appeared to have a significant indirect impact on Russian foreign policy toward China regarding border issues, with the federal government reluctant to agree to initiatives that would be rejected at the regional level. For example, despite years of discussion, the Russian government failed to institute a measure—already put in place by the Chinese—to allow visa-free access to cities in the border regions. Second, regional leaders in the 1990s and early 2000s disregarded or obstructed the implementation of national-level policy directives relevant to Russian-Chinese relations. Regional leaders, for example, impeded the completion of the demarcation of the Russian-Chinese border, deliberately engaging in go-slow activities. Similarly, the leadership in Primorskii krai refused to support efforts, endorsed by the federal government, for the Tumen River Economic Development Area. Third, the weakening of centralized controls in the 1990s gave regional authorities the ability to affect the course of Russian policy toward China through local initiatives, some of which were in outright violation of federal policy. In Khabarovsk krai, officials forbade Chinese vessels to navigate freely along the Amur River, a clear contravention of the 1991 border agreement. The periodic sweeps to arrest illegal migrants in Primorskii and Khabarovsk krais—Operation Foreigner—were undertaken at the initiative of the regional leaderships. The regional authorities also had considerable autonomy to process visas and set labor quotas, thus controlling the movement of Chinese into the border regions, with subsequent implications for the development of Russian-Chinese economic linkages.

During the 1990s, the regional leaders in the Russian border region—like their counterparts elsewhere—were engaged in an ongoing power struggle with the federal government over the distribution of political authority and the allocation of scarce resources. The weakened Russian state was severely challenged in its efforts to project power in an area thousands of miles from Moscow. The paucity of cross-border agreements concluded between Russia and China indicated the inability of the Russian state to implement such measures, as well as a deference to Russian regional concerns. Both the Yeltsin and the Putin administrations made concerted efforts to include regional elites in the Russian Far East in consultations on Russian-Chinese relations, regularly including regional leaders as members of Russian delegations to China on state visits. At the same time, however, the federal government, while making some conciliatory gestures to Far Eastern elites, made it clear that it was not willing to acquiesce to actions that would strain ties with China. China, moreover, was assertive in indicating that it would not tolerate extended displays of anti-Chinese sentiment from the Far Eastern regions. The delaying tactics of regional leaders slowed down but did not prevent the demarcation of the border. Inflammatory statements about Chinese immigration (although not just by regional leaders) in the summer of 2002 evoked a critical response from the Putin administration and an official disavowal by the Russian Foreign Ministry. In early 2003, the Putin administration was signaling that compromise would be a component of any solution regarding the three remaining disputed islands that were excluded from the 1991 border agreement. Ultimately, Russian regional interests had to be subordinated to those of the Russian state, which needed to maintain a cordial relationship with China.

Domestic actors did play a role in Russian foreign policy toward China, but the relationship between domestic groups and the Russian government was more entangled than suggested by pluralist models, which presumed the influence of autonomous associations in a civil society. The Russian government had multiple reasons to keep the defense-related industries operative: These sectors represented the highest achievements of Soviet technology and their preservation was a matter of national security as well as national pride. In addition, their demise would have posed a massive threat to the regime in the form of unemployment on a mass scale. The Russian government, rather than the Russian energy sector, was the primary advocate of energy collaboration with China, a movement that was not universally endorsed by the industry. Regional elites played a significant role in Russian foreign policy interactions with China. But the inability of regional elites directly to shape policy indicated the limitations of their influence, as well as the refusal of the federal government to conflate regional and national interests.

Governmental Type as a Determinant of Foreign Policy Behavior

During the 1980s, theorists of international relations directed increased attention to the premise—the intellectual origins of which can be traced to Immanuel Kant—that democratic states are predisposed by virtue of their regime type to pursue a different foreign policy than nondemocratic states. Reduced to its most simplified formulation, this approach postulates that democratic states practice a peaceful foreign policy; or in a more refined format, known as the democratic peace hypothesis, "democracies do not make war on each other."[12] As previously noted, analysts had long attributed Soviet foreign policy behavior to the distinctive "totalitarian" features of the Soviet government. In view of this, the alacrity with which Western observers embraced the democratic peace proposition in the 1990s as a predictor of Russian foreign policy behavior was perhaps not surprising. To put it baldly, a democratic Russia would have a democratic foreign policy. As Michael McFaul has noted: "The pacific motives underlying Russia's foreign policy for most of its first years of independence are a result of factors and political groups emerging from its peaceful transition from communist rule to democracy. Russian foreign policy is what it is because those in political power were liberal politicians and economic groups with pacific interests."[13]

Adherents to the democratic peace hypothesis tended to have an overtly prescriptive goal: to ensure that Russia would forge friendly ties with the West, and with the United States in particular. Considerably less attention, however, was directed to the question of the implications of Russian regime type for its foreign policy relationship with other states. Since China was an authoritarian regime, the democratic peace proposition did not in itself predict that Russia and China would not engage in aggression behavior, but the inference was clear that a democratic Russia would be more inclined than the Soviet Union to seek a pacific relationship with China. Leaving aside the issue as to whether Russia could in fact be considered a democracy, it was true that the Russian Federation in the 1990s and early 2000s sought a peaceful relationship with China. But the evidence does not indicate that this choice was a consequence of Russia's emergent governmental structure. Rather, as with a number of other policies, the Yeltsin administration, after an initial period of several months, pursued the foreign policy approach that had been forged in the Gorbachev era.

Did Individual Leaders Matter?

Russian foreign policy behavior in the 1990s was often viewed as dependent on the individual personalities and corresponding ideological orientation of its leaders. This perspective tended to overlap with that of the democratic peace hypothesis in the sense that the individual leadership of Boris Yeltsin was viewed as an indispensable component of a democratic Russia. According to Michael McFaul: "Had Boris Yeltsin lost the 1996 presidential election, Russian foreign policy would have followed a very different course."[14] The Clinton administration adopted this position early in Yeltsin's presidency and subsequently invested considerable effort into providing support for Yeltsin's personal leadership, viewing him as a bulwark in providing Russia with a pro-American foreign policy.[15]

The attention directed to the Atlanticist and Eurasianist perspectives on Russian foreign policy behavior in the 1990s, moreover, tended to obscure a fundamental convergence in their views: both groups were preoccupied above all with establishing a foreign policy approach toward the United States. The emphasis of the Eurasianists on a multipolar world, with the establishment of linkages with Russia's neighbors to the East and South, was perceived as a means of counterbalancing the United States. The cultivation of ties with China in this instance was instrumental, seen as a means to an end. Outside of specialized circles, the Russian elite was largely uninformed and uninterested in China. But if the Russian-Chinese relationship aroused limited interest, it also, as noted in Chapter 1, provoked little controversy. No leading politician (with the possible exception of Vladimir Zhirinovskii) or political party at the national level challenged the foreign policy approach toward China developed by the Yeltsin administration. Other members of the Liberal Democratic Party, moreover, supported a policy of strong ties with China. This position was taken, for example, by Aleksei Mitrofanov, the vice chairman of the State Duma Committee on Foreign Affairs from 1993 to 1995, and of the Geopolitics Committee from 1995 to 1999.[16]

The continuity in Russian foreign policy toward China in its first decade, which reflected a near consensual unanimity among Russia's political elite, casts doubt on the notion that another leadership would have pursued a notably divergent policy. The role of individual personalities does not appear as a decisive factor in shaping the Russian Federation's foreign policy toward China. Boris Yeltsin appeared to be a typical representative of his political class in his relative lack of interest in China. Yeltsin oversaw the strengthening of ties with China, but this was a process that took place in the absence of individuals with an expertise on China within the presidential staff.

Moreover, Russian interactions with China in the 1990s do not lend credence to the sentiment, widespread in certain foreign policy circles, that the replacement of Andrei Kozyrev with Evgenii Primakov in January 1996 represented a significant shift in the Russian foreign policy orientation.[17] Rather, the incremental development of Russian foreign policy ties with China makes it difficult to draw a clear-cut line of differentiation between the personal foreign policy agendas of these two foreign ministers. After the first few months of 1992, Kozyrev suppressed his tendencies to criticize the Chinese for their errant ways, presiding over the strengthening of the relationship. Kozyrev was considerably more cosmopolitan than Yeltsin and more ideologically predisposed toward the West, with a personal inclination to disdain China as an historical anachronism. Nonetheless, Kozyrev orchestrated a foreign policy approach toward China characterized by a continuous upgrading of linkages. As Allen C. Lynch has noted, Kozyrev pursued a style of Russian diplomacy (not just confined to the Russian-Chinese relationship) that was more complex and balanced than was generally acknowledged.[18] There is no doubt that Primakov was more oriented toward China than his predecessor, and clearly far preferred by the Chinese leadership. The Russian-Chinese relationship continued to strengthen during Primakov's term as foreign minister, but it is not convincing that this was a consequence of his personal leadership. Although Andrei Kozyrev was considered an Atlanticist and Evgenii Primakov an Eurasianist, Primakov's tenure as minister of foreign affairs built upon the foundations that had been laid down under Kozyrev. The essential constancy in the Russian foreign policy toward China, moreover, was maintained with Igor Ivanov's assumption of the position of foreign minister in 1998 and continued into the Putin administration.

Despite Vladimir Putin's repositioning of Russian foreign policy closer to the United States in the aftermath of the terrorist attacks of September 11, 2001, the Putin presidency fundamentally adhered to the foreign policy strategy toward China laid out in the Yeltsin era. However, Russian-Chinese relations under Putin diverged from those of the Yeltsin administration in one significant respect. The overall policy line remained the same, but the means by which it was implemented changed. Putin's efforts to bring order to the organizational chaos that had plagued the Yeltsin administration began to reap some dividends, with a consequent effect on Russian foreign policy decision making. In addition, Putin proved to be more of a modern man than Yeltsin, less interested in geopolitical strategizing in an effort to regain Russia's lost status and more directed toward developing the means to bring Russia into the global economy of the twenty-first century. Putin was more interested in developing bilateral economic linkages with China than Yeltsin had been, and was more concerned to develop economic interactions that were not carryovers from the Soviet era but conformed to the dictates of a market economy. The process of establishing economic subcommittees—largely stalled under Yeltsin—was accelerated, and the meetings of the Russian and Chinese prime ministers devoted greater attention to efforts to stimulate economic cooperation, especially in the sphere of energy. Putin's actions highlighted the role of individual leadership as an intangible and not easily quantified component of a state's capabilities. A weak state such as Russia was constrained in its foreign policy behavior by a number of structural factors that limited its range of action (see below). Nonetheless, a skillful leader retained some margin of choice over a potential range of actions, making it possible to play a weak hand to maximum advantage.

Structural Attributes of the Russian Federation

During the 1990s, the structural circumstances of the Russian Federation virtually mandated that any rational leadership would seek amicable ties with China. Four attributes in particular can be distinguished as key in framing the policy choices available to the Russian leadership: (1) economic conditions; (2) the state of the Russian military; (3) demographic factors; and (4) the physical environment imposed on Russia by geography. The precipitous fall in Russian gross domestic product (GDP) in the 1990s indicated Russia's decline as a major economic power. As Chapter 4 indicates, Russia's GDP in 2001 was less than half that of Mexico. The task of Russia's economic rejuvenation presented an enormous challenge to the Russian government. At the same time, the drop in GDP, as well as the transition from a state-administered economy to laissez-faire market practice, meant that the federal government was left with sharply diminished budgetary resources. The allocation of government revenues to the development of the Russian-Chinese relationship was not a high priority. The Russian Federation lacked the financial means to carry out even mundane tasks. The border demarcation was impeded by political resistance from Far Eastern elites but also by the lack of fuel oil to power Russian boats in the Amur River. Under such circumstances, more ambitious undertakings, such as the establishment of cross-border infrastructure and special economic zones—were beyond the financial capabilities of the state.

The decline in government revenues left the Russian military as a shadow of its former self. The problems of the Russian military in its first decade were legion: undernourished recruits bearing out-of-date weapons with limited training, the lack of funds for procurement of new weaponry, the diversion of limited revenues to the seemingly endless conflict in Chechnya, and so forth. By the end of the decade, Sukhoi fighter jets being sold to India and China were more sophisticated than those possessed by the Russian military, which was making do with upgrades of its Sukhoi fighter planes. The Sino-Soviet rift, with its accompanying militarization of the border, had been immensely costly to the Soviet Union, serving as a motivating factor in Gorbachev's efforts to defuse the conflict. The same dynamic applied in the 1990s. The Russian Federation was financially unable to maintain a large contingent of troops along the Russian-Chinese border; hostile relations with China were simply unthinkable.

In the 1990s, Russia experienced a demographic crisis manifest in such indicators as rising mortality and falling fertility rates, and an increased incidence of HIV/AIDs, tuberculosis, and drug and alcohol abuse. The deterioration in Russia's human capital placed further constraints on Russia's ability to project power.[19] The key demographic issue in Russia's relationship with China, however, was the population of the Russian Far East and Siberian regions, a situation that reflected the convergence of demography with political, economic, and geographic factors. These sparsely populated areas saw an accelerated decline in population in the 1990s, leading to dire—but not wholly fantastic—forecasts that Russia could lose control of the region west of the Ural mountains. As Putin himself acknowledged in July 2000, without efforts to develop the area, the Russian population would end up speaking Japanese, Chinese, or Korean in the future (see Chapter 6). As long as the Soviet Union was a closed, essentially autarchic state, the status of these areas remained largely a domestic issue. The opening up of the region in the 1990s brought with it the movement of Chinese across the border and pressures to establish economic ties with China and to integrate into the Asian Pacific region. High regional unemployment rates coexisted with serious labor shortages, with Russian citizens unwilling to perform certain jobs. The efforts of the regime to apply a Stolypin solution making use of massive immigration of Russians into the area were ineffectual, leaving the government with few options but to contemplate the use of migrant labor or to resign itself to the economic stagnation of the region.

Even with the loss of the Soviet republics, the Russian Federation remained the world's largest state. Its location, spanning Europe and Asia—apparently conforming to Halford MacKinder's notion of the "heartland"—mandated its geopolitical significance.[20] The physical location and size of China (only slightly smaller than the United States) and its 4,250-kilometer border with Russia similarly ensured the importance of their bilateral relations. If Russia and China had simply been noncontiguous states, located on separate continents, they still would have been motivated to pursue the goal of checking U.S. hegemony. Geography, however, served as a key determinant of the Russian-Chinese relationship that had shaped interactions between the two states from their earliest encounters. The first contacts of imperial China with tsarist Russia differed from those with other Western states because the Russians arrived on land rather than by sea. Geographical contiguity also meant that both states shared interests—sometimes convergent and at other times opposing—in Central Asia. In the final analysis, neither state could ignore the physical reality of the lengthy border.

In the 1990s, Russian weakness was met by Chinese ascendance. As Chapter 4 notes, China's GDP in 2002 was about four times larger than Russia's. A modest nuclear power with an estimated 20–25 intercontinental ballistic missiles, China sought military modernization throughout the decade, emerging (thanks largely to Russia's contribution) with a significantly enhanced air and naval capability. This, combined with a population of an estimated 1.3 billion people, made China a force to be reckoned with at the global and especially the regional level. The Chinese leadership had access to considerably greater resources than its Russian counterpart, with correspondingly more choices in the deliberation of foreign policy goals. China's aggregate power was greater than that of Russia. The politics of economic scarcity left Russia with limited options, dictating that it seek friendly ties with its increasingly powerful neighbor.

Realism and Russian Foreign Policy Toward China

Critics of the realist approach have rightly pointed out that political realism, in its treatment of the state as a unitary actor, falls into anthropomorphism with its depiction of the state as a conscious, directed entity. As Michael McFaul has noted, speaking of Russian foreign policy: "In democracies, 'states' do not have foreign policy objectives. Rather, individual political leaders, parties, and interest groups have foreign policy objectives."[21] These foreign policy objectives, however, are inevitably shaped by the domestic circumstances of the state. On the one hand, adherents to the "innenpolitik" approach, which stresses the influence of domestic factors on foreign policy, can point to the role of internal domestic attributes in structuring foreign policy outcomes.[22] On the other hand, classical realism treats these attributes as components of state power that condition the actions of the state as a unitary rational actor. Viewed from this perspective, classical realism in fact credibly explains certain fundamental aspects of Russian interactions with China in its first decade. Russian foreign policy toward China was conducted according to a highly developed sensitivity to Russia's relative power capabilities. As Robert Jervis has noted, structural constraints impose set foreign policy behaviors upon a state; only when environmental constraints are less severe do differences in behavior emerge that can be explained at the decision-making level.[23] Russia's reduced aggregate power dictated that it seek amicable ties with China. The consensual agreement among Russia's political elites indicated that this policy could not be explained with reference to ideological preferences or special group interests. In this sense, the broad outline of Russian foreign policy toward China conformed to assumptions of classical realism, with its focus on rational state behavior. Despite the lack of institutionalization in foreign policy administration, Russian foreign policy toward China in its first decade was essentially pragmatic and purposeful, based on an assessment of Russia's need for security as a prerequisite to the goal of national rejuvenation.[24]

Neorealist Assessments

With the collapse of the Soviet Union and the demise of the Cold War, many observers welcomed the coming of a "new world order" based on international institutions and global interdependence. As neorealist Kenneth Waltz commented: "Some students of international politics believe that realism is obsolete."[25] This perspective was obviously not shared by Waltz or other adherents to neorealism who continued to maintain that systemic factors, specifically the uneven distribution of power capabilities, were the key to understanding international politics.[26] Indeed, the interactions between Russia and China in the international realm conformed closely to basic precepts of neorealist analysis. Both states displayed an acute awareness of the distribution of power in the international system, as well as their relative positions in the global hierarchy. Russia and China, true to neorealist predictions, sought to challenge the unipolar world system through the establishment of a new balance of power based on multipolarity. As Chapter 7 indicates, the two states united in an effort to constrain the predominant power of the United States in the international order. Their intent to work to establish a multipolar world order first appeared in the 1994 Russian-Chinese joint communiqué and was reiterated in subsequent documents signed by the presidents of the two states. The occasions in which either Russia or China appeared to veer from this quest indicated, on closer examination, the controlling role exercised by the United States over the international economic order and the global economic institutions. Chinese opposition to the NATO air strikes on Yugoslavia, for example, did not prevent Premier Zhu Rongji from traveling to Washington in April 1999 in the hopes of striking a final deal on China's admittance to the World Trade Organization (WTO). Putin's bandwagoning movements toward the United States in the aftermath of the September 11, 2001, terrorist attacks appeared to be based on a pragmatic recognition that the United States served as a gatekeeper to entrance into global economic institutions and integration into the global capitalist marketplace. In these circumstances, the Chinese and Russian leaderships acquiesced to the reality of U.S. preponderance. But that reality also contributed to their motivation to work, within circumscribed limits, toward the construction of counterweights to U.S. hegemony.

There is no doubt that Russian-Chinese interactions on international issues were motivated by calculations of the systemic distribution of power. The neorealist approach is convincing in its portrayal of Russian-Chinese efforts to constrain U.S. hegemony. Nonetheless, the neorealist explanation in itself is not sufficient to account for the emergence of the Russian-Chinese relationship. The problem of geostrategic assessments has not been that they are inaccurate, but that they have typically been reductionist in relying on systemic explanations as the major determinant of the Russian-Chinese relationship. This tendency was exacerbated by the geostrategic orientation of Russian analysts who, continuing in the Soviet tradition, were reluctant to discard the fantasy of Russia as a great power.[27] U.S. commentary, moreover, also focused on the geostrategic implications of Russian interactions with China, to the exclusion of other aspects of the relationship. Thus, for example, the *New York Times* editorial on the July 2001 Friendship Treaty was entitled "Triangular Diplomacy," evoking vocabulary from the Nixon era.[28] This perspective neglects the role played by bilateral—and to a lesser extent regional—factors in the evolution of Russian-Chinese relations.

Why the Strategic Partnership?

Despite their contiguous location, Russia and China had distinctly separate cultural traditions, with few convergent links. The political legacy of Marxism-Leninism separated as well as united the two states. In the 1990s, Russian leaders were attempting to disavow the Marxist-Leninist heritage, which China at least in theory formally upheld. Even the expressed interest of some Russian political parties, such as the Communist Party and Civic Union, in China as a successful model of economic growth indicated a highly selective—in fact distorted—appraisal of the Chinese experience that downplayed the extent to which China had abandoned state planning for capitalist practice. An aging group of Chinese elites could lay claim to a knowledge of the Soviet Union as a result of their personal experiences during the 1950s, but the majority of Chinese directed their focus on the outside world to the United States and its Western allies.

The impetus to the development of ties between Russia and China did not derive from a shared sense of values and norms, but from an awareness on both sides—sometimes reluctantly arrived at—that a cordial relationship conformed to their national interests. As previously noted, a number of analysts considered the Russian-Chinese relationship in systemic terms, based on calculations of counterbalancing U.S. unilateralism. An alternative explanation, rooted in domestic considerations, was to view Russian arms sales to China as the cornerstone of the partnership.[29] The Russian transfer of weapons and their related technologies to China did serve to increase linkages between the two states. As Chapter 5 notes, Russian-Chinese military relations, absent of their commercial impetus, were limited in substantive content. However, the evolution of the strategic relationship between Russia and China is not amenable to a single-factor explanation.

The emphasis placed on Russia and China as strategic partners in the international realm or as regional actors working to influence security outcomes in Central Asia tended to overshadow the importance of the Russian-Chinese relationship at the bilateral level. In fact, bilateral concerns constituted the core issues of Russian interactions with China. In the first instance, the two states were inextricably linked by the fate of geography, which provided the physical context of their relationship. In the second, Russian foreign policy behavior toward China was conditioned by Russia's domestic constraints, notably its economic weakness, which compelled it toward a harmonious relationship with China. The essential resolution of the border conflict and the demilitarization of the Russian-Chinese border were of key importance to Russia in guaranteeing security along the 4,250-kilometer border.

Compared to Russia, China's leaders operated in a less constricted environment, which gave them a correspondingly larger range of options as to the delineation of foreign policy objectives. Fortunately for Russia, Chinese foreign policy was rooted in a pragmatic appreciation of the need to place foreign policy goals in the service of the national quest for economic modernization. China's leaders had no interest in diverting funds to maintain high troop levels along the Russian-Chinese border, or in policies that might increase the chances for instability in the border regions. Furthermore, the establishment of cordial ties with Russia proved to be advantageous to China in other foreign policy venues. Russian cooperation was vital to China's efforts to establish the Shanghai Cooperation Organization as a regional security structure in Central Asia. Russian arms sales aided in the modernization of China's air and naval capabilities and bolstered China's status as a regional power, placing increased pressure on Taiwan and the states of Southeast Asia. As it became evident that the United States had no intention of accepting Russia as an equal partner in the international arena, the Russian leadership returned to geostrategic assessments of the balance of power that pitted Russia with China against the United States. Thus, systemic factors relating to the global distribution of power prevailed over the collapse of the communist order, as China turned out to be less isolated than originally envisioned.

An Enduring Partnership?

Efforts to predict the course of the Russian-Chinese relationship are peril-
ous, as its future evolution will be determined by the interaction of a series of
internal domestic and external international factors. Both Russia and China
face serious economic and demographic problems that will test the ability of
their leaderships. China has moved further along the capitalist road than
Russia, but both states seek a successful transition to the market economy.
The collapse of the communist system presents a post-communist leadership
in Russia with the daunting task of constructing a new political, economic,
and social order. The demise of the same edifice, however, burdens the ostensibly still-communist leadership in China with the challenge of maintaining its position as a viable representative of an almost obsolete political system.
The international system is still in the process of transformation following
the end of the Cold War. For the next several decades, however, barring
cataclysmic events, the preeminent position of the United States as a unilateral superpower seems assured.

At present, two issues appear to be of particular importance regarding the
future development of the Russian relationship with China. First, the gap
between Russian and Chinese aggregate power appears likely to widen in
the following decades, with Russia increasingly inferior to China in terms of
relative power capabilities. For the past several decades, China has placed a
priority on the maintenance of stability as a foreign policy objective. Whether
China, having succeeded in the task of national modernization, would turn
to a more assertive, possibly aggressive, foreign policy strategy, is a matter
of obvious potential concern for Russia. As many analysts have noted, Russian arms sales to China are contributing to the military prowess of a potential future competitor.[30] Less attention, however, has been paid to the role of
Russia's nuclear arsenal as a deterrent to Chinese aspirations. In the 1990s,
the Russian leadership, realizing Russia's declining strength in conventional
weaponry, turned to nuclear weapons as the main means of safeguarding its
security. According to the April 2000 Russian Federation Military Doctrine,
nuclear weapons were seen "as a factor in deterring aggression," which the
Russian Federation reserved the right to use "in response to large-scale aggression utilizing conventional weapons in situations critical to the national
security of the Russian Federation."[31] Russian arms sales to China were an
evident example of the subordination of long-range security concerns to short-
term economic expediency. At the same time, the Russian leadership presumably calculated that arms and technology transfers to China did not
constitute a national security threat, not because of their "eternal friendship"
but due to the continued existence of Russia's nuclear capability.[32]

Nonetheless, an ascendant China, assuming a preeminent position in the Asian Pacific region, would place considerable pressure on Russia, quite apart from the overt use of military means. In this context, the second key issue in Russia's future interactions with China is the status of the Russian Far East, Transbaikal, and Siberian regions. Russia's claim on these far-flung areas is tenuous, both on historical, political, and economic grounds. China's historical case is not especially strong either, but geography, along with Chinese political and economic dominance, guarantees China's increased influence in the region. The Russian leadership faces a serious, almost overwhelming, task. Russia's imperative need is to institute a policy of economic development in these areas, which will incorporate them into the Russian Federation as constituent participant units and not as semi-colonial outposts. A Soviet-style economic autarchy is no longer a possibility for the region, which faces integration into the global economy. The continued erosion of Russian control in these areas will invariably rebound to the advantage of China.

Simultaneously, a domestic policy created for the development of the Russian Far East and Transbaikal areas must include a realistic appraisal of its external relations with neighboring states in the Asian Pacific region. Russia is dependent on Chinese cooperation in order to institute a workable migration policy, which will inevitably bring increased numbers of Chinese into the area. The opening up of the region to forms of foreign economic cooperation and investment (which will presumably be mandated in any agreement Russia makes for accession to the WTO) also means an increased Chinese economic presence. As a pragmatic matter, Russia must seek to expand its economic linkages with other Asian states—notably Japan and South Korea—to prevent the area from turning into an economic appendage of China. But there is no escaping the fate imposed on Russia by geography, which means that Russia cannot avoid encounters with China.

Russia's weakness does not mandate that the Russian leadership adopt a policy of slavish subservience to China. But it does underscore the critical importance for Russia of effective leadership and skillful diplomacy in its interactions with China, both on matters dealing with Russia in Asia and on overall issues of Russian-Chinese relations. In its first decade, the Russian Federation established, assessed in an aggregate context, a successful foreign policy relationship with China, distinguished by its pragmatic attention to Russian interests. The challenge for the Russian Federation is to maintain this legacy in the future in its foreign policy interaction with the People's Republic of China.

Appendix

Treaty of Good-Neighborly Friendship and Cooperation Between the People's Republic of China and the Russian Federation

The People's Republic of China and the Russian Federation (hereinafter referred to as "the two parties to the treaty"), Based on the historical tradition of good-neighborly friendship between their two peoples, Holding that the Sino-Russian joint declarations and statements signed by their two leaders between 1992 and 2000 are of great significance in developing their bilateral relations, Firmly believing that consolidating friendship, good-neighborliness, and mutual cooperation between the two countries is in the fundamental interest of their peoples and helps to preserve Asian and world peace, security, and stability, Reiterating their commitments undertaken under the "UN Charter" and other international treaties in which they participate, Hoping to promote the establishment of a fair and rational new international order based on observing the universally acknowledged principles and norms of international law, Working to raise relations between the two countries to a totally new level, And resolving that the friendship between their peoples will pass down for all generations, Are agreed on the following:

Article 1. The two parties to the treaty will enduringly and comprehensively develop a strategic cooperation partnership of good-neighborliness, friendship, cooperation, and trust as equals, in accordance with the universally acknowledged principles and norms of international law and with the principles of mutual respect for sovereignty and territorial integrity, mutual nonaggression, mutual noninterference in internal affairs, mutual benefit as equals, and peaceful coexistence.

Article 2. The two parties will not use force or the threat of force in their mutual relations, nor will they adopt economic or other means of putting pressure on each other; differences between them can only be resolved by peaceful means in accordance with the provisions of the "UN Charter" and other universally acknowledged principles and norms of international law. The two parties reiterate that they undertake not to be the first to use nuclear weapons, nor will they aim strategic nuclear missiles at each other.

Article 3. The two parties respect each other's political, economic, social, and cultural development paths chosen according to their national condition, and will ensure that relations between the two countries will remain enduringly stable.

Article 4. China supports Russia's policy on issues of preserving the national unity of the Russian Federation and its territorial integrity. Russia supports China's policies on issues of preserving the national unity and territorial integrity of the People's Republic of China.

Article 5. Russia reiterates that there is no change in its principled stance on the Taiwan issue expounded in the political documents signed and approved by the two heads of state between 1992 and 2000. Russia holds that there is only one China in the world, and the government of the People's Republic of China is the sole legitimate government representing the whole of China, and that Taiwan is an indivisible part of China. Russia opposes Taiwan independence in any form.

Article 6. The two parties point out with satisfaction there are no territorial demands between them, and they are resolved to actively work to turn the building of their border into a border of everlasting peace and friendship for all generations. The two parties will observe the international principles on the inviolability of territory and national borders and will strictly abide by the national border between them. In accordance with the "PRC-USSR Agreement on the Eastern Section of the Sino-Soviet Border" signed on 16 May 1991, the two parties will continue to hold negotiations to resolve questions of border demarcation on which Sino-Russian unanimity has not yet been reached through consultation. Prior to these issues being resolved, the two parties will maintain the status quo in sections of the border on which unanimity has not yet been reached through consultation.

Article 7. The two parties will adopt measures in accordance with current agreements to enhance trust in the military field and mutual reduction of military forces in the border regions. The two parties will expand and deepen measures for trust in the military field, so as to strengthen their own security and consolidate regional and international security. Based on the principle of reasonable sufficiency of weapons and armed forces, the two parties will make efforts to ensure their national security. The military and military technology cooperation carried out by the two parties in accordance with the relevant agreements is not aimed at any third country.

Article 8. Neither party will participate in any alliance or bloc which damages the sovereignty, security, and territorial integrity of the other party, and will not adopt any similar action, including not concluding a similar treaty with any third country. Neither party to the treaty will permit a third country to use its territory to damage the national sovereignty, security, and territorial integrity of the other party. Neither party to the treaty will permit the establishment on its territory of an organization or group that harms the sovereignty, security, and territorial integrity of the other party, and will prohibit such activities.

Article 9. If one party to the treaty believes that there is a threat of aggression menacing peace, wrecking peace, and involving its security interests and is aimed at one of the parties, the two parties will immediately make contact and hold consultations in order to eliminate the threat that has arisen.

Article 10. The two parties will use and perfect the mechanism for holding periodic meetings at various levels, and first of all at the highest and high levels, to hold periodic exchanges of views and coordinate their stances on bilateral relations and major and urgent international issues of common concern, so as to strengthen their strategic cooperation partnership of trust as equals.

Article 11. The two parties advocate strict adherence to the universally acknowledged principles and norms of international law, oppose any action of using force to put pressure or intervene under any pretext in the internal affairs of sovereign states, and are ready to actively work to strengthen international peace, stability, development, and cooperation. The two parties oppose actions that may threaten international stability, security, and peace, and will cooperate in preventing international conflicts and in their political solution.

Article 12. The two parties will work together to preserve global strategic balance and security, and will vigorously promote adherence to relevant basic agreements for ensuring the preservation of strategic stability. The two parties will actively promote the process of nuclear disarmament and reduction of chemical weapons, advance the strengthening of the system for banning biological weapons, and take steps to prevent the proliferation of weapons of mass destruction, the means of carrying them, and their related technology.

Article 13. The two parties will step up cooperation in the United Nations and its Security Council and specialized agencies. The two parties will make efforts to strengthen the United Nations as the highest authoritative and most universal international organization in handling international affairs, and especially its core role in peace and development, and ensure the main responsibility of the UN Security Council in the field of preserving international peace and security.

Article 14. The two parties will vigorously promote stability with their peripheral regions, establish an atmosphere of mutual understanding, trust, and cooperation, and spur efforts to establish a mechanism for multilateral cooperation suited to the actual security and cooperation issues in these regions.

Article 15. In accordance with the relevant agreements and other documents between their governments for dealing with creditors' rights and debts, the two parties recognize the legitimate rights and interests regarding assets and other property belonging to one party that is in the territory of the other party.

Article 16. The two parties will carry out cooperation on the basis of mutual benefit in the economic and trade, military technology, science and technology, energy, transport, nuclear power, finance, aviation and space, information technology, and other fields of common interest, promote the development of border and local economic and trade cooperation, and create the necessary good conditions for this in line with their national laws. The two parties will vigorously advance and develop exchanges and cooperation in the fields of culture, education, public health, information, tourism, sports, and legal system.

Article 17. The two parties will carry out cooperation in international financial institutions and economic organizations and forums; in accordance with the provisions of the charters of these institutions, organizations, and forums, they will promote the accession of one party to these institutions of which the other party is already a member (participant country).

Article 18. In accordance with their international obligations and national laws and regulations, the two parties will carry out cooperation in promoting the attainment of human rights and basic freedoms. In accordance with their international obligations and national laws and regulations, the two parties will take effective steps to ensure the legitimate rights and interests of legal and human entities of one party in the territory of the other party, and will provide each other with the necessary assistance in civil and criminal adjudication. The departments concerned of the two parties will, in accordance with their relevant laws, investigate and resolve problems and disputes involving a legal or human entity of one party engaged in cooperation and management activities in the territory of the other party.

Article 19. The two parties will cooperate in protecting and improving the environment, in preventing cross-border pollution, in the fair and rational use of biological resources in waters in the border area and in the north Pacific and border river courses, and will work together to protect rare plants and animals and the natural ecological system in the border areas, and cooperate in preventing natural disasters and major accidents arising from technical causes and in eliminating their consequences.

Article 20. In accordance with their national laws and their international obligations, the two parties will actively cooperate to crack down on terrorism, separatism and extremism, and to crack down on organized crime and criminal activities such as illegal trafficking in narcotics, amphetamines, and weapons. The two parties will cooperate in cracking down on illegal immigration, including illegal traffic in humans through their territory.

Article 21. The two sides attach importance to the development of exchanges and cooperation between their central (federal) legislative and law enforcement organs. The two parties will vigorously promote exchanges and cooperation between their judicial organs.

Article 22. This treaty does not affect the rights and obligations of the two parties as parties to other international treaties, nor is it aimed at any third country.

Article 23. In order to implement this treaty, the two parties will actively advance the framing of treaties in specific fields of interest to both of them.

Article 24. This treaty needs to be ratified, and will come into force on the day that instruments of ratification are exchanged. The exchange will take place in Beijing.

Article 25. This treaty is valid for 20 years. It will be automatically extended for a further five years if, one year before its expiry, neither party has informed the other party in writing that it requests termination, and the treaty will continue in force accordingly.

This treaty is signed in Moscow on 16 July 2001 in two copies, both in Chinese and Russian, and the two languages are equally valid.

> [Signed] Jiang Zemin, on behalf of the People's Republic of China
> Vladimir Putin, on behalf of the Russian Federation.

Source: Xinhua, 16 July 2001 in FBIS-CHI-2001–0716.

Notes

Notes to Chapter 1

1. See Elizabeth Wishnick, *Mending Fences: The Evolution of Moscow's China Policy from Brezhnev to Yeltsin* (Seattle: University of Washington Press, 2001). Wishnick's book examines the shifts in Moscow's relations with China over time, beginning with the Soviet Union's China policy at the nadir of the relationship in 1969. Also Sherman W. Garnett, ed., *Rapprochement or Rivalry?: Russia–China Relations in a Changing Asia* (Washington, DC: Carnegie Institute for International Peace, 2000). The book is a compilation of articles from American, Russian, and Chinese scholars that focuses on aspects of the Russian-Chinese strategic partnership and the Russian Far East. For a Russian perspective, see Dmitri Trenin, *Russia's China Problem* (Moscow: Carnegie Endowment for International Peace, 1999). An earlier version was published in Russian as *Kitaiskaia problema Rossii* (The China problem of Russia) (Moscow: Carnegie Moscow Center, 1998). Also, Alexander Lukin, *The Bear Watches the Dragon: Russia's Perceptions of China and the Evolution of Russian-Chinese Relations Since the Eighteenth Century* (Armonk, NY: M.E. Sharpe, 2003).

2. See F. Stephen Larrabee and Theodore W. Karasik, *Foreign and Security Policy Decisionmaking Under Yeltsin* (Santa Monica, CA: Rand, 1997); Neil Malcolm, Alex Pravda, Roy Allison, and Margot Light, *Internal Factors in Russian Foreign Policy* (Oxford: Oxford University Press, 1996); Neil Malcolm, "Russian Foreign Policy Decision-Making," in Peter Shearman, ed., *Russian Foreign Policy Since 1990* (Boulder, CO: Westview Press, 1995); 23–51; Robert H. Donaldson and Joseph L. Nogee, *The Foreign Policy of Russia: Changing Systems, Enduring Interests*, 2d ed. (Armonk, NY: M.E. Sharpe, 2002), Chapter 5; Roger E. Kanet and Susanne M. Birgerson, "The Domestic-Foreign Policy Linkage in Russian Politics: Nationalist Influences on Russian Foreign Policy," *Communist and Post-Communist Studies* 30, no. 4 (1997): 335–44; and Scott Parish "Chaos in Russian Foreign Policy Decision-Making," *Transition* (17 May 1996): 30–33, 64.

3. By the end of his presidency, Boris Yeltsin's behavior had attained a legendary status, including an episode at Shannon airport in Ireland in 1994 when an apparently inebriated Yeltsin failed to get off the plane, leaving the Irish prime minister and his entourage waiting on the tarmac, and a 1997 appearance in Stockholm where Yeltsin claimed that Japan and Germany possessed nuclear weapons. For a discussion of U.S. president Bill Clinton's interactions with Yeltsin, see Strobe Talbott, *The Russia Hand: A Memoir of Presidential Diplomacy* (New York: Random House, 2002).

4. For further discussion, see Robert H. Donaldson and John A. Donaldson, "The Arms Trade in Russian-Chinese Relations: Identity, Domestic Politics, and Geopolitical Positioning," *International Studies Quarterly* 47, no. 4 (December 2003): 709–32.

5. For a discussion of Russian attitudes toward China, see Lukin, *The Bear Watches the Dragon*, Chapters 4 and 6. Also Trenin, *Russia's China Problem*, 9–10.

6. Yeltsin issued various decrees, for example in November 1992 and in March 1995, specifying the Foreign Ministry the responsible agency for the coordination of foreign policy activity.

7. One exception was the demographer Emil Pain, who served as a presidential advisor to Boris Yeltsin for part of the 1990s.

8. See G. Kireev, "Demarcation of the Border with China," *International Affairs* 45, no. 2 (1999): 98–109; and G. Kireev, "The Serpentine Path to the Shanghai G-5," *International Affairs* 49, no. 3 (2003): 85–92.

9. Russia was not able to establish an organization functionally equivalent to the Chinese Ministry of Foreign Trade and Economic Cooperation (MOFTEC). The Russian Ministry of Foreign Economic Relations (MFER) proved to be a bastion of conservative thinking. In 2002, President Putin was developing a plan to transfer responsibilities for the promotion of foreign economic links from the Economic Development and Trade Ministry (the renamed MFER) to the Foreign Ministry. See Andrei Zolotov, Jr., "Putin Lectures Ambassadors on Policy," *Moscow Times*, 15 July 2002.

10. Evgenii Bazhanov, "Russian Policy Toward China," in Shearman, ed., *Russian Foreign Policy Since 1990*, 166.

11. Rather, elites tended to diverge on the question of how closely to develop ties with China, with the conservatives more likely to advocate an outright alliance. See Lukin, *The Bear Watches the Dragon*, Chapters 4 and 6.

12. See "Zakliuchenie po itogam parlamentskikh slushanii 'o problemakh rossiisko-kitaiskikh otnoshenii i perspectivakh ikh resheniia,'" 25 aprelia 1999 g. (Conclusions on the results of the parliamentary hearings "about problems of Russian-Chinese relations and perspectives of their resolution," 25 April 1994), Committee on International Affairs of the Federation Council and State Duma of the Russian Federation.

13. See Lukin, *The Bear Watches the Dragon*: 287–88.

14. Zhirinovskii, engaging in his usual propensity for provocation and bombast, simultaneously denounced China (along with a host of other states) as the enemy, while calling for the development of ties between Russia and China. His flirtation with Taiwan—encouraged by the Taiwanese leadership—aroused criticism on the part of the Chinese leadership, which protested his visits to Taipei.

15. See Allen S. Whiting, "Chinese Nationalism and Foreign Policy After Deng," *China Quarterly*, no. 142 (June 1995): 295–316; John W. Garver, "The Chinese Communist Party and the Collapse of Soviet Communism," *China Quarterly*, no. 133 (March 1993): 1–26; and David M. Lampton, *"Same Bed, Different Dreams: Managing U.S.–China Relations 1989–2000* (Berkeley and Los Angeles: University of California Press, 2001), Chapter 1.

16. Xinhua, 17 July 2001.

17. Omri, Part 1, no. 59 (25 March 1997).

18. Lampton, *Same Bed, Different Dreams*, 330.

19. Dmitri Trenin, "The China Factor: Challenge and Chance for Russia," in Garnett, ed., *Rapprochement or Rivalry?*, 47.

20. In comparison, the February 1950 treaty signed between the Soviet Union and

China was entitled the Treaty of Friendship, Alliance and Mutual Assistance Between the USSR and the People's Republic of China.

21. For an exposition of this view, see Donaldson and Donaldson, "The Arms Trade in Russian-Chinese Relations"; and Stephen G. Brooks and William C. Wohlforth, "American Primacy in Perspective," *Foreign Affairs* 81, no. 4 (July–August 2002): 28.

22. For a discussion of geostrategic perceptions held by Russian analysts, see Lukin, *The Bear Watches the Dragon*, Chapter 4.

Notes to Chapter 2

1. For an extended discussion of Russian-Chinese interactions in the border regions, see S.C.M Paine, *Imperial Rivals: China, Russia and Their Disputed Frontier* (Armonk, NY: M.E. Sharpe, 1996); also John P. LeDonne, *The Russian Empire and the World, 1700–1917: The Geopolitics of Expansion and Containment* (New York: Oxford University Press, 1997), 155–223.

2. John K. Fairbank, Edwin O. Reischauer, and Albert M. Craig, *East Asia: The Modern Transformation* (Boston: Houghton Mifflin, 1964), 43–55, 171–73.

3. For a discussion of the Maoist strategy see, Benjamin I. Schwartz, *Chinese Communism and the Rise of Mao* (New York: Harper and Row, 1951), Chapter 13; Stuart R. Schram, *The Political Thought of Mao Tse-tung*, rev. ed. (New York: Frederick A. Praeger, 1969), 15–149.

4. See Richard C. Thornton, *China: A Political History, 1917–1980* (Boulder, CO: Westview, 1983), 95–105. On the other hand, as Thornton (p. 132) also notes, Mao refused to comply with the Soviet request that he engage in combat with the Japanese in North China after the German invasion of the Soviet Union. For a discussion of the CCP's relationship to Moscow, arguing that the CCP was more submissive than previously believed, see John Lewis Gaddis, *We Now Know: Rethinking Cold War History* (New York: Clarendon Press, 1997), 58–60; and, more extensively, Michael M. Sheng, *Battling Western Imperialism: Mao, Stalin and the United States* (Princeton, NJ: Princeton University Press, 1998).

5. Harriet L. Moore, *Soviet Far Eastern Policy 1931–1945* (Princeton, NJ: Princeton University Press, 1945), 266.

6. See Adam Ulam, *Expansion and Coexistence: Soviet Foreign Policy 1917–73*, 2d ed. (New York: Praeger, 1974), 483–92; Harvey W. Nelson, *Power and Insecurity: Beijing, Moscow and Washington, 1949–1988* (Boulder, CO: Lynne Reinner, 1989), 4–5; Robert M. Slusser, "Soviet Far Eastern Policy, 1945–1950," in Yonosuke Nagai and Akira Iriye, eds., *The Origins of the Cold War in Asia* (New York: Columbia University Press, 1977), 123–46. Brian Murray, making use of recently declassified documents in the Russian archives, concluded that the materials generally confirm accounts detailing the lack of Soviet support for the CCP in the mid- to late 1940s. Brian Murray, "Stalin, the Cold War, and the Division of China: A Multi-Archival Mystery," *Working Paper No. 12*, Cold War International History Project, Woodrow Wilson International Center for Scholars (June 1995). The contrary view, stressing the close relationship between Mao and Stalin, is set out in Sheng, *Battling Western Imperialism*, and Michael Sheng, "The United States, the Chinese Communist Party, and the Soviet Union, 1948–1950: A Reappraisal," *Pacific Historical Review* 63, no. 4 (November 1994): 521–37.

7. Mao Tse-tung. *Selected Works of Mao Tse-tung*, vol. 4 (Peking: Foreign Languages Press, 1969), 415.

8. For the text of the treaty, see Max Beloff, *Soviet Policy in the Far East, 1944–1951* (Oxford: Oxford University Press, 1953), 260–67. While the Soviet Union surrendered its territorial claims in Manchuria, it did pressure China to yield to joint-stock ventures in Xinjiang province in mineral extraction, agreements that were not nullified until the death of Stalin. By Mao's own account, negotiations between the Soviet Union and China were arduous, with Stalin reluctant to relinquish territorial gains. See John Gittings, "New Light on Mao: His View of the World," *China Quarterly* 50 (October–December 1974): 759. Also Tim Weiner, "Stalin–Mao Alliance Was Uneasy, Newly Released Papers Show," *New York Times*, 10 December 1995: 8.

9. See Donald S. Zagoria, *The Sino-Soviet Conflict, 1956–1961* (New York: Atheneum, 1966); William E. Griffith, *The Sino-Soviet Rift* (Cambridge, MA: MIT Press, 1964); G.F. Hudson, Richard Lowenthal, and Roderick MacFarquhar, *The Sino-Soviet Dispute* (New York: Praeger, 1961); Herbert J. Ellison, ed., *The Sino-Soviet Conflict: A Global Perspective* (Seattle: University of Washington Press, 1982); Dennis J. Doolin, *Territorial Claims in the Sino-Soviet Conflict: Documents and Analysis*, Hoover Institution Studies, No. 7, 1965; and Douglas T. Stuart and William T. Tow, *China, the Soviet Union, and the West* (Boulder, CO: Westview Press, 1982).

10. The Chinese also asserted that Mongolia should be considered part of China, a claim that China had surrendered in the 1950 Treaty of Friendship, Alliance, and Mutual Assistance.

11. See, for example, Nelson, *Power and Insecurity*, 72–73; Thornton, *China: A Political History*, 344–45; Arkady Shevchenko, *Breaking with Moscow* (New York: Knopf, 1985), 165–68; Lowell Dittmer, *Sino-Soviet Normalization and Its International Implications, 1945–1990* (Seattle: University of Washington Press, 1992), 189–94; and Elizabeth Wishnick, *Mending Fences: The Evolution of Moscow's China Policy from Brezhnev to Yeltsin* (Seattle: University of Washington Press, 2001), 34–36.

12. Li Zhisui, *The Private Life of Chairman Mao* (New York: Random House, 1994), 565; also see Gerald Segal, "China and the Great Power Triangle," *China Quarterly* 83 (September 1980): 490–509.

13. Considerably more attention has been paid by Western analysts to the unfolding of the Sino-Soviet split than to its repair. For discussions of Sino-Soviet relations in the 1970s and 1980s, see Wishnick, *Mending Fences*; Dittmer, *Sino-Soviet Normalization*; Stuart and Tow, *China, the Soviet Union and the West*; Thomas G. Hart, *Sino-Soviet Relations: Reexamining the Prospects for Normalization* (Aldershot, England: Gower, 1987); and Herbert J. Ellison, "Changing Sino-Soviet Relations," *Problems of Communism* 36 (May–June 1987): 17–29.

14. *Pravda* and *Izvestia*, 29 July 1986, 1–3, in *Current Digest of the Soviet Press*, vol. 38, no. 30, 27 (August 1986): 1–8. In addition, Gorbachev offered Soviet support in the construction of a railroad linking Urumqi with Kazakhstan, invited the Chinese to participate in Soviet space exploration, and indicated Soviet acceptance of China's request that the main navigation channel serve as the boundary line at the disputed border in the Amur River.

15. Gorbachev was formally invited to China in February 1989 during Soviet foreign minister Eduard Shevardnadze's visit to Beijing. The Vietnamese announced on April 5, 1989, that they would withdraw all their troops from Cambodia by the end of September 1989.

16. This interpretation was given to Gorbachev in his meeting with Zhao Ziyang but was also articulated by Chinese premier Li Peng. See Moscow Domestic Service, 16 May 1989, in FBIS-SOV-89–093, 16 May 1989, 21–22; and comments by Li Peng in Moscow Television Service, 16 May 1989, in FBIS-SOV-89–093, 16 May 1989, 20–21; also see Willy Wo-Lap Lam, *South China Morning Post*, 17 May 1989, no. 16, p. 1, in FBIS-CHI-89–094, 17 May 1989.

17. Tass, 18 May 1989, in FBIS-SOV-89–095, 18 May 1989, 16–18.

18. For a discussion of Western interpretations of the Sino-Soviet dispute, see Donald W. Treadgold, "Alternative Western Views of the Sino-Soviet Conflict," in Herbert J. Ellison, ed., *The Sino-Soviet Conflict*, 325–55. Perhaps Richard Lowenthal presents the most fully developed ideological interpretation of the dispute. See his *World Communism: The Disintegration of a Secular Faith* (New York: Oxford University Press, 1964); and Richard Lowenthal, "Diplomacy and Dialectics of a Dispute," in Hudson, Lowenthal, and MacFarquhar, *The Sino-Soviet Dispute*, 9–34.

19. "Russia: Ten Years After," at www.ceip.org/files/programs/russia/tenyears/panel12.htm.

20. Moscow Television Service, 6 June 1989, in FBIS-SOV-89–197S, 6 June 1989.

21. "Gorbachev Expresses Regret on China Strife," *New York Times*, 16 June 1989, A9; Frances X. Cline, "Gorbachev Mutes His Voice on China," *New York Times*, 13 June 1989, A5.

22. See Patrick Lescot, AFP, 28 December 1989, in FBIS-CHI-89–249, 29 December 1989; Chang Chuan, "Wang Zhen Shouts Abuse at Gorbachev," *Cheng Ming*, no. 148 (1 February 1990): 8, in FBIS-CHI-90–017, 25 January 1990; Willy Wo-Lap Lam, "Deng Forecasts Gorbachev Downfall," *South China Morning Post*, 25 January 1990, 1, in FBIS-CHI-90–017, 25 January 1990; Lo Ping, "Notes on a Northern Journey: Top-Secret Documents of the CPC on Repudiating Gorbachev," *Cheng Ming*, no. 148 (1 February 1990): 6–8; and Lo Ping, "Notes on a Northern Journey: Lamentations of a Secret Document," *Cheng Ming*, no. 150 (1 April 1990): 6–8, in FBIS-CHI-90–064, 3 April 1990.

23. Kyodo, 25 July 1989, in FBIS-CHI-89–141, 25 July 1989.

24. AFP, 28 December 1989; also see Lo Ping, "Top-Secret Documents of the CPC."

25. *The Economist*, 3 March 1990, 31.

26. See Tso Ni, "Chinese Pilots Will Be Trained in the Soviet Union," *Cheng Ming*, no. 163 (1 May 1991): 15–16, in FBIS-CHI-91–084; Lo Ping, "Notes on the Northern Journey: Communist China Set to Establish PRC-USSR-DPRK Alliance," *Cheng Ming*, no. 150 (1 June 1991): 16–18, in FBIS-CHI-91–108, 5 June 1991; and Ho Po-shih, "Central Document Initiates Across-the-Board Adjustment of China's Policy Toward Soviet Union," *Tangtai*, no. 3 (15 June 1991): 18, in FBIS-CHI-91–121, 24 June 1991.

27. Xinhua, 19 May 1991.

28. "A New Milestone of Sino-Soviet Good-Neighborly and Friendly Relations—Congratulating General Secretary Jiang Zemin's Completely Successful Visit to the Soviet Union," *Renmin Ribao*, 20 May 1991, in FBIS-CHI-91–098, 21 May 1991.

29. Reports from Japan fueled this speculation by indicating that the leaders of the coup (as well as several thousand KGB and CPSU functionaries) had sought to flee to China following its failure, reports denied by the Chinese authorities. In particular, the Hong Kong press had a field day dealing with allegations of CCP complicity. See for example, Lo Ping, "Notes on the Northern Journey: CPC Secretly Assists Gang of

Eight in Soviet Union," *Cheng Ming*, no. 167 (1 September 1991): 8–10, in FBIS-CHI-91–173, 6 September 1991; Tsai Yung-mei, "Beijing's Reactions to Great Changes in Soviet Union," *Kai Fang*, no. 15 (15 September 1991): 22–24 in FBIS-CHI-91–189, 30 September 1991; Ouyang Wei, "Joy, Anger, Sorrow of CPC in Reaction to Soviet Coup as Anti-Peaceful Evolution is Stepped Up," *Pai Hsing*, no. 248 (16 September 1991): 6–7, in FBIS-CHI-91–183, 20 September 1991; Ting Mei, "CPC Gets Involved in Soviet Coup," *Chiushih Nientai*, no. 260 (1 September 1991): 20, in FBIS-CHI-91–171, 4 September 1991; Ho Po-shih, "CPC Issues Successive Emergency Circulars Ordering Entire Party to Guard Against Changes," *Tangtai*, no. 6 (15 September 1991): 8–12, in FBIS-CHI-91–185, 24 September 1991; and "Soviet Coup Shocks Beijing: CPC Members Consider Resignation from Party, Jiang Zemin Criticized by Deng Xiaoping for Wavering," *Pai Hsing*, no. 249 (1 October 1991): 3–4, in FBIS-CHI-91–195, 8 October 1991. Also see *Izvestia*, 5 September 1991: 3, in FBIS-SOV-91–172, 5 September 1991.

30. Xinhua, 20 August 1991.

31. John Kohut, *South China Morning Post*, 23 August 1991.

32. For further discussion, see Allen S. Whiting, "Chinese Nationalism and Foreign Policy After Deng," *China Quarterly*, no. 142, (June 1995): 295–316; John W. Garver, "The Chinese Communist Party and the Collapse of Soviet Communism," *China Quarterly* 133 (March 1993): 1–26; and David M. Lampton, *Same Bed, Different Dreams: Managing U.S.–China Relations 1989–2000* (Berkeley and Los Angeles: University of California Press, 2001), Chapter 1.

33. Ho Po-shih, "What Does CPC Say Internally in Wake of Changing Situation in Soviet Union?" *Tangtai*, no. 10 (15 January 1992): 41–52, in FBIS-CHI-92–026, 7 February 1992.

34. China extended diplomatic recognition to Latvia, Lithuania, and Estonia in early September 1991, after their declarations of independence in the wake of the failed August coup attempt.

35. Interview with Stanislav A. Mouravsky and Anatoly A. Slusar, Foreign Policy Association, Moscow, Russia, 28 June 1994.

36. Itar-Tass, 16 September 1992; also see Alexander Lukin, *The Bear Watches the Dragon: Russia's Perceptions of China and the Evolution of Russian–Chinese Relations Since the Eighteenth Century* (Armonk, NY: M.E. Sharpe, 2003), 267–71. Following the collapse of the Soviet Union, Taiwanese diplomacy sought to gain a foothold in the newly emergent sovereign states of the region, achieving its greatest success in establishing consular ties with Latvia (subsequently broken by Latvia in 1994 in exchange for diplomatic recognition with the PRC). For further discussion, see Czeslaw Tubilewicz, "The Baltic States in Taiwan's Post–Cold War Flexible Diplomacy," *Europe–Asia Studies* 54, no. 5 (2002): 791–810.

37. Moscow Russian Television Network, 18 December 1992, in FBIS-SOV-92–245, 21 December 1992; Kyodo, 18 December 1992, in FBIS-CHI-92–245, 21 December 1992.

38. See Yeltsin's comments in Moscow Russian Television Network, 18 December 1992, in FBIS-SOV-92–245, 21 December 1992; and R. Zaripov, A. Kabannikov, and V. Shutkevich, "The Forbidden City Can Rest Easy: It Seems Boris Nikolayevich Has Promised the Chinese Spare Parts for Su-27 Fighters," *Komsomolskaia Pravda*, 19 December 1992, 5 in FBIS-SOV-92–245, 21 December 1992.

39. Itar-Tass, 19 December 1992.

40. Xinhua, 3 September 1994.

41. Itar-Tass, 28 June 1994.

42. Xinhua, 3 September 1994.

43. The Dalai Lama visited Russia in 1994 as a religious leader of Russian Buddhists, but his subsequent efforts to return were rejected by the Russian government.

44. Chinese president Jiang Zemin visited Moscow in May 1995 in an unofficial capacity (although he did meet with Boris Yeltsin during his stay), attending ceremonies commemorating the fiftieth anniversary of the allied victory in World War II.

45. Xinhua, 25 April 1996.

46. Xinhua, 23 April 1997.

47. Itar-Tass, 23 November 1998.

48. See, for example, the Russian-Chinese 1999 joint statement. Itar-Tass, 10 December 1999.

49. Konstantin Makienko, "Preliminary Estimates of Russian Performance in Military-Technical Cooperation with Foreign States in 2000," *Eksport Vooruzheniy* (January–February 2001): 5.

50. Three islands were excluded from the 1991 border agreement: Bolshoi Ussuriiskii and Tarabarovskii islands in the region of Khabarovsk in the Amur River, and Bolshoi island in the upper reaches of the Argun River in Chita oblast.

51. The Russian-Iranian treaty was followed by a military-technical agreement in October 2001 providing for extensive transfers of arms and technology to Iran.

52. "Vos'maia vstrecha" (The eighth meeting), *Rossiiskaia Gazeta*, 14 July 2001: 1.

53. Simon Saradzhyan, "Moscow Mending Ties with Old Ally Beijing," *Moscow Times*, 26 February 2001. Also interview with Dmitri Trenin, Deputy Director, Carnegie Moscow Center, Moscow, Russia, 26 January, 2001.

54. "Vos'maia vstrecha."

55. Xinhua, 17 July 2001.

56. Xinhua, 27 May 2003.

57. Konstantin Makienko, *Voenno-tekhnicheskoe sotrudnichestvo Rossii i KNR v 1992–2002 godakh: dostizheniia, tendentsii, perspektivy* (Military-technical cooperation between Russia and the PRC 1992–2002: results, tendencies and prospects) Document Number 2, Russian Office of the Center for Defense Analysis, October 2002, 40–45.

Notes to Chapter 3

1. S.C.M. Paine, *Imperial Rivals: China, Russia and Their Disputed Frontier* (Armonk, NY: M.E. Sharpe, 1996), 352.

2. For a copy of the agreement see "Soglashenie ot 16 Maia 1991 goda mezhdu Soiuzom Sovetskikh Sotsialisticheskikh Respublik i Kitaiskoi Narodnoi Respublikoi o sovetsko-kitaiskoi gosudarstvennoi granitse na ee Vostochnoi chasti" (The agreement of May 16, 1991, between the Union of Soviet Socialist Republics and the People's Republic of China on the Soviet-Chinese state border on its Eastern part) in *Nekotorye problemy demarkatsii rossiisko-kitaiskoi granitsy, 1991–1997 gg. Sbornik statei i dokumentov* (Some problems of the demarcation of the Russian-Chinese border 1991–1997: A collection of articles and documents), (Moscow: Nevavisimaia Gazeta, 1997): 14–21.

3. The first two islands have an overall area of some 350 square kilometers; the third island is about 58 square kilometers in area. Damanskii island was allotted to the Chinese.

4. The agreement was also ratified in February 1992 by the Standing Committee of the National People's Congress.

5. See G. Kireeev, "Demarcation of the Border with China," *International Affairs* 45, no. 2 (1999): 98–109.

6. In the Khanka district of Primorskii krai, the border was adjusted so that China received 2.6 square kilometers of land from Russia, while Russia acquired 0.9 square kilometers, of land from China. In the Ussuri district, the border marker was moved several hundred meters to China's advantage. See Kireev, "Demarcation"; Georgi F. Kunadze, "Border Problems Between Russia and Its Neighbors," in Gilbert Rozman, Mikhail G. Nosov, and Koji Watanabe, eds., *Russia and East Asia: The 21st Century Security Environment*, vol. 3. EastWest Institute (Armonk, NY: M.E. Sharpe, 1999), 133–49; and Hiroshi Kimura, Shaojun Li, and Il-Dong Koh, "Frontiers Are the Razor's Edge: Russia's Borders with its Eastern Neighbors," in Rozman, Nosov, and Watanabe, eds., *Russia and East Asia*, 150–71.

7. These protocols, approved by the Boundary Demarcation Commission in April 1999, formally established the boundary on the eastern and the western sections of the Sino-Russian border.

8. See Akihiro Iwashita, "The Influence of Local Russian Initiatives on Relations with China: Border Demarcation and Regional Partnership," *Acta Slavica IAPONICA* 19 (2002): 1–18; Menkesili island is, in fact, not an island but a sandbar. Also see Yutaka Akino, "Moscow's New Perspectives on Sino-Russian Relations," at http://src.-h.slav.hokudai.ac.jp.

9. Xinhua, 18 July 2000.

10. Itar-Tass, 22 January 2003.

11. Xinhua, 27 May 2003.

12. Iwashita, "The Influence of Local Russian Initiatives."

13. A major difference between the two territorial issues is that the Kurile islands are inhabited, while Russians did not reside on the river islands on a permanent basis. For a comparison of the Russian-Chinese and Russian-Japanese border negotiations, see Kimura, Li, and Koh, "Frontiers Are the Razor's Edge," 160–64.

14. See Akino, "Moscow's New Perspectives," and Iwashita, "The Influence of Local Russian Initiatives." For further discussion of the border issue in Russian-Chinese relations, see Akihiro Iwashita, "Opyt prigranichnogo sotrudnichestva Rossii i KNR za poslednie 10 let" (The experience of border cooperation of Russia and the PRC in the past 10 years), in Akihiro Iwashita, ed., *The Sino-Russian "Strategic Partnership," Current Views from the Border and Beijing*, Slavic Research Center Occasional Papers No. 91, Slavic Research Center, Hokkaido University (2003): 55–75; Akihiro Iwashita, "The Russo-Chinese 'Strategic Partnership' and Border Negotiations: Then and Now," *Bulletin of the Graduate Schools*, Yamuguchi Prefectural University, no. 2 (2001): 1–10. Readers of Japanese are referred to Akihiro Iwashita, *Chu Ro kokkyou 4000 kilo* (The Sino-Russian 4000 kilometer border) (Tokyo: Kadokawa Shoten, 2003).

15. *Izvestia*, 22 April 1992, in FBIS-SOV-92–079, 23 April 1992.

16. With the collapse of the Soviet Union, moreover, the Russian military removed a large number of troops and equipment from the CIS states, including along the border areas.

17. In addition, Russia was allowed 3,810 battle tanks, 5,670 armored infantry fighting vehicles, 4,510 artillery systems of 122-mm and higher caliber, 96 tactical missile launchers, 290 combat aircraft, 434 helicopter gunships, 680 armed infantry

fighting vehicles for border troops, and 70 combat helicopters. G. Kireev, "The Serpentine Path to the Shanghai G-5," *International Affairs* 49, no. 3 (2003): 90.

18. In November 2001, Vitaly Vorobyev, head of the joint delegation of the CIS monitoring group on compliance with the arms reduction agreements, indicated that all the involved states were maintaining levels of military hardware and personnel below the established limits. Itar-Tass, 10 November 2001.

19. Ilya Bulavinov, "Boundless Friendship of Russia and China," *Kommersant*, 25 April 1997, in EVP Press Digest 04/25/97 (Part 1, 2).

20. "Out of Control," *Moscow Times*, 11 December 2001. According to Shramchenko, military radars once lost track of a plane used by Russian leaders during a flight to Japan for an hour and a half.

21. Galina Vitkovskaya, "Russia: Cross-Border Migration in the Russian Far East," *Writenet Country Papers*, October 1997 at www.unhcr.ch/refworld/country/writenet/wrirus03.htm.

22. Felix K. Chang, "The Unraveling of Russia's Far Eastern Power," *Orbis* 43, no. 2 (Spring 1999): 267.

23. Itar-Tass, 23 October 1998.

24. In 2000, when Uzbekistan attended the meeting as an observer, the organization adopted the nomenclature "Shanghai Forum."

25. Some of these activities had already been initiated before the Dushanbe meeting, including the first meeting of foreign ministers, the appointment of special envoys, and the initial development of links to coordinate law enforcement activities.

26. For a copy of the charter, see "Khartia Shankhaiskoi organizatsii sotrudnichestva" (Charter of the Shanghai cooperation organization). In *Moskovskii zhurnal mezhdunarodnogo prava*, no. 1 (49) (January–March 2003): 272–83.

27. Xinhua, 5 July 2000.

28. For copies of these documents, see "Shankhaiskaia konventsiia o bor′be s terrorizmom, separatizmom i ekstremizmom" (Shanghai convention about the struggle with terrorism, separatism, and extremism) and "Soglashenie mezhdu gosudarstvami—chlenami Shankhaiskoi organizatsii sotrudnichestva o regional′noi antiterroristicheskoi strukture" (Agreement between member states of the Shanghai cooperation organization about the Regional anti-terrorist structure) in *Moskovskii zhurnal mezhdunarodnogo prava*, no. 1 (49) (January–March 2003): 295–305, 285–94.

29. "Khartia Shankhaiskoi organizatsii sotrudnichestva," 273.

30. For a discussion of Chinese interests in the promotion of the SCO, see Zhao Huasheng, "Establishment and Development of the Shanghai Cooperation Organization," *SIIS Journal*, no. 3 (2002), and Zhao Huasheng "New Situation in Central Asia and Shanghai Cooperation Organization," *SIIS Journal*, no. 2 (2003), at www.siis.org.cn.

31. Originally the 2003 meeting was scheduled to be held in Almaty. It was moved to Moscow because the leaders of the member states were already scheduled to visit Russia for the celebrations of the three-hundredth anniversary of St. Petersburg.

32. Itar-Tass, 23 September 2003.

33. Mao Chieh, "Profound Significance of Five-Nation Cooperation," *Ta Kung Pao*, 6 July 2000, in FBIS-CHI-2000–0706.

34. See Elizabeth Wishnick, "Growing U.S. Security Interests in Central Asia," Strategic Studies Institute, U.S. Army War College (October 2002) at www.carlisle.army/mil/usassi/welcome.htm. Also E. Wayne Merry, "Moscow's Retreat and Beijing's Rise as a Regional Great Power," *Problems of Post-Communism* 50, no. 3 (May–June

2003): 17–31; and Akihiro Iwashita, "The Shanghai Cooperation Organization and Its Implications for Eurasian Security: A New Dimension of 'Partnership' after the Post–Cold War Period," paper presented at the international summer symposium, "Russia's Integration into the World Economy and Community," Slavic Research Center, Hokkaido University, July 2003.

35. RFE/RL Newsline, vol. 7, no. 100, Part I, 29 May 2003.

36. The historical legacy of World War II exercised a lingering influence on Japanese relations with both Russia and China. Russia's occupation of the Kurile islands inhibited the Russian-Japanese relationship, while Sino-Japanese relations still reflected tensions due to the Japanese invasion and occupation of China.

37. Xinhua, 2 December 2002.

38. www.apecsec.org.sg/graphics/apec_map_indi.jpg.

39. As communist party states, two other APEC members, China and Vietnam, bore the legacy of state planning, but their economic reform movements had progressed further than Russia's toward a reliance on market mechanisms.

40. In 2003 there were ten members of ASEAN (Indonesia, Malaysia, the Philippines, Singapore, Thailand, Brunei, Vietnam, Laos, Myanmar, and Cambodia) and ten dialogue partners (Australia, Canada, Chile, the European Union, India, Japan, New Zealand, Russia, South Korea, and the United States).

41. Xinhua, 2 December 2002, and 27 May 2003.

42. Interfax, 19 June 2003.

43. In 1989, an estimated 2,600 Uighurs lived in the Russian republic. There are no indications that this number has increased significantly. Personal communication from Murray Feshbach.

44. This same phrase was incorporated into the Shanghai Convention on Rebuffing Terrorism, Separatism, and Extremism adopted by the SCO in 2001.

Notes to Chapter 4

1. The extent of GDP decline in Russia in the 1990s is a hotly debated topic, not amenable to easy assessment. For World Bank estimates, see CAS Annex B6, Key Economic Indicators—Russian Federation; and CAS Annex A2–1, Russian Federation at a Glance, both at www.worldbank.org.ru. On World Bank figures, also see Joseph E. Stiglitz, *Globalization and its Discontents* (New York: W.W. Norton, 2002), 151–52.

2. For a discussion of the impact of the Asian financial crisis on the Russian economy, see Stiglitz, *Globalization and Its Discontents*, Chapter 5.

3. CAS Annex B6, Key Economic Indicators—Russian Federation, at www.worldbank.org.ru.

4. www.worldbank.org.

5. Sergei Karaganov, "Novaia vneshnaia politika" (A new foreign policy), *Moskovskie Novosti*, no. 8 (29 February–6 March 2000): 11.

6. Russian foreign trade statistics include automobiles—i.e., imported luxury vehicles—within the commodity category of machinery and equipment.

7. *The World Factbook, 2002*, at www.cia.gov/cia/publications/factbook.

8. www.worldbank.org. Allen C. Lynch provides comparisons between Russian and Chinese economic performance in "Roots of Russia's Economic Dilemmas: Liberal Economics and Illiberal Geography," *Europe–Asia Studies* 54, no. 1 (2002): 31–49.

9. *The World Factbook, 2002*, at www.cia.gov/cia/publications/factbook.

10. *The World Factbook, 1999,* at www.cia.gov/cia/publications/factbook.

11. For a pessimistic appraisal of the future prospects of the Chinese economy (as well as the ability of the Chinese Communist Party to maintain control of the Chinese state), see Gordon G. Chang, *The Coming Collapse of China* (New York: Random House, 2001).

12. *The World Factbook, 2002,* at www.cia.gov/cia/publications/factbook. World Bank estimates were higher, placing Chinese growth in GDP for 2001 at 7.3 percent, the same estimate as the Chinese government. See www.worldbank.org.

13. These percentages are derived from Russian customs statistics. *Tamozhennaia statistika vneshnei torgovli Rossiiskoi Federatsii, 2000* (Customs statistics of foreign trade of the Russian Federation, 2000) (Moscow: State Customs Committee of the Russian Federation, 2001), 7, 10; *Tamozhennaia statistika vneshnei torgovli Rossiiskoi Federatsii, 2000,* 7, 9.

14. http://english.peopledaily.com.cn; Itar-Tass, 1 February 2003. According to Chinese customs statistics, moreover, China would surpass Italy as Russia's third largest trading partner.

15. Itar-Tass, 21 November 1998. This assessment placed total trade turnover at 9.48 billion dollars, well above the official projection of 6.846 billion dollars.

16. In 2000, for example, Chinese customs statistics assessed the value of Russian fish imports to China as more than 7.5 times that of Russian statistics of fish exports to China. *China Customs Statistics Yearbook 2000* (Beijing: Customs General Administration of the People's Republic of China, 2001), 127; *Tamozhennaia statistika vneshnei torgovli Rossiiskoi Federatsii, 2000,* 416.

17. *China Customs Statistics Yearbook, 2001,* 131. Chinese and Russian customs categories are the same, a reflection of the shared Soviet economic inheritance. But Russia, unlike China, does not provide a breakdown by state for category number 88: aircraft, spacecraft and their parts.

18. For these reasons, Table 4.1, outlining Chinese-Russian trade volumes, and Table 4.4, indicating the commodity composition of Chinese-Russian trade, use Chinese rather than Russian customs trade statistics.

19. *China Customs Statistics Yearbook, 1998,* 152; *Chinese Customs Statistics Yearbook, 2001,* 130.

20. Russia was hardly a trailblazer in this respect, being the tenth member of the CIS to conclude a bilateral trade agreement with China.

21. The Chinese have followed former Soviet usage in translating the head of the government (*zhongli* in Chinese) into English as "premier," rather than "prime minister."

22. The structural analogy is not comparable, since Al Gore was the U.S. vice president.

23. See Xinhua, 23 August 2002; Xinhua, 2 December 2002; and Xinhua, 27 May 2002.

24. Xinhua, 23 August 2002.

25. RFE/RL Newsline, vol. 7, no. 99, Part I, 28 May 2003.

26. Soviet statistics for the late 1980s appear to have been adjusted for inflation. Although the proportions of increase in trade value are higher with Soviet trade statistics, they are not out of line with the figures on Soviet-Chinese trade turnover recorded by the Chinese State Statistical Bureau. For comparable Chinese statistics (recorded in dollars) see *Zhongguo Duiwai Jingji Tongji Nianjian 1979–1991* (Almanac of China's Foreign Economic Relations and Trade 1979–1991) (Beijing: China Statistical Information and Consultancy Service Center, 1992), 93, 98, 103, 108.

27. Delays in the border crossing were also a consequence of different rail gauges between Russia and China, necessitating the individual movement of freight cars onto new truck wheel assemblies.

28. Itar-Tass, 30 August 1994.

29. See Viktor B. Supian and Mihail G. Nosov, "Reintegration of an Abandoned Fortress," in Gilbert Rozman, Mikhail G. Nosov, and Koji Watanabe, eds., *Russia and East Asia: The 21st Century Security Environment*, vol. 3, EastWest Institute (Armonk, NY: M.E. Sharpe, 1999): 75.

30. Clifford Gaddy and Barry Ickes, "Russia's Virtual Economy," *Foreign Affairs* 77, no. 5 (September–October 1998): 56.

31. Xinhua, 23 February 1993; Xinhua, 22 June 1998.

32. Xinhua, 22 June 1998.

33. Itar-Tass, 19 June 1998.

34. Itar-Tass, 19 February 1999.

35. Russia also agreed to charge only 4 percent interest per year on the loan for the station, compared with the 7 percent interest proposed by France. In addition, the Chinese down payment for the project was only 75,000 dollars, half in barter goods, with another 75,000 dollars provided at the completion of the contract. See *China Economic Review* 8, no. 8 (August 1998): 14–16; and Yevgenia Borisova, "Ministry Costs Russia Billions," *Moscow Times*, 16 March 2001.

36. Igor Sotnikov, "A Good Neighbor Leads to Wealth," *Rossiiskaia Gazeta*, 24 July 2001, 7, in FBIS-CHI-2001–0724.

37. Ibid.

38. See Marshall I. Goldman, *Lost Opportunity: Why Economic Reforms in Russia Have Not Worked* (New York: W.W. Norton, 1994), especially 64–144.

39. As Chapter 2 notes, Boris Yeltsin's comments on his first trip to China in December 1992 indicated that he was surprised at the level of development of the Chinese economy.

40. Yuri Luzhkov, the mayor of Moscow, was one of the few Russian politicians to defend the shuttle traders. In 1996, he noted that at least one-fourth of the Moscow retail trade was provided by shuttle traders. See *Delovoy Mir*, 30 July 1996, in FBIS-SOV-208–S, 30 July 1996. For a general discussion of Russian attitudes toward China, including the impact of the shuttle trade, see Alexander Lukin, *The Bear Watches the Dragon* (Armonk, NY: M.E. Sharpe, 2003), Chapters 3–4.

41. RFE/RL Newsline, vol. 6, no. 157, Part 1, 21 August 2002; and Itar-Tass, 21 August 2002. However, Kasyanov also noted that the goods, although of low quality, were inexpensive, which raised the question (not typically considered in criticisms of the shuttlers) as to whether lower-income Russian consumers would be willing (or able) to pay higher prices for better-quality products. According to Mikhail Alexseev, the consumer goods provided by Chinese shuttle traders to Primorskii krai in the 1990s were for the most part superior to those available during the Soviet era and presented in greater variety. See Mikhail Alexseev, "Chinese Migration in the Russian Far East," in Judith Thornton and Charles E. Ziegler, eds., *Russia's Far East: A Region at Risk,* NBR and University of Washington Press (Seattle, WA: 2002), 329.

42. John Helmer, *Journal of Commerce*, 10 November 1997.

43. Aleksandr Ptashkin, "First Half Over: Russia Gradually Being Squeezed Out of Chinese Power Generation Market," *Trud*, 28 August 1997, 4; in FBIS-SOV-97–244, 4 September 1997.

44. "Rossiiskii nezavisimyi institut sotsial'nykh i natsional'nykh problem" (Rus-

sian independent institute of social and national problems), *Grazhdane Rossii: kem oni sebia oshchushchaiut i v kakom obshchestve oni khoteli by zhit'*? (Citizens of Russia: whom do they feel themselves to be and what kind of society would they like to live in?). Cited in Lukin, *The Bear Watches the Dragon*, 198–99.

45. In addition, Russia signed an agreement in 1995 with Taiwan providing for the shipment of 5,000 drums of low-radiation nuclear waste to Russia. The agreement, however, was subsequently stalled due to lack of legislation within Russia (eventually passed by the State Duma in June 2001) to permit nuclear waste storage.

46. Originally, the project was designated for Liaoning province, but was moved to Jiangsu province.

47. Russia was supplying 70–80 percent of the equipment for the plant, but the German company Siemens and several Finnish companies were also participants in the project.

48. Itar-Tass, 21 October 1999.

49. Ibid.

50. Chinese customs statistics indicated that Chinese imports of aircraft and spacecraft from Russia totaled 389.3 million dollars in 1998, 397.6 million dollars in 1999, 60,516 dollars in 2000, and 1,478,048 dollars in 2001. However, the classification does not distinguish between aviation and aerospace equipment. The failure of Russian customs statistics to present a breakdown of aviation exports by individual states suggests that aerospace equipment figured heavily in the export mix. See *Chinese Customs Statistics Yearbook, 1998*, 153; *Chinese Customs Statistics Yearbook, 1999*, 130; *Chinese Customs Statistics Yearbook, 2000*, 128; and *Chinese Customs Statistics Yearbook, 2001*, 131.

51. AFP, 25 November 1999, in FBIS-CHI-1999–1125.

52. Ibid.

53. Koptev was a member of the Russian delegation that accompanied Boris Yeltsin during his November 1997 trip to Beijing, as well as participating in the bilateral talks led by Vice Prime Minister Ilya Klebanov in August 1999 and March 2000.

54. Glonass, in fact, was not operational. In 2000, only ten of the twenty-four satellites necessary for the system to function had been placed in orbit, and these were at the end of their service lives. See Sergei Putilov, "The Military Are Concerned About Space," *Vremya MN*, 14 September 2001, in FBIS-SOV-2001–0914; and Simon Saradzhyan, "Klebanov Details China Space Deal," *Moscow Times*, 9 March 2000.

55. In the late 1990s, a discussion also developed in Chinese space circles over the possibility of purchasing the Mir space station. See K'ang Chien-wen, "Call from Space—Chinese Space-Flight Prospects in the New Century," *Ta Kung Pao*, 31 December 1999, E3, in FBIS-CHI-2000–0130.

56. See Itar-Tass, 13 August 2002; Itar-Tass, 21 August 2002.

57. Other American corporations—for example, Radio Shack, *Popular Mechanics*, and the LEGO company (in addition to Pizza Hut)—paid to have cosmonauts promote their products on board the Space Station Alpha.

58. See Michael Cabbage, "China's Great Leap Forward: Space," *Orlando Sentinel*, 9 December 2001, at www.orlandosentinel.com.

59. Itar-Tass, 3 April 2003.

60. Saradzhyan, "Klebanov Details Space Deal."

61. Interfax, 10 September 2001.

62. Lyuba Pronina, "Plane Makers Ply Old Markets for New Deals," *Moscow Times*, 3 October 2002.

63. Xinhua, 23 August 2002.

64. Daniel Yergin, Dennis Eklof, and Jefferson Edwards, "Fueling Asia's Recovery," *Foreign Affairs* 77, no. 2 (March–April 1998): 41. For further discussion of China's energy policy, see Gaye Christoffersen, "China's Intentions for Russian and Central Asian Oil and Gas," *National Bureau of Asian Research Analysis* 9, no. 2 (March 1998); Felix K. Chang, "Chinese Energy and Asian Security," *Orbis* 45, no. 2 (Spring 2001): 211–40; and Keun-wook Paik, "Energy Cooperation in Sino-Russian Relations: The Importance of Oil and Gas," *Pacific Review* 9, no. 1 (1996): 77–95.

65. The 1999 figures were related by Vice Prime Minister Viktor Khristenko. See RFE/RL Newsline, vol. 4, no. 50, Part I, 10 March 2000. The figures for 2000 were presented in Xinhua, 11 January 2001. China's oil imports dropped to 60 million tons in 2001 but increased again to almost 70 million tons in 2002. Xinhua, 4 April 2003.

66. RFE/RL Newsline, vol. 4, no. 50, Part I, 10 March 2000.

67. See Christoffersen, "China's Intentions," 19–23.

68. This development was facilitated by Prime Minister Viktor Chernomyrdin's long association with the Soviet gas industry and first Vice Prime Minister Boris Nemtsov's concurrent positions as minister of Fuel and Energy and chairman of the Russian side of the bilateral commission designated to deal with Russian-Chinese economic affairs.

69. See Fiona Hill and Florence Fee, "Fueling the Future: The Prospects for Russian Oil and Gas," *Demokratizatsiya* 10, no. 4 (Fall 2002): 462–87.

70. Interfax, 23 February 1999. Prior to meeting with Zhu Rongji in February 1999, Prime Minister Primakov voiced the same sentiment.

71. Hill and Fee, "Fueling the Future," 479–83.

72. Xinhua, 2 December 2002; Xinhua, 27 May 2003.

73. For a discussion of Russia's energy situation, see Peter Rutland, "Lost Opportunities: Energy and Politics in Russia," *National Bureau of Asian Research Analysis* 8, no. 5 (December 1997).

74. RFE/RL Newsline, vol. 4, no. 50, Part I, 10 March 2000.

75. *Moscow Times*, 26 September, 2002, 6; Valeriy Yazev "Spasatel'nyi krug dlia nefteotrasli" (Life saver for the oil sector), *Rossiiskaia Gazeta*, 18 February 1999, 2. Yazev was the chairman of the Duma Committee on Fuel Resources. According to Mark N. Katz, Russian oil producers' costs ranged as high as twelve dollars a barrel, compared to one and a half dollars a barrel for Saudi Arabia. Mark N. Katz, "Big Decisions Loom for Russian Oil Production," at http://iicas.org/articles/library/libr_rus_28_11_01_2_bz.htm.

76. The Mongolian government also agreed to oil and gas pipelines passing through Mongolia, but the Chinese government was unwilling to consider third-country transit for any energy transfers from Russia.

77. The field was projected to contain between 1.5 and 2 trillion cubic meters of gas; estimates of the cost of the project varied between 10 and 12 billion dollars.

78. In addition, by mid-2000 a proliferating number of Russian energy companies, including Gazprom, were demanding a right to participate in the project.

79. Shell and Exxon-Mobil also received 15 percent shares, with PetroChina assuming a 55 percent share in the undertaking.

80. "China Debt to Finance a Gas Line?" *Moscow Times*, 7 August 2001, 6.

81. Ibid.

82. In May 1999, the Russian oil and gas company Sakhanetegaz and CNPC signed an agreement on preparing a feasibility study on the construction of a gas pipeline

from fields in Western Yakutia to China. In June 2003, a delegation from Sinopec, China's second largest energy firm, toured the Sakhalin-2 oil and gas project, expressing an interest in importing liquefied natural gas from the site.

83. Hill and Fee, "Fueling the Future," 480.

84. *Moscow Times*, 19 July 2002, 6.

85. In late 1997, CNPC purchased 60 percent of the shares of the Aktobemunaigaz Company in Kazakhstan. Subsequently, the Kazakh employees claimed that the company had dismissed 2,000 workers without compensation, giving rise to a situation that eventually necessitated mediation by the Chinese and Kazakh governments.

86. Interfax, 25 July 2002.

87. www.yukos.com/new_rm/China.asp.

88. Efforts by CPNC to purchase state shares in the Russian oil firm Slavneft in December 2002 set off a furor among Russian politicians who objected to foreign ownership of the company, citing harm to Russia's strategic interests.

89. RFE/RL Newsline, vol. 7, no. 8, Part I, 14 January 2003. Reports of the financial contribution offered by Japan varied somewhat.

90. For a discussion of the role of MOFTEC in Chinese foreign policy decision making, see Lu Ning, "The Central Leadership, Supraministry Coordinating Bodies, State Council Ministries, and Party Departments," in David M. Lampton, ed., *The Making of Chinese Foreign and Security Policy in the Era of Reform, 1978–2000* (Stanford, CA: Stanford University Press, 2001), 39–60; and Margaret M. Pearson, "The Case of China's Accession to GATT/WTO," in Lampton, ed., *The Making of Chinese Foreign and Security Policy*, 336–70.

91. Nicholas R. Lardy, *Integrating China into the Global Economy* (Washington, DC: Brookings Institution Press, 2002). For discussions on the impact of WTO membership on China, see Joseph Fewsmith, "The Political and Social Implications of China's Accession to the WTO," *China Quarterly* 167, no. 3 (September 2001): 573–91; William B. Abnet and Robert B. Cassidy, "China's WTO Accession: The Road to Implementation," *NBR Special Report*, no. 3 (November 2002); and Minxin Pei, "Future Shock: The WTO and Political Change in China," *Policy Brief* 1, no. 3 (February 2001) at www.ceip.org.

92. See the comments of Sergei Tsyplakov, Russia's trade representative in China, in Interfax, 30 December 2002.

93. Xinhua, 5 June 2002.

94. According to a report in *Pravda.ru*, the Chinese side agreed to lower its demands and revise its requests to open the Russian market to Chinese labor as a result of the first round of bilateral negotiations. See http://english.pravda.ru, 10 June 2002.

95. Interfax, 17 June 2003.

96. For a discussion of Soviet interest in the Chinese economic reforms in the Gorbachev era, see Lukin, *The Bear Watches the Dragon*, Chapter 2.

97. See Ibid., Chapters 3, 4, and 6; and Goldman, *Lost Opportunity*, Chapter 9.

98. At a textile factory in Partizansk in Primorskii krai, for example, Russian seamstresses in a South Korean–owned firm received on average twenty-one cents an hour (compared to eleven cents an hour for Chinese workers). Russell Working, "Fashion Sweatshops Flourish in Far East," *Moscow Times*, 19 March 1999.

99. Russian trade statistics placed Russian-Chinese trade for 2002 at 9.214 billion dollars (compared to Chinese assessments of 11.927 billion dollars). The value of Russian-Italian trade was assessed at 9.655 billion dollars and Russian-German trade at 14.621 billion dollars. See *Tamozhennaia statistika vneshnei torgovli Rossiiskoi*

Federatsii, 2000, 7–10. Various estimates placed the value of unofficial trade between Russia and China in the vicinity of 10 billion dollars a year in the early 2000s. See, for example, *Pravda.ru*, 27 May 2003, at www.pravda.ru; and comments of President Hu Jintao on Chinese-Russian trade in RFE/RL Newsline, vol. 7, no. 99, Part I, 28 May 2003.

100. This development, at least, is predicted by adherents of integration theory and neofunctionalism. For a discussion of basic premises of these theories, see James E. Dougherty and Robert L. Pfaltzgraff, Jr., *Contending Theories of International Relations: A Comprehensive Survey*, 5th ed. (New York: Longman, 2001), Chapter 10.

Notes to Chapter 5

1. Formally, Jiang Zemin served as the chairman of the MAC, but day-to-day operational authority rested with Liu.

2. The timing of Chi's visit, shortly before the August 1991 coup attempt, sparked subsequent rumors—apparently unfounded—that the Chinese had been party to, or at least briefed on, efforts to depose of Mikhail Gorbachev.

3. Technically, the Chinese purchased twenty-four Su-27 fighter jets. An additional two aircraft were included for testing and research purposes. Interview with Konstantin Makienko, deputy director, Center for the Analysis of Strategies and Technologies (CAST), Moscow, Russia, 29 January 2001.

4. Kyodo, 16 December 1992, in FBIS-CHI-92–242, 16 December 1992.

5. Chiang Yao, "Why Does China Increase Its Military Expenditures?" *Cheng Ming*, no. 183 (1 January 1993): 19–20, in FBIS-CHI-93–002, 5 January 1993.

6. R. Zaripov, A. Kabannikov, and V. Shutkevich, "The Forbidden City Can Rest Easy: It Seems Boris Nikolayevich Has Promised the Chinese Spare Parts for Su-27 Fighters," *Komsomolskaia Pravda*, 19 December 1992, 5, in FBIS-SOV-92–245, 21 December 1992.

7. *Ostankino*, 18 December 1992, in FBIS-SOV-92–245, 23 December 1992. This figure, however, presumably reflected contracted orders rather than actual deliveries.

8. See Pavel Popov and Georgii Bovt, "Russian Military Hardware to Be Shipped to China," *Kommersant Daily*, 20 November 1992, 8, in FBIS-SOV-92–226, 23 November 1992; and Chiang Yao, "Why Does China Increase Its Military Expenditures?"

9. *South China Morning Post*, 25 June 1993. The Chinese ability to view an assortment of Russian advanced weapon systems was enhanced by a secret exhibition held on the outskirts of Beijing in May. See also Pavel Felgenhauer, "An Uneasy Partnership: Sino-Russian Defense Cooperation and Arms Sales," in Andrew J. Pierre and Dmitri V. Trenin, eds., *Russia in the World Arms Trade* (Washington, DC: Brookings Institution Press, 1997), 87–103.

10. *Komsomolskaia Pravda*, 13 November 1993, 3, in FBIS-SOV-93–219, 16 November 1993.

11. Chou Te-hui, "Russia Supplies Beijing with an Arms Sales List," *Lien Ho Pao*, 26 April 1994, 2, in FBIS-CHI-94–080, 26 April 1994, 18.

12. Reports on Chinese arms purchases from Russia are subject to considerable variation, as to both quantity and monetary value. Many Western sources have reported that the Su-27 technology transfer agreement included a Chinese commitment to purchase seventy-two Su-27 fighter jets from Russia, a figure that apparently reflected the inadvertent double counting of the actual total. China purchased twenty-six Su-27s in 1992 (including the two aircraft provided for testing and research

purposes) and an additional twenty-two Su-27s in 1995 as a component of the licensing agreement. Interview with Konstantin Makienko, CAST, Moscow, Russia, 29 January 2001. Also see Konstantin Makienko, "U.S. Congressional Research Service Report on Russia's Place in the Arms Market," *Eksport Vooruzhenii* (September–October 2001): 2–6; and Konstantin Makienko, *Voenno-tekhnicheskoe sotrudnichestvo Rossii i KNR v 1992–2002 godakh: dostizheniia, tendentsii, perspektivy* (Military-technical cooperation between Russia and the PRC 1992–2002: results, tendencies, and prospects), Document No. 2, Russian Office of the Center for Defense Analysis, October 2002, 10, 41–42.

13. See comments of Aleksei Boygatyrev, chief of Sukhoi aviation company's press service, Interfax, 22 December 1997; and the remarks of Aleksandr Kotelkin, general director of Rosvooruzheniye (the state arms exports agency), Itar-Tass, 30 August 1997; also Itar-Tass, 13 November 1997; Interfax, 18 April 1997; and Makienko, *Voenno-tekhnicheskoe sotrudnichestvo*, 10.

14. RFE/RL Newsline, vol. 2, no. 17, 27 January 1998.

15. *Jamestown Foundation Monitor*, vol. 4, no. 22, 3 February 1998.

16. Itar-Tass, 10 August 1998.

17. Itar-Tass, 22 October 1998.

18. Itar-Tass, 25 August 1999; Itar-Tass, 16 January 2000.

19. Christiaan Virant, "China, Russia Hammer Out Arms Deals," Reuters, 22 October 1998, in Johnson's Russia List, No. 2444, 22 October 1998.

20. Interfax, 9 June 1999.

21. Estimates of the quantity of Su-30MKK fighter jets sold varied, but most accounts listed the number as either thirty-eight or forty. See Makienko, *Voenno-tekhnicheskoe sotrudnichestvo*, 10, 42–43.

22. Itar-Tass, 24 August 1999; Itar-Tass, 25 August 1999.

23. As with the 1999 order, estimates ranged between thirty-eight and forty on the number of planes sold.

24. The Israeli cancellation was a reluctant response to U.S. pressures. The Russian alternative would make use of Beriev advanced radar systems, and as with the AWACS proposal, be mounted on Russian Il-76 aircraft. The delay in signing the contract apparently indicated Chinese doubts as to Russia's technological capability actually to produce the aircraft. Reportedly, the Chinese demanded a massive upgrading of the aircraft's electronics and radar systems prior to finalizing the order. See Fred Weir, "Can Russia Deliver on Arms Sales?" *Christian Science Monitor*, 29 November 2000.

25. For a detailed listing of Chinese arms purchases from Russia from 1992 to 2000 (including a breakdown of air, naval, and land armaments), see Makienko, *Voenno-tekhnicheskoe sotrudnichestvo*, 41–49.

26. The Su-30MK2 was an upgraded variant of the original Su-30MKK fighter jet. As usual, media reports varied as to the precise quantity of aircraft contracted. CAST estimates placed the order at twenty-four aircraft. See www.cast.ru.

27. Liu was quoted as stating that "he would die with everlasting regret if China did not build an aircraft carrier." Reportedly, the Chinese purchased the technical documentation for an aircraft carrier from the Nevsky design office, an action that was completed without prior authorization from Rosvooruzheniye, the Russian arms export agency. During the 1990s, China also sought to buy an aircraft carrier, an endeavor that encountered substantial U.S. opposition and apparently served to deter third parties—including Russia—from making a sale. Chinese entrepreneurs bought

the obsolete Kiev and Minsk carriers of the former Soviet fleet, as well as the uncompleted Varyag from Ukraine, to be recycled as tourist attractions. These purchases aroused some suspicion in the international community as well as pleas in the Hong Kong press that the Varyag be reconstructed as a functional aircraft carrier. See Nayan Chanda, "No Cash Carrier," *Far East Economic Review*, 10 October 1996: 20; Alexander Zhilin, "Generals Do Arms Business First," *Moscow News*, no. 13 (7–13 April 1995); and Jiang Feng, "Can the 'Varyag' Become a Chinese Aircraft Carrier?" *Ta Kung Pao*, 25 April 2002, in FBIS-CHI-2002–0425.

28. Leslie Shepherd, "Russia Arms Sales Earn Needed Cash," AFP, 4 July 1998; see also Felgenhauer, "An Uneasy Partnership," 87–103.

29. Numerous assessments of the value and volume of Russian arms transfers exist, using a variety of methodologies to derive their calculations. Formally the Russian government does not release data on the value of arms shipments, but periodic statements by Russian officials, most notably those associated with the state arms trading agency Rosoboronexport (or its predecessor Rosvooruzheniye), and managers of Russian defense enterprises, provide information on the value of annual arms sales. Estimates of arms and technology shipments, however, whether from Rosoboronexport or other sources (SIPRI, the International Institute of Strategic Studies [IISS], the U.S. Congressional Research Service, etc.) are inherently ambiguous: it is not clear to what extent the monetary sales reported reflect signed contracts or actual deliveries, involve barter deals, or shipments to pay off loans. Certain transactions also go unrecorded, such as those involving the illicit sale of weaponry and licensing agreements. For example, Grigoriy Rapota, the Russian minister of trade, reported in a 2000 interview that while the official government figure for arms exports in 1996 was almost 3.5 billion dollars, 900 million dollars of this amount went for debt repayment and another 500 million dollars was conducted in barter payments, leaving only 2.1 billion dollars in hard currency revenues. *Yaderny Kontrol*, 14 April 2000: 40–44, in FBIS-SOV-2000–0716.

30. The Congressional Research Service 2002 report on arms transfers ranked Russia second behind the United States in arms exports. SIPRI, however, adopting a more controversial stance, claimed that Russia had overtaken the United States as the world's ranking supplier of armaments for both 2001 and 2002. This projection tended to be disavowed even by Russian officials, who noted that the methodology used by SIPRI was based on a calculation of the volume of arms transfers and not the actual contract price. See Thorn Shanker, "Global Arms Sales to Developing Nations are Tumbling, Study Finds," *New York Times*, 8 August 2002, A8; *SIPRI Yearbook 2002* (Oxford: Oxford University Press, 2002), 374–79; Lyuba Pronina, "Russia Is Top Arms Dealer," *Moscow Times*, 17 June 2002; Ivan Safronov, "Does Russia Sell More Weapons Than Any Other Country?" *Kommersant*, no. 100 (June 2002), Johnson's Russia List, Number 6310, 15 June 2002; and Itar-Tass, 9 June 2003.

31. Technically, there is a category in Russian trade statistics (commodity code number 93) entitled "arms and ammunition: accessories and parts thereof." But this category is narrowly defined to include such items as rifles and other firearms with their cartridges, not military weaponry.

32. Interfax, 28 February 2000. Fradkov further noted that budget revenues from arms exports in 1999 exceeded 3 billion dollars.

33. Percentages extrapolated from *SIPRI Yearbook 2002*, 376.

34. Interview with Konstantin Makienko, deputy director, CAST, Moscow, Russia,

29 January 2001. Also see Konstantin Makienko, "Preliminary Estimates of Russia's Arms Exports in 2001," *Eksport Vooruzheniy* (November–December 2001): 6–8; and Konstantin Makienko, "Indiisko-Kitaiskoe getto" (The Indian-Chinese ghetto), *Ekspert*, no. 40 (26 October 1998): 20–25.

35. See Ruslan Pukhov, "Tri chetverti voennogo eksporta Rossii daet aviaprom" (Three-quarters of the military exports of Russia are by the aviation industry), *Vremia Novostei*, 11 June 2003; Lyuba Pronina, "Weapons Exports Hit Record \$4.8Bln," *Moscow Times*, 19 February 2003; Lyuba Pronina, "Arms Export Boom Is Losing Steam," *Moscow Times*, 9 June 2003; Itar-Tass, 7 May 2003; and RFE/RL Newsline, vol. 7, no. 79, Part I, 25 April 2003.

36. Pronina, "Arms Exporter Rakes in Record 4.3 Bln." Rosoboronexport garnered the overwhelming share of arms exports revenues in 2002—an estimated 85 percent— but deliveries by independent arms exporters constituted an additional 15 percent of Russian arms exports. See Pukhov, etal. "Preliminary Estimates of Russia's Arms."

37. However, according to a November 2000 arrangement reached during Prime Minister Kasyanov's visit to Beijing, Russia agreed by 2002 to repay the former Soviet debt to China, long the subject of negotiation, through the supply of weaponry. Starting in 1999, Russia began shipping arms for debt repayment, including Sa-15, Tor-M1, and S-300 missile systems.

38. Subsequently, however, Russia was able to reduce the submarine contract to 50 percent barter. Pavel Felgenhauer, "Russia Too Busy Arming to Care About Consequences," *St. Petersburg Times*, 14–20 July 1997.

39. Similarly, workers at the Severnyi plant in St. Petersburg were compensated with flasks, lighters, and fluffy stuffed dogs in return for a Chinese order of S-300 surface-to-air missiles. Such indignities were commonplace in the 1990s and by no means confined to Russian interactions with China. In another notorious example, Malaysia supplied Russia with palm oil in return for its purchase of MiG-29 jets.

40. Ksenia Gonchar, *Russia's Defense Industry at the Turn of the Century*, Brief 17, Bonn International Center for Conversion, November 2000: 40.

41. "The Challenges of Globalization and the Russian Defense Industry Complex," Press Conference with Ruslan Pukhov and Maxim Pyadushkin, Press Development Institute, 17 December 2002, at www.cast.ru.

42. See Igor Khripunov, "Russia's Weapons Trade: Domestic Competition and Foreign Markets," *Problems of Post-Communism* 46, no. 2 (March–April 1999): 39–48; Ian Anthony, ed., *Russia and the Arms Trade* (Oxford: Oxford University Press, 1998); and Alexander A. Sergounin and Sergey V. Subbotin, *Russian Arms Transfers to East Asia in the 1990s* (Oxford: Oxford University Press, 1999).

43. Anton Surikov, "Beijing Is Purchasing War for Itself: Who Is Upset by the Military-Technical Cooperation of Russian and China?" *Pravda-5*, 17 September 1996: 3, in FBIS-SOV-211-S, 17 September 1996. Surikov was the director of the Information and Analysis Center of the Institute for Defense Studies.

44. David Lague and Susan V. Lawrence, "In Guns We Trust," *Far Eastern Economic Review*, 12 December 2002, in *CDI Russia Weekly*, no. 234, 6 December 2000.

45. A report by Andrei Bagrov, "V kazhdom propellere dyshit skandal" (Each propeller reeks of scandal), in the 18 July 1996 edition of *Kommersant Daily*, detailed improprieties allegedly committed by Mikhail Simonov, general director of the Sukhoi Design Bureau regarding the sale of the Su-27 production license to China. Simonov refuted these allegations in an interview on the Moscow Russian Television Network recorded in FBIS-SOV-96–147, 30 July 1996. Some Western commentators have

asserted that Sukhoi transferred the Su-27 license without official authorization. The article in *Kommersant* did not make this accusation directly, which does not seem credible. Negotiations over the sale of the license were ongoing between Russia and China for several years and took place in the presence of Russian governmental officials, including representatives of Rosvooruzheniye. For additional reports of the Su-27 licensing sale, see Stephen J. Blank and Alvin Z. Rubinstein, "Is Russia Still a Power in Asia?" *Problems of Post-Communism* 45, no. 2 (March–April 1997): 38; and Sherman W. Garnett, *Limited Partnership: Russia-Chinese Relations in a Changing Asia* (Washington, DC: Carnegie Endowment for International Peace, 1998), 27. For reports of Chinese infractions of Russian export regulations, see Blank and Rubinstein, "Is Russia Still a Power in Asia?"; Stephen Blank, "Russia's Secret Arms Market," *World and I* 13, no. 10 (October 1998): 304; Stephen Blank, "The Dynamics of Russian Weapon Sales to China," 4 March 1997, at www.army.mil/usassi; Zhilin, "Generals Do Arms Business First"; Felgenhauer, "An Uneasy Partnership"; and Alexei Baliyev, "Velikaia druzhba prirastaet kalashnikovom" (Great friendship growing through Kalashnikovs), *Rossiiskaia Gazeta*, 5 October 1996, 23.

46. One particularly egregious example was the charge that members of the "family" —close associates of Boris Yeltsin including his daughter Tatyana Dyachenko— restructured Rosvooruzheniye in 1996 in order to get access to the hard currency revenue from arms exports to finance Yeltsin's 1996 presidential campaign. See Kevin P. O'Prey, "Arms Exports and Russia's Defense Industries: Issues for the U.S. Congress," in *Russia's Uncertain Economic Future*, Compendium of Papers Submitted to the Joint Economic Committee, Congress of the United States (Washington, DC: Government Printing Office, 2002), 385–410; and Sergounin and Subbotin, *Russian Arms Transfers*, 67.

47. Zhilin, "Generals Do Arms Business First."

48. See Pukhov, "Tri chetverti voennogo eksporta Rossii daet aviaprom"; CAST News, 9 June 2003, at www.cast.ru; and Pronina, "Arms Export Boom Is Losing Steam."

49. Interfax, 27 January 1997.

50. Igor Chernyak, "Magnificence and Poverty of the Miracle Aircraft of the Twenty-First Century," *Komsomolskaia Pravda*, 17 September 1996, 6, in FBIS-UMA-96-201–S, 17 September 1996.

51. Simon Saradzhyan, "Fighter Export Deals Ignite Sukhoi Profits," *Moscow Times*, 18 June 2001; Lyuba Pronina, "Sukhoi Claims a Banner Year," *Moscow Times*, 28 December 2001.

52. Pronina, "Arms Export Boom Is Losing Steam."

53. For assessments by Russian analysts, see Raffi Katchadourian, "Arms Exports Battle for Future," *The Russia Journal*, 20–26 January 2001; Alexei Nikolsy "Defense Sector Has Exhausted Its Resources," *Vedomosti*, 17 April 2002, at www.wps.ru; and Gennady Voskresenskiy, "The Time of Finances and Business: Exports Are Increasing, Potential Is Declining," *Vremya MN*, 12 March 2002, at FBIS-SOV-2002-0315.

54. Interviews conducted by Kevin O'Prey with staff in Russian defense enterprises indicated that they preferred to work with Western firms in the high-technology sphere, considering cooperation with China to be "degrading." Their disdain, however, was not sufficient to deter them from contracts with China. O'Prey, "Arms Exports," 391.

55. Alexander A. Sergounin and Sergey V. Subbotin, "Sino-Russian Military-Technical Cooperation: a Russian View," in Ian Anthony, *Russia and the Arms Trade* (Oxford: Oxford University Press, 1998), 196; also O'Prey, "Arms Exports," 403.

56. O'Prey, "Arms Exports," 391.

57. See Yuriy Kirshin, "The Role of the Ministry of Defence in the Export of Conventional Weapons," in Anthony, ed., *Russia and the Arms Trade*, 117–23.

58. See Tai Ming Cheung, "The Influence of the Gun: China's Central Military Commission and Its Relationship with the Military, Party, and State Decision-Making Systems," in David M. Lampton, ed., *The Making of Chinese Foreign and Security Policy in the Era of Reform, 1978–2000* (Stanford, CA: Stanford University Press, 2001), 61–90.

59. See Felgenhauer, "An Uneasy Partnership," 91. Proceeds from Russian arms sales to China in the late summer of 1997 were reportedly used to pay the salary arrears of Russian officers. Also Sherman W. Garnett, *Limited Partnership: Russia–China Relations in a Changing Asia* (Washington, DC: Carnegie Endowment for International Peace, 1998), 23.

60. See comments by Lieutenant General Nikolai Zlenko of the Ministry of Defense in Simon Saradzhyan, "Putin Forms Arms Sales Powerhouse," *Moscow Times*, 8 November 2000, and Reuben Johnson; "Changing of the Guard . . . Again," *Moscow Times*, 2 December 2000.

61. Xinhua, 24 December 2001. In January 2003, the Putin administration, announcing a one-third increase in 2003 military spending, also put forth a proposal in which research and development on new equipment would be financed by profits earned by defense companies on arms exports. See Lyuba Pronina, "Military Spending Boosted by 33%," *Moscow Times*, 17 January 2003.

62. For further discussion, see Robert H. Donaldson and John A. Donaldson, "The Arms Trade in Russian-Chinese Relations: Identity, Domestic Politics, and Geopolitical Positioning," *International Studies Quarterly* 47, no. 4 (December 2003): 709–732.

63. See Garnett, *Limited Partnership*, 25–27; Dmitri Trenin, *Russia's China Problem* (Washington, DC: Carnegie Endowment for International Peace, 1999), 36–38; interview with Konstantin Makienko, Moscow, Russia, 29 January 2001; RFE/RL Newsline, vol. 6, no. 34, Part I, 21 February 2002; and O'Prey, "Arms Exports and Russia's Defense Industries," 391.

64. See O'Prey, "Arms Exports and Russia's Defense Industries," 391; and Sergounin and Subbotin, *Russian Arms Transfers*, 92.

65. Makienko, *Voenno-tekhnicheskoe sotrudnichestvo*, 25. In fact, China did not appear interested in large-scale purchases of land-based weaponry, preferring to concentrate on enhancing its aviation and naval capabilities.

66. However, Russia did not possess any fighter jets of the Su-30 series, which were produced solely for export and beyond the financial means of the Russian military to purchase. In 2003, plans were released for the upgrading of twenty Su-27s for the Russian air force. See Simon Saradzhyan, "Air Force to Upgrade 20 Su-27s in 2003," *Moscow Times*, 16 January 2003. For a comparison of weaponry sold to China and to India see Makienko, *Voenno-tekhnicheskoe sotrudnichestvo*, 48–54; also Konstantin Makienko, "V soiuze s Indiei, v dolgu pered Kitaem" (In alliance with India, in debt to China), *Kommersant Vlast'*, no. 1, 15 January 2002, 30–31; and Konstantin Makienko, "Indiia—ideal'nyi partner" (India—an ideal partner), *Vedomosti* 11 December 2002.

67. Russia signed no-first-use agreements with the United States and the United Kingdom, and agreements on the prevention of dangerous military activity with Canada, Greece, the United States, and the Czech Republic. China had similar agreements on preventing dangerous military activities with Kazakhstan, Kyrgyzstan, and Tajikistan.

68. See Itar-Tass, 11 July 2002; Itar-Tass, 9 August 2002; and Xinhua, 9 July 2002.

69. See, for example, Aleksandr V. Nemets and John L. Scherer, *Sino-Russian Military Relations* (Washington: Portcullis eBooks, 2000). Nemets and Scherer also argue that "every weapon or weapon-related technology in the Russian arsenal (has become) available to China," p. 4.

70. Trenin, *Russia's China Problem*, 38.

71. The June 2003 murder of two Kremlin defense industry executives connected with the Almaz-Antei air defense consortium indicated the difficulties of defense sector reform.

72. Ruslan Pukhov, "India Remains Russia's Only Partner in Arms Creation," *Vremia Novostei*, 31 July 2003, at www.cast.ru.

73. For a discussion of the impact of Chinese weapons purchases from Russia on Taiwan and Southeast Asia, see Makienko, *Voenno-tekhnicheskoe sotrudnichestvo*, 29–37.

Notes to Chapter 6

1. On the Chinese side, the Inner Mongolian autonomous region shares a border with Chita and Amur oblasts; Heilongjiang province has a border with Amur oblast, the Jewish Autonomous oblast, Khabarovsk krai, and Primorskii krai; and a small section of Jilin province also borders on Primorskii krai. The 55-kilometer segment of the Russian-Chinese border on its western edge links Altai krai with Xinjiang province.

2. See Viktor B. Supian and Mikhail G. Nosov, "Reintegration of an Abandoned Fortress," in Gilbert Rozman, Mikhail G. Nosov, and Koji Watanabe, eds., *Russia and East Asia: The 21st Century Security Environment*, EastWest Institute (Armonk, NY: M.E. Sharpe, 1999), 72.

3. The situation of the Russian Far East in the post-Soviet era has received considerable scholarly attention. For books on the topic (or relevant chapters within edited volumes), see Judith Thornton and Charles E. Zeigler, eds., *Russia's Far East: A Region at Risk* (Seattle: University of Washington Press, 2002); Rozman, Nosov, and Watanabe, eds., *Russia and East Asia*; Elizabeth Wishnick, *Mending Fences: The Evolution of Moscow's China Policy from Brezhnev to Yeltsin* (Seattle, WA: University of Washington Press, 2001); and Sherman W. Garnett, ed., *Rapprochement or Rivalry?: Russia–China Relations in a Changing Asia* (Washington, DC: Carnegie Endowment for International Peace, 2000).

4. Akihiro Iwashita, "The Influence of Local Russian Initiatives on Relations with China: Border Demarcation and Regional Partnership," *Acta Slavica IAPONICA*, vol. 19 (2002): 4. Also see Akihiro Iwashita, "The Russian-Chinese 'Strategic Partnership' and Border Negotiations: Then and Now," *Bulletin of the Graduate Schools*, Yamaguchi Prefectural University, no. 2 (2001); and Akihiro Iwashita, "Opyt prigranichnogo sotrudnichestva Rossii i KNR za poslednie 10 let" (The experience of border cooperation between Russia and the PRC for the past 10 years), in Akihiro Iwashita, ed., *The Sino-Russian "Strategic Partnership," Current Views from the Border and Beijing*, Slavic Research Center. Hokkaido University. Occasional Papers, no. 91 (2003).

5. Iwashita, "The Influence of Local Russian Initiatives," 10–13; Georgi F. Kunadze, "Border Problems Between Russia and Its Neighbors," in Rozman, Nosov, and Watanabe, eds., *Russia and East Asia*, 138.

6. Zakhar Vinogradov and Andrey Savelyev, "Who Is Thickening the Fog over the Tumen River?" *Komsomolskaia Pravda*, 12 March 1997, in FBIS-SOV-97–048.

7. Rozov was not unemployed, as he was quickly hired to work for Nazdratenko. For a presentation of Rozov's position, see his article "Mnenie" (Opinion) in *Trud*, 15 January 1997, 5.

8. Yeltsin's foreign policy advisor, Dmitrii Ryurikov, also announced in April 1996 that the demarcation process had been temporarily frozen. Omri, no. 80, Part I, 23 April 1996.

9. Nazdratenko was a thorn in the side of the foreign ministry staff. In the words of an unnamed diplomat: "The whole country may suffer because of this moron and the Chinese may swallow the whole of Primorskii krai, God forbid." Stanislav Kondrashov, "Natisk na vostok po-rossiiskoi" (Onslaught in the East in the Russian style), *Izvestia*, 11 November 1996, 4.

10. Interfax, 30 April 1996.

11. According to Georgi F. Kunadze, a former Russian vice minister, the Primorskii krai administration dropped its objections to the land transfer in a compromise of sorts. After China agreed to adjust the borderline in Khasan so that the graveyards would remain in Russian territory, the federal government made a deal with politicians in the krai to suspend efforts to get rid of Nazdrantenko. Georgi F. Kunadze, "Border Problems Between Russia and Its Neighbors," in Rozman, Nosov, and Watanabe, eds., *Russia and East Asia*, 138.

12. Yeltsin subsequently disbanded the Amur River Border Guard Flotilla in June 1998.

13. For further discussion of these issues, see Kunadze, "Border Problems Between Russia and Its Neighbors," in Rozman, Nosov, and Watanabe, eds., *Russia and East Asia*, 133–49.

14. Omri, No. 142, Part I, 17 December 1996.

15. Various officials within the Yeltsin government were openly critical of the border agreement, including Prime Minister Sergei Stepashin during his tenure as minister of the Interior.

16. See G. Kireev, "Demarcation of the Border with China," *International Affairs* 45, no. 2 (1999): 98–109.

17. RIA, 22 July 2000 in FBIS-SOV-2000–0720.

18. Itar-Tass, 13 July 2000.

19. According to Gilbert Rozman, the members of a closed session of the Far East and Transbaikal Parliamentary Association were assured prior to Yeltsin's April 1996 trip to China that Yeltsin and Foreign Minister Primakov had agreed with Nazdratenko not to complete the border demarcation. In public statements as prime minister, however, Primakov took care to uphold the 1991 border agreement, maintaining that its implementation was vital to the Russian national interest. See Gilbert Rozman, "Troubled Choices for the Russian Far East: Decentralization, Open Regionalism, and Internationalism," *Journal of East Asian Affairs* 11, no. 2 (Summer–Fall 1997): 560.

20. Interfax, 16 May 2001.

21. Ekaterina Motrich, "Demographic Potential and Chinese Presence in the Russian Far East," *Far Eastern Affairs* 30, no. 1 (2002): 67.

22. *Heilongjiang Tongji Nianjian 2001* (Statistical Yearbook of Heilongjiang, 2001) (Heilongjiang: Heilongjiang Province Statistical Bureau, 2001), 35.

23. Sergei Shakrai, "Strategy Needed for Relationship with China," *Izvestia*, 20 May 1994, 4, in FBIS-SOV-94–098. For a study that argues that the Siberian regions

need to reduce their population, see Fiona Hill and Clifford Gaddy, *The Siberian Curse: How Communist Planners Left Russia Out in the Cold* (Washington, DC: Brookings Institution Press, 2003).

24. Emil Pain, "Nelegaly na beregakh Amura" (Illegals on the banks of the Amur), *Rossiiskie Vesti*, 6 May 1997, 3. For an account of the historical presence of Asians in the Russian Far East, also see Viacheslav Karlusov and Andrei Kudin, "The Chinese Presence in the Russian Far East: A Historical and Economic Analysis," *Far Eastern Affairs*, 2002–04–01FEA-No. 002: 62–76, at http://80–dlib.eastview.com.

25. In the 1930s, an estimated 200,000 Koreans lived in the Russian Far East, some of whom (or their descendants) began to return in the 1990s, primarily to Primorksii krai. Galina Vitkovskaya, "Lawlessness, Environmental Damage, and Other New Threats in the Russian Far East," in Rozman, Nosov and Watanabe, eds., *Russia and East Asia*, 186.

26. Dismal working conditions in the former labor camps led to a series of strikes among Chinese workers, who objected to being treated like the former prisoners.

27. Omri, no. 166, Part I, 25 August 1995.

28. Interview with Boris Nemtsov, Davis Center for Russian and Eurasian Studies, Harvard University, Cambridge, Massachusetts, 11 February 1998; Sergei Rogov, *Russia as the Eurasian Bridge: Challenges of Russia's Integration into the World Community*, Center for Naval Analyses, CIM 587/November 1998, 47.

29. Omri, no. 207, Part I, October 24, 1995.

30. Pain, "Nelegaly na beregakh Amura," 3.

31. Publications of the Carnegie Moscow Center dealing with Chinese immigration include Galina Vitkovskaya and Dmitri Trenin, eds., *Perspectivy Dal'nevostochnogo Regiona: mezhstranovoe vzaimodeistvie* (Perspectives of the Far Eastern region: cross-border cooperation) (Moscow: Carnegie Endowment for International Peace, 1999); Galina Vitkovskaya and Dmitri Trenin, eds., *Perspectivy Dal'nevostochnogo Regiona: naselenie, migratsiia, rynki, truda* (Perspectives of the Far Eastern region: population, migration, and labor markets), Working Papers, Issue 2 (Moscow: Carnegie Center for International Peace, 1999); Galina Vitkovskaya and Sergei Panarin, *Migratsiia i bezopasnost' v Rossii* (Migration and security in Russia) (Moscow: Carnegie Endowment for International Peace, 2000); Galina Vitkovskaya, "Does Chinese Immigration Endanger Russian Security?" *Carnegie Briefings*, Issue 8, (August 1999). Many of these publications can also be found on the Web site of the Moscow Carnegie Center at http://pubs.carnegie.ru. Also see Galina Vitkovskaya, Zhanna Zaionchkovskaia, and Kathleen Newland, "Chinese Migration into Russia," in Garnett, ed., *Rapprochement or Rivalry?*, 347–68; Galina Vitkovskaya, "Lawlessness, Environmental Damage, and Other New Threats in the Russian Far East," in Rozman, Nosov, and Watanabe, eds., *Russia and East Asia*, 179–99; Galina Vitkovskaya, "Russia: Cross Border Migration in the Russian Far East," *Writenet Country Papers*, October 1997; Mikhail Alexseev, "The 'Yellow Peril' Revisited: The Impact of Chinese Migration in Primorskii Krai," Memo No. 94, *Ponars* (Program on New Approaches to Russian Security), 1999; Mikhail Alexseev, "Chinese Migration in the Russian Far East," in Thornton and Zeigler, eds., *Russia's Far East*, 319–48; and Elizabeth Wishnick, "Russia in Asia and Asians in Russia," *SAIS Review* 20, no. 1 (Winter–Spring 2000): 87–101.

32. The Carnegie migration study estimated in 1996 that the number of Chinese in the border regions of Russia stretching from Primorskii krai to Irkutsk oblast was in the range of 200,000–300,000 people. Vitkovskaya and Zaionchkovskaia, "Novaia

Stolypinskaia politika" (A new Stolypin policy), in Vitkovskaya and Trenin, eds., *Perspectivy Dal'nevostochnogo Regiona: mezhstranovoe vzaimodeistvie*, 98.

33. Pain made a similar argument. He noted that operations to identify and expel illegal immigrants routinely uncovered only 5,000–6,000 persons per year in the Russian Far East, and that estimates of several million Chinese in the region were nonsensical given that the combined population of the cities of Vladivostok, Blagoveshchensk, and Nakhodka, where the immigrants concentrated, was only about 1.8 million. See Pain, "Nelegaly na beregakh Amura," 3.

34. V.G. Gelbras estimated the Chinese community in Moscow to be between 20,000–25,000 in the late 1990s. His research further indicated that the provincial origin of Chinese in Moscow differed significantly from Chinese in the Russian Far East. Whereas most Chinese in the Russian Far East migrated from the three Manchurian provinces, Chinese living in Moscow arrived from a wide range of locations in China including the coastal regions and southern China. See "Russia–China: The Chinese Community in Moscow," Johnson's Russia List, No. 6401, 14 August 2002.

35. Vitkovskaya, "Does Chinese Migration Endanger Russian Security?"

36. In the late 1990s, the head of the Primorskii krai visa office estimated that 60 percent of all illegal Chinese immigrants to Russia were simply using the country as a temporary stopover en route to Europe, Canada, or the United States. Vitkovskaya, "Lawlessness, Environmental Damage, and Other New Threats," in Rozman, Nosov, and Watanabe, eds., *Russia and East Asia*, 182.

37. In 1999, the Jewish autonomous oblast reduced the number of Chinese contract workers by 400 persons, allowing for 1,400 legal entrants. Itar-Tass, 3 February 1999.

38. Anatolii Novikov, "Inostrantsy v Khabarovskom krae: problemy i resheniia" (Foreigners in Khabarovsk krai: problems and resolutions), in Vitkovskaya and Trenin, eds., *Perspektivy Dal'nevostochnogo Regiona: naselenie, migratsiia, rynki truda*, 32–35. In the same volume see also, Stanislav Khodkov, "Immigratsiia i immigratsionnaia politika v Khabarovskom krae" (Immigration and immigration policy in Khabarovsk krai), 27–31.

39. Alexseev, "The 'Yellow Peril' Revisited," 1.

40. *Primorskii krai v 1998 godu* (Primorksii krai in 1998) (Vladivostok: Goskomstat, 1999), 21.

41. Alexseev, "Chinese Migration in the Russian Far East," in Thornton and Zeigler, eds., *Russia's Far East*, 323.

42. Lilia Larina, "Obraz Kitaia i Kitaitsev v predstavlenii Dal'nevostochnikov" (Images of China and Chinese in the perception of Far Eastern residents), in Vitkovskaya and Trenin, eds, *Perspektivy Dal'nevostochnogo Regiona: naselenie, migratsiia, rynki truda*, 97; see also Alexander Lukin, "The Image of China in Russian Border Regions," *Asian Survey* 38, no. 9 (September 1998): 821–30; Vitkovskaya and Zaionchkovskaia, "Novaia Stolypinskaia politika," in Vitkovskaya and Trenin, eds., *Perspectivy Dal'nevostochnogo Regiona: mezhstranovoe vzaimodeistvie*, 80–120; Alexander Lukin, *The Bear Watches the Dragon: Russia's Perception of China and the Evolution of Russian-Chinese Relations Since the Eighteenth Century* (Armonk, NY: M.E. Sharpe, 2003), 164–93; and Mikhail A. Alexseev, "Economic Valuations and Interethnic Fears: Perceptions of Chinese Migration in the Russian Far East," *Journal of Peace Research* 40, no. 1 (January 2003): 89–106.

43. *RFE/RL*, vol. 3, no. 130, Part I, 6 July 1999.

44. This comment of Ishaev's was somewhat misleading. While Russian state statistics indicated that the population of Khabarovsk krai decreased by 752,000 between

1993 and 1997, an estimated 468,000 people left the krai, with the remainder of the decrease—284,000 people—due to natural deaths, which considerably exceeded births. See Vitkovskaya and Zaionchkovskaia, "Novaia Stolypinskaia politika," in Vitkovskaya and Trenin, eds., *Perspectivy Dal'nevostochnogo Regiona: mezhstranovoe vzaimodeistvie*, 88.

45. Aleksandr Babakin and Aleksandr Shinkin, "Tridtsat' shest' granits Rossii" (The thirty-six borders of Russia), *Rossiiskaia Gazeta*, 10 July 1999, 4. Ishaev made these remarks at a meeting of border region leaders held with Prime Minister Sergei Stephasin in July 1999.

46. Xinhua, 30 June 1994.

47. David Kerr, "Opening and Closing the Sino-Russian Border: Trade, Regional Development and Political Interest in Northeast Asia," *Europe–Asia Studies* 48, no. 6 (1996): 960.

48. Omri, no. 207, Part I, 24 October 1995.

49. Nikolai Svanidze, "Li Pen zaiavliaet: Kitai ne pooshchriaet pereselenie svoikh grazhdan v Rossii" (Li Peng declares: China will not encourage the settlement of its citizens in Russia), *Nezavisimaia Gazeta*, 19 February 1998, 1.

50. Elizabeth Wishnick, "Chinese Perspectives on Cross-Border Relations," in Garnett, ed., *Rapprochement or Rivalry?*, 240–42; and Wishnick "Russia in Asia," 96.

51. Sergei Litvinov, "Our Border Guards Are the Most Steadfast," *Nezavisimoye Voyennoye Obozreniye*, 19–25 March 1999, no. 10: 1–2, in FBIS-SOV-1999–0425.

52. Xinhua, 23 September 1999.

53. RFE/RL Newsline, vol. 6, no. 113, Part I, 18 June 2002.

54. RFE/RL Newsline, vol. 5, no. 183, Part I, 27 September 2002. Also see Minister of Foreign Affairs Igor Ivanov's answers to questions posed by Internet users in "Esli vy poteriali grazhdanstvo" (If you have lost your citizenship), *Rossiiskaia Gazeta*, 16 November 2002.

55. This perspective was first articulated by researchers associated with the Moscow Carnegie Center, including demographers Galina Vitkovskaya and Zhanna Zaionchkovskaia, and the center's deputy director, Dmitri Trenin (see note 31). For additional examples of this position see Vilya Gelbras, *Kitaiskaia realnost' Rossii* (The Chinese reality of Russia). (Moscow: Izd-vo Muravei, 2001); and *Novoe osvoenie Sibiri i Dal'nego Vostoka* (The new emancipation of Siberia and the Far East), Council on Foreign and Defense Policy at www.svop.ru/yuka/896.html.

56. RFE/RL Newsline, vol. 5, no. 62, Part I, 29 March 2001.

57. *Novoe osvoenie Sibiri i Dal'nego Vostoka.*

58. M. Alekseev, "V nashem dome poselilsia zamechatel'nyi sosed . . ." (A remarkable neighbor has settled in our home), *Ekonomika i Zhizn'*, no. 39 (September 2002): 1–3.

59. Karlusov and Kudin, "The Chinese Presence in the Russian Far East," 71.

60. *Regiony Rossii, 2000, Tom 2* (Regions of Russia, 2000, vol. 2) (Moscow: Goskomstat: 2000), 863; Kunio Okada, "The Japanese Economic Presence in the Russian Far East," in Thornton and Zeigler, *Russia's Far East*, 433–34.

61. Itar-Tass, 30 June 2003.

62. Ibid.

63. The first figure is presented in Russell Working, *Vladivostok News*, 26 June 1998, at http://srchome.slav.hokudai.ac.jp/eng/Russia/feast-e.html. The second is derived from statistics presented in *Primorskii krai v 1998 godu* (Primorskii krai in 1998) (Vladivostok: Goskomstat, 1999), 176.

64. Nadezhda Mikheeva, "Foreign Trade of the Russian Far East with the People's Republic of China: Development and Problems," at http://src-h.slav.hokudai.ac.jp/eng/Russia/feast-e/html.

65. *Khabarovskii krai v 1998 godu* Chast 1(Khaborovsk krai in 1998 Part 1) (Khabarovsk: Goskomstat, 1999), 114.

66. Natalia Pisarenko, "Vneshneekonomicheskie sviazi Khabarovskogo kraia i KNR," (Foreign economic links between Khabarovsk krai and the PRC), in Vitkovskaya and Trenin, eds., *Perspektivy Dal'nevostochnogo Regiona: naselenie, migratsiia, rynki truda*, 82.

67. Interpress Service, 2 April 1999, on Johnson's Russia List, No. 3226, 2 April 1999.

68. Elena Borodina, "Russian Far East: International Trade in 2001," at www.bisnis.doc.gov/bisnis/country/020509trade_rfe.htm.

69. Extrapolated from Table 6.3 and *Zhongguo Duiwai Jingji Maoyi Nianjian 2002* (Yearbook of China's Foreign Economic Relations 2002) (Beijing: Chinese State Statistical Bureau, 2002), 840.

70. These figures are extrapolated from Tables 4.1 and 6.3.

71. See Elizabeth Wishnick, "Chinese Perspectives on Cross-Border Relations," in Garnett, ed., *Rapprochement or Rivalry?*, 227–56; and in the same volume, Gilbert Rozman, "Turning Fortresses into Free Trade Zones," 177–202.

72. Shinkin, "Tridtsat' shest' granits Rossii."

73. This arrangement paired Amur oblast with Shanghai, Primorskii krai with Jilin, Bashkortostan with Liaoning, Altai with Xinjiang, and Novosibirsk with Heilongjiang.

74. Rajon Menon and Charles E. Zeigler, "The Balance of Power and U.S. Foreign Policy Interests in the Russian Far East," *NBR Analysis* 11, no. 5 (December 2000): 21. In February 2003, the regional administrations of Amur oblast and Heilongjiang province reportedly agreed on the bridge's construction. In December 2002, however, regional protests erupted in Altai krai over a decision to build a road linking Altai krai to Xinjiang province, with local residents expressing fears that it would result in increased migration to the krai.

75. *Primorskii krai v 1998 godu*, 146.

76. See Gaye Christofferson, "The Greater Vladivostok Project: Transnational Linkages in Regional Economic Planning," *Pacific Affairs* 67, no. 4 (Winter 1994/1995): 513–31; and Daniel Aldrich, "If You Built It, They Will Come: A Cautionary Tale About the Tumen River Projects," *Journal of East Asian Affairs* 11, no. 1 (January 1997): 299–326.

77. The Web site of the East-West Intermodel Corridor is located at www.ahwg.org.

78. Itar-Tass, 11 March 1999.

79. Elizabeth Wishnick, "Prospects for Russian-American Economic Cooperation in the Russian Far East," *Russian Regional Report*, 20 August 1999.

80. *Primorskii krai v 1999 godu* (Primorskii krai in 1999) (Vladivostok: Goskomstat, 2000), 153, 186.

81. *Sotsial'no-ekonomicheskoe razvitie svobodnoi ekonomicheskoi zony "Nakhodka" v 2000 godu* (Social and economic development of the free economic zone "Nakhodka" in 2000) (Vladivostok: Goskomstat, 2001), 13.

82. U.S. businesses involved with the East-West project had strong reservations about the leadership of Primorskii krai. At a dinner hosted for Prime Minister Sergei Stepashin in Seattle in June 1999, local investors as well as Washington State governor

Gary Locke indicated their distaste for the presence of Nazdratenko, considering him a "crook," a "thug," and the "godfather of Vladivostok." *RFE/RL*, vol. 3, no. 144, Part I, July 27, 1999.

83. In March 2003, the Chinese offered to lease the port of Po'set, or Zarubino in Primorskii krai, a notion promptly rejected by the Russian side. Interfax, 31 March 2003; Interfax, 2 April 2003.

84. Ruslan Pukhov, "Arms Are More than Gold," *Gazeta Wyborcza*, 17 December 2001, 9, at www.cast.ru. For a discussion of the situation of defense industries in the Russian Far East, see Evgenia Gydkova, "Problemy konversii oboronnoi promyshlennosti Rossiiskogo Dal'nego Vostoka" (Problems of the conversion of the defense industry of the Russian Far East), in Vitkovskaya and Trenin, eds., *Perspectivy Dal'nevostochnogo Regiona: naselenie, migratsiia, rynki truda*, 72–76; and Katherine G. Burns, "Security Implications of Defense Conversion in the Russian Far East," in Thornton and Zeigler, eds., *Russia's Far East*, 267–89.

85. Itar-Tass, 5 August 1999.

86. Interpress Service, Moscow, 2 April 1999, Johnson's Russia List, no. 3226, 2 April 1999.

87. BBC Monitoring, Johnson's Russia List, no. 4422, 25 July 2000.

88. In May 2003, Nazdratenko was ousted from his position as head of the State Fisheries Committee, with Putin appointing him a deputy secretary of the Security Council.

89. Itar-Tass, 6 February 1999.

90. Itar-Tass, 3 June 2002.

91. Although the displacement of Russians by Chinese laborers in agriculture aroused tensions, public opinion surveys invariably indicated that Chinese worked harder than Russians and were willing to perform jobs that Russians, even unemployed Russians, often rejected. Their wages were also significantly lower—one and a half to two times less on average—than those of Russians with the same qualifications. See Vitkovskaya and Zaionchkovskaia, "Novaia Stolypinskaia Politika," in Vitkovskaya and Trenin, eds., *Perspectivy Dal'nevostochnogo Regiona: mezhstranovoe vzaimodeistvie*, 110; and Larina, "Obraz Kitaia i kitaitsev," in Vitkovskaya and Trenin, eds., *Perspektivy Dal'nevostochnogo Regiona: naselenie, migratsiia, rynki truda*, 97.

92. See Sarah Karush, "Hardworking Chinese Harvest the Steppe," *Moscow Times*, 15 August 2002.

93. See Jennifer Duncan and Michelle Ruetschle, "Agrarian Reform and Agricultural Productivity in the Russian Far East," in Thornton and Zeigler, eds., *Russia's Far East*, 193–220.

94. Irina Aksenova, "Dal'nii Vostok obosoblen i razobshchen" (The Far East is detached and disconnected), *Rossiiskaia Gazeta*, 26 November 2002.

95. See Lukin, "The Image of China in Russia's Border Regions," 833–38; and *The Bear Watches the Dragon*, especially Chapter 3.

96. Alexseev, "Economic Valuations and Interethnic Fears." The Council on Foreign and Defense Policy report on Siberia and the Russian Far East also makes this point. Its authors note that "since Chinese (and for the future Korean and other Eastern) migration is unavoidable, it is necessary to adopt measures ahead of time to avert the transformation of the southern part of Siberia and the Far East into a zone of ethnic and future social-political confrontation." At www.svop.ru/yuka/892.shtml.

Notes to Chapter 7

1. Xinhua, 3 September 1994.
2. For a discussion of the concept of the strategic relationship and its genesis, see Sean Kay, "What Is a Strategic Partnership?" *Problems of Post-Communism* 47, no. 3 (May–June 2000): 15–24.
3. Tass, 18 May 1989, in FBIS-SOV-89–095, 18 May 1989.
4. Chris Yeung, *South China Morning Post*, 1 April 1991, 7, in FBIS-CHI-91–062, 1 April 1991.
5. Xinhua, 19 May 1991.
6. Richard Sakwa, *Russian Politics and Society* (London and New York: Routledge, 1993), 295.
7. Vladimir Kashirov and Georgiy Shmelyov, Tass, 16 March 1992, in FBIS-SOV-92–053, 18 March 1992.
8. See Alexander Rahr, "'Atlanticists' versus 'Eurasians' in Russian Foreign Policy," *RFE-RL Research Report*, vol. 1, no. 22 (29 May 1992): 17–23; Suzanne Crow, "Competing Blueprints for Russian Foreign Policy," *RFE-RL Research Report*, vol. 1, no. 50, (18 December 1992): 45–50; and Bobo Lo, *Russian Foreign Policy in the Post-Soviet Era: Reality, Illusion and Mythmaking* (New York: Palgrave Macmillan, 2002), especially Chapter 3.
9. Vladimir Lukin, "Our Security Predicament," *Foreign Policy*, no. 88 (Fall 1992): 57–76; this phrase has been a favorite of Lukin's. See also Vladimir Nadein, "Vladimir Lukin obviniaet MID v vernosti 'brezhnevskoi diplomatii'" (Vladimir Lukin accuses the Ministry of Foreign Affairs of fidelity to "Brezhnevian" diplomacy), *Izvestia*, 5 February 1994.
10. *Wen Wei Po*, 19 December 1992, in FBIS-CHI-92–245, 21 December 1992.
11. Xinhua, 18 December 1992.
12. Itar-Tass, 1 February 1994; Xinhua, 27 May 1994.
13. Xinhua, 3 September 1994.
14. Xinhua, 25 April 1996.
15. The concept of the "strategic relationship," however, has also been employed by the United States. See Kay, "What Is a Strategic Partnership?"
16. Xinhua, 25 April 1996.
17. See, for example, Andrei Kozyrev, "The Lagging Partnership," *Foreign Affairs* 73, no. 3 (May–June 1994): 63–64.
18. Evgenii Primakov, "Na gorizonte—mnogopoliusnyi mir" (On the horizon—a multipolar world), *Nezavisimaia Gazeta*, 10 October 1996.
19. In addition, Primakov's professional background appealed to the Chinese. His credentials included a tenure as the director of the Institute for Oriental Studies, director of the Institute of World Economy and International Affairs (IMEMO), membership in Gorbachev's Presidential Council, and the heading of Russia's External Intelligence Service in the Yeltsin era.
20. Itar-Tass, 23 April 1997.
21. Pavel Felgenhauer, *Moscow Times*, 15 February 1996. Also see the statements made by Arkadii Vol'skii, president of the Russian Union of Industrialists and Entrepreneurs, "Anatolii Chubais preduprezhdaet" (Anatolii Chubais warns), *Trud*, 5 February 1997; and Viktor Ilyukhin, head of the Security Committee of the Russian Duma, Interfax, 20 March 1997.
22. Interfax, 24 April 1997.

23. Michael H. Armacost and Kenneth B. Pyle, "Japan and the Engagement of China: Challenges for U.S. Policy Coordination," *NBR Analysis*, vol. 12, no. 5 (December 2001): 30–32; and David M. Lampton, *Same Bed Different, Dreams: Managing U.S.–China Relations 1989–2000* (Berkeley and Los Angeles: University of California Press, 2001), 230–31.

24. Lampton, *Same Bed, Different Dreams*, 46–55. Also see Gerrit W. Gong, ed., *Taiwan Strait Dilemmas: China–Taiwan–U.S. Policies in the New Century* (Washington, DC: CSIS Press, 2000).

25. Xinhua, 25 October 1998.

26. Xinhua, 24 November 1998.

27. Itar-Tass, 1 April 1999.

28. Xinhua, 10 May 1999.

29. Itar-Tass, 8 May 1999.

30. RFE/RL Newsline, May 10, 1999.

31. See He Jinzhe, "Eight-Nation Draft Resolution is Full of 'Mines,'" *Renmin Ribao* (Guangzhou South China News Supplement), 11 June 1999: 2, in FBIS-CHI-1999–0611.

32. Interfax, 24 April 1998.

33. Russia and China both abstained from Resolution 1239 regarding relief assistance to Kosovo refugees, adopted on May 14, 1999, shortly after the May 7, 1999, NATO bombing of the Chinese embassy in Belgrade.

34. Conservative elements of the Chinese leadership (who also were likely to be opposed to China joining the WTO) urged the cancellation of Zhu's trip. Lampton, *Same Bed, Different Dreams*, 58–59.

35. Itar-Tass, 9 May 1998.

36. Zhang Baoxiang, "Beiyue jiajin zhiding xin zanlue" (NATO steps up the formulation of a new strategy), *Renmin Ribao*, 7 August 1998, 6.

37. www.usembassy.it/file9904/alia/99040613.htm.

38. Ai Yu, "Kosovo Crisis and Stability in China's Tibet and Xinjiang," *Ta Kung Pao*, 2 June 1999, in FBIS-CHI-1999–0624.

39. In a 1999 survey on cross-strait relations, 44.8 percent of the respondents identified themselves as Taiwanese, 13.1 percent as Chinese, 39.9 percent as both, and 2.2 percent as "don't know." Loh I-cheng, "The Gordian Knot in Cross-Strait Relations: The Question of Taiwan's Participation in International Organizations," in Gong, ed., *Taiwan Strait Dilemmas*, 57.

40. Much has been written about the unauthorized entry of Russian troops into Kosovo and their seizure of the Pristina airport before NATO troops arrived. It appears likely that this move was a freelance operation by the Russian military command undertaken without the knowledge of the Ministry of Foreign Affairs or the Yeltsin government. In any case, the action would seem to have been a response to NATO's unwillingness to accord Russia a peacekeeping role.

41. Aleksandr Sabov, "Vmeste s voinoi zakonchilsia i mir?" (Has peace also ended along with the war?), *Rossiiskaia Gazeta*, 13 July 1999.

42. Bing Jinfu, "Tianxia reng butaiping" (Under heaven there is still not peace), *Renmin Ribao*, 2 July 1999.

43. Itar-Tass, 10 December 1999.

44. Michael J. Green and Toby F. Dalton, "Asian Reactions to U.S. Missile Defense," *NBR Analysis* 11, no. 3 (November 2000): 12–13; Also see Arthur S. Ding,

"China's Concerns About Theater Missile Defense: A Critique," *Nonproliferation Review* 6, no. 4 (Fall 1999): 93–101.

45. www.fas.org/spp/starwars/congress/1997_r/hr105–308p1.htm.

46. Michael McDevitt, "Beijing's Bind," *Washington Quarterly* 23, no. 3 (Summer 2000): 178.

47. Tom Sanderson, "Chinese Perspectives on US Ballistic Missile Defense," at www.stimson.org.

48. For further discussion of Russian reactions to missile defense, see Amy F. Woolf, *National Missile Defense: Russia's Reaction*, CRS Report for Congress, Congressional Research Service, August 10, 2001; and Green and Dalton, "Asian Reactions to U.S. Missile Defense."

49. Quoted in Woolf, "Russia's Reaction," 7.

50. Itar-Tass, 23 November 1998.

51. Xinhua, 16 April 1999.

52. Itar-Tass, 10 December 1999.

53. Joint Statement on Strategic Stability, Clinton-Putin Summit, 3–5 June 2000, Moscow, Russia at http://usinfo.state.gov/topical/pol/arms/stories/00060407.htm.

54. See Pavel Felgenhauer. "'Nice Visit' a Boost for Putin," *Moscow Times*, 8 June 2000; Robert E. Hunter, "Guiding Missile Defense," *Moscow Times*, 16 June 2002.

55. See Pavel Felgenhauer, "ABM Proposal an Old Ploy," *Moscow Times*, 22 June 2000; and Itar-Tass, 11 June 2000.

56. Xinhua, 8 June 2000.

57. AFP, 6 June 2000, in FBIS-CHI-2000–0606; also see RFE/RL Newsline, 7 June 2000; and Yu Bin, "Strategic Outdistancing . . . or Else," *Comparative Connections*, China–Russia Relations (July 2000), at www.csis.org.

58. Vladimir Putin's first meeting as Russian president with Jiang Zemin took place a few weeks earlier in Dushanbe, Tajikistan, at the annual meeting of the "Shanghai Five." Missile defense was apparently an item of discussion.

59. Xinhua, 18 July 2000.

60. As Chapter 2 notes, Russia signed friendship treaties with a number of CIS states in the 1990s, an unsubstantial treaty with North Korea in February 2000 and a cooperation treaty with Iran in March 2001.

61. "Vos'maia vstrecha" (The eighth meeting), *Rossiiskaia Gazeta*, 14 July 2001, 1.

62. The Shanghai Cooperation Organization (SCO), of course, can be viewed as an example of China's commitment to multilateralism in the Central Asian region. Moreover, India, Pakistan, and Iran have all indicated an interest in SCO membership. See Li Tzu-Ching, "Jiang ni ZhongE jiemeng zhi Mei" (Jiang plans an alliance of China with Russia to restrict the United States), *Zheng Ming*, no. 257 (March 1999): 13–15. Also see Andrew C. Kuchins, "Russia's Relations with China and India: Strategic Partnerships Yes; Strategic Alliances No," *Demokratizatsiya* 9, no. 2 (Spring 2001), 259–275; and Andrew C. Kuchins, "Russia's Strategic Partnerships and Global Security," Memo no. 165, *Ponars*, 2000.

63. Simon Saradzhyan, "Moscow Mending Ties with Old Ally Beijing," *Moscow Times*, 26 February 2001.

64. See RFE/RL Newsline, 18 January 2000; also Yu Bin, "Strategic Outdistancing . . . or Else."

65. See, for example, Pavel Felgenhauer, "Isolating Uncle Sam," *Moscow Times*, 19 July 2001; Constantine C. Menges, "Russia, China and What's Really on the Table,"

Washington Post, 29 July 2001, in Johnson's Russia List, no. 5374, 31 July 2001; Martin Sieff, "Russia–China Pact Echoes 1939," UPI, 16 July 2001, in Johnson's Russia List, no. 5349, 17 July 2001; "Triangular Diplomacy" (ed.), *New York Times,* 18 July 2001. For more extensive commentary on the treaty, see Jeanne L. Wilson, "Strategic Partners: Russian-Chinese Relations and the July 2001 Friendship Treaty," *Problems of Post-Communism* 49, no. 3 (May–June 2002): 3–18; Elizabeth Wishnick, "Russia and China: Brothers Again?" *Asian Survey* 41, no. 5 (September–October 2001): 797–812; and A. Lukin, "China: Advancing Bilateral Cooperation," *International Affairs,* 01–01–2002(IAF-No.001) at http://80–dlib.eastview.com.

66. Jane Perlez, "White House Unconcerned About China–Russia Accord," *New York Times,* 17 July 2001. Other State Department officials, in a more diplomatic vein, noted that the treaty did not represent a threat to the United States, which viewed good relations between Russia and China as a positive development.

67. Interfax, 12 July 2001. When queried as to why there was no mention of the ABM issue in the treaty, Losyukov replied that it was not a topic for a treaty because "such a treaty is signed for decades and the topic may stop being acute within 20 years."

68. For example, National Security Advisor Condeleezza Rice, Secretary of Defense Donald Rumsfeld, Deputy Secretary of Defense Paul Wolfowitz, and CIA Director George Tenet all labeled Russia as a "threat" to the United States. In a somewhat different context, Secretary of State Colin Powell specified that "the approach we have to Russia . . . shouldn't be terribly different than the very realistic approach we had to the old Soviet Union in the late '80's." See Joseph Ferguson, "Spy Mania and Familiar Rhetoric," *Comparative Connections,* U.S.-Russian Relations (January 2001), at www.csis.org.

69. Perhaps Dmitri Trenin, deputy director of the Carnegie Moscow Center, has most forcefully made this argument. See Dmitri Trenin, "Vladimir Putin's Autumn Marathon: Toward the Birth of a Russian Foreign Policy Strategy," *Briefing Papers,* Issue 11 (November 2001), at http://pubs.carnegie.ru; Dmitri Trenin, "Nenadezhnaia strategiia" (An unreliable strategy), *Pro et Contra* 6, nos. 1–2 (Winter–Spring 2001): 50–65; Dmitri Trenin, "Novyi kurs Putina: povorot zakreplen. Chto dal'she? (Putin's new course: the turn has been strengthened. What's next?) *Briefing Papers* 4, no. 6 (June 2002), at http://pubs.carnegie.ru; and Dmitri Trenin "How Durable Is the New U.S.-Russian Partnership: A Perspective from Moscow," 12 December 2001, at http://ceip.org. For further commentary on Putin's foreign policy since September 11, 2001, see Peter Rutland, "Putin's Levitation Act," *Russia and Eurasia Review* 1, no. 1 (4 June 2002); Angela Stent, "Russia: Farewell to Empire?" *World Policy Journal* 19, no. 3 (Fall 2002), at www.worldpolicy.org; and Celeste A. Wallander, "Russia's Relationship with China After September 11," Memo no. 214, *Ponars,* 2002.

70. See Bao Lisheng, "Three Evil Forces Threatening Xinjiang's Stability," *Ta Kung Pao,* 10 August 2001, in FBIS-CHI-2001–0810.

71. Xinhua, 12 October 2001.

72. Itar-Tass, 24 October 2001.

73. Itar-Tass, 16 December 2001; Pavel Felgenhauer, "Vashington stavit Rossiiu na mesto" (Washington puts Russia in its place), *Moskovskie Novosti,* 18 December 2001, 5.

74. AFP, 13 December 2001, in FBIS-CHI-2001–1213; Elisabeth Rosenthal, "China Voices Muted Distress at U.S. Blow to ABM," *New York Times,* 14 December 2001.

75. Li Gang, "The End of the ABM Treaty," *Ta Kung Pao,* 23 December 2001, in FBIS-CHI-2001–1224. According to Yan Zheng and Ma Jian in *People's Daily:*

"Although the attitude of the Russian leadership appears to be tough, since Russia's all-round national strength is not what it was, and it requires a great deal of U.S. technical and fund support in order to develop its economy, it cannot fall out with the United States on the NMD issue." "Russia's All-Round Countering of NMD," *Renmin Ribao*, 23 February 2001, in FBIS-CHI-2001–0223.

76. Itar-Tass, 18 December 2001.

77. See David E. Powell, "Despite a Pact, Putin Saves Face But Gains Little," *Boston Globe*, 19 May 2002; Pavel Felgenhauer, "A Worthless Scrap of Paper," *Moscow Times*, 16 May 2002.

78. The joint declaration signed by Bush and Putin at their May 2002 summit also included a reference to plans for the United States and Russia, within the framework of the NATO–Russia council, "to explore opportunities for intensified practical cooperation on missile defense in Europe." Itar-Tass, 24 May 2002.

79. Itar-Tass, 28 May 2002. The concept has been commonplace among Russian politicians in the post-Soviet era.

80. Interfax, 17 April 2002; Itar-Tass, 6 June 2002.

81. "Gaodu pingjia Ezhong hezuo chengguo: Eluosi zongtong Pu jing jieshou benbao kaofang" (Russian-Chinese cooperation has resulted in a high degree of achievements: Russian president Putin in Beijing gives an interview to *Renmin Ribao*), *Renmin Ribao*, June 1, 2002, 3.

82. Interfax, 8 June 2002; Itar-Tass, 8 June 2002.

83. Itar-Tass, 5 June 2002.

84. AFP, 24 May 2002, in FBIS-SOV-2002–0524.

85. See, for example, Tan Weibing, "Nuclear Disarmament: Why Did Russia Make Large Concessions, Can the U.S.-Russia Offensive Strategic Weapons Treaty Agreement Really Make the World 'More Peaceful'?" *Liaowang*, no. 21 (20 May 2002): 56–57, in FBIS-CHI-2002–0524.

86. See Ma Jian, "Eluosi yu Xifang 'kao er bulong'" (Russia and the West: draw near but remain apart), *Renmin Ribao*, 31 May 2002: 7; Xinhua, 16 May 2002.

87. "Vystuplenie Prezidenta Putina na sammite Rossiia NATO" (Speech of President Putin at Russia–NATO summit), Rome, 28 May 2002, at www.nato.int/docu/speech/2002.

88. Willy Wo-Lap Lam, "Moscow Tilts West, Beijing Worries," *China Brief* 2, Issue 12, 6 June 2002.

89. See Ren Yujun, "Meiguo: jie fankong zhiji, mou quanqiu baye" (The United States makes use of opposition to terrorism as a means of achieving global hegemony), *Renmin Ribao*, 22 March 2002; also Halford MacKinder, *Democratic Ideals and Reality: A Study in the Politics of Reconstruction* (New York: H. Holt, 1942).

90. Vladim Socor, "War Draws Central Asia's 'Stans' Closer to the U.S.," *Wall Street Journal Europe*, 18 January 18, 2002, Johnson's Russia List, no. 6029, 18 January 2002; RFE/RL Newsline, 7 December 2001; Mikhail Khodaryonok, "'Starshego brata' sdali za milliard dollarov" (Big brother dumped for one billion dollars), *Nezavisimaia Gazeta*, 30 January 2002.

91. Vladimir Isachenkov, "U.S. Should Leave Asia," *AP*, 12 February 2002; Interfax, 18 March 2002.

92. Xinhua, 4 February 2002.

93. Xinhua, 11 February 2002.

94. United Nations Security Council, Resolution 1441, adopted at Security Council Meeting 4644, 8 November 2002, at www.un.int/usa/sres-iraq.htm.

95. Joint Statement by China, France, and Russia Interpreting UN Security Council Resolution 1441 (2002) at www.staff.city.ac.uk/p.willetts/IRAQ/FRRSCHST.HTM.

96. Xinhua, 2 December 2002.

97. John Litchfield and Anne Penketh, "France, Germany and Russia Defy the US by Declaring That War Is Unjustified," *Independent*, 11 February 2003 at www.commondreams.org/headlines03/0211–01.htm.

98. Elizabeth Bryant, "Russia, France, Germany Warn Against War," *Washington Times*, 5 March 2003.

99. See Doug Stuck, "Powell Makes Few Gains on Asia Tour," *Washington Post*, 26 February 2003: A16; John Pomfret, "Beijing Is Cool to Powell's Pleas," *Washington Post*, 25 February 2003: A19.

100. Xinhua, 27 February 2003.

101. Elizabeth Bryant, "Russia, France, Germany Warn Against War," *Washington Times*, 5 March 2003.

102. Xinhua, 6 March 2003.

103. Itar-Tass, 11 March 2003.

104. Xinhua, 23 May 2003.

105. Agreed Framework Between the United States of America and the Democratic People's Republic of Korea, 21 October 1994 at www.ceip.org/files/projects/npp/resources/koreaaf.htm.

106. See Stephen Blank, "Russian Policy and the Changing Korean Question," *Asian Survey* 35, no. 8 (August 1995): 711–26; and G. Toloraia, "Korean Peninsula and Russia," *International Affairs*, no. 1 (2003) at www.ciaonet.org.

107. Itar-Tass, 12 April 1994, in FBIS-SOV-94–070, 12 April 1994; and *Yonghap*, 29 January 1994, in FBIS-CHI-04–021, 1 February 1994.

108. KCNA, 20 July 2000, in FBIS-SOV-2000–0720.

109. Kim had previously been to China but not on a formal state visit. Kim's aversion to air travel meant that his Russian trip involved a nearly month-long journey crossing Siberia on a specially outfitted armored train.

110. Itar-Tass, 4 August 2001.

111. The 1996 Russian-Chinese joint statement noted the commitment of the two sides "to strengthen security, stability and economic cooperation in North-Eastern Asia," while the 1998 statement indicated that "solving the problems of the Korean peninsula is vitally important to ensuring stability in the Asia Pacific region." Xinhua, 25 April 1996; Xinhua, 28 November 1998.

112. Xinhua, 2 December 2002.

113. Xinhua, 27 February 2003.

114. John Ruwitch, "China and Russia Lack Clout to Dictate to North Korea," Reuters, 17 January 2003, in Johnson's Russia List, Number 7024, 19 January 2003; Alexander Pikayev, "The North Korean 'Threat' and How to Counter It," *Briefing Papers* 5, Issue 1 (January 2003) at www.carnegie.ru.

115. Russia and Cuba abstained on the vote, while China voted in its favor.

116. See Minxin Pei, "A Docile China Is Bad for Global Peace," *Financial Times*, 12 March 2003.

117. Xinhua, 23 May 2003.

118. China agreed in November 1991 to abide by the Missile Technology Control Regime, thus preventing the transfer of certain M-series ballistic missiles to Iran. In September 1997, China pledged to halt future sales of anti-ship cruise missiles to Iran. During the U.S.–China summit in October 1998, China and the United States

concluded a confidential agreement that China would not provide any new nuclear assistance to Iran. See Bates Gill, "Two Steps Forward, One Step Back: The Dynamics of Chinese Nonproliferation and Arms Control Policy Making in an Era of Reform," in Lampton, ed., *The Making of Chinese Foreign and Security Policy*; also see Michael D. Swaine, "Ballistic Missile Development," in Richard J. Ellings and Aaron L. Friedberg, eds., *Strategic Asia: Power and Purpose, 2001–02* (Seattle, WA: National Bureau of Asian Research, 2001), 299–360.

119. The Iranian shopping list included a variety of missile systems, including S-300 missiles, Moskit and Yakhont anti-ship missiles, and Su-27 and Su-30 fighter planes.

120. Steve Holland, "Putin, Bush Sign Landmark Nuclear Arms Treaty," Reuters, 24 May 2002.

121. Xinhua, 23 May 2003.

122. "Gaodu pingjia Ezhong," *Renmin Ribao*, June 1, 2002, 3.

123. Xinhua, 2 December 2002.

124. Xinhua, 23 May 2003.

125. Mikhail Gorbachev, *Perestroika: New Thinking for Our Country and the World* (New York: Harper and Row, 1987), 190–209.

126. Dmitri Trenin, "Sealing a New Era in U.S.-Russian Relations," *Moscow Times*, 27 May 2002. Trenin has also been a vocal critic of the concept of "multipolarity," arguing that it is a dead-end road for Russia, rooted in obsolescent illusions of Russian power.

127. Pei, "A Docile China."

128. Interfax, 22 May 2003.

Notes to Chapter 8

1. For a discussion of constructivism, see Jeffrey T. Checkel, "The Constructivist Turn in International Relations Theory," *World Politics* 50, no. 2 (1998): 324–48.

2. For a classic exposition, see Graham Allison and Philip Zelikow, *Essence of Decision: Explaining the Cuban Missile Crisis*, 2d ed. (New York: Longman, 1999).

3. The appointment of Arkadii Vol'skii, the president of the Union of Industrialists and Entrepreneurs, to chair the Russian side of the committee, was also a retrograde decision. Vol'skii had emerged as an advocate of the Chinese model, but as noted in Chapter 1, his vision of its relevance for Russia was essentially conservative, rooted in a desire to preserve Russia's state industries.

4. Alexander Lukin, *The Bear Watches the Dragon: Russia's Perception of China and the Evolution of Russian-Chinese Relations Since the Eighteenth Century* (Armonk, NY: M.E. Sharpe, 2003), 317.

5. Karl Friedrich and Zbigniew Brzezinski, *Totalitarian Dictatorship and Autocracy* (New York: Praeger, 1956), 9–10.

6. See H. Gordon Skilling, "Interest Groups and Communist Politics," *World Politics* 18, no. 3 (April 1966): 435–51; and H. Gordon Skilling and Franklyn Griffiths, eds., *Interest Groups in Soviet Politics* (Princeton, NJ: Princeton University Press, 1971).

7. For further discussion of the role of domestic factors in Russian foreign policy decision making, see Allen C. Lynch, "The Realism of Russia's Foreign Policy," *Europe–Asia Studies* 53, no. 1 (2001): 7–8; Neil Malcolm, Alex Pravda, Roy Allison,

and Margot Light, *Internal Factors in Russian Foreign Policy* (Oxford: Oxford University Press, 1996); and Robert H. Donaldson and Joseph L. Nogee, *The Foreign Policy of Russia: Changing Systems, Enduring Interests*, 2d ed. (Armonk, NY: M.E. Sharpe, 2002), Chapter 5. Michael McFaul has been perhaps the most vocal proponent of the argument that Russia's foreign policy is a product of domestic politics. See, for example, Michael McFaul, "Russia's Many Foreign Policies," *Demokratizatsiya* 7, no. 3 (Summer 1999): 393–412; and Michael McFaul, "A Precarious Peace: Domestic Politics in the Making of Russian Foreign Policy," *International Security* 22, no. 3 (Winter 1997): 5–36.

8. A classic example is the work of Robert A. Dahl with its emphasis on the role of independent associations in democratic society. See Robert A. Dahl, *Dilemmas of Pluralist Democracy: Autonomy vs. Control* (New Haven, CT: Yale University Press, 1982); and Robert A. Dahl, *Who Governs? Democracy and Power in an American City* (New Haven, CT: Yale University Press, 1961).

9. As noted in Chapter 7, Russia canceled the agreement in 2000. For further discussion, see Robert H. Donaldson and John A. Donaldson, "The Arms Trade in Russian-Chinese Relations: Identity, Domestic Politics, and Geopolitical Positioning," *International Studies Quarterly* 47, no. 4 (December 2003), 709–32.

10. Alexander A. Sergounin and Sergey V. Subbotin, *Russian Arms Transfers to East Asia in the 1990s* (Oxford: Oxford University Press, 1999), 17, 23. Also Xinhua, 5 March 1992, in FBIS-CHI-92–044, 5 March 1992; Xinhua, 23 June 1992, in FBIS-CHI-92–122, 24 June 1992; and CNA, 12 August 1992 in FBIS-CHI-92–156, 12 August 1992.

11. For an account that emphasizes the influence of regional elites on Russian foreign policy toward China, see Elizabeth Wishnick, *Mending Fences: The Evolution of Moscow's China Policy from Brezhnev to Yeltsin* (Seattle: University of Washington Press, 2001), Chapters 1, 9.

12. For a discussion of the democratic peace literature, see James E. Dougherty and Robert L. Pfaltzgraff, Jr., *Contending Theories of International Relations: A Comprehensive Survey*, 5th ed. (New York: Longman, 2001), 313–21. Also James Lee Ray, *Democracy and International Conflict: An Evaluation of the Democratic Peace Proposition* (Columbia: University of South Carolina Press, 1995); and Michael Brown, Sean Lynn-Jones, and Steven Miller, eds., *Debating the Democratic Peace* (Cambridge, MA: MIT Press, 1996).

13. Michael McFaul, "A Precarious Peace: Domestic Politics in the Making of Russian Foreign Policy," *International Security* 22, no. 3 (Winter 1997): 5.

14. McFaul, "A Precarious Peace," 24.

15. See Strobe Talbott, *The Russia Hand: A Memoir of Presidential Diplomacy* (New York: Random House, 2002).

16. Lukin, *The Bear Watches the Dragon*, 225.

17. For further discussion, see Lynch, "The Realism of Russia's Foreign Policy"; and Paul Kubicek, "Russian Foreign Policy and the West," *Political Science Quarterly* 114, no. 4 (Winter 1999–2000): 547–68.

18. Lynch, "The Realism of Russia's Foreign Policy," 9.

19. See Rajan Menon, "Structural Constraints on Russian Diplomacy," *Orbis* 45, no. 4 (Fall 2001): 579–96.

20. See Colin Gray, "The Continued Primacy of Geography," *Orbis* 40, no. 2 (Spring 1996): 247–59. Also Allen C. Lynch, "Roots of Russia's Economic Dilemmas: Liberal Economics and Illiberal Geography," *Europe–Asia Studies* 54, no. 1 (2002): 31–49.

21. McFaul, "Russia's Many Foreign Policies," 393.

22. See Gideon Rose, "Neoclassical Realism and Theories of Foreign Policy," *World Politics* 51, no. 1 (1998): 144–72. For the classic exposition of realism, see Hans J. Morgenthau, *Politics Among Nations: The Struggle for Power and Peace*, 5th ed. (New York: Alfred A. Knopf, 1973).

23. Robert Jervis, "Perception and Misperception in International Politics," in Paul R. Viotti and Mark V. Kauppi, eds., *International Relations Theory: Realism, Pluralism, Globalism, and Beyond*, 3d ed. (Boston: Allyn and Bacon, 1999), 259.

24. The sensitivity of Russian foreign policy to realist indicators of power has also been noted by Lynch, "The Realism of Russia's Foreign Policy," and Kubicek, "Russian Foreign Policy and the West."

25. Kenneth N. Waltz, "Structural Realism After the Cold War," *International Security* 25, no. 1 (Summer 2000): 5.

26. Waltz's theory of international relations is set forth in Kenneth N. Waltz, *Theory of International Politics* (Reading, MA: Addison-Wesley, 1979); for an alternative neorealist presentation, see John J. Mearsheimer, *The Tragedy of Great Power Politics* (New York: W.W. Norton, 2001).

27. See Lukin, *The Bear Watches the Dragon*, Chapter 4; Trenin, *Russia's China Problem* (Moscow: Carnegie Moscow Center, 1998), 38; and Bobo Lo *Russian Foreign Policy in the Post-Soviet Era: Reality, Illusion and Mythmaking* (New York: Palgrave Macmillan, 2002).

28. "Triangular Diplomacy" (ed.), *New York Times*, 18 July 2001.

29. Donaldson and Donaldson, in "The Arms Trade in Russian-Chinese Relations," consider ties between the two states as an outright "alliance" that "embodies a relationship that is primarily based on sales of arms from Russia to China." Also see Stephen G. Brooks and William C. Wohlforth, "American Primacy in Perspective," *Foreign Affairs* 81, no. 4 (July–August 2002): 28.

30. For an extensive discussion of this point, see Donaldson and Donaldson, "The Arms Trade in Russian-Chinese Relations." Also Alexander D. Voskressenski, "Russia's Evolving Grand Strategy Toward China," in Sherman W. Garnett, ed., *Rapprochement or Rivalry? Russia–China Relations in a Changing Asia* (Washington, DC: Carnegie Endowment for International Peace, 2000), 117–46.

31. "Russia's Military Doctrine," at www.armscontrol.org/act/2000_05/dc3ma00.asp?print.

32. For a discussion of nuclear deterrence from a neorealist perspective, see the argument made by Kenneth N. Waltz, in Scott D. Sagan and Kenneth N. Waltz, *The Spread of Nuclear Weapons: A Debate Renewed* (New York: W.W. Norton, 2003), Chapters 2, 4.

Bibliography

Books and Articles

Abnet, William B., and Robert B. Cassidy. 2002. "China's WTO Accession: The Road to Implementation." *NBR Special Report*, no. 3 (November).

Admidin, Andrei, and Elena Devaeva. 1999. "Economic Cooperation Between the Russian Far East and Northeast Asia." *Far Eastern Affairs*, no. 1: 29–38.

Akino, Yutaka. 1996. "Moscow's New Perspectives on Sino-Russian Relations." At http://src.-h.slav.hokudai.ac.jp.

Aldrich, Daniel. 1997. "If You Built It, They Will Come: A Cautionary Tale About the Tumen River Project." *Journal of East Asian Affairs* 11, no. 1 (January): 299–326.

Alexseev, Mikhail. 2002. "Chinese Migration in the Russian Far East: Security Threats and Incentives for Cooperation in Primorskii Krai." In Judith Thornton and Charles E. Zeigler, eds., *Russia's Far East: A Region at Risk*, 319–47. Seattle, WA: The National Bureau for Asian Research.

———. 2003. "Economic Valuations and Interethnic Fears: Perceptions of Chinese Migration in the Russian Far East." *Journal of Peace Research* 40, no. 1 (January): 89–106.

———. 1999. "The 'Yellow Peril' Revisited: The Impact of Chinese Migration in Primorskii Krai." Memo No. 94, *Ponars*.

Allison, Graham, and Philip Zelikow. 1999. *Essence of Decision: Explaining the Cuban Missile Crisis.* 2d ed. New York: Longman.

Anthony, Ian, ed. 1998. *Russia and the Arms Trade.* Oxford: Oxford University Press.

Armacost, Michael H., and Kenneth B. Pyle. 2001. "Japan and the Engagement of China: Challenges for U.S. Policy Coordination." *NBR Analysis*, vol. 12, no. 5 (December): 3–63.

Bazhanov, Evgenii. 1995. "Russian Policy Toward China." In Peter Shearman, ed., *Russian Foreign Policy Since 1990*, 159–78. Boulder, CO: Westview Press.

Beloff, Max. 1953. *Soviet Policy in the Far East, 1944–1951.* Oxford: Oxford University Press.

Blank, Stephen J. 1997. "The Dynamics of Russian Weapon Sales to China." March 4 at www.army.mil/usassi.

———. 1995. "Russian Policy and the Changing Korean Question." *Asian Survey* 35, no. 8 (August): 711–26.

———. 1998. "Russia's Secret Arms Market." *World and I* 13, no. 10 (October): 300–18.

Blank, Stephen J., and Alvin Z. Rubinstein, eds. 1997. *Imperial Decline: Russia's Changing Role in Asia*. Durham, NC: Duke University Press.

———. 1997. "Is Russia Still a Power in Asia?" *Problems of Post-Communism* 45, no. 2 (March–April): 37–46.

Brooks, Stephen G., and William C. Wohlforth. 2002. "American Primacy in Perspective." *Foreign Affairs* 81, no. 4 (July–August): 20–33.

———. 2000/2001. "Power, Globalization, and the End of the Cold War." *International Security* 25, no. 3 (Winter): 5–53.

Brown, Michael, Sean Lynn-Jones, and Steven Miller, eds. 1996. *Debating the Democratic Peace*. Cambridge, MA: MIT Press.

Burns, Katherine G. 2002. "Security Implications of Defense Conversion in the Russian Far East." In Judith Thornton and Charles E. Zeigler, eds., *Russia's Far East: A Region at Risk*, 267–89. Seattle: University of Washington Press.

Chang, Felix K. 2001. "Chinese Energy and Asian Security." *Orbis* 45, no. 2 (Spring): 211–40.

———. 1999. "The Unraveling of Russia's Far Eastern Power." *Orbis* 43, no. 2 (Spring): 257–84.

Chang, Gordon G. 2001. *The Coming Collapse of China*. New York: Random House.

Checkel, Jeffrey T. 1998. "The Constructivist Turn in International Relations Theory." *World Politics* 50, no. 2: 324–48.

Cheung, Tai Ming. 2001. "The Influence of the Gun: China's Central Military Commission and Its Relationship with the Military, Party, and State Decision-Making Systems." In David M. Lampton, ed., *The Making of Chinese Foreign and Security Policy in the Era of Reform, 1978–2000*, 61–90. Stanford, CA: Stanford University Press.

Christoffersen, Gaye. 1998. "China's Intentions for Russian and Central Asian Oil and Gas." *NBR Analysis* 9, no. 2 (March): 3–34.

———. 1994/1995. "The Greater Vladivostok Project: Transnational Linkages in Regional Economic Planning." *Pacific Affairs* 67, no. 4 (Winter): 513–31.

Crow, Suzanne. 1992. "Competing Blueprints for Russian Foreign Policy." *RFE-RL Research Report* 1, no. 50 (December 18): 45–50.

Dahl, Robert A. 1982. *Dilemmas of Pluralist Democracy: Autonomy vs. Control*. New Haven, CT: Yale University Press.

———. 1961. *Who Governs? Democracy and Power in an American City*. New Haven, CT: Yale University Press.

Ding, Arthur S. 1999. "China's Concerns About Theater Missile Defense: A Critique." *Nonproliferation Review* 6, no. 4 (Fall): 93–101.

Dittmer, Lowell. 1992. *Sino-Soviet Normalization and Its International Implications, 1945–1990*. Seattle: University of Washington Press.

Donaldson, Robert H., and John A. Donaldson. 2003. "The Arms Trade in Russian-Chinese Relations: Identity, Domestic Politics, and Geopolitical Positioning." *International Studies Quarterly* 47, no. 4 (December): 709–32.

Donaldson, Robert H., and Joseph L. Nogee. 2002. *The Foreign Policy of Russia: Changing Systems, Enduring Interests*. 2d ed. Armonk, NY: M.E. Sharpe.

Doolin, Dennis J. 1965. *Territorial Claims in the Sino-Soviet Conflict: Documents and Analysis*. Hoover Institution Studies, no. 7: 13–77.

Dougherty, James E., and Robert L. Pfaltzgraff, Jr. 2001. *Contending Theories of International Relations: A Comprehensive Survey*. 5th ed. New York: Longman.

Doyle, Michael W., and G. John Ikenberry, eds. 1997. *New Thinking in International Relations Theory*. Boulder, CO: Westview Press.

Duncan, Jennifer, and Michelle Ruetschle. 2002. "Agrarian Reform and Agricultural Productivity in the Russian Far East." In Judith Thornton and Charles E. Zeigler, eds., *Russia's Far East: A Region at Risk*, 267–89. Seattle: University of Washington Press.

Ellings, Richard J., and Aaron L. Friedberg, eds. 2001. *Strategic Asia: Power and Purpose, 2001–02*. Seattle, WA: National Bureau of Asian Research.

Ellison, Herbert J., ed. 1987. "Changing Sino-Soviet Relations." *Problems of Communism* 36 (May–June): 17–29.

———. 1982. *The Sino-Soviet Conflict: A Global Perspective*. Seattle: University of Washington Press.

Fairbank, John K., Edwin O. Reischauer, and Albert M. Craig. 1964. *East Asia: The Modern Transformation*. Boston, MA: Houghton Mifflin.

Felgenhauer, Pavel. 1997. "An Uneasy Partnership: Sino-Russian Defense Cooperation and Arms Sales." In Andrew J. Pierre and Dmitri V. Trenin, eds., *Russia in the World Arms Trade*, 87–103. Washington, DC: Brookings Institution Press.

Fewsmith, Joseph. 2001. "The Political and Social Implications of China's Accession to the WTO." *China Quarterly* 167, no. 3 (September): 573–91.

Friedrich, Karl, and Zbigniew Brzezinski. 1956. *Totalitarian Dictatorship and Autocracy*. New York: Praeger.

Gaddis, John Lewis. 1997. *We Now Know: Rethinking Cold War History*. New York: Clarendon Press.

Gaddy, Clifford, and Barry Ickes. 1998. "Russia's Virtual Economy." *Foreign Affairs* 77, no. 5 (September–October): 53–67.

Garnett, Sherman W. 1998. *Limited Partnership: Russia-China Relations in a Changing Asia*. Washington, DC: Carnegie Endowment for International Peace.

———, ed. 2000. *Rapprochement or Rivalry?: Russia-China Relations in a Changing Asia*. Washington, DC: Carnegie Endowment for International Peace.

Garver, John W. 1993. "The Chinese Communist Party and the Collapse of Soviet Communism." *China Quarterly* 133 (March): 1–26.

Gelbras, Vilya G. 2001. *Kitaiskaia realnost' Rossii* (The Chinese reality of Russia). Moscow: Izd-vo Muravei.

Gill, Bates. 2001. "Two Steps Forward, One Step Back: The Dynamics of Chinese Nonproliferation and Arms Control Policy Making in an Era of Reform." In David M. Lampton, ed., *The Making of Chinese Foreign and Security Policy in the Era of Reform, 1978–2000*, 257–88. Stanford, CA: Stanford University Press.

Gittings, John. 1974. "New Light on Mao: His View of the World." *China Quarterly* 50 (October–December): 750–66.

Goldman, Marshall I. 1994. *Lost Opportunity: Why Economic Reforms in Russia Have Not Worked*. New York: W.W. Norton.

Gonchar, Ksenia. 2000. *Russia's Defense Industry at the Turn of the Century*. Brief 17, Bonn International Center for Conversion, November.

Gong, Gerrit W., ed. 2000. *Taiwan Strait Dilemmas: China-Taiwan-U.S. Policies in the New Century*. Washington, DC: CSIS Press.

Gorbachev, Mikhail. 1987. *Perestroika: New Thinking for Our Country and the World*. New York: Harper and Row.

Gray, Colin. 1996. "The Continued Primacy of Geography." *Orbis* 40, no. 2 (Spring): 247–59.

Green, Michael J., and Toby F. Dalton. 2000. "Asian Reactions to U.S. Missile Defense." *NBR Analysis* 11, no. 3 (November): 3–59.

Griffith, William E. 1964. *The Sino-Soviet Rift*. Cambridge, MA: MIT Press.

Gydkova, Evgenia. 1999. "Problemy konversii oboronnoi promyshlennosti Rossiiskogo Dal'nego Vostoka" (Problems of the conversion of the defense industry of the Russian Far East). In Galina Vitkovskaya and Dmitri Trenin, eds., *Perspectivy Dal'nevostochnogo Regiona: naselenie, migratsiia, rynki truda* (Perspectives of the Far Eastern region: population, migration, and labor markets), 72–76. Working Papers, Issue 2. Moscow: Carnegie Center for International Peace.

Hart, Thomas G. 1987. *Sino-Soviet Relations: Reexamining the Prospects for Normalization* Aldershot, England: Gower.

Hill, Fiona, and Florence Fee. 2002. "Fueling the Future: The Prospects for Russian Oil and Gas." *Demokratizatsiya* 10, no. 4 (Fall): 462–87.

Hill, Fiona and Clifford Gaddy. 2003. *The Siberian Curse: How Communist Planners Left Russia Out in the Cold*, Washington, DC: Brookings Institution Press.

Hudson, G.F., Richard Lowenthal, and Roderick MacFarquhar. 1961. *The Sino-Soviet Dispute*. New York: Praeger.

Iwashita, Akihiro. 2002. "The Influence of Local Russian Initiatives on Relations with China: Border Demarcation and Regional Partnership." *Acta Slavica IAPONICA*, vol. 19, 1–18.

———. 2003. "Opyt prigranichnogo sotrudnichestva Rossii i KNR za poslednie 10 let" (The experience of border cooperation between Russia and the PRC for the past 10 years). In Akihiro Iwashita, ed., *The Sino-Russian "Strategic Partnership": Current Views from the Border and Beijing*, 55–75. Slavic Research Center Occasional Papers no. 91, Slavic Research Center, Hokkaido University.

———. 2001. "The Russo-Chinese 'Strategic Partnership' and Border Negotiations: Then and Now." *Bulletin of the Graduate Schools*. Yamuguchi Prefectural University, no. 2: 1–10.

———. 2003. "The Shanghai Cooperation Organization and Its Implications for Eurasian Security: A New Dimension of 'Partnership' After the Post–Cold War Period." Paper presented at the International Summer Symposium, "Russia's Integration into the World Economy and Community." Slavic Research Center, Hokkaido University, July.

Jervis, Robert. 1999. "Perception and Misperception in International Politics." In Paul R. Viotti and Mark V. Kauppi, eds., *International Relations Theory: Realism, Pluralism, Globalism and Beyond*, 257–68. 3d ed. Boston: Allyn and Bacon.

Kanet, Roger E., and Susanne M. Birgerson. 1997. "The Domestic-Foreign Policy Linkage in Russian Politics: Nationalist Influences on Russian Foreign Policy." *Communist and Post-Communist Studies* 30, no. 4: 335–44.

Karlusov, Viacheslav, and Andrei Kudin. 2002. "The Chinese Presence in the Russian Far East: A Historical and Economic Analysis." *Far Eastern Affairs* (2002–04–01FEA-no. 002): 62–76.

Kay, Sean. 2000. "What Is a Strategic Partnership?" *Problems of Post-Communism* 47, no. 3 (May–June): 15–24.

Kerr, David. 1996. "The New Eurasianism: The Rise of Geopolitics in Russia's Foreign Policy." *Europe–Asia Studies* 47, no. 6 (September): 977–88.

———. 1996. "Opening and Closing the Sino-Russian Border: Trade, Regional Development and Political Interest in Northeast Asia." *Europe–Asia Studies* 48, no. 6: 931–58.

Khripunov, Igor. 1999. "Russia's Weapons Trade: Domestic Competition and Foreign Markets." *Problems of Post-Communism* 46, no. 2 (March–April): 39–48.

Kimura, Hiroshi, Shaojun Li, and Il-Dong Koh. 1999. "Frontiers Are the Razor's Edge: Russia's Borders with its Eastern Neighbors." In Gilbert Rozman, Mikhail G. Nosov, and Koji Watanabe, eds., *Russia and East Asia: The 21st Century Security Environment*, 150–71. Vol. 3. EastWest Institute. Armonk, NY: M.E. Sharpe.

Kireev, G. 1999. "Demarcation of the Border with China." *International Affairs* 45, no. 2: 98–109.

———. 2003. "The Serpentine Path to the Shanghai G-5." *International Affairs* 49, no. 3: 85–92.

Kirshin, Yuriy. 1998. "The Role of the Ministry of Defense in the Export of Conventional Weapons." In Ian Anthony, ed., *Russia and the Arms Trade*, 117–23. Oxford: Oxford University Press.

Khodkov, Stanislav. 1999. "Immigratsiia i immigrationnaia politika v Khabarovskom krae" (Immigration and immigration policy in Khabarovsk krai). In Galina Vitkovskaya and Dmitri Trenin, eds., *Perspectivy Dal'nevostochnogo Regiona: naselenie, migratsiia, rynki truda* (Perspectives of the Far Eastern region: population, migration, and labor markets), 27–31. Working Papers, Issue 2. Moscow: Carnegie Center for International Peace.

Kozyrev, Andrei. 1994. "The Lagging Partnership." *Foreign Affairs* 73, no. 3 (May–June): 59–71.

Kubicek, Paul. 1999/2000. "Russian Foreign Policy and the West." *Political Science Quarterly* 114, no. 4: 547–68.

Kuchins, Andrew C. 2001. "Russia's Relations with China and India: Strategic Partnerships Yes; Strategic Alliances No," *Demokratizatsiya*, vol. 9, no. 2 (Spring): 259–75.

———. 2000. "Russia's Strategic Partnerships and Global Security." Memo no. 165, *Ponars.*

Kunadze, Georgi F. 1999. "Border Problems Between Russia and Its Neighbors." In Gilbert Rozman, Mikhail G. Nosov, and Koji Watanabe, eds., *Russia and East Asia: The 21st Century Security Environment*, Vol. 3, 133–49. EastWest Institute. Armonk, NY: M.E. Sharpe.

Lam, Willy Wo-Lap. 2002. "Moscow Tilts West, Beijing Worries." *China Brief* 2, no. 12 (June 6) (www.jamestown.org).

Lampton, David M. 2001. *Same Bed, Different Dreams: Managing U.S.–China Relations 1989–2000*. Berkeley and Los Angeles: University of California Press.

———, ed. 2001. *The Making of Chinese Foreign and Security Policy in the Era of Reform, 1978–2000*. Stanford, CA: Stanford University Press.

Lardy, Nicholas R. 2002. *Integrating China into the Global Economy*. Washington, DC: Brookings Institution Press.

Larina, Lilia. 1999. "Obraz Kitaia i kitaitsev v predstavlenii Dal'nevostochnikov" (Images of China and Chinese in the perception of Far Eastern residents). In Galina Vitkovskaya and Dmitri Trenin, eds., *Perspectivy Dal'nevostochnogo Regiona: naselenie, migratsiia, rynki truda* (Perspectives of the Far Eastern region: population, migration, and labor markets), 95–97. Working Papers. Issue 2, Moscow: Carnegie Center for International Peace.

Larrabee, F. Stephen, and Theodore W. Karasik. 1997. *Foreign and Security Policy Decisionmaking Under Yeltsin*. Santa Monica, CA: Rand.

LeDonne, John P. 1997. *The Russian Empire and the World, 1700–1917: The Geopolitics of Expansion and Containment*. New York: Oxford University Press.

Li, Tzu-Ching. 1999. "Jiang ni ZhongE jiemeng zhi Mei" (Jiang plans an alliance of China with Russia to restrict the United States). *Zheng Ming*, no. 257 (March): 13–15.

Li, Zhisui. 1994. *The Private Life of Chairman Mao*. New York: Random House.

Lo, Bobo. 2002. *Russian Foreign Policy in the Post-Soviet Era: Reality, Illusion and Mythmaking*. New York: Palgrave Macmillan.

Loh, I-cheng. 2000. "The Gordian Knot in Cross-Strait Relations: The Question of Taiwan's Participation in International Organizations." In Gerrit W. Gong, ed., *Taiwan Strait Dilemmas: China–Taiwan–U.S. Policies in the New Century*, 33–57. Washington, DC: CSIS Press.

Lowenthal, Richard. 1961. "Diplomacy and Dialectics of a Dispute." In G.F. Hudson, Richard Lowenthal, and Roderick MacFarquhar, eds., *The Sino-Soviet Dispute*, 9–34. New York: Praeger.

———. 1964. *World Communism: The Disintegration of a Secular Faith*. New York: Oxford University Press.

Lu, Ning. 2001. "The Central Leadership, Supraministry Coordinating Bodies, State Council Ministries, and Party Departments." In David M. Lampton, ed., *The Making of Chinese Foreign and Security Policy in the Era of Reform, 1978–2000*, 39–60. Stanford, CA: Stanford University Press.

Lukin, Alexander. 2003. *The Bear Watches the Dragon: Russia's Perceptions of China and the Evolution of Russian-Chinese Relations Since the Eighteenth Century*. Armonk, NY: M.E. Sharpe.

———. 2002. "China: Advancing Bilateral Cooperation." *International Affairs* (01–01–2002 IAF-no.001).

———. 1998. "The Image of China in Russia's Border Regions." *Asian Survey* 38, no. 9 (September): 821–30.

Lukin, Vladimir. 1992. "Our Security Predicament" *Foreign Policy* 88 (Fall): 57–76.

Lynch, Allen C. 2001. "The Realism of Russia's Foreign Policy." *Europe–Asia Studies* 53, no. 1: 7–31.

———. 2002. "Roots of Russia's Economic Dilemmas: Liberal Economics and Illiberal Geography." *Europe–Asia Studies* 54, no. 1: 31–49.

McDevitt, Michael. 2000. "Beijing's Bind." *Washington Quarterly* 23, no. 3 (Summer): 177–86.

McFaul, Michael. 1997. "A Precarious Peace: Domestic Politics in the Making of Russian Foreign Policy." *International Security* 22, no. 3 (Winter): 5–36.

———. 1999. "Russia's Many Foreign Policies." *Demokratizatsiya* 7, no. 3 (Summer): 393–412.

McFaul, Michael, and Sarah E. Mendelson. 2000. "Russian Democracy—A U.S. National Security Interest." *Demokratizatsiya* 8, no. 3 (Summer): 330–53.

MacKinder, Halford. 1942. *Democratic Ideals and Reality: A Study in the Politics of Reconstruction*. New York: H. Holt.

Makienko, Konstantin. 2002. "Indiia—ideal'nyi partner" (India—an ideal partner). *Vedomosti*, December 11.

———. 1998. Indiisko-Kitaiskoe getto" (The Indian-Chinese ghetto). *Ekspert*, no. 40 (October 26): 20–25.

———. 2000. "Preliminary Estimates of Russian Performance in Military-Technical Cooperation with Foreign States in 2000." *Eksport Vooruzheniy* (January–February): 5–7.

————. 2001. "Preliminary Estimates of Russia's Arms Exports in 2001." *Eksport Vooruzheniy* (November–December): 6–8.

————. 2002. "Russia in the Combat Aircraft Market." *Russia/CIS Observer* (July) at www.cast.ru.

————. 2001. "U.S. Congressional Research Service Report on Russia's Place in Arms Market," *Eksport Vooruzheniy* (September–October): 2–6.

————. 2002. *Voenno-tekhnicheskoe sotrudnichestvo Rossii i KNR v 1992–2002 godakh: dostizheniia, tendentsii, perspektivy* (Military-technical cooperation between Russia and the PRC 1992–2002: results, tendencies and prospects). Document no. 2. Moscow: Russian Office of the Center for Defense Analysis, October.

Malcolm, Neil. 1995. "Russian Foreign Policy Decision Making." In Shearman, Peter, ed. *Russian Foreign Policy Since 1990*. Boulder, CO: Westview Press.

Malcolm, Neil, Alex Pravda, Roy Allison, and Margot Light. 1996. *Internal Factors in Russian Foreign Policy*. Oxford: Oxford University Press.

Mao Tse-tung. 1969. *Selected Works of Mao Tse-tung*. Vol. IV. Peking: Foreign Languages Press.

Mearsheimer, John J. 2001. *The Tragedy of Great Power Politics*. New York: W.W. Norton.

Menon, Rajon. 2001. "Structural Constraints on Russian Diplomacy." *Orbis* 45, no. 4 (Fall): 579–96.

Menon, Rajon, and Charles E. Zeigler. 2000. "The Balance of Power and U.S. Foreign Policy Interests in the Russian Far East." *NBR Analysis* vol. 11, no. 5 (December): 5–28.

Merry, Wayne E. 2003. "Moscow's Retreat and Beijing's Rise as a Regional Great Power." *Problems of Post-Communism* 50, no. 3 (May–June): 17–31.

Mikheeva, Nadezhda. 1997. "Foreign Trade of the Russian Far East with the People's Republic of China: Development and Problems." At http://src.h.slav.hokudai.ac.jp/eng/Russia/feast-e/html.

Motrich, Ekaterina. 2002. "Demographic Potential and Chinese Presence in the Russian Far East." *Far Eastern Affairs* 30, no. 1: 67–78.

Moore, Harriet L. 1945. *Soviet Far Eastern Policy 1931–1945*. Princeton, NJ: Princeton University Press.

Morgenthau, Hans J. 1973. *Politics Among Nations: The Struggle for Power and Peace*. 5th ed. New York: Alfred A. Knopf.

Murray, Brian. 1995. "Stalin, the Cold War, and the Division of China: A Multi-Archival Mystery." *Working Paper No. 12*. Cold War International History Project. Woodrow Wilson International Center for Scholars, June.

Nelson, Harvey W. 1989. *Power and Insecurity: Beijing, Moscow and Washington, 1949–1988*. Boulder, CO: Lynne Reinner.

Nemets, Alekrandr V., and John L. Scherer. 2000. *Sino-Russian Military Relations*. Washington, DC: Portcullis eBooks.

Novikov, Anatolii. 1999. "Inostrantsy v Khabarovskom krae: problemy i resheniia" (Foreigners in Khabarovsk krai: problems and resolutions). In Galina Vitkovskaya and Dmitri Trenin, eds., *Perspectivy Dal'nevostochnogo Regiona: naselenie, migratsiia, rynki truda* (Perspectives of the Far Eastern region: population, migration, and labor markets), 32–35. Working Papers, Issue 2, Moscow: Carnegie Center for International Peace.

Okada, Kunio. 2002. "The Japanese Economic Presence in the Russian Far East." In Judith Thornton and Charles E. Zeigler, eds., *Russia's Far East: A Region at Risk*, 419–40. Seattle: University of Washington Press.

O'Prey, Kevin P. 2002. "Arms Exports and Russia's Defense Industries: Issues for the U.S. Congress." In *Russia's Uncertain Economic Future*, 385–410. Compendium of Papers Submitted to the Joint Economic Committee, Congress of the United States. Washington, DC: Government Printing Office.

Paik, Keun-wook. 1996. "Energy Cooperation in Sino-Russian Relations: The Importance of Oil and Gas." *Pacific Review* 9, no. 1: 77–95.

Paine, S.C.M. 1996. *Imperial Rivals: China, Russia and Their Disputed Frontier*. Armonk, NY: M.E. Sharpe.

Parish, Scott. 1996. "Chaos in Russian Foreign Policy Decision-Making." *Transition* (May 17): 30–33, 64.

Pearson, Margaret M. 2001. "The Case of China's Accession to GATT/WTO." In David M. Lampton, ed., *The Making of China's Foreign and Security Policy in the Era of Reform*, 336–70. Stanford, CA: Stanford University Press.

Pei, Minxin. "Future Shock: The WTO and Political Change in China." *Policy Brief* 1, no. 3 (February 2001): 1–7.

Pierre, Andrew J., and Dmitri V. Trenin, eds. 1997. *Russia in the World Arms Trade*. Washington, DC: Brookings Institution Press.

Pikayev, Alexander. 2003. "The North Korean 'Threat' and How to Counter It." *Briefing Papers* 5, no. 1 (January). At www.carnegie.ru.

Pisarenko, Natalia. 1999. "Vneshneekonomicheskie sviazi Khabarovskogo kraia i KNR" (Foreign economic links between Khabarovsk krai and the PRC). In Galina Vitkovskaya and Dmitri Trenin, eds., *Perspectivy Dal' nevostochnogo Regiona: naselenie, migratsiia, rynki truda* (Perspectives of the Far Eastern region: population, migration, and labor markets), 82–84. Working Papers, Issue 2, Moscow: Carnegie Center for International Peace.

Pukhov, Ruslan, Konstantin Makienko, and Maxim Pyadushkin. 2002. "Preliminary Estimates of Russia's Arms Exports in 2002." *Eksport Vooruzheniy* (November–December): 2–5.

Ray, James Lee. 1995. *Democracy and International Conflict: An Evaluation of the Democratic Peace Proposition*. Columbia: University of South Carolina Press.

Rogov, Sergei. 1998. *Russia as the Eurasian Bridge: Challenges of Russia's Integration into the World Community*. Center for Naval Analyses. CIM 587/November.

Rose, Gideon. 1998. "Neoclassical Realism and Theories of Foreign Policy." *World Politics* 51, no. 1: 144–72.

Rozman, Gilbert, Mikhail G. Nosov, and Koji Watanabe, eds. 1999. *Russia and East Asia: The 21st Century Security Environment*. EastWest Institute. Armonk, NY: M.E. Sharpe.

———. 1997. "Troubled Choices for the Russian Far East: Decentralization, Open Regionalism, and Internationalism." *Journal of East Asian Affairs* 11, no. 2 (Summer–Fall): 537–69.

———. 2000. "Turning Fortresses into Free Trade Zones." In Sherman W. Garnett, ed., *Rapprochement or Rivalry? Russia–China Relations in a Changing Asia*, 177–202. Washington, DC: Carnegie Endowment for International Peace.

Rutland, Peter. 1997. "Lost Opportunities: Energy and Politics in Russia." *NBR Analysis* 8, no. 5 (December): 5–30.

———. 2002. "Putin's Levitation Act." *Russia and Eurasia Review* 1, no. 1 (June 4). At www.jamestown.org.

Sakwa, Richard. 1993. *Russian Politics and Society.* London and New York: Routledge.

Sanderson, Tom. 2001. "Chinese Perspectives on US Ballistic Missile Defense." At www.stimson.org.

Schram, Stuart R. 1969. *The Political Thought of Mao Tse-tung.* Rev. ed. New York: Frederick A. Praeger.

Schwartz, Benjamin I. 1951. *Chinese Communism and the Rise of Mao.* New York: Harper and Row.

Segal, Gerald. 1980. "China and the Great Power Triangle." *China Quarterly,* no. 83. (September): 490–509.

Sergounin, Alexander A. and Sergey V. Subbotin. 1998. "Sino-Russian Military-Technical Cooperation: A Russian View," in Ian Anthony, ed. *Russia and the Arms Trade.* Oxford: Oxford University Press.

Sergounin, Alexander A., and Sergey V. Subbotin. 1999. *Russian Arms Transfers to East Asia in the 1990's.* Oxford: Oxford University Press.

Sheng, Michael M. 1998. *Battling Western Imperialism: Mao, Stalin and the United States.* Princeton, NJ: Princeton University Press.

———. 1994. "The United States, the Chinese Communist Party, and the Soviet Union, 1948–1950: A Reappraisal." *Pacific Historical Review* 63, no. 4 (November): 521–37.

Shevchenko, Arkady. 1985. *Breaking with Moscow.* New York: Knopf.

Skilling, H. Gordon. 1966. "Interest Groups and Communist Politics." *World Politics,* vol. 18, no. 3 (April): 435–51.

Skilling, H. Gordon, and Franklyn Griffiths, eds. 1971. *Interest Groups in Soviet Politics.* Princeton, NJ: Princeton University Press.

Slusser, Robert M. 1977. "Soviet Far Eastern Policy, 1945–1950." In Yonosuke Nagai and Akira Iriye, eds., *The Origins of the Cold War in Asia,* 123–46. New York: Columbia University Press.

Stent, Angela. 2002. "Russia: Farewell to Empire?" *World Policy Journal,* vol. 19, no. 3 (Fall): 83–94.

Stiglitz, Joseph E. 2002. *Globalization and its Discontents.* New York: W.W. Norton.

Stuart, Douglas T., and William T. Tow. 1982. *China, the Soviet Union, and the West.* Boulder, CO: Westview Press.

Swaine, Michael D. 2001. "Ballistic Missile Development." In Richard J. Ellings and Aaron L. Friedberg, eds., *Strategic Asia: Power and Purpose, 2001–02,* 299–360. Seattle, WA: National Bureau of Asian Research.

Talbott, Strobe. 2002. *The Russia Hand: A Memoir of Presidential Diplomacy.* New York: Random House.

Thornton, Judith, and Charles E. Zeigler, eds. 2002. *Russia's Far East: A Region at Risk.* Seattle: University of Washington Press.

Thornton, Richard C. 1983. *China: A Political History, 1917–1980.* Boulder, CO: Westview Press.

Toloraia, G. "Korean Peninsula and Russia." *International Affairs,* no. 1 (2003). At http://ciaonet.org.

Treadgold, Donald W. 1982. "Alternative Western Views of the Sino-Soviet Conflict." In Herbert J. Ellison, ed., *The Sino-Soviet Conflict : A Global Perspective.* Seattle: University of Washington Press.

Trenin, Dmitri. 2000. "The China Factor: Challenge and Chance for Russia." In Sherman Garnett, ed., *Rapprochement or Rivalry?: Russia–China Relations in a Changing Asia,* 39–70. Washington, DC: Carnegie Endowment for International Peace.

———. 1998. *Kitaiskaia problema Rossii* (The China problem of Russia). Moscow: Carnegie Moscow Center.

———. 2001. "Nenadezhnaia strategiia" (An unreliable strategy). *Pro et Contra* 6, nos. 1–2 (Winter–Spring): 50–65.

———. 2002. "Novyi kurs Putina: povorot zakreplen. Chto dal'she?" (Putin's new course: the turn has been strengthened. What's next?) *Briefing Papers* 4, no. 6 (June).

———. 1999. *Russia's China Problem.* Washington, DC: Carnegie Endowment for International Peace.

———. 2001. "Vladimir Putin's Autumn Marathon: Toward the Birth of a Russian Foreign Policy Strategy." *Briefing Papers*, no. 11 (November).

Tubilewicz, Czeslaw. 2002. "The Baltic States in Taiwan's Post–Cold War 'Flexible Diplomacy.'" *Europe–Asia Studies* 54, no. 5: 791–810.

Ulam, Adam. 1974. *Expansion and Coexistence: Soviet Foreign Policy, 1917–73*, 2d ed. New York: Praeger.

Vitkovskaya, Galina. 1999. "Does Chinese Immigration Endanger Russian Security?" *Carnegie Briefings.* Issue 8, August.

———. 1999. "Lawlessness, Environmental Damage, and Other New Threats in the Russian Far East." In Gilbert Rozman, Mikhail G. Nosov, and Koji Watanabe, eds., *Russia and East Asia: The 21st Century Security Environment*, 179–99. Vol. 3. EastWest Institute. Armonk, NY: M.E. Sharpe.

———. 1997. "Russia: Cross Border Migration in the Russian Far East." *Writenet Country Papers*, October.

Vitkovskaya, Galina, and Sergei Panarin. 2000. *Migratsiia i bezopasnost' v Rossii* (Migration and security in Russia). Moscow: Carnegie Endowment for International Peace.

Vitkovskaya, Galina, and Dmitri Trenin, eds. 1999. *Perspectivy Dal'nevostochnogo Regiona: mezhstranovoe vzaimodeistvie* (Perspectives of the Far Eastern region: cross-border cooperation). Moscow: Carnegie Endowment for International Peace.

———, eds. 1999. *Perspectivy Dal'nevostochnogo Regiona: naselenie, migratsiia, rynki truda* (Perspectives of the Far Eastern region: population, migration, and labor markets). Working Papers, Issue 2, Moscow: Carnegie Center for International Peace.

Vitkovskaya, Galina, and Zhanna Zaionchkovskaia. 1999. "Novaia stolypinskaia politika na Dal'nem Vostoke Rossii: nadezhdy i realii" (A new Stolypin policy for the Russian Far East: hopes and realities). In Vitkovskaya, Galina and Dmitri Trenin, eds., *Perspectivy Dal'nevostochnogo Regiona: mezhstranovoe vzaimodeistvie* (Perspectives of the Far Eastern region: cross-border cooperation), 80–120. Moscow: Carnegie Endowment for International Peace.

Vitkovskaya, Galina, Zhanna Zaionchkovskaia, ánd Kathleen Newland. "Chinese Migration into Russia." In Sherman W. Garnett, ed., *Rapprochement or Rivalry? Russia–China Relations in a Changing Asia.* Washington, DC: Carnegie Endowment for International Peace.

Voskressenski, Alexander. 2000. "Russia's Evolving Grand Strategy Toward China." In Sherman W. Garnett, ed., *Rapprochement or Rivalry? Russia–China Relations in a Changing Asia*, 117–46. Washington, DC: Carnegie Endowment for International Peace.

Wallander, Celeste A. 2002. "Russia's Relationship with China After September 11," Memo no. 214, *Ponars.*

Waltz, Kenneth N. 1979. *Theory of International Politics.* Reading, MA: Addison-Wesley.

———. 2000. "Structural Realism After the Cold War." *International Security* 25, no. 1 (Summer): 5–41.

Waltz, Kenneth N., and Scott D. Sagan. 2003. *The Spread of Nuclear Weapons: A Debate Renewed*. New York: W.W. Norton.

Whiting, Allen S. 1995. "Chinese Nationalism and Foreign Policy After Deng." *China Quarterly* 142 (June): 295–316.

Wilson, Jeanne L. 2002. "Strategic Partners: Russian-Chinese Relations and the July 2001 Friendship Treaty." *Problems of Post-Communism* 49, no. 3 (May–June): 3–18.

Wishnick, Elizabeth. 2000. "Chinese Perspectives on Cross-Border Relations." In Sherman W. Garnett. ed., *Rapprochement or Rivalry? Russia–China Relations in a Changing Asia*, 227–56. Washington, DC: Carnegie Endowment for International Peace.

———. 2002. "Growing U.S. Security Interests in Central Asia." Strategic Studies Institute, U.S. Army War College (October), at www.carlisle.army/mil/usassi/welcome.htm.

———. 2001. *Mending Fences: The Evolution of Moscow's China Policy from Brezhnev to Yeltsin*. Seattle: University of Washington Press.

———. 2002. "One Asia Policy or Two? Moscow and the Russian Far East Debate Russia's Engagement in Asia." *NBR Analysis* 13, no. 1 (March): 39–101.

———. 2001. "Russia and China: Brothers Again?" *Asian Survey* 41, no. 5 (September–October): 797–812.

———. 2000. "Russia in Asia and Asians in Russia." *SAIS Review* 20, no. 1 (Winter–Spring): 87–101.

Woolf, Amy F. 2001. *National Missile Defense: Russia's Reaction*. CRS Report for Congress. Congressional Research Service, August 10.

Yergin, Daniel, Dennis Eklof, and Jefferson Edwards. 1998. "Fueling Asia's Recovery." *Foreign Affairs* 77, no. 2 (March–April): 34–50.

Zagoria, Donald S. 1966. *The Sino-Soviet Conflict, 1956–1961*. New York: Atheneum.

Zhao Huasheng. 2002. "Establishment and Development of the Shanghai Cooperation Organization." *SIIS Journal*, no. 3, at www.siis.org.cn.

———. 2003. "New Situation in Central Asia and Shanghai Cooperation Organization." *SIIS Journal*, no. 2, at www.siis.org.cn.

Statistical Yearbooks

China Customs Statistic Yearbook, 1998, 1999, 2000, 2001. Beijing: Customs General Administration of the People's Republic of China, 1999, 2000, 2001, 2002.

Heilongjiang tongji nianjian 1993, 1994, 1995, 1996, 1997, 1998, 1999, 2000, 2001, 2002 (Statistical yearbook of Heilongjiang, 1993–2002). Heilongjiang: Heilongjiang Province Statistical Bureau, 1993–2002.

Khabarovskii krai v 1998 godu, chast 1 (Khaborovsk krai in 1998, Part 1). Khabarovsk: Goskomstat, 1999.

Narodnoe khoziaistvo SSSR v 1990 g. (Economy of the USSR in 1990). Moscow: State Statistical Committee of the USSR, 1991.

Primorskii krai v 1998 godu, Chast 1 (Primorksii krai in 1998, Part 1). Vladivostok: Goskomstat, 1999.

Primorskii krai v 1999 godu (Primorskii krai in 1999). Vladivostok: Goskomstat, 2000.

Regiony Rossii, tom 2, 1993, 1994, 1995, 1996, 1997, 1998 (Regions of Russia, vol. 2, 1993–1998). Moscow: Goskomstat, 1993–1998.

SIPRI Yearbook 2002. Oxford: Oxford University Press, 2002.

Sotsial'no-ekonomicheskoe razvitie svobodnoi ekonomicheskoi zony "Nakhodka" v 2000 godu (Social-economic development of the free economic zone "Nakhodka" in 2000). Vladivostok: Goskomstat, 2001.

Tamozhennaia statistika vneshnei torgovli Rossiiskoi Federatsii 1998, 1999, 2000, 2002, 2003 (Customs statistics of foreign trade of the Russian Federation, 1998–2003) Moscow: State Customs Committee of the Russian Federation, 1998–2003.

Vneshniaia torgovlia SSSR 1922–1981 (Foreign trade of the USSR) Moscow: Ministry of Foreign Trade, 1982.

Vneshniaia torgovlia SSSR v 1985 (Foreign trade of the USSR in 1985) Moscow: Ministry of Foreign Trade, 1986.

The World Factbook, 1999. At www.cia.gov/cia/publications/factbook.

The World Factbook, 2002. At www.cia.gov/cia/publications/factbook.

World Military Expenditures and Arms Transfers: 1991–1992, 1993–94, 1995, 1996. U.S. Arms Control and Disarmament Agency. Washington, DC: Government Printing Office. 1993, 1995, 1996, 1997.

World Military Expenditures and Arms Transfers, 1999–2000. Washington, DC: U.S. Department of State. Bureau of Verification and Compliance, 2001.

Zhongguo duiwai jingji maoyi nianjian 1994/95, 1996/97, 1997, 1998/99, 1999/2000, 2000, 2001, 2002 (Almanac of China's foreign economic relations and trade, 1994–2002) Beijing: Chinese State Statistical Bureau, 1995–2002.

Zhongguo duiwai jingji tongji nianjian 1979–1991 (Chinese foreign economic statistics 1979–1991). Beijing: China Statistical Information and Consultancy Service Center, 1992.

Documents

"Khartia Shankhaiskoi organizatsii sotrudnichestva" (Charter of the Shanghai cooperation organization). *Moskovskii zhurnal mezhdunarodnogo prava*, no. 1 (49) (January–March, 2003): 272–83.

Novoe osvoenie Sibiri i Dal'nego Voctoka (The new emancipation of Siberia and the Far East). Council on Foreign and Defense Policy. At www.svop.ru/yuka/896.html.

"Shankhaiskaia konventsiia o bor'be s terrorizmom, separatizmom i ekstremizmom" (Shanghai convention about the struggle with terrorism, separatism, and extremism). *Moskovskii zhurnal mezhdunarodnogo prava*, no. 1 (49) (January–March, 2003): 295–305.

"Soglashenie mezhdu gosudarstvami-chlenami Shankhaiskoi organizatsii sotrudnichestva o Regional'noi antiterroristicheskoi strukture" (Agreement between member states of the Shanghai cooperation organization about the Regional antiterrorist structure). *Moskovskii zhurnal mezhdunarodnogo prava*, no. 1, (49) (January–March, 2003): 285–94.

"Soglashenie ot 16 Maia 1991 goda mezhdu Soiuzom Sovetskikh Sotsialisticheskikh Respublik i Kitaiskoi Narodnoi Respublikoi o sovetsko-kitaiskoi gosudarstvennoi granitse na ee Vostochnoi chasti" (Agreement of May 16, 1991, between the Union of Soviet Socialist Republics and the People's Republic of China on the Soviet-Chinese state border on its Eastern part). *Nekotorye problemy demarkatsii rossiisko-kitaiskoi granitsy, 1991–1997 gg. Sbornik statei i dokumentov* (Some problems of

the demarcation of the Russian-Chinese border 1991–1997: A collection of articles and documents). Moscow: *Nezavisimaia Gazeta*, 1997: 14–21.

"Zakliuchenie po itogam parlamentskikh slushanii 'o problemakh Rossiisko-Kitaiskikh
otnoshenii i perspektivakh ikh resheniia,'" 25 aprelia 1999 g. (Conclusions on the
results of the parliamentary hearings "about problems of Russian-Chinese relations
and perspectives of their resolution," 25 April 1994). Committees on International
Affairs of the Federation Council and State Duma of the Russian Federation.

Newspapers and Magazines

Asia Times
Boston Globe
Cheng Ming (Zheng Ming)
China Economic Review
Chiushih Nientai (Jiushi Niandai)
Christian Science Monitor
Delovoy Mir
Economist
Far Eastern Economic Review
Financial Times
Izvestia
Journal of Commerce
Kai Fang
Kommersant
Komsomolskaia Pravda
Liaowang
Moscow News
Moscow Times
Moskovskie Novosti
New York Times
Nezavisimaia Gazeta
Orlando Sentinel
Pai Hsing
Renmin Ribao
Rossiiskaia Gazeta
South China Morning Post
Ta Kung Pao
Tangtai
Trud
Vedomosti
Vremya MN
Washington Post
Yaderny Kontrol

List Serves, Internet Media and Research Resources, and Translation Services

AFP
CDI Russia Weekly

Comparative Connections
Current Digest of the Soviet Press
EVP Press Digest
Interfax
Itar-Tass
Jamestown Foundation Monitor
Johnson's Russia List
Omri
Reuters
RFE/RL Newsline
Russian Regional Report
Tass
UPI
World News Connection
Xinhua

Index

A-50E early warning aircraft, 99
  See also military-technical
    relationship; weapons trade
Admiralteiskie Wharf shipyards,
    104, 108
  See also economic issues, Russia;
    military-industrial complex,
    Russia; military-technical
    relationship; weapons trade
Aerospace cooperation, 33, 79–81
  See also Russian-Chinese economic
    cooperation
Afghanistan, 52, 54, 165, 167, 171
  and Soviet invasion, 19–20
  and threat of Islamic extremism, 52
  and U.S. led incursion, 38
Agreement on the Eastern Part of the
    Soviet-Chinese Border (1991),
    44, 57
  impact in the Russian Far East, 12,
    28, 32, 38, 116–120
  importance to Russian national
    interest, 12
  and 2001 Friendship Treaty, 37
  See also border demarcation; border
    negotiations, Soviet era; Russian
    Far East; Transbaikal area
Agreement on the Western Part of the
    Russian-Chinese Border (1994),
    27, 44
  See also border demarcation

AHC Sukhoi, 106–107
  See also economic issues, Russia;
    Khabarovsk krai; military-
    industrial complex, Russia;
    military-technical relationship;
    Sukhoi; weapons trade
al-Qaeda, 54, 165–67, 171
Albright, Madeleine, 155
Alexseev, Mikhail, 126, 142
Amur oblast, 132, 137
Amur river, 44, 118–119
Anti-Ballistic Missile (ABM) Treaty,
    34, 112, 150, 159–161, 165,
    167–168
  See also missile defense; national
    missile defense (NMD); National
    Missile Defense Act of 1999;
    theater missile defense (TMD)
Arbatov, Georgy, 98
Argun river, 44–45
Arkhipov, Ivan, 20, 70
Armenia, 156
Armitage, Richard, 163
Asia Pacific Economic Cooperation
    (APEC), 56–57
Asian financial crisis, 31, 61, 63
Asian Pacific region, 59–60, 114
Association of South East Asian
    Nations (ASEAN), 57
ASEAN Regional Forum (ARF), 57
Atlanticists, 146, 148, 192–93

Jeanne L. Wilson is a professor of political science at Wheaton College in Norton, Massachusetts, and a research associate at the Davis Center for Russian and Eurasian Studies, Harvard University. Her research interests include Russian-Chinese foreign policy relations and the comparative implications (political, economic, and societal) of the Russian and Chinese experiences as states in transition from state socialism to market capitalism.